Learn Office 2010

A Practical Course in

Windows 7 and Office 2010

ISBN 978-0-9563141-6-1

Blackrock Education Centre, Kill Avenue, Dún Laoghaire, Co Dublin, Ireland.

Tel: (+353 1) 230 2709, Fax: (+353 1) 236 5044
E-mail: becbooks@blackrockec.ie
Websites: wwwbecpublishing.com *and* www.blackrockec.ie

First published 2012

Microsoft® Windows®, Microsoft® Office®, Microsoft® Word®, Microsoft® Access®, Microsoft® Excel®, Microsoft® PowerPoint®, Microsoft® Internet Explorer® and Microsoft® Outlook® are either registered trademarks or trademarks of the Microsoft Corporation. The use of Winzip and the Winzip trademark is with the kind permission of Winzip Computing Incorporated.

Other products mentioned in this manual may be registered trademarks or trademarks of their respective companies or corporations.

The companies, organisations, products, the related people, their positions, names, addresses and other details used for instructional purposes in this manual and its related support materials on the manual's support website www.becpublishing.com are fictitious. No association with any real company, organisations, products or people are intended nor should any be inferred.

Every effort has been made to ensure that this book contains accurate information. However, Blackrock Education Centre, its agents and the authors shall not be liable for any loss or damage suffered by readers as a result of any information contained herein.

Credits	
BEC Director	*Proofreading*
Pat Seaver	Claire Rourke
	Lorna Bointon
BEC Production	
Carrie Fonseca	*Line Drawings*
	Annette Bolger
Original Text	
Lorna Bointon	*Text Design*
Alan Bourke	Liz White
Adapted for Office 2010	*Cover Design*
Lorna Bointon	Karolina Mosz
Editing and Formatting	
Claire Rourke	

Contents

Note to Reader

Learn Office 2010: The Definitive Guide to Windows 7 and Office 2010 has been written to enable the absolute beginner to arrive at an understanding of basic computer applications. It has been written in clear English with step-by-step instructions to be easily understood as either a self-study guide or for the tutor- led environment. It is applicable for both desktop PCs and laptops.

The ***Before You Begin*** section, unique to the Blackrock Education Centre computer manuals, has been written for those students who are absolute beginners. It starts with the basics of how to switch the computer on and off, it explains the use of the **mouse**, the **taskbar**, and introduces the student to the **keyboard** and the **cursor**. The student is then introduced to the **windows**, **the ribbon**, **settings** and the **Help function**.

Each new topic is fully and carefully explored, complemented with numerous exercises for student practice. Small amounts of additional information have been included to enhance the students' understanding of very important topics.

Particular attention is given to ensuring that the content of the manual reflects the view on the screen. The manual has large-format A4 pages and is fully illustrated with screen shots throughout. The placing of the graphics and text side by side make this an ideal training manual.

This manual will use Microsoft Outlook to teach the use of the e-mail, with an opportunity to practise creating and sending an e-mail. It will also offer interactive website training at www.becpublishing.com. There are also **FREE** online resources available to download from the website.

There is a full **glossary** of computer terms and the manual is clearly indexed.

Before
You Begin

Before
You Begin

Section 1 ▶ The Computer Workplace

1.1 Introduction

The Before You Begin section is designed for those using a computer for the first time or at beginner level. It contains practical information that will help make basic computer terminology familiar and will outline the most common pieces of computer equipment. Spending time on becoming comfortable with the foundation skills mentioned below will help your progression to learn other skills.

Section 3 deals with the use of laptops, in particular the battery power, the mouse pad and keyboard, and the care and handling of the laptop while in use. The remaining sections apply whether a laptop or a desktop PC is being used.

1.2 Getting Set Up

1.2.1 Switching on the Computer

The first thing to do to set up is to switch on the computer (see Section 3 if you are using laptop). On a typical desktop computer, there is a power button situated on the system box. Check the computer's power cable is plugged into the wall socket and press the power button. Generally, the various lights will flash and the computer monitor will be activated. If not press the power switch on the monitor.

Text will appear on the screen to say that Windows is starting up. Depending on the way in which the computer was set up, you may need to 'log in' using a password that has been set up for you. If not, the computer will continue to 'start up'.

This takes a few minutes until a screen similar to the one on the right opens.

1.3 Where You Work

When the computer has finished starting up, the screen that is presented is referred to as the desktop. Similar to the way in which a real office desk is used, on a computer desktop you can sort and manage computer files, open and edit documents. The small pictures on the desktop with the text underneath are called icons, and these represent documents or programs stored on the computer.

Icons

1.4 The Mouse

The mouse is the principal means of controlling the computer. It is a small, box device that you move around with your hand. By moving the mouse, you control the cursor, which is a small arrow that is displayed on the screen. This enables you to open, close and manipulate computer applications.

The cursor

Generally, a mouse has three basic parts: a left button, a right button and a scroll wheel in the middle. As you move the mouse on the mat, the cursor moves on the screen in tandem with the mouse. Move the mouse to the right and the cursor moves to the right, etc. When the cursor is placed in a particular position, e.g. over an icon, pressing a button causes the computer to perform an action related to the icon.

Using the mouse may appear simple at first. Learning how to use it properly takes practise and it is crucial for confident and easy use of the computer.

Four actions are performed with the mouse – pointing, clicking, dragging and scrolling.

1.4.1 Pointing

You point to an icon or a button that you want to use, by moving the mouse. A white arrow moves on the screen representing the action of the mouse.

Practice: Point to the **Recycle Bin** icon.

Recycle Bin

note

Sometimes a box with text is displayed (depending on your computer settings) when you point to an icon or button. This is known as a **screen tip**, which gives a short explanation of the button or icon.

1.4.2 Clicking

Left-click and right-click are used to describe which mouse button to use. To left-click on an object, firstly point to it. Then quickly press and release the left mouse button. You will hear the button click. Clicking is also referred to as selecting.

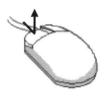

A **single click** either:
- Select an object.
- Perform an action.

Practice: Point and left-click the mouse on the Recycle Bin icon. The icon darkens, or is highlighted. This shows that you have selected it. To deselect it, move the cursor to a blank area on the screen away from the recycle bin icon and left-click.

Practice: Point and right-click the mouse on the Recycle Bin icon. This time a pop-up menu appears. Without clicking either mouse button, move the cursor to a blank area on the screen away from the icon and left-click to hide the pop-up menu.

Double click

A **double-click** means left-clicking twice in rapid succession.
- Double-clicking performs a different action, e.g. opening a folder, a file or an application.

Practice:
- Double-click the **Computer** icon. The **Computer** window opens.
- Point and click on the **Close X** button at the top right-hand corner to close the window.

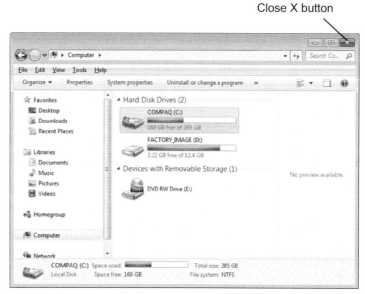

Close X button

1.4.3 Dragging

To drag an object means to move it on the desktop from one location to another. For example, point to an icon on the desktop, click and hold down the left mouse button. Then, while still holding down the left mouse button, move the mouse on the mouse mat (this drags the icon on the desktop).

Practice:
- Place the tip of the pointer on an icon, e.g. the Recycle Bin, on the desktop.
- Hold down the left mouse button and move/drag the mouse.
  An outline (or ghost image) of the icon moves with the mouse.
- Release the button to 'drop' the icon in its new position. (It may spring back to its original position, depending on how your computer has been set up.)

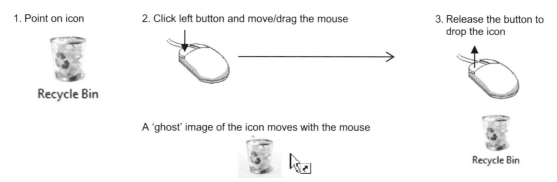

1. Point on icon   2. Click left button and move/drag the mouse   3. Release the button to drop the icon

Recycle Bin

A 'ghost' image of the icon moves with the mouse

Recycle Bin

1.4.4 Scrolling

Scrolling means moving up or down to view different parts of a document or window. For example, if you are working in Microsoft Word and have come to the bottom of the page, it is easy to scroll up to view the top of the page.

To scroll with the mouse, do the following:
- Rest your finger on the mouse wheel and roll away from your hand to move up and roll towards your hand to move down.

note

Scrolling is only possible when working with documents or windows that take up more space than is available on the display screen.

1.5 The Taskbar

The **taskbar** is a bar that appears along the bottom of the desktop. Depending on your computer settings, the taskbar will either remain visible all the time on the desktop or be hidden from view. If it is hidden move the cursor on the desktop to the bottom of the screen and the taskbar will pop up.

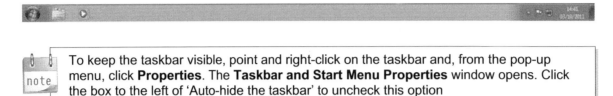

> note
>
> To keep the taskbar visible, point and right-click on the taskbar and, from the pop-up menu, click **Properties**. The **Taskbar and Start Menu Properties** window opens. Click the box to the left of 'Auto-hide the taskbar' to uncheck this option

1.5.1 Taskbar Buttons

The taskbar contains a number of icons in the form of buttons. A button can be clicked to perform a specific action. Some buttons are always on the taskbar while others appear on it from time to time, depending on what you are working on.

Think of the items on the taskbar as if they were drawers in a real desk where things can be put away when they are not being used.

Practice:
- Click the **Start** button once and then click it again.
- Double-click the time displayed at the bottom right-hand side of the taskbar.
  The **Date and Time Properties** window opens, displaying a calendar and a clock along with other items.
- Point and click the **Close X** at the top right hand corner to close the window.

The taskbar in the illustration on the right shows some more examples of taskbar buttons.

1.6 Cursors

The cursor on the screen changes automatically into different shapes, depending on the action being performed. The cursor shape gives the user a visual indication of what is happening.

- The **arrow**, or normal select, cursor is probably the most common. It is used to select objects, to click buttons and to choose options in menus and on toolbars.

- The busy cursor (or hourglass) appears when the computer is engaged in an activity that will take a few moments to complete. You should wait until the action is completed and the pointer resumes its original shape.

- In some windows, a question mark button appears beside the Close X button on the top right of the box. When you click this button and then point to an object or menu, the cursor changes into the help cursor and a pop-up explanation, in a box, is displayed.

1.7 Turning Off the Computer

To turn off the computer do the following:
- Left-click (click with the left mouse button) the **Start** button.
- Move the cursor to the **Shut Down** button.
- Left-click the button.
  The computer will take a few moments to shut down.

Section 2 ▶ The Keyboard

2.1 The Keyboard

The keyboard and the mouse are the main 'controls' for interacting with your computer, i.e. for instructing the computer to do something for you, such as, 'go online' to browse the internet, typing a letter, looking at photos from a digital camera.

The keyboard is referred to as a QWERTY keyboard – taken from the layout of the first row of letters. The keys for letters of the alphabet are arranged in the centre of the main keys on three rows. Above these is a row of keys for numbers. Various other character/symbol keys are arranged around the letter keys, though some are included on the number keys.

Most computer keyboards have an additional numeric keypad to the far right of the standard keys. There is also an extra row of keys at the top, called Function keys, which are used by some programs or applications.

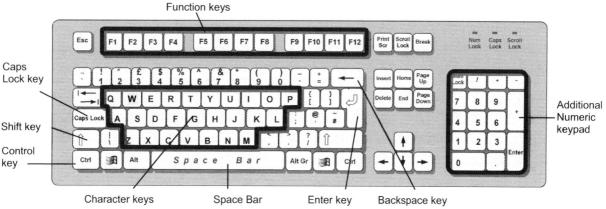

In addition, there are some extra keys that are frequently used in computer work, mostly located around the edges of the character keys.

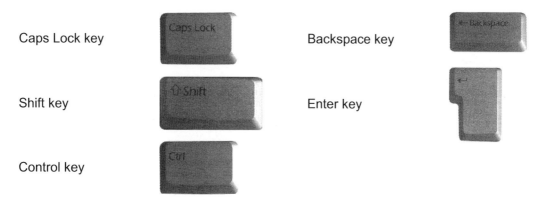

Caps Lock key   Backspace key

Shift key   Enter key

Control key

2.2 Basic Typing Skills

To understand how the keys work, practise and repeat the short keyboard exercise below using a program called **WordPad** – a small application, for creating documents.

To open WordPad, do the following:

- Left-click the **Start button** on the taskbar at the bottom of the desktop.
- Point to **All Programs**.
- Point to **Accessories**.
- Click **WordPad**.
  The **WordPad** application will open in the centre of the screen.

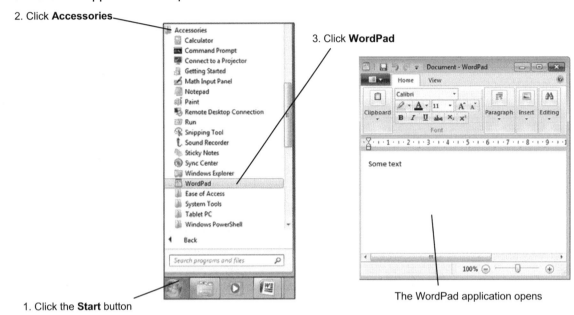

2. Click **Accessories**

3. Click **WordPad**

1. Click the **Start** button

The WordPad application opens

Basic typing

1. Type your first name using the **character keys**. Notice how the first letter is not in capitals.

Backspace key – to delete the typed text

2. Delete the text by clicking on the **Backspace key** until all the letters are gone.

Shift key – to create a single capital letter

3. Press down the **Shift key** with one finger and click the first letter of your name with another finger. Release the Shift key. The letter should appear on the WordPad page as a capital letter. Continue to type the rest of the characters of your first name by pressing the character keys.

Space bar – to create a space between words

4. To type your surname you will need to leave a space after your first name. Press the **space bar** once. Then follow instruction 7 to type your surname.

Enter key – to create a new line

5. To make a new line, press the **Enter key** once. Type the first line of your address. (Make sure the first word has a first capital letter and use the space bar to create a space between words.)
6. Repeat instruction 9 to type the remaining lines of your address.

Caps Lock key – to type in all capitals

7. Press the Enter key twice. Press the **Caps Lock key**. (A light should appear on the keyboard indicating that the caps lock key is turned on.)
8. Type Ireland. Notice how all the letters are in capitals. Read the text which you have typed to check it.

If there are any spelling errors, move the cursor to the right of the incorrect letter and left-click. You should see a black line – a **flashing cursor**. Press the Backspace key to delete the mistake and then retype the correct character, etc.

Some of the keys on the keyboard display more than one symbol – one above the other. For example, on the row of numeric keys above the character keys, the number 8 key also has an asterisk, above the 9 and 0 keys there are brackets. (The position of the symbols might vary slightly from one keyboard to another.)

To type these symbols hold down the Shift key (as you do when typing a capital letter).

1. In the open WordPad file, click after the last letter of IRELAND and click the Enter key a couple of times to move down the page.
2. Click key 8, press the space bar, click the key 9, press the space bar and click on the key 0. Press the Enter key.

Shift key – to type the special symbol on a key
3. Hold down the Shift key and, keeping it held down, press the keys 8, 9 and 0 again, clicking the space bar between each. This time the symbols above the numbers will be displayed.

Wherever there is a symbol above another on a key, use the procedure above to type that symbol. The exception to this rule is the euro symbol.

Control (CTRL) and Alt keys – to type the euro symbol
1. Within the open WordPad file, use two fingers to press down the CTRL and Alt keys and, keeping them held down, click the number 4 key. The euro symbol will be typed on the WordPad page.

Practise this drill again. Spend time locating and typing some of the other most commonly used symbols, as shown below.

question mark	?	single and double quotation mark	' "
comma	,	sterling symbol	£
full stop	.	dollar symbol	$
apostrophe	'	percentage symbol	%
colon and semi-colon	: ;	underscore	_
ampersand	&	the 'at' symbol	@
exclamation mark	!	forward slash	/

2.3 Click and Type

The **I-beam** cursor in Microsoft Office 2007 is associated with the way the text will be aligned on the page. The alignment icons appear beside or under the I-beam to indicate how the text will be aligned.

Left aligns the text

Left aligns the text and applies a left indent

Centre aligns the text

Right aligns the text

You can place text anywhere in a document by hovering the mouse over the page. This will enable you to view the alignment options. Double-click when you see the alignment option you require and type some text.

This process is known as click and type. Click and type automatically applies the alignment and/or indentation.

Section 3 ▶ Using a Laptop

3.1 Using a Laptop

The work undertaken and the way in which the programs work is the same whether you are working on a laptop or a desktop computer. However, there are some specific guidelines for working with a laptop.

Care should be taken when moving the laptop, avoiding knocks, in particular when it is switched on and there are processes running – i.e. applications or background system processes. Any knock or bang at this stage can damage the internal hard drive which will be spinning during this time. While it is a portable device it should remain stable when in use.

3.1.1 Battery Power

A power supply and cable comes with a new laptop. The laptop power – which keeps the machine turned on – differs from the desktop PC in that there is an internal battery which needs to be charged so that the machine can be used without having to plug it into a wall socket (for example, if it is being used in the garden or in a meeting). This battery is charging when the power supply is plugged in. When the laptop is not plugged in, you will need to keep a check on the battery performance to determine how much time you have to work remotely.

A battery power indicator is usually available on the taskbar at the bottom of the screen (see Section 1.5) and an alert as to the remaining performance time is displayed if the power is running low. If you tend to use the laptop a lot outside of an office or the home, it is advisable to invest in a high performance battery.

3.2 The Touchpad

The touchpad is built into a laptop below the keyboard. This is the rectangular shape and the two buttons normally found on a mouse are also built in.

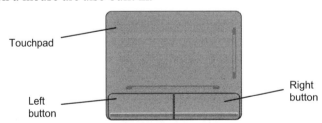

The touchpad might take a little getting used to if you are familiar with using a standard mouse. As you move your finger on the touchpad, the cursor, usually in the shape of a small arrow, moves on the screen in tandem. Move your finger to the right and the cursor moves to the right, etc. Similar to a conventional mouse, the left button is most frequently used to interact with the computer programs and icons. (See Section 1.4 for practice using the mouse.)

Dragging using the touchpad, while the same in principal as using an external mouse, is a little different in practice:

- Move the cursor on the screen to the **Computer** icon and double-click on the left mouse button on your laptop, to open the Computer window.
- Move the cursor to the top of the **Computer** window. (Make sure the arrow is in an empty area.)
- With one finger hold down the left mouse button and with the other hand glide your finger across, up or down the touchpad.
- The **Computer** window will follow in tandem.
- Click the **Close X** button to close the Computer window.

 Wherever an instruction mentions to move the mouse on the mouse mat, replace the action with moving your finger on the touchpad. An external mouse can also be attached to the computer and can be used as described in Section 1.4.

3.3   The Keyboard

The keyboard on a laptop is very similar to that which would be used with a desktop computer (see Section 2). The layout has the same QWERTY appearance and the special keys (Shift key, Control key, Backspace key, Enter key, Space bar, Function keys, etc.) will also be in similar positions to those on a desktop computer keyboard.

The main difference in using a laptop keyboard is that there isn't an additional numeric keypad to the right of the main keys. This numeric keypad is incorporated into the main keyboard and is accessed by pressing a function key, which is normally to the bottom left of the keyboard, followed by the required number key. The numbers can be seen in the bottom right-hand corner of the **7, 8, 9, 0, u, i, o, p, j, k, l, ;, m, ,, .** and **/** keys.

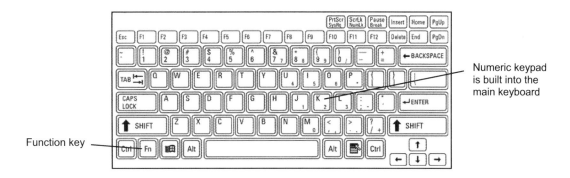

Numeric keypad is built into the main keyboard

Function key

Section 4 ► Windows

4.1 Windows

Windows are the visual means with which you interact with the software on the computer, access files and create documents. A window is a panel that appears on the desktop.

To practise working with a window, do the following:

- Click the **Computer** icon.
  The **Computer** window opens.

Close X button
Maximise button
Minimise button
Address bar

Windows have some common features:

- An **Address bar**, which displays the file location.
- A **Close X button** on the top right hand corner, which is used to close the window.
- Windows can be **minimised**, i.e. temporarily hidden from the desktop.
- When a window has been minimised, the title bar is visible as a button on the taskbar.
  To restore the window, click the button on the taskbar once – the window will reopen to the same size it was before it was minimised.
- Windows can be **maximised**, i.e. enlarged to fill the entire screen.
- To maximise a window click the maximise button.
- Windows can be moved around the desktop and **resized**.
- You can have more than one window open at the same time.

Practice Sequence	
1	Ensure the Computer window is open on the desktop.	☐
2	Double-click the Recycle Bin.	☐
3	Both windows are now open on the desktop.	☐
4	By clicking with the left mouse button on the title bar, move each of the windows, one at a time, around the desktop to reposition them beside each other, one above the other, etc.	☐
5	Note that when you click on a title bar the bar becomes darker in colour. The title bar of the other window becomes lighter. The window with the darker title bar is known as the **active** window.	☐
6	To close each window, click the **Close X** button on the top right-hand side.	☐

note
If, when a window filled the screen – i.e. the window was as large as the full screen – when it was opened, its size can be reduced by clicking the **Restore** button. This makes it possible to see other windows that are open (and the desktop).

Restore button

4.2 Scrolling in a Window Containing Folders and Files

When a window is opened on screen, some of the files or folders may be hidden from view. The horizontal and vertical scroll bars are used to access the hidden contents of a window.

To view the full list of contents in a window, do the following:

- Click the down scroll arrow on the vertical scroll bar to scroll to the bottom of the list.
  Click the up scroll arrow on the vertical scroll bar to scroll to the top of the list.
  Alternatively, click and drag the scroll box up or down on the vertical scroll bar.

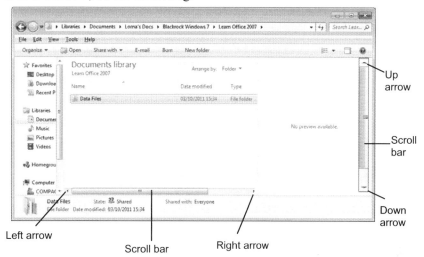

To view the full list of details for files or folders in a window:

- To view the columns on the right-click the right scroll arrow on the horizontal scroll bar.
- To view the columns on the left-click the left scroll arrow on the horizontal scroll bar.
  Alternatively, click and drag the scroll box right or left on the horizontal scroll bar.

4.3 Scrolling in an Application Window

When a document is opened in an application, such as Microsoft Word, the page on the screen represents an A4 page. There may be one or more pages in the document and, therefore, the entire document may not be visible at once. Use the vertical scroll bar as described in Section 3.2 to scroll down or up to view the complete document.

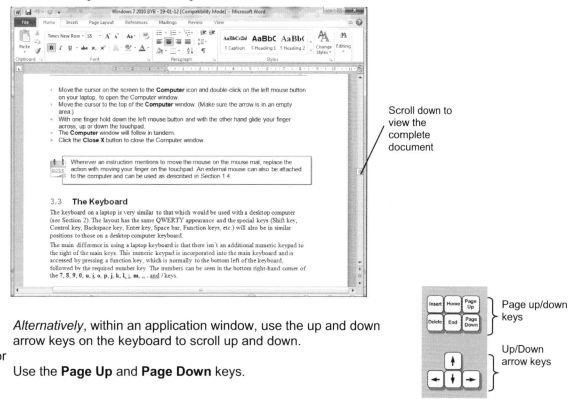

Alternatively, within an application window, use the up and down arrow keys on the keyboard to scroll up and down.

or

Use the **Page Up** and **Page Down** keys.

Section 5 ► The Ribbon

5.1 Ribbon

The ribbon is a feature of the Office 2010 applications – Word, Excel, PowerPoint and Access. On opening an application, the ribbon is at the top of the screen. It provides all of the commands that will be needed while working, such as saving a file, formatting, spell checking, etc. The illustrations below show how each of the application ribbons appear on opening a new or existing file.

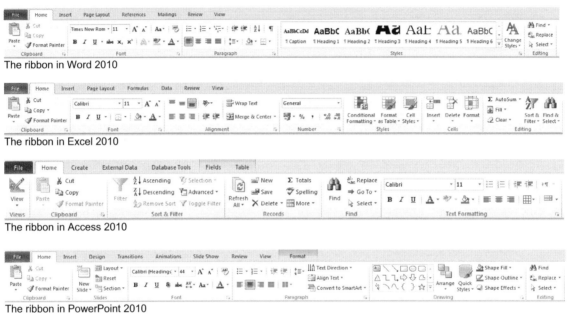

The ribbon in Word 2010

The ribbon in Excel 2010

The ribbon in Access 2010

The ribbon in PowerPoint 2010

The ribbon is organised into sections by **tabs**.

Tabs

Related groups of commands

- The tabs are the headings displayed across the top of the ribbon, such as Home, Insert, Page Layout, etc.
- Underneath a tab related commands are grouped together.
- The tab headings indicate a particular category of activity – for example, by clicking the Page Layout tab the various commands required to change the page size, the margins, etc. are displayed.
- Click on a tab to **activate** it or bring it (and the related command buttons) to the forefront of the ribbon.

5.2 Showing Additional Options

Additional options and settings, which don't appear on the ribbon, are available for each group of related commands by clicking the title at the bottom of a group. For example, by clicking Font, the Font window opens with additional options relating to the formatting of text.

5.3 The File Menu

The File menu is displayed on the top left of the ribbon in each application.

* Click the **File** menu to access a menu for opening and saving files, printing, etc.
* You can also easily access the most recent documents that you have been working on.
* The File menu also provides access to the Word Options feature which helps users to customise applications.

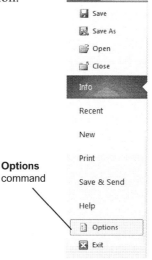

Options command

5.4 Context-Sensitive Tabs

Some tabs, such as the Picture Tools or Table Tools, do not appear on the ribbon until a particular feature is being used.

For example, if a picture is inserted into the document, the Format tab appears on the ribbon providing groups of commands to edit the picture. When the picture is no longer selected, the Format tab will be hidden until the picture is selected again.

The same applies when a table is inserted into the document; the Table Tools – Design and Layout tabs are available on the ribbon.

5.5 Quick Access Toolbar

By default, the Quick Access Toolbar is positioned at the top of the application window above the File menu. (The position can be changed.) It is named because the most commonly used commands – e.g. save, undo and open – can be accessed by clicking the appropriate icon. Further options can be accessed by clicking the arrow on the right of the toolbar. The icons on this toolbar can be changed to suit your needs.

Section 6 ▶ Settings

6.1 Default Settings

When the computer has been switched on and the setup process completed, the desktop will be displayed in a particular way, i.e. the icons will be a particular size and arrangement, the cursor size will be a set size, and the colour scheme and graphics of the desktop background will also be preset.

These preset values for the different features are referred to as the default settings. So, for example, when you switch on a new computer, what you see on the screen has been preset in the factory. However, you can change the preset values to suit your individual preferences or needs. You might like to increase the size of the cursor on the screen if it seems too small or change the desktop background to a different picture or colour scheme.

Changing computer settings is covered in more detail in Module 2, but you may wish to start customising your own workspace to suit your needs, by changing some of the settings below.

To practise changing a default setting, do the following:

Hiding and Showing the Taskbar

The Taskbar will either be temporarily hidden or always visible on the desktop.
To set either of these options, do the following:

- Right-click on a clear part of the taskbar.
  A pop-up menu appears.
- Click **Properties**.
  The **Taskbar and Start Menu Properties** window opens.
- Click in the box to the left of **Auto-hide the taskbar**.
- Click **OK**.
  When the tick appears in this box, the taskbar will be hidden when not in use. When there is no tick in this box, the taskbar will be always visible on the desktop.

Changing the Desktop Background Image

To change the image that appears on the desktop from the default setting, do the following:
- On a blank area of the desktop right-click (click with the right mouse button).
- Click **Personalize** from the pop-up menu.
  The **Personalization** window opens.
- Select the Desktop Background option.
- Select a Windows Desktop Backgrounds from the list.
- Select an image. Click **Save Changes**.

Use the **Browse** button to locate the picture

If the picture is not listed, or you would like to use a picture that you have loaded onto your computer, do the following:
- Click the **Browse** button.
The **Browse** window opens.
- Locate the picture.

Select a folder and click OK

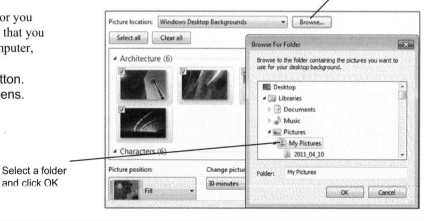

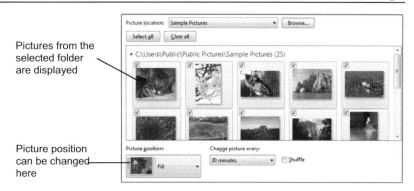

Pictures from the
selected folder
are displayed

Picture position
can be changed
here

Increasing the Size of the Icons on the Desktop

To increase the size of the desktop icons, do the
following:

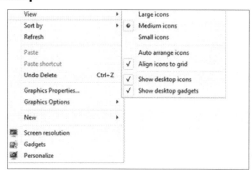

- Right-click on a blank area of the desktop.
- Click **View** from the pop-up menu.
- A sub-menu appears.
- From the choices presented, click
  the box next to **Large icons**.

Increasing the Size of the Cursor

To increase the size of the cursor, do the following:

- Right click the desktop and select **Personalize**.
- From the list on the left-hand side of the window click **Change Mouse Pointers** (another name
  for cursor).

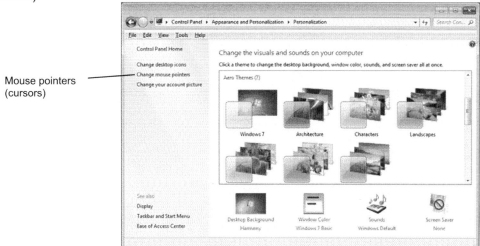

Mouse pointers
(cursors)

The **Mouse Properties** window opens.
- Click the **Pointers** tab and from the
  drop-down list under scheme select **Windows
  Standard** (large) or **Windows Standard** (extra large)
  depending on your preference.
- Click **OK** and see the effect of the change.

Follow the steps again to change the cursor to
a different size.

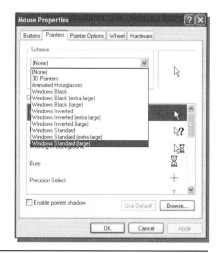

6.2   Application Default Settings

When you open a new document, all the document settings, such as font, text size and page layout, appear with preset values. These are the application default settings.

These default settings can be changed to suit the way in which you work or the documents you create most often. The way in which they are changed, however, varies from one application to the next.

The default font size for a new document in Word is typically set to 12. If you find this too large, you can make 10 the default.

- In the **Home** menu, click the icon (arrow) to the right of **Font**, to open the **Font** window.

This icon is called the Dialog Box Launcher

Arrow icon indicates the Dialog Box launcher

- Set the font size to **10**.
- Click the **Default** button at the bottom of the window.
- Click **Yes** in the confirmation window that opens.
  In each new document you open, the font size will be set to 10.

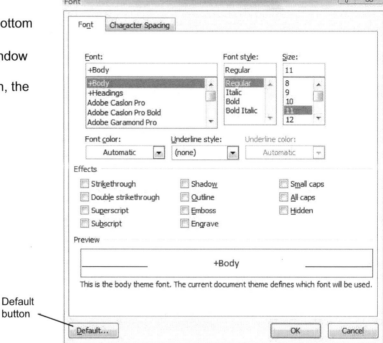

Default button

Section 7 ▶　　　The Help Function

7.1　Online Help

When you are using the computer, there are comprehensive Help systems available to assist you with problems that may arise during the course of your work.

System help assists you with using the computer. It is available in the Start menu.

Application help assists you with a specific application. It can be accessed within each of the Office applications by clicking on the question mark button on the right of the ribbon.

In both cases, there are different types of help available – such as looking up a glossary, taking a tour or tutorial, step-by-step instructions with worked examples, selecting from an index or accessing online help when your computer is connected to the internet.

7.2　System Help

The Help and Support system can be used to access general information about your computer system as well as for specific queries. Information can be accessed using the search facility, an index or a table of contents.

To access the System Help, do the following:
- Click the **Start** button and choose the **Help and Support** item on the menu.
  The **Help and Support Center** window opens.

Forward and Back buttons enable you to move back and forth between articles that have been opened

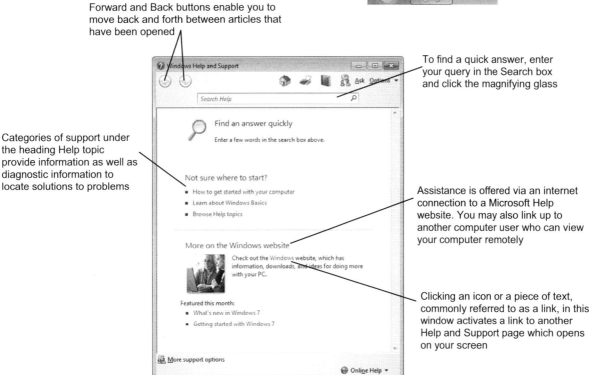

To find a quick answer, enter your query in the Search box and click the magnifying glass

Categories of support under the heading Help topic provide information as well as diagnostic information to locate solutions to problems

Assistance is offered via an internet connection to a Microsoft Help website. You may also link up to another computer user who can view your computer remotely

Clicking an icon or a piece of text, commonly referred to as a link, in this window activates a link to another Help and Support page which opens on your screen

For example, if information on installing a digital camera is needed, you would use the Help and Support window as follows.

- Click the **Start** button.
- From the menu select **Help and Support**.
- Under the **Not sure where to start?** heading, click the **Browse Help Topics** item.
- Select a topic from the list of links.
  A window opens showing a list of categories related to your search.

7.3 Using the Browse Help Option

Another way to access information using the Help and Support window is to use the **Browse Help** option.

- On the **Help and Support Center** toolbar, click the **Browse Help** button.
  A list of contents is displayed.
- Select a link to a Help topic.
- A further page of sub-topics will be displayed. Click a sub-topic.
- A page of text will be displayed for the selected topic (further links may also be displayed).

Browse button

7.4 Application Help

When you are working in an Office 2010 application, you can get help on a particular problem by searching either the Help content on your computer (installed with the application) or through Microsoft Office Online, when your computer is connected to the internet. The application help feature in Office 2010 is accessed by clicking the question mark button on the right of the ribbon. The example below shows the help system in Microsoft Word, but the process is the same for each of the applications.

To access the help system when working in an application, do the following:

- Click the **Microsoft Office Help** icon on the ribbon.
- The **Help** window opens on the Home page, displaying a table of contents in the main section, with the most common help categories.
- If the help topic you are looking for is available in the list on the home page, clicking it will provide a further list of related topics to choose from.
- Click until you find the information you need.
  To keep the **Help** window active or on top of the application window – if you want to refer to the instructions as you carry out a step-by-step procedure – click the drawing pin button will switch between keeping the window on top or behind.

Drawing Pin button

Keep on top

Not on top

7.5   Using the Search Option

7.5.1 Simple Search

There is a simple Search facility within the Help and Support Center that enables you to type specific search word(s).

To look for help on installing a digital camera, do the following:

- Type a topic into the **Search box**, for example, 'digital cameras'.
- Click the magnifying glass.
  A window with topics related to **Digital Camera** will be displayed.
- Click the most appropriate text link to access the information you require.

7.5.2 Searching for Help Content Stored on Your Computer: Browse Word Help

There is a simple **Search** facility within the Help window which enables a search on specific word(s).

To find information do the following:

- Type a topic into the **Search** box, for example, **printing**.
- Click the **Search** button.
  The help content stored on your computer is searched for any occurrences of the word 'printing' and the results are displayed in the main section of the Help window.
- Use the **Next** button to go to the next page of results.
- Click the most appropriate text link to access the information you require.
  Typically, background information and step-by-step instructions will be presented.

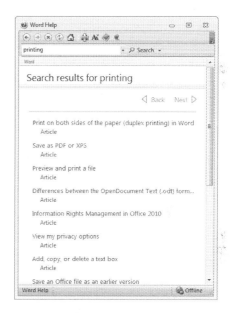

7.5.3 Searching for Help Content Stored on Your Computer: Table of Contents

You can return to the **Table of Contents** list at any time.

- Click the **Table of Contents** icon.
  The **Table of Contents** list opens in a pane on the left of the main pane.
- Click a topic.
  The help content stored on your computer is searched for any occurrences of the word 'printing' and the results are displayed in the main section of the **Help** window.
- Use the **Next** button to go to the next page of results.
- Click the most appropriate text link to access the information you require.
  Typically, background information and step-by-step instructions will be presented.

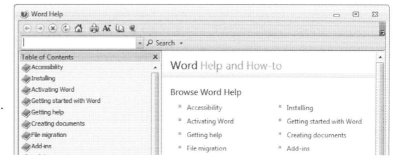

7.5.4 Searching for Help Content on the Internet: Show Content from Office Online

If your computer is connected to the internet, you can include the vast number of help resources in the search, along with the help content stored on your computer.

- Click the **Connection Status** button at the bottom right of the Help window.

- From the pop-up menu, select **Show content from Office Online**.
  A tick mark will be placed beside it and a new search will be carried out displaying results which will include web pages. Click the most appropriate text link to access the information you require. If you click a web page symbol, the help topic will be displayed in a browser window (e.g. printing).

When only the content stored on your computer is being searched, the **Connection Status** will display **Offline**.

When the search includes online content, the **Connection Status** will display **Connected to Office.com**.

7.5.5 Searching for Help Content in a Specific Location

A specific location or type of help information (such as, visual or audio demonstrations, additional templates, etc.) can be searched for.

- In the **Help** window, click the down arrow beside the **Search** button to display a list of options. The list is divided into two sections, i.e. **Content from Office.com** and **Content from this computer**.
- Click the relevant heading to search in that location.

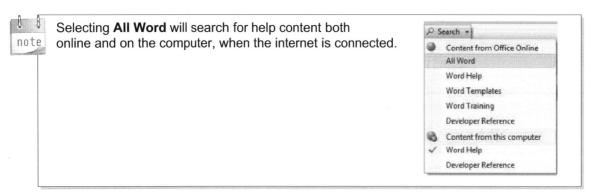

Selecting **All Word** will search for help content both online and on the computer, when the internet is connected.

7.6 Wizards

'Wizard' is a term used to describe a set of instructions that leads you through the steps to perform a task. The wizard asks you various questions about the available options. When you make your choices, the wizard then performs the task for you. Wizards are usually available for complex tasks that involve many steps, such as creating a table or performing a mail merge. (See **Tables** and **Mail Merge** in Module 3.) The advantage of using a wizard is that it simplifies a complex procedure – you just follow the steps. Automating the task also saves time. The disadvantage of using a wizard is that you may have less control over the final result, as your choice of options may be limited.

module **1**

Concepts of Information and Communication Technology

module 1
Concepts of ICT

Module Goals for Module 1

Concepts of Information and Communication Technology (ICT) requires the candidate to understand the main concepts of ICT at a general level and to know about the different parts of a computer.

The candidate shall be able to:

- Understand what hardware is, know about factors that affect computer performance and know about peripheral devices.

- Understand what software is and give examples of common applications software and operating system software.

- Understand how information networks are used within computing, and be aware of the different options to connect to the internet.

- Understand what Information and Communication Technology (ICT) is and give examples of its practical applications in everyday life.

- Understand health and safety and environmental issues in relation to using computers.

- Recognise important security issues associated with using computers.

- Recognise important legal issues in relation to copyright and data protection associated with using computers.

Section 1 ▶   Basic Concepts

1.1   Types of Computer

1.1.1 Mainframe Computers

Mainframe computers have become more commonly known as **enterprise servers** as major organisations, such as banks, government departments and supermarket chains, use them to handle large amounts of information. They are room-sized computers that work at high speed and have very large storage capacities. The cost of installing, running and maintaining mainframe computers runs into hundreds of thousands of euro a year.

Mainframe computers are usually connected to a large number of terminals – screens and keyboards – such as you may see in banks. Some terminals are known as 'dumb' terminals as they cannot operate on their own – all the processing is carried out by the mainframe computer. Other terminals, while still relying on the mainframe, have a certain amount of processing power that can be used locally by the user. These are known as 'intelligent' terminals.

1.1.2 Servers

Servers are a type of computer that stores and retrieves large amounts of information. Different types of server are used to handle different types of information. For example, a **web server** processes information from web pages and applications, a **file server** stores a large collection of files and a **database server** manages information in a database. Other uses for a server include storing common documents, files and software in a network (see Section 4.1).

1.2 Personal Computers

1.2.1 Desktop Computers

The most common type of **personal computer** is a desktop computer, so called because it fits on a desk and is not portable. PCs are manufactured under different brand names throughout the world but are also referred to as **IBM-compatible** computers. This indicates that, although brand names may differ, they can run the same programs and applications as similar computers made by **IBM**, the American company whose PCs became the business standard. PCs are different from **Macintosh** computers, which use a different operating system and are made by **Apple**.

Computers can be connected together, i.e. **networked**, to share programs and information between users. Organisations like universities, government departments and businesses use networks to share information and manage data.

As PCs have become a universal office and home machine, their cost has dropped from thousands of euro to just hundreds for a basic machine. The desktop PC is now the most widely used small computer. Modern desktop computers can facilitate many tasks, from composing simple letters to video editing and are used widely in the business and academic worlds.

1.2.2 Laptop Computers

Laptop computers – which are also called notebooks – are small, portable, computers that can be carried around and used, as the name suggests, on your lap. They are characterised by small screens and small keyboards. Most modern laptops can be connected to a standard monitor, mouse and keyboard, and, in this way, the disadvantages of working with a small screen and keyboard for extended periods may be overcome. Because of high manufacturing costs, laptop computers are usually more expensive than desktop PCs of similar capacity. Modern laptops can do the same jobs as a desktop PC. They are mainly used by people who do not work in a fixed location, such as sales representatives, journalists, photographers and university lecturers.

1.2.3 Tablet PCs

Tablet PCs are A4-sized computers that have no keyboard and run a modified version of the full computer operating software, often with extensions to enable handwriting recognition, etc. They can be written on directly with a stylus. The main function of tablet PCs is to conduct light business functions, note-taking, e-book reading and to provide wireless internet access. They are mainly used by stock controllers, graphic designers and digital artists, though are also used by people who may have difficulty using a traditional desktop computer.

1.3 Hand-Held Devices

Hand-held devices comprise a range of computers that are portable and can easily fit in the hand. They include mobile phones, palmtop computers, personal digital assistants (PDAs), mp3 players, portable media players and hand-held game consoles. These types of computer can often perform many of the functions of a PC or laptop, such as accessing the Internet, sending and receiving e-mails, playing music, making phone calls, managing a diary and address book, playing video games, and so on. Hand-held devices differ from PCs and laptops in that they do not have large hard drives or large screens or keyboards. Instead, hand-held devices have smaller, or external, memories and often rely on touchscreen technology or a small keyboard to input information. In general, hand-held devices are intended to give the user freedom of movement and access to information and communication.

With advances in technology, hand-held devices are becoming increasingly **convergent**, covering a multitude of uses. For example, Apple's **iPhone** offers mobile phone capability, as well as audio and video playback and a full suite of productivity applications, such as e-mail and access to the internet.

1.3.1 Personal Digital Assistant (PDAs)

These are a fully functional computer that can be held in one hand and provide a number of functions related to personal organisation. They may download e-mail, play music, manage a diary and address book, handle databases, facilitate note taking and so on. PDAs typically use a pointing device, similar to a small pen, to input data through screen menus, icons and sometimes very minute keyboards. With developments in palmtop computers, PDAs and mobile telephones, the dividing line between them all is becoming less obvious and a multipurpose small computer, referred to as a pocket PC, is now available.

1.3.2 Mobile Phones/Smartphones

These are phones that do not require a fixed land line to make calls. They also use wireless technology to access the Internet, where users can access the full range of options, including m-banking and checking news websites. Mobile phones are becoming ever more sophisticated. Higher end models are sometimes referred to as **smartphones** as they can run complex operating systems, such as Symbian or Windows Mobile, and offer similar applications to a PC.

1.3.3 Palmtop Computers

Palmtop computers have a very small screen size and keyboard size and this has obvious limitations. Essentially, they are personal information managers (PIM). As they are very small in size, they do not usually have disk drives. Instead, they have slots that allow them to be connected to other devices to transfer information. They are usually used in conjunction with a desktop or laptop. In some palmtops, the keyboard has been replaced by an electronic pen and handwriting recognition software. Palmtops can offer some of the functionality of a laptop, such as word processing, e-mail and spreadsheets, in a much-reduced size. Files can be transferred from palmtops to desktops or laptops for further editing or storage.

1.4 PC Components

1.4.1 Main Parts of a PC

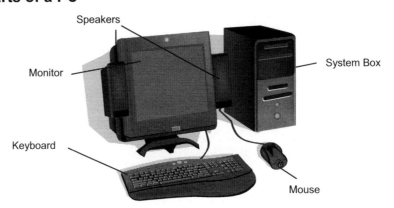

- The **central processing unit (CPU)** – which is also called the **microprocessor** – is the brain of the computer and is located on the motherboard.
- The **system box**, or **base unit**, houses the **power supply**, **hard disk** and a **CD-ROM or DVD** drive or drives. These are all connected to the **motherboard**, where an array of microchips, such as the **CPU** and **RAM (Random Access Memory)** store and process data. Special plugs called **ports** are attached to electronic cards that fit into slots in the motherboard and to which peripheral devices are connected. The base unit may be either horizontal, known as a **desktop** case, or vertical, known as a **tower** case (as in the illustration).
- The **hard disk** is the main data storage area used by a computer. Hard disks are used to store the applications that make a computer work. Data can be retrieved much faster from a hard disk than from CD-ROMs. They cannot be easily removed from the system box, so they are referred to as fixed storage.
- The **CD-ROM drive** and/or **DVD drive** opens from the system box to accept CDs or DVDs. The drive is used either to read existing data from a disc or to write (called 'burning') data onto a blank disc. The main difference between a CD and a DVD is the amount and type of data which can be stored. CDs are generally used for audio and can hold 650MB, roughly equivalent to 80 minutes of audio playback time. DVDs are generally used for video and can hold 4.7GB, which is about 120 minutes of video playback time. Some DVDs can store data on both sides of the disc, enabling twice the capacity. CDs and DVDs can also store data other than audio and video, such as documents and digital photos.
- A **USB port** is a special plug that enables users to connect external devices to their computer. USB (Universal Serial Bus) has become a standard interface for many devices, including digital cameras, mp3 players, printers, audio speakers, Flash memory sticks and external hard drives. USB ports can also connect essential components, such as a keyboard or a mouse, to a base unit.
- The **keyboard** and **mouse** enable the user to input data into the computer.
- The **monitor** is a display unit, like a TV screen. It displays the task being performed by the computer.
- Other items, e.g. printers, scanners, modems, which can be added on to the basic computer, are known as **peripheral devices** or, more commonly, **peripherals.** These are covered in detail in Section 2.4 of this module.

1.4.2 Ports

Hardware ports on a computer provide an interface for the transfer of information between it and other devices. They are physical connectors which accept a cable with a specific type of plug.

The most common types are listed below.

- **Serial ports** are a legacy device and have largely been superseded by superior technologies, such as USB. Serial ports can send or receive one bit of data at a time.

- **Parallel ports**, which have become largely redundant, can send or receive multiple bits of data simultaneously. Because their main use was connecting printers to computers, they are often called **printer ports**.

- **Network ports** are used to connect a computer to a network. They generally have one or two small LEDs indicating a network connection is present.

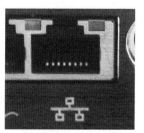

- **USB** (**Universal Serial Bus**) is the replacement for the old serial and parallel ports. It has numerous advantages, such as:
  - Greatly increased data transfer speed compared to serial or parallel ports.
  - The ability to chain devices together – for example a USB mouse can be plugged into a USB keyboard, which in turn can be plugged into a computer.
  - Smaller USB devices can draw power through the USB connection, helping reduce the amount of cabling, plugs and power sockets needed.

- **FireWire** is similar to USB and is commonly used in Apple computers, and in audio/video devices, such as digital camcorders. It offers higher data transfer speeds than USB and does not need a computer to control it.

1.5 Factors Impacting Computer Performance

1.5.1 The Central Processing Unit

The **central processing unit** (CPU) is a microchip, containing millions of electronic components, that interprets and executes instructions and performs calculations. Along with the processor and other components, the **clock speed**, or operating frequency, determines how fast the computer carries out the instructions it receives. In general terms, the faster the clock speed, the more

1

efficient the computer. The clock speed is measured in megahertz (MHz) or gigahertz (GHz), with megahertz being the smallest unit of measurement and gigahertz the largest. The clock speed of current computers may be as high as 3.2 GHz (billions of cycles per second).

A common PC microprocessor is the **Pentium 4**, made by Intel, but there are several other types of CPU made by different manufacturers.

1.5.2 Memory (RAM Capacity)

The computer programs used on a computer are loaded into **RAM** (random access memory) from the hard disk. Work created on a computer is also held in RAM until it is saved. Anything contained in RAM is instantly available. The computer does not have to look for the information on the hard disk. RAM can only store data when a computer is switched on and everything in RAM vanishes when the computer is switched off.

The amount of RAM installed on a computer may affect the speed at which the computer operates. The system software takes up an appreciable part of the available RAM. Thus, if there is not enough RAM available for what a user wants to do, the computer uses some space on the hard disk as **temporary** or **virtual memory**. It takes much longer to access data in virtual memory than RAM and this slows down the computer.

1.5.3 Hard Disk

The speed at which the hard disk can access and save information has an effect on the overall speed of a computer when it is using the hard disk. This is connected with the speed at which the disk rotates, commonly 5,000 to 10,000 rpm. As a general rule, the faster the speed of rotation, the faster the computer can save or gain access to data.

To illustrate the speed difference between the hard disk and other media, it takes the computer roughly 10 times longer to access data from a CD-ROM than from a hard disk. However, access speed can also be limited by the capacity of the storage medium. The more information that is stored, the longer it can take to locate and retrieve programs and data.

1.5.4 Bus Speed

A further factor influencing a computer's efficiency is the speed at which data is sent from one part of the computer to another. The **System Bus** transfers data in much the same way as a transport system shares and conveys passengers and goods over a transport network. Dedicated connections between components carry different types of information, such as data and memory locations. Bus speeds are described in terms of the number of 'bits' of information that can be transferred at a single time. Typical speeds are 66, 100, 133 and 400 megahertz (MHz). 400 MHz is equivalent to 400 million bits of information per second. PCI Express, for example, can transfer up to 8Gb (gigabits) per second.

1.5.5 Graphics Card Processor

The **graphics card** is a piece of hardware that is dedicated to processing graphic screen displays. The graphics accelerator card is a specialised variation of the standard graphics card which has its own processor and memory, meaning that that this workload can be taken away from the CPU.

Graphic accelerators are generally optimised for producing the 3D graphics used in areas such as Computer Aided Design and gaming. As operating systems become more complex visually, they are being increasingly used to help in drawing the normal desktop display as well.

1.5.6 Number of Applications Being Used

The more tasks that are being worked on at any one time in RAM, the more the CPU resources that are engaged. The number of applications open and the volume of work being executed can affect a computer's performance. The less processing resources and memory that are available, the fewer tasks that can be performed at the same time.

Section 2 ▶   Hardware

2.1   Definition

Hardware refers to the physical parts of the computer – such as the screen, system box, keyboard and cables – which come with the computer when you buy it. The word 'hardware' can describe a complete computer or a part of it, such as the printer or scanner. Hardware can do nothing without software.

2.2   Memory and Storage

2.2.1   Types of Memory

Random access memory (RAM) is the main working memory of the computer. RAM is measured in gigabytes (GB), so a computer could be said to have 2GB of RAM. RAM is empty when the computer is first switched on. The system software, such as Windows, is loaded into it so that a computer can carry out all the functions required. If a word processing program is being used to produce a document, the word processing program is first loaded into RAM and the document being prepared is also stored in RAM as it is worked on. If the computer is switched off before the document has been saved, everything held in RAM is lost and will need to be recreated. RAM can be described as **volatile** memory.

Read-only memory (**ROM**) is stored on memory chips. Data is permanently burned into these chips when they are manufactured and they usually cannot be altered. The information and instructions held in ROM are there before the computer is switched on and still there when the power is off. Unlike RAM, a computer cannot write to ROM memory. It can only be read from, and can be described as **non-volatile** memory. This kind of memory is typically used to store instructions telling a computer how to start up. ROM must be available immediately when the computer is switched on. Only small amounts of data are stored in ROM compared with the large amounts in RAM.

2.2.2   How Computer Storage is Measured

A computer must be able to 'remember' the information it is working with. The information is 'remembered' by being stored, either temporarily or permanently. All information processed by the computer is handled and stored in digital form using **binary code**. This code only uses a series of two digits, 0 and 1. In our daily work, we normally use a number system that has 10 digits, 0 to 9, the **decimal system**. Below is how you and a computer count from 0 to 9.

You:	0	1	2	3	4	5	6	7	8	9
Computer:	0000	0001	0010	0011	0100	0101	0110	0111	1000	1001

A single digit – **0** or **1** – is called a **bit**. Bits are grouped together, typically in sets of eight, to make **bytes**. Computer memory is measured using the following sequence.

1 Bit	1 Byte	1 Kilobyte (KB)	1 Megabyte (MB)	1 Gigabyte (GB)	1 Terabyte (TB)
A single digit: 0 or 1	8 bits (e.g. can represent the letter A)	1,024 bytes (1 thousand)	1,048,576 bytes (1 million)	1,073,741,824 bytes (1 thousand million)	1,099,511,627,776 bytes (1 trillion)

2.2.3 Types of Storage Media

The programs used and work produced on a computer must be stored before it is switched off so that they are available again. The next time the computer is switched on, they can be loaded into RAM and work can continue. This kind of mechanical storage is often referred to as **secondary memory**. Common examples include the following.

- **Hard disk:** There are two main types of hard disk: internal and external. Internal hard disks are located within the computer system box. They are usually composed of several metal (hard) magnetically coated disks encased in a sealed metal box. The capacity of a typical hard disk in a laptop is 160GB 250GB for external hard disks and 500GB for desktops. Larger sizes are readily available. Extra hard disks can be added to the computer, either internally or externally. External hard disks are separate to the system box and are attached to it by cables.

- **CD (compact disc):** While hard disks are magnetic, a compact disc (CD) is an optical disc that uses a laser to read the information held on it. It can store up to 700MB of data. CD-R (compact disc recordable) is a write once, read many times CD format that allows one-time recording on a disc. CD-RW (compact disc rewriteable) is a CD format that allows repeated recording on a disc. A CD-ROM is a pre-recorded compact disc that cannot be recorded to. CDs are most suitable for storing large files and for programs that mix text, graphics and audio, such as illustrated encyclopaedias, interactive games and computer-based training programmes.

- **DVD (digital versatile disc):** This is a high-capacity development of the CD that can store gigabytes of information. While CDs were originally designed for recorded music, DVDs have always had many uses. As a format, it has replaced the standard videocassette, for example, as it can store an entire feature film with very high picture quality. Like CD-ROMs, standard DVDs, such as those containing films, cannot be recorded to by users, but various recordable formats such as DVD-R are available.

- **USB flash drives**: These are a small (they can normally fit on a keyring), convenient storage device that plug into the USB. They can hold from 1GB to 32GB of information.

- **Online file storage** refers to the increasingly common method of storing files over the internet. Certain websites allow registered users to transfer their files to the internet where they can be shared openly or accessed only by the owner. Once the file is online, it may also be transferred back to the user's computer as though it were stored on any other device. Online storage is most often used to share files with other computer users. This is especially true of digital photos, videos and music. Large files are usually not stored online as they take a long time to transfer to and from the internet.

- **Network drives** If a computer is part of a network, then access storage can be used that is physically located on another computer. For example, a network server computer in an office may have several hard disks of huge capacity that are **shared** and thus available to other computers on the network. Users can transfer files to and from these shared locations in the same way as they would with the hard disks in their own **local** computers. The files are transmitted over **network cables** or via a **wireless network connection**.

● Portable digital devices such as digital cameras, mobile phones and hand-held games consoles often use removable **memory cards** for storage. The type of memory technology most often used on these cards is **flash memory**, and the cards themselves are often referred to as **flash cards**. There are various card formats and capacities, for example CompactFlash and SD. All the varieties of card are by necessity physically small.

A 1GB **microSD** card is shown on the right at actual size. Capacities at the time of writing range from 128MB to 16GB. Many PCs have inbuilt **card readers** which can accept a variety of memory card formats. The cards then become visible as emovable drives and files can be copied on and off as normal. Memory cards from digital cameras can be used in special vending machines to print physical copies of digital photos.

The illustration below shows how different drives are represented on the computer screen.

2.3　Common Input Devices

Computers are programmed to work on information (data) that is entered by users through various devices. Devices that are connected to a computer are referred to as **peripherals**. Below are some of the most common input devices. There are many other specialist peripheral devices manufactured to input information into computers.

2.3.1　Mouse

The mouse is a small device that the hand can fit over easily. As the mouse is moved on a mouse mat, it transmits information to the computer, which moves the **cursor** on the screen accordingly.

The typical mouse has three buttons. When a mouse button is clicked over an item, it can activate a program, select a particular function, etc. A wheel mounted between the forward buttons is used for scrolling through long documents. Mice use laser light shining from underneath to track movement. They are normally connected to the computer with a USB cable, but some use radio or infrared technology to communicate with the computer and are called cordless mice.

2.3.2　Keyboards

Keyboards have character keys derived from the arrangement used on a typewriter. The standard keyboard is known as a **QWERTY** keyboard (from the first six letters on the top row of letter keys). Most keyboards have a numeric keypad on the right-hand side, as well as extra function keys that are used to perform pre-programmed functions.

2.3.3　Trackballs

Trackballs are essentially a mouse turned upside down. Users rotate a ball that is mounted on a small box to move the cursor about the screen. The trackball saves the space normally taken up by the mouse mat. There are buttons beside the trackball which duplicate the functions of the mouse buttons. They are often used in applications such as Computer Aided Design, as they provide extremely precise control.

2.3.4 Scanners

Scanners are an optical input device. They use light-sensing processes to capture images which are then translated into a digital code for processing by the computer.

- **Flatbed** scanners look like a very small photocopier. They scan images such as graphics, photographs or text, and convert them into digital information that can be understood by a computer. The images and text can be manipulated using specialist software and printed or stored for later use.

- **Barcode readers** scan barcodes, such as those used on grocery items. The computer is pre-programmed to recognise the various codes represented by the bars and transfers them into numeric information, such as prices.

- **OCR scanners (optical character recognition)** are used to recognise printed or written text characters by a computer. They use a photo-scanning technology that scans text character by character and is commonly used to process cheques and credit card slips, and to sort mail. Optical character recognition can be used to scan documents that can then be converted into speech.

In the office, scanners are often included in **multifunction devices**, which also perform laser printing and faxing functions.

2.3.5 Touchpads

Touchpads are a small touch-sensitive device (2.5cm to 5cm square) that replaces the mouse on a typical laptop computer. When a user's fingertip is moved over its surface, the result is similar to using a mouse or trackball. Touchpads are also used on some keyboards as an alternative to the mouse. (See BYB, Section 3.)

2.3.6 Joysticks

Joysticks are a hand lever that can be moved in various directions to control movement on the screen. Most joysticks include a number of buttons that are pressed to perform various actions. Joysticks are commonly used in flight simulators or to control computer-operated machines.

2.3.7 Digital Cameras

These cameras digitise images and store them onto a removable **flash memory** card, as opposed to film. These images can then be transferred to a computer for editing and printing. When connected to the computer, most modern digital cameras are identified by the computer as an external storage device or as an additional drive and can be explored the same as any other drive.

2.3.8 Microphones

As well as enabling sound to be recorded on a computer, microphones can also be used to enable speech to control computer functions when the appropriate software is installed. Speech can be digitised, converted into text and placed in a word processing program.

2.3.9 Styluses

Styluses are used with some PDA and similar hand-held devices. It is a small implement that is held and used to write directly onto a touch-sensitive screen. Special handwriting recognition software can then convert the handwriting into text as if it had been typed on a keyboard.

2.3.10 Webcams

Web cameras, or webcams, are small digital cameras connected to a computer that are capable of capturing still pictures or streaming video. They can be used, for example, for video conferencing or with internet telephony applications.

2.3.11 Graphics Pads and Tablets

These have a flat rectangular base that is sensitive to either light or touch and a special pen. As the pen is moved over the flat base, it records the strokes made by the pen and replicates them on the screen. For example, they can produce artwork in a more natural way than using a mouse.

2.4 Common Output Devices

Computers can output information in various ways using different pieces of peripheral equipment.

2.4.1 Monitors

Monitors, or screens, provide the visual interface to the operation of a computer. They display a standard graphical paradigm that provides visual feedback about what actions are being performed and what is occurring in the use of the machine.

Below are some of the common attributes of modern monitors.

- They use flat, light LCD or plasma displays.

- The **size** is measured diagonally between opposite corners of the screen. Common sizes are 17" and 19". Larger sizes are often used for graphics and full-page layout work where one or more pages can be shown full-size on the monitor. **The resolution** is the number of dots or **pixels** that can be displayed on the monitor. The typical display was 640 pixels across the screen and 480 pixels from top to bottom. This is known as VGA (video graphics array) resolution. The next generation of monitors had a resolution standard of 800 by 600 pixels and were referred to as SVGA (super VGA). The higher resolution of 1,024 by 768 pixels, or XVGA (extended VGA), is the standard today, though resolutions higher than XVGA are common. A monitor with higher resolution will display more of a document than one with a lower resolution on the same size screen, but the text will appear smaller.

- The **quality of the colour** displayed by a monitor depends on the construction of the monitor itself as well as the electronic circuitry in the computer. It is common to describe colour quality by the number of colours that can be displayed. Early computer monitors could only display 4 or 16 colours, but 256 colours gradually became the standard used in software. Computers and their monitors are now able to display thousands, even millions, of colours, giving photographic quality to the display.

2.4.2 Printers

Printers enable documents produced on a computer to be printed on paper or other material. Such documents are often referred to as **printouts** or **hard copies**. Below are some of the most common printers used today.

- **Dot matrix** printers are also called impact printers. They use a print head with pins that produce dots on the page by striking through an inked ribbon. The greater the number of pins and the greater the number of times they strike a particular area, the better the quality of the print but the slower the printing speed. Carbon copies can be produced with these printers. In more recent times, they have been used for small printouts, such as with ticket machines or at supermarket checkouts. They are still widely used with accounting software where multipart stationery produces multiple copies of documents.

- **Inkjet** printers work by shooting minute jets of ink directly onto the paper. They can use different coloured inks to produce high-quality colour images. Most inkjet printers use separate black ink for ordinary text. Inkjet printers are inexpensive to buy, but running costs are high, with cartridges having to be replaced after a few hundred copies. When a printer uses a single cartridge containing all the colours, the whole cartridge has to be replaced when one colour runs out. Some printers use separate cartridges for the different colours, up to six in some cases, but then several cartridges have to be replaced on a regular basis. For maximum print quality, specialist art paper has to be used, adding to the expense. Carbon copies cannot be produced by inkjet printers as there is no mechanical striking action involved. Inkjet printers are quiet to use but are slower than laser printers.

- **Laser** printers work in the same way as photocopiers. Instead of a lens, they use a laser to place an electrical charge in the shape of the text and/or graphics to be printed on a rotating drum. The charged area of the drum attracts fine black powder (toner) to itself and the powder is pressed onto the paper as the drum rotates. The paper is then heated to seal the image onto the paper.

1

Laser printers produce high-quality images, usually only in black and white (or greyscale) because of cost. Colour laser printers typically cost two or three times as much to buy as an equivalent black and white model. An office-quality laser printer is much more expensive than a small inkjet printer, but it is quieter and of more robust construction and it is designed for heavy use. It is also much faster than an inkjet printer and running costs are lower, as a toner cartridge typically produces around 5,000 pages before it needs to be replaced. As with inkjet printers, carbon copies cannot be produced.

2.4.3 Speakers

Multimedia applications have made the use of loudspeakers with computers essential and they are standard equipment in modern computers. Small loudspeakers are usually supplied, but a computer can be connected to an external amplifier and larger loudspeakers, if required. Modern flat-screen LCD monitors are supplied with speakers built in to the side panels.

2.4.4 Headphones

Headphones are small personal speakers that users wear over their ears. Those that fit inside the ear are also called **earbuds** or **earphones**. Headphones are appropriate when users don't want to disturb those around them, such as in a classroom or on a train.

2.5 Input/Output Devices

Some devices can be classified as both input and output devices. These include touchscreens and electronic musical devices.

2.5.1 Touchscreens

Touchscreens enable a computer to be controlled by directly touching the screen. No mouse or other device is needed. Touch-sensitive screens are used in information booths for public access where a mouse or other device would be impractical.

2.5.2 Electronic Musical Devices

These instruments can be connected to a computer via the soundcard and the input manipulated with special software. The results can be transferred to CD or stored on the computer's hard disk for further editing or playback. Typical examples include sequencers and synthesisers.

Section 3 ▶ Software

3.1 Definition
The term software collectively describes programs that are executed on a computer, for example **operating system software** and **application software**.

3.2 Operating and Application Software

3.2.1 Operating System Software
This is a program that holds all the instructions that make the computer work, e.g. the start-up procedure, monitor display and the use of hard disks, etc. for storing data.

The operating system also manages other programs, such as word processors, games and internet browsers. It accepts instructions from them, passes them to the CPU, arranges the display on the monitor, takes the results from the CPU and sends them to be stored on the hard disk or to the printer for printing. The operating system is permanently stored on the hard disk and is automatically started when the computer is switched on. Without an operating system, a computer would be like a car without an engine.

Common examples of operating systems are:
* **Microsoft Windows**, variants of which, e.g. **Windows Vista** and **Windows 7**, are the most common operating systems in use on PC compatible computers.
* **Ubuntu** and **Fedora**, which are Linux-based and run on PC-compatible computers.
* **MacOS**, which runs on Apple and Intel hardware.
* **Symbian**, which runs on many portable devices, such as smartphones.

3.2.2 Applications Software
Applications software is all the other software that runs on a computer. This is the software most users recognise as the applications with which they do their work. The Microsoft Office 2010 suite of programs, which you are learning to use as part of this course, is an example of applications software. The suite is made up of the following applications.

Software Type	Product Name	Function of Software
Word Processor	Word	Preparing documents, such as reports and letters.
Spreadsheet	Excel	Manipulating numbers and performing mathematical functions.
Database	Access	Keeping track of information, such as details of members of a club.
Presentation	PowerPoint	Making slide shows for presentations.
E-Mail	Outlook	Sending and receiving email messages.

Other common applications include those listed below.

Software Type	Product Name	Function of Software
Web Browser	Internet Explorer	Accessing the Internet and viewing content on web pages.
Photo Editor	Picture Manager	Managing and editing digital photographs.
Computer Games	Games for Windows	Playing games on the computer, either single-player or multi-player.

There is a considerable range of applications software available to address different needs within organisations and businesses. Personnel management systems are available to record and track employee profiles, entitlements, salary, assignments, etc. Management information systems in a customer services division of a company would typically record a customer needs profile, product support record, levels of access to online information, contact details and other relevant information.

There are also applications, such as customer relationship management systems, that generate, maintain and update customer contact information. Additionally, there are telesales management systems that can monitor connections made, call durations and compile response rates of prospective clients, etc. Accounting software can maintain financial records, produce cash flow statements, balance sheets, maintain ledgers and, depending on their sophistication, prepare quarterly reports, tax returns, forecasts, etc.

In the home, e-mail and web browsing applications are also commonly used, along with photo editing software that can be used to work with photographs downloaded from a digital camera. Games are also applications, often played online against other players all over the world.

3.2.3 Contrasting Operating Systems and Applications Software
An operating system, such as Windows, and an application, such as Word are both examples of computer software. The difference between them is that without the operating system the applications are useless – it provides the platform on which they can run.

3.3 Enhancing Accessibility
Accessibility refers to the ease with which various components of a computer, either hardware or software can be used. Certain disabilities can prevent users from being able to perform various functions. For example, if a user is visually impaired, they may have difficulty seeing what is on the screen. A range of options is available to enhance accessibility for those users who may have difficulty using a computer conventionally. Most come as part of the Windows operating system.

- **Voice recognition software** takes the place of a keyboard and mouse, enabling users to speak into a microphone. The software then converts what is said into text, performs the command that has been stated, etc.
- **Screen readers** are software applications that convert screen information to another output format that is accessible to users with a visual impairment. Screen readers are regularly used to convert text in an active document to digitised voice.
- **Screen magnifiers** are software applications that enlarge the content displayed on the screen so that it can be seen more easily.
- **On-Screen keyboards** are virtual keyboards that are displayed on the screen and enable users to type with a pointing device or joystick.

Section 4 ▶ Information Networks

1

4.1   Types of Network

4.1.1   LAN, WLAN and WAN

In a **local area network (LAN)**, a number of computers are networked, i.e. linked together, by means of cables within a limited area, often in the same building. Company offices are often networked in this way.

A **wireless local area network (WLAN)** is similar to a LAN but the computers are not linked with cables. In a wireless network, computers can communicate using radio waves that send signals to each other through the air. This gives users in the network greater flexibility as they can move around within the network area. WLANs are becoming more common as the popularity of laptops increases. WLANs can be found in homes and offices as well as public places, like cafes, where users can access the internet.

In a **wide area network (WAN)**, computers, as well as computer networks, are linked together over a large distance.

The WAN operates in the same way as a local area network, but on a much larger scale. Many organisations operate WANs to link their offices in different parts of the country or even different parts of the world.

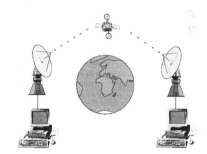
Satellite communication

Worldwide coverage is provided largely by satellite communications. Data is transmitted across the world using satellite technology. The satellite transmits the data, which can then be received in a distant location without the need for extensive land lines or undersea cables.

4.1.2   Client/Server Computers

In most networks, there are two types of computer involved, a **client** and a **server**. The client computer is the one that users sit at and interact with. The server computer is responsible for storing data which it sends to and receives from the client computer. Data that the server computer stores is available to all the client computers connected to the network. For example, a server computer has a certain file stored on it that a particular user wants to update. The user can download that file, change it, then upload it back on to the server computer. Once it is uploaded to the server computer, the updated file is available to everyone else on the network.

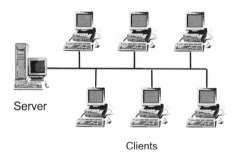
Server

Clients

4.1.3   Peer to Peer Networks

Peer to Peer (P2P) is a network arrangement in which there is no independent server. Instead, each computer in the network is a server in itself. P2P networks are perhaps best known for facilitating the illegal sharing of copyrighted data, such as music and films. Security in a P2P network can often be an issue and is ideal only when everyone connected to the network knows the other users, e.g. in a home network.

4.2   The Internet

4.2.1   The Internet

The internet is a worldwide network of computers that are linked by telecommunications networks. Any computer that has the appropriate software, hardware and a telecommunication connection can access it. The computer on your desk can be – and probably is – one of them. Below is a list of the requirements for a basic dial-up connection to the internet.

* A **computer**: Any computer can be used to connect to the internet. The special communication language used on the internet enables all types of computers to communicate with each other.

* A **router**: This is a piece of hardware that provides the physical access point between an individual computer and the internet. Generally, the router will connect to the internet via a telephone socket, wireless or satellite connection. The computer connects to the router by cable or wireless connection.

* A **browser**: This is a piece of software, such as Netscape Communicator, Microsoft Internet Explorer or Mozilla Firefox, that enables the computer to interpret the signals that come from the internet.

* An **Internet service provider (ISP) account**: This is a company, typically a telecommunications company, that connects your computer to the internet.

* A standard **telephone line**, unless a wireless or satellite connection is being used.

4.2.2   Uses of the Internet

The internet is most commonly used as a means of global communication to send e-mails or instant messages, share photos and videos, take part in chat room discussions or write blogs. The internet is also an excellent source of reference material and gives access to large amounts of information on every subject imaginable. In addition, the internet is quickly replacing older, more conventional types of media, such as the newspaper, radio and TV. As the internet is much more flexible and interactive than traditional media, publishers and advertisers can offer individually customised content to users.

4.3   Intranets and Extranets

4.3.1   Intranets

An intranet enables internal communication and sharing of information within an organisation. A website constructed for a company intranet looks and acts just like any other site, but the information is only available to employees within the company and special software protects it from unauthorised access. Intranets operate exactly the same way as the internet, i.e. a browser is used to view information. Intranets enable companies to post up-to-date, relevant and important information in an area accessible to only staff.

4.3.2   Extranets

An extranet is an extension to an organisation's intranet. For example, it enables external access to different parts of a company's intranet. Typically, customers may have access to online ordering or account enquiries. Normally, you can only gain access to an extranet if you have a valid username and password. The username and password you enter will determine your level of access and the parts of the extranet you can view.

4.4   Connecting to the Internet

4.4.1   Use of the Telephone Network in Computing

The telephone system developed in the twentieth century is called the **public switched telephone network (PSTN)** or **public switched data network (PSDN)**. It was designed for transmitting voices as analogue signals across cables in a continuously varying electrical signal, but is now also used for the transmission of data.

With the rise of the internet and the need to transmit data more quickly, the rate at which data could be transmitted over telecommunication networks was an important research issue. Several systems were developed, most of which centred on the compression of data. Listed below are three of the most important milestones.

*   The **integrated services digital network (ISDN)**: This was designed to transmit digital signals that computers use. While these signals are transferred down ordinary telephone lines, special technology installed at either end of the line assists in faster transfer rates. ISDN is much faster than PSDN, although it still supplies information at a rate far below the capacity that a computer can deal with. The basic transfer rate of information across an ISDN line is 64 Kbps (kilobits per second). 128 Kbps is available, but often at extra cost. Additional ISDN lines can be combined to give increased speed. The ISDN enables a user to use the internet and the phone line at the same time, although they will be charged for two calls.

*   **Asymmetric digital subscriber line (ADSL)**: This is a high-speed data communications technology that enables the use of existing analogue telephone lines for fast access to the internet. The connection is permanently live so there is never a need to dial up the connection. The data transfer rate varies widely from one service provider to another. Data is received more quickly than it is transmitted. A typical rate would be 2Mbps in and 512Mbps out.

*   **Fibre optics**: This is the more recent, popular choice for the high-end users of data transfer technology. It transfers modulated light beams as signals along optical fibres at speeds of 2Gbps. The fibre optic cable can carry significantly more information than electromagnetic or radio-based signal systems, as it is a higher frequency signal. There is also the advantage of the signal not being corrupted by electromagnetic interference.

4.5   Data Transfer

4.5.1   Uploading and Downloading

Uploading and downloading describe the transfer of files between computers that are indirectly connected via the internet. **Uploading** means transferring a file to a remote location and **downloading** is the opposite, the transfer of a file from a remote location to a local computer.

Files are normally downloaded by clicking on links in web pages, but they can also be transferred by other means, such as BitTorrent or **FTP (File Transfer Protocol)** applications.

Uploading can also take place via FTP, or via web pages, such as when submitting video to YouTube.

4.5.2   Transfer Rate

The **transfer rate** is a measure of the average amount of data transferred between two pieces of data transmission equipment over a period of time. Generally, it is measured in multiples of bits or bytes per second. In everyday terms, it is the speed at which a computer can send and receive information over a network, be it a LAN, WAN or the internet.

The transfer rate governs how quickly web pages appear and how long downloads and uploads take. Examples of transfer rates are shown in the table on page 46.

Rate	Description	Example
bps	Bits per second	800 bps is the minimum requirement for transmitting recognisable speech.
Kbps	Kilobits (thousands of bits) per second	A 56K modem has a theoretical maximum rate of 56Kbps
Mbps	Megabits (millions of bits) per second	ADSL broadband internet connection can download at up to 8Mbps depending on the service.
Gbps	Gigabits (billions of bits) per second	PC2100 SDRAM memory, a type of RAM used in many computers, has a transfer rate of around 21Gbps.

4.6 Internet Connections

4.6.1 Dial-Up and Broadband Connections

Internet connections are divided into two categories: **dial-up** and **broadband**.

Dial-up connections require the computer to actually dial a special phone number to establish a connection to the internet. Dial-up connections typically have low transfer rates measured in Kbps. The cost of a dial-up connection varies according to the rate for the number that is dialled and how long the connection (which is like a telephone call) lasts.

Broadband connections can refer to any number of technologies that offer high-speed internet access. Broadband connections have high transfer rates measured in Mbps, and are always live, so there is no need to dial a phone number to connect to the internet. This also means that there is usually a flat fee for the connection, which can be bundled with telephone services. Because of the nature of a broadband connection – high-speed and always on – computers that use them to access the internet are at a higher risk of intruder attack as they are visible, to a greater or lesser extent, to any other computer on the internet anywhere else in the world. This raises security implications, and means that precautions, such as strong passwords, firewalls and anti-virus software, should be used.

4.6.2 Options for Internet Connection

A computer can be connected to the internet in a variety of ways. The method used can depend on the choice of **Internet Service Providers (ISP)** available, or it can be dictated by cost or by geographical location. For example, users in remote areas may only be able to access a dial-up internet service using their telephone line and be forced to use a wireless or satellite service for high-speed internet. Even users in semi-urban or urban areas may have their choice dictated if their local exchange has not been upgraded or they are too far away from it.

Common types of internet connection are listed below.

Dial-up Connections

- **Modems**: Dial-up connections are the slowest type of connection. They use the standard telephone line, with data transmission to and from the computer passing through a **modem**. This is a device that converts the analogue signal that is carried by a phone line into the digital form understood by a computer, or vice versa. Telephone calls cannot be made or received while a computer is using the line. The typical transfer rate is 56Kbps.

- **ISDN (Integrated Services Digital Network)**: These connections are a slight improvement on dial-up, as it is a digital transmission system. Multiple lines can be bundled to provide greater speed and it enables voice and data transmission simultaneously. The typical transfer rate is 128Kbps.

Broadband Connections

- **Wireless Internet**: This uses a special **router** that can receive and broadcast signals via a remote antenna, which is in turn directly connected to the internet. This technology is commonly used where 'wired' connections are unavailable. It is relatively fast but susceptible to interruption. Mobile phones also use wireless technology to access the internet. Wireless in this context is not the same as a wireless network within the home or office. In that situation, the actual internet connection could be ADSL or any other technology, with the connection shared inside the building using a wireless network. The typical transfer rate is 2Mbps.

- **Satellite Internet**: This enables internet access to extremely remote areas. This is an expensive solution that offers relatively slow transfer rates. It is also, like wireless, a very **latent** solution. This means that while an upload or download is fast once it has started, it can take a long time to start. This makes it unsuitable for applications like VoIP or online gaming. The typical transfer rate is up to 500Kbps.

- **Cable Internet**: This is an internet connection using a dedicated 'cable', perhaps supplied by a cable television provider and bundled with a television service. It is a high-speed connection, but is not dedicated, in other words the connection is shared by a number of other users. The typical transfer rate is up to 50Mbps.

- **ADSL (Asymmetric Digital Subscriber Line)**: This is a high-speed service, so named because the download speed is typically much faster than the upload speed. The typical transfer rate is up to 24Mbps.

- **Optic Fibre**: Utilising laser light to transfer data, this technology can offer transfer rates of up to 100Mbps.

- **Mobile Phones**: These are phones that do not require a fixed land line to make calls. They also use wireless technology to access the internet, where users can access the full range of services, including accessing news websites and m-banking (mobile-banking). With m-banking, users can check balances, pay bills and order statements, etc. Mobile phones are becoming ever more sophisticated.

1

Section 5 ▶   ICT in Everyday Life

5.1   Definition
Information and Communication Technology (ICT) is a catch-all phrase used to describe a range of technologies for gathering, storing, producing, manipulating, printing, retrieving, processing, analysing and transmitting information. It encompasses computers, computer networks and consumer electronics as well as mass-media technologies, such as digital television and satellite communications. ICT is actively promoted by the United Nations as a tool for economic and social development.

5.2   Internet Services for Consumers
It is difficult to think of a profession that has not benefited from the invention of the computer. Information and communication technology has enabled businesses, governments and education institutes to perform their various functions with greater efficiency and accuracy than ever before. Below are a few examples of how computers help people perform jobs and manage organisations.

- Many businesses use computers to manage their employees' records, as well as for accounting and payroll functions.

- Insurance companies use computers to process claims. In this way, more than 95 per cent of claims are resolved automatically.

- Governments use computers to analyse census information and keep track of public records.

- Hospitals use computers to diagnose, monitor and treat patients.

- Schools and universities use computers to keep track of student registrations and academic records.

Not only can businesses and governments perform their jobs more efficiently using computer technology, with the internet, they can also provide a better, more convenient and individually tailored service to their customers and citizens.

5.2.1   E-Commerce
E-commerce refers to the buying and selling of products through an electronic system, such as the internet. Not all aspects of e-commerce are necessarily electronic, for example, after a customer makes a purchase, their item is shipped by post. E-commerce is used by all types of businesses to sell all types of products, including clothing, toys, computers, electronic equipment, airline tickets, food, jewellery, books and medicine.

Most e-commerce websites operate like high-street shops but, with e-commerce, businesses can provide an individually customised shopping experience for their customers by, for example, enabling customers to select preferences, such as size or brand, and then filtering out any products that do not fit those preferences. E-commerce is an effective way for businesses to create relationships with their customers as businesses can create profiles based on a customer's buying habits. With these profiles, businesses can reward customers, as well as entice them to return to their website, by sending out personalised offers and reductions on other products.

There are also other e-commerce websites that don't fit into the traditional model of a shop. Auction websites enable anyone who has a registered account to buy and sell items online. Other types of e-commerce include music and video websites that enable users to download purchased content, as well as websites that offer their content on a subscription basis, such as journals and other publications.

5.2.2 E-Banking

E-Banking enables financial institutions to provide services to their customers through the internet or other electronic media, such as mobile phones, which may also be called mobile banking (m-banking). E-banking enables customers to perform a range of financial transactions from any location where there is access to an appropriate network. Typically, these transactions include transferring funds between accounts, obtaining account balances and transaction summaries, making account payments, ordering chequebooks, setting up standing orders and receiving notification of account transactions via SMS. As e-banking technology becomes more advanced, the types of transactions that a bank can provide to its customers will become more sophisticated and give greater flexibility and convenience. E-banking is very flexible and convenient for many customers who, for whatever reason, do not have the time to physically go to a bank to perform transactions. E-banking is also an ideal way to keep up with account activity as balances and transaction statements can be obtained instantly. This enables customers to budget and control financial transactions with far greater accuracy than ever before.

For customers to use an e-banking system, they must usually have held an account with a bank for a specified period of time before going through a registration process which provides them with access to e-banking. The technology behind e-banking is very secure and most financial institutions go to great lengths to ensure the security of their customers. Quite often, e-banking is more secure than regular banking as there is nothing tangible, such as a paper document, that might reveal a customer's details. Security cannot ever be guaranteed and it is up to users to ensure that they have followed any necessary security procedures.

5.2.3 E-Government

This is the electronic system that many local and state governments use to provide services to their citizens. E-government enables citizens to register for access to public records, such as census information, government budgets, specific articles of legislation, etc. With e-government, it is possible to perform any number of functions related to government, such as file income tax returns, register to vote, change and update personal information (such as a postal address), apply for government benefits (like grants or scholarships), renew a driver's licence, and request and submit forms.

5.2.4 E-Learning

This refers to the system of education that schools – typically third-level institutions such as universities – provide to registered users. E-learning benefits its users through flexibility as there is no need for learners to go to a physical classroom. It is quite common for people to take e-learning courses from institutions in other countries.

E-learning is cost-effective for both students and institutions. It offers institutions a multi-distribution stream for materials and accessibility to a widespread pool of students. It offers students easy and convenient access to learning materials, that are delivered often in an attractive multimedia presentation or interactive application, and does not necessitate the purchase of expensive manuals and books. E-Learning also enables learners to participate in courses during out-of-work time and from a location that is convenient for themselves. As such, there are considerable savings for the participant as work time is not lost, and childcare arrangements and travel are kept to a minimum. E-learning courses can provide learners with the opportunity to obtain full degrees or certificates over several years. Some e-learning courses also provide continuing education courses that are shorter and do not lead to a professional qualification but which give the learner a chance to acquire a new appreciation for a subject or learn a hobby or craft, such as painting or photography.

E-learning courses typically take place on the internet and learners are provided with registration details so that they can access a specific website. In that website, there is usually an area where tutors can submit lectures for learners to read in their own time, as well as an area for students to submit assignments, ask questions and participate in discussions. With most e-learning courses, there are no traditional books, but only readings in an electronic format which students can print out. However, many e-learning courses do require that certain paper documents are sent and received by post.

5.3   Teleworking

With the development of better telecommunications and better security software, many people now work from home. This is called teleworking and it is fast becoming a popular option with many organisations. Below are some advantages of teleworking.

- Some tasks are easier to focus on away from the bustle of an office.

- Parents can plan their work around the family schedule as more flexible working hours are possible.

- Many employers allow teleworkers to nominate their own working hours and have agreed schedules and timeframes for the completion of projects.

- Commuting is reduced or eliminated altogether, meaning employees do not have expensive travel bills and do not waste valuable time commuting. This can enable them to have a wider choice of areas in which to live.

- Companies that avail of teleworking for their employees make considerable savings on overheads, such as office space, heating, parking and canteens.

However, there are some disadvantages to teleworking.

- There are few opportunities for employees to meet and develop work communities. There is little chance to meet new people through their work and new employees can feel isolated.

- It is difficult to generate a culture of teamwork with teleworking groups.

- As the employee is working from home, it can be difficult to establish boundaries between family, friends and work.

- Many modern homes are small and space is limited. The teleworker must dedicate a certain amount of this space to their work, thus giving the family less living space.

- In some areas, people running a business from home or using space for office use have to pay local taxes.

5.4   Communication

5.4.1   E-Mail

E-mail is a method of sending and receiving mail messages over the internet. You must have internet access in order to use e-mail. It is possible to get internet and e-mail access for free, the only cost being the telephone charges.

E-mail has revolutionised communication between individuals, businesses and organisation in the following ways.

- It enables fast, low-cost communication around the world. An e-mail message or document can usually be sent to any destination in the world for the cost of a local call.

- You can send and receive messages or documents in electronic form, edit them and forward them to someone else.

- You can correspond with friends easily and quickly.

- An e-mail message can be sent to a number of people simultaneously.

- An e-mail inbox holds a user's messages in a single place enabling the messages (and any attached documents) to be kept, re-read or opened any number of times.

- E-mail speeds up communication. As writing conventions are very informal, a reply can be sent to a message by typing a few words and clicking a button on a screen.

5.4.2 Instant Messaging

Instant messaging (IM) enables computer users to 'chat' using special software in real time. It is one of the oldest forms of communication using a computer. Messages entered are sent instantly to the other user, who can then reply. Files can also be transferred. On a broadband internet connection, there is no cost involved in using IM and it provides an experience closer to a normal conversation than e-mail. IM has several other features which users can take advantage of, such as sending and receiving photos, music, video, enabling webcams for video reception and transmission, along with enabling voice conversations. Some of these features are not always free and require an additional paid subscription service.

5.4.3 Voice over Internet Protocol

Voice over internet protocol (VoIP) refers to the use of the internet, and digital equipment connected to it, to transmit voice traffic as opposed to using a traditional telephone. The advantage of VoIP is usually cost. A business may have its own private network connecting offices worldwide – if telephone traffic can be transmitted over the same network as computer data, then that business will not have to incur the costs involved by a person in one country calling someone in another country using the normal telephone system. The business will use normal desktop telephones that connect directly into its data network.

5.4.4 Really Simple Syndication

The huge amount of ever-changing content on the web means that it is increasingly difficult for internet users to keep up with the various websites and other internet resources they may be interested in. Really Simple Syndication (RSS) addresses this problem. Many if not all popular websites now provide one or more feeds or channels to which can subscribe. New items on these sites will then pop up on users' screens automatically, without the need for users to actively go and check the websites periodically themselves.

5.4.5 Blogs

A web log, or blog, is a website where postings are made by one or more individuals, and appear with the newest at the top of the page. They are commonly used to air personal opinions or as a diary, but can also be used as a forum for help and information on any subject. They are mostly text-based but can contain images or any other type of embedded content. Users generally register, for free, to start a blog account and can choose whether to make the blog available to the public or restrict access to only certain people. In addition, most blogs have RSS feeds, so they are easy to keep up with. Many businesses use blogs to establish better relationships with their customers by writing in such a way as to give a better understanding of what they do and who they are. Businesses can also keep customers informed of new products and can write more extensively about techniques and features of their products. Blogs are not limited to personal journals and businesses and can cover every topic imaginable from music to cooking, travel, sports, fashion, etc. Some of the more popular blogs also generate substantial incomes for the writers through third-party advertisements.

5.4.6 Podcasts

The term podcast is an acronym for Portable On-Demand Broadcast. Podcasting is an extension of the RSS concept, where content – which is often music or video, but which can in fact be any type of file – can be subscribed to and automatically downloaded. In a typical scenario, users might obtain episodes of a television show as podcasts, and view them on a PDA.

5.4.7 Virtual Communities

A virtual community is an online group of people who communicate using a variety of software technologies rather than through physical contact or more traditional means. Some examples of the ways people can interact are listed below.

- **Social Networking Websites**: Websites such as Facebook and Bebo are immensely popular. Facebook offers linked communities which users can join, for example based around a school or geographic region. Bebo gives users the opportunity to create customised profiles with plug-in components such as a drawing module, the results of which can be uploaded to other Bebo users.

- **Internet Forums**: These are a structured, moderated way of communicating and are commonly used for online support and providing technical assistance. A forum will cover a broad subject, such as offering help and support for printers made by a manufacturer. It may be divided into multiple topics, with users able to create threads under these topics to ask their particular question. Replies are then posted within these threads. Most forums are moderated to remove offensive content and ensure that discussions are broadly related to the main focus of the forum. Users are usually also required to register with a valid e-mail address.

- **Chat rooms**: These are virtual rooms that enable many users to connect and chat together at the same time in a more informal and less regulated way than would be the case with forums. Normally, chat rooms are based around a broad topic.

- **Online Computer Games**: Online gaming can take many forms. Many people use online gambling sites, for example playing poker for money against other users anywhere in the world. MMO or Massively Multiplayer Online games, such as **Everquest** and **Second Life**, enable millions of players to interact in artificial worlds, some with their own economies and currency. In the case of Second Life, real-world companies have begun introducing themselves into the virtual world, advertising and offering goods and services.

5.5   Publishing Content Online

Computer users with internet connections have the ability to publish and share their own content online. There are many websites that let registered users upload data, such as video clips, audio clips, podcasts and written documents, to share with the general public or just to specific people. Some of these websites only allow certain types of content, such as videoclips, to be uploaded while others allow any type of content.

Content-sharing websites generally act as servers that **host** the data for users. This means that the website will store the content for users and make it available through the Internet. Usually, these websites publish users' content on the site's own web pages. However, users are generally allowed to display any hosted content on other websites and share it openly.

The explosion in high-speed internet and digital audio and video devices has made it extremely easy for anyone to publish audio, digital photographs, video and make it available to other internet users. Video can be uploaded to sites such as YouTube, while photo galleries can be created on Flickr.

5.6   Online Precautions

Online communities are mostly populated by friendly people, but, as in the real world, there are also individuals who are abusive or potentially dangerous. To minimise exposure to problem situations, there are some common-sense steps that can be taken.

- Disclose as little personal information as possible. Use an invented name and never give real address details, phone numbers or age and gender details.

- Create an e-mail account on a free service such as Gmail, and use this account if an e-mail address is required, for example when registering for a forum.

- Ensure that children are monitored and use moderated forums and chat rooms.

- Information posted is publicly available, and subject to the same laws as any publicly made comments.

- Be wary of websites that offer rewards or prizes in exchange for personal details. There are many websites that offer some kind of contest or sweepstakes that you can possibly win by entering your personal details. These websites often collect personal details for direct marketing purposes.

Section 6 ▶   Health

6.1   Ergonomics

Ergonomics is the study of the interaction of people with equipment and machines. The main concern of ergonomics is that people can work with machines safely and efficiently. Stress-related illness can result from improper working conditions and practices. To avoid these and other problems and create a good working environment, simple precautions should be taken in the computer work environment. Some of these are:

- Making sure the work area is comfortable and that an adequate temperature is maintained.
- Making sure that adequate lighting is available to reduce headaches and eye strain as well as mental fatigue and low morale.
- Installing appropriate lighting fixtures to reduce glare and ensure an even distribution of illumination that eliminates shadows.
- Taking regular breaks to stretch and relax muscles in addition to using eye relaxation techniques, like focusing on objects outside a window.
- Using an adjustable chair that conforms to current health standards.
- Ensuring that the mouse and keyboard are positioned so that they do not cause discomfort.
- Fitting a monitor filter to eliminate glare and eye strain.
- Keeping pathways clear of cables.
- Ensuring that there is adequate ventilation.
- Complying with local fire and safety regulations.
- Examining plugs, sockets and leads for defects and have any necessary repairs carried out by qualified personnel.

You should refer to your local health and safety authority for more detailed recommendations and any legal requirements you need to comply with.

6.2   Precautions

The illustrations on the next page are given as examples of a good arrangement for computer users. Please note that these recommendations are only general guidelines; always follow the manufacturer's guidelines and local health authority recommendations.

- Be in a position to look down, not up, at the monitor.
- Place the monitor on the desk rather than on top of the CPU box for the correct viewing level and to avoid neck strain.
- Set the monitor back on the desk to avoid eye strain.
- Position the monitor to avoid glare from lighting or from windows.
- Fit windows with adjustable blinds to remove any reflections from the screen.
- Use a document holder beside the screen and at the same level to minimise head and eye movements.
- Use the mouse on a mouse mat so that it will move smoothly.
- Use a chair with adjustable height and backrest facilities.
- A footrest should be provided if required.
- Under-desk knee and thigh clearances should be adequate for different users.
- The elbow angle should be between 90° and 110°.
- Have the keyboard and mouse at the correct level for the individual user.

- Use a desk lamp to provide local illumination where necessary.
- Ensure cables are safely secured.
- Supply adequate power points and do not overload them.
- Ensure that there are appropriate ventilation arrangements.

Desktop Computers

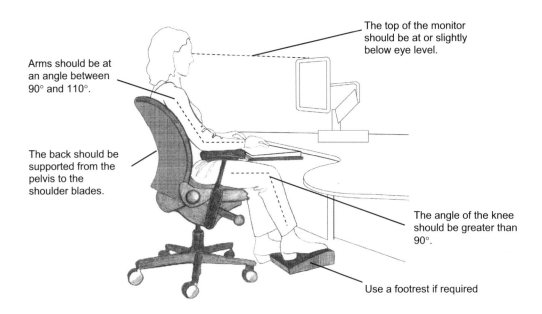

The top of the monitor should be at or slightly below eye level.

Arms should be at an angle between 90° and 110°.

The back should be supported from the pelvis to the shoulder blades.

The angle of the knee should be greater than 90°.

Use a footrest if required

Laptop Computers

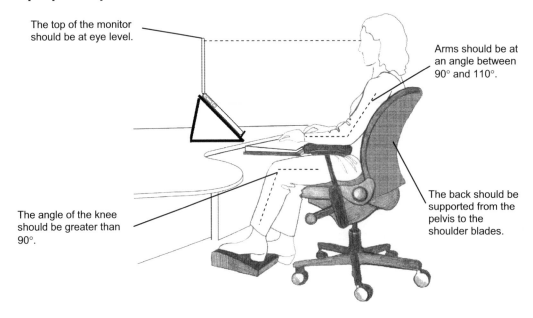

The top of the monitor should be at eye level.

Arms should be at an angle between 90° and 110°.

The angle of the knee should be greater than 90°.

The back should be supported from the pelvis to the shoulder blades.

6.3   The Environment

6.3.1   Recycling

With the increased use of digital documents, the demand for paper should be reduced. However, this is not the case and the international demand for paper is higher than ever, which is putting unsustainable demands on the world's forests supplies. The solution to this problem is to recycle or use paper that has been made from wood harvested in managed forests.

As computer equipment, including printer cartridges, expire or become obsolete, they have to be disposed of. Inappropriate disposal is contributing to the build-up of non-biodegradable waste. One of the ways computer users can help the environment is by using recycled printer cartridges and to consider upgrading to replace computer components rather than replacing their computers.

6.3.2   Energy Saving Options

Computers consume energy in the form of electricity. Most computer equipment is supplied with hardware that can be configured to enable energy-efficient running. It is important that computer users are aware of these features and learn to adjust the settings in order to minimise power consumption. This logo is shown on energy-efficient computer products.

Some of the energy efficient settings available in Windows 7 include:

- Automatically turning off the monitor after a certain period of time.
- Automatically putting the computer or monitor into **sleep mode**, also called **standby mode**, which when the computer is not in use for a short period of time, such as during a break. This setting works by reducing the power usage of the computer hardware without shutting down entirely. Touching the keyboard or mouse will bring the computer out of sleep mode.
- Automatically putting the computer into **hibernate mode** when the computer is not in use for a long period of time, such as overnight. This setting reduces the power usage of the computer hardware to the point where it is almost completely off.
- Turning off, also called **shutting down**, the computer hardware when not in use for extended periods of time.

6.3.3   Configuring Power Settings

To adjust the power settings in Windows 7 to enable energy-efficient options, do the following:

- From the **Start Button** click **Control Panel**.
  The Control Panel window opens.
- Click **Power Options**.

 If using Category View, some users may have to click **System and Security** to access Power Options.

The **Power Options** window opens.

- In the **Select a power plan** window, select a power scheme (usually **Recommended Settings**).

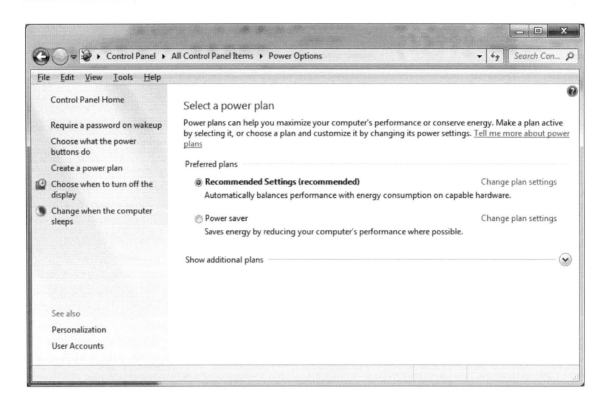

- To make changes to the chosen power plan, select **Change Plan Settings**.

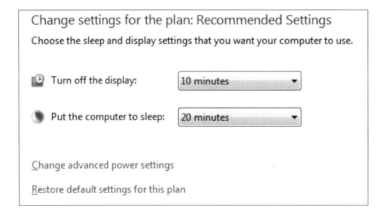

- Select a time for *sleep* and *display* settings and click **Save Changes**

Section 7 ▶ Security

7.1 Identity and Authentication

7.1.1 Usernames and Passwords

When a person's data is entered into a computer system, it is the responsibility of the computer owner to ensure that the data is kept confidential. This confidentiality is covered by data protection legislation and is dealt with in more detail in Section 7.2.

Data in any organisation should be available only to those who have and need access rights to ensure the privacy of people whose details are kept in databases. These rights must be linked to a system of security clearance controlled by someone in authority. In order to control access rights, all computers or networks must be configured so that users are required to enter a username. This is a special word or group of characters that uniquely identifies the user. As well as a username, a unique password should also be entered. A password is similar to an ATM PIN but is made up of characters and numbers.

This system of usernames and passwords protects data from being accessed by unauthorised people. As many computer systems are now accessible over the internet, the need for security is self-evident.

7.1.2 Good Password Policies

Users are often lazy with passwords and use their surnames, or easily guessed words, such as 'password'. A determined intruder could gain access to a system with insecure passwords very easily. It is sensible to follow some basic guidelines for choosing passwords. On many systems, rules such as those below are actively enforced.

- Do not share passwords with other users.
- Do not use words in the dictionary, or easily guessed passwords, such as 'password', 'letmein' or 'access'.
- Change passwords regularly.
- Use a password at least 8 characters in length.
- Use a mix of both upper and lower case letters and numbers and non-alphabetic characters.
- Use numbers in place of letters. For example, use 'B1@ckr0ck' instead of 'blackrock'.

7.2 Information Security

7.2.1 Preventing Data Theft

Security involves not only the physical security of the computer equipment, but also the security of the data contained on the hard disk and other storage media. After a computer malfunction or accident, hardware is easily replaced but data may be damaged and rendered completely useless. Companies can go out of business after a complete data loss.

It is essential that organisations and their employees are proactive in protecting important information. This is best achieved by introducing an information security policy. This policy might include recommendations such as:

- Well-documented company procedures for backing up data.
- Employees being aware of their responsibilities when working with sensitive data.
- Procedures for reporting and dealing with security incidents.
- Using passwords and usernames.

- Using BIOS passwords if available, so that the computer will not even start unless the correct password is supplied.
- Keeping sensitive data in an encrypted area of the hard drive, or password-protect document files containing this type of data.
- Use a security cable fastened to a desk or wall.
- The appointment of a person solely responsible for data security.
- Banning the use of all personal storage devices, including USB memory sticks and camera memory cards, from the workplace.

7.2.2 Backups

Information on a computer is stored electronically. Because of this, there is always a possibility that it can be lost due to a malfunction in the system or through human error. To avoid total loss of data, it is important to have copies of all important files stored on disks or other removable media. These copies are called backups.

Backups can be made in several ways. Copies can be made to tape, USB drive, external hard disks or burned onto a CD or DVD. The data from some files may also be kept as hard copy. These backups should be kept in a safe and secure place, e.g. locked away in fireproof containers or off the premises in a remote location.

7.2.3 Firewalls

A computer connected to the internet is also connected to millions of other computers worldwide. This carries a huge risk of unauthorised access by malicious individuals or criminal organisations. Firewalls act as a barrier between individual computers, or computer networks, and the wider internet, essentially making them invisible. Firewalls can exist in hardware, for example inside a broadband router, or in software. They can be configured to provide alerts if attempted intrusions occur.

7.3 Viruses and Other Types of Malware

7.3.1 Malware and Computer Viruses

A virus is a computer program written with the intention of secretly causing damage to the files on a computer, or stealing information stored on a computer (or network), or enabling the computer to be controlled remotely without the owner's knowledge.

The term 'virus' refers to one particular type of malware, but is usually incorrectly used to describe a number of different types of program, such as **Trojans**, **worms**, and **spyware** (see Module 2).

Malware can infect a computer in many ways, including:
- Infected e-mail attachments.
- Distributing illegal software across network connections.
- Through malicious websites.
- Through security loopholes in operating systems.

7.3.2 Protection Against Malware

Antivirus software is used to detect and remove malware. The process of removing a problem file is called disinfecting or cleaning. These applications use virus definition libraries, which are databases of all known malware programs, to recognise problems. New viruses, Trojans and assorted other undesirable programs are created every day, so it is important to keep the database that your antivirus software uses up to date. Antivirus software vendors maintain central databases which are updated regularly, and modern antivirus software will keep itself updated automatically via the internet.

Section 8 ▶ Copyright and Law

1

8.1 Copyright

Copyright is defined as a group of legal rights that protect creative works from being used, reproduced, performed or disseminated without permission from the creator of the work. Commercial software is covered by copyright similar to printed media, such as books. You are obliged to look after your software and not enable others to copy it. You should purchase and register your own software for your own use.

- Program or application disks should be copied only for the purposes of backing up and safekeeping as specified in the licence agreement. If the original disks are damaged or become corrupted, the backup copies can be used to reinstall the software.

- Sharing or lending program disks may be in breach of licensing agreements.

- Transferring or copying software over a network should only be carried out under the terms of the software license agreement. **Single user** or **stand-alone** copies of software should not be used on networks. **Site licences** are available for most network requirements.

- **Software piracy**, i.e. the illegal duplication, distribution, sale and use of software, is a criminal offence.

- Copyright legislation may also apply to shareware and freeware (see Section 8.4).

The internet enables access to a vast library of information in various formats. Material downloaded from the internet is the property of the person or organisation that put it there. Whether in paper or digital format, all graphics, text, audio and video files on the internet are protected by copyright and the owner's permission must be sought if the material is to be used for any purpose other than that stated by them.

8.1.1 Disks and Copyright

Material stored on removable media, such as CDs and USB flash drives, must be checked for copyright before it is distributed. Commercial software produced on these media is likely to require your commitment to a licensing agreement.

8.2 Recognising Licensed Software

Most commercial software is distributed with a **product ID number**. This unique number usually identifies the product item and distinguishes it from other versions of the same product that are licensed to users.

Some commercial software also requires an activation key. Where an activation key is used, it is normally entered as part of the installation process and the process will not continue without a valid key, the aim being to deter piracy. This key can sometimes be validated online.

When software has been installed, users can perform a registration process to inform the software supplier that a valid copy of the software has been installed and that it qualifies for updates. A valid Product ID will also often be requested if users access technical support for the software.

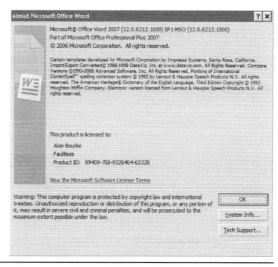

It is common practice amongst software developers to provide access to an application's product ID number through the Help function. Typically, with Microsoft Office applications, clicking on the word **Help** on the application's Menu bar and selecting the **About** menu item on the drop-down list will present you with a window containing the number.

All software is supplied under a licence. Most open-source software is supplied under the GPL or Gnu Public Licence, for example. Vendors such as Microsoft have their own licensing agreements which can also be viewed from the About Microsoft window in the Help menu.

8.3   End-User Agreements

When a software package is purchased, you are not paying for ownership but for the right – a licence – to use the product. It is important to read the licensing agreement displayed on the packaging or in the accompanying documentation. It is also common practice among software companies to display the agreement on screen at some stage when the software is being installed on the computer. No matter where the licence agreement is displayed, you are legally obliged to adhere to it if you use the software.

Most copies of software are single-user copies. This means that the purchaser may only use the software on one computer. A site licence can be purchased if the software is to be installed on a number of computers. Only one copy of the software is supplied, but the site licence legally entitles the purchaser to install it on a specified number of computers. The cost of a site licence is generally much lower than the cost of buying individual copies of the software for each machine.

8.4   Shareware, Freeware, Public Domain and Open Source Software

8.4.1   Shareware

Many computer programmers and hobbyists write software programs and allow them to be distributed freely as shareware. Distribution may be via the internet or on CDs distributed with magazines. Shareware is copyrighted software that enables you a try-it-out period before you make the purchase. Payment for shareware is based on an honour system. If you wish to continue using the software after the trial period, you are required to send a payment, usually nominal, to the author. To encourage payment, many shareware programs will only function for a limited period or some functions may be disabled. Paid-up users may get additions and free updates. The quality of shareware is variable, but some programs, such as early versions of the popular image-editing program Paint Shop Pro®, are of professional standard. Current versions of this program are no longer shareware.

8.4.2   Freeware

Freeware is similar to shareware. It is also distributed freely, but no payment is expected. Some authors may ask for feedback or for a reciprocal action ('Do something nice for someone' or 'Send me a postcard'). As with shareware, freeware comes in an 'as is' condition. Some developers freely distribute the first version of their product to benefit from users' reactions in the development of the program. Freeware authors often retain all the rights to their software under copyright legislation. Copying and distributing further copies of the material may not be allowed.

8.4.3 Public Domain Software

Public domain software is software which is not copyrighted. It is the property of whoever is using it, and can be copied and/or modified as if that user had created it themselves.

8.4.4 Open Source Software

Open source software is computer software which is, like public domain software, available for free and which can be shared, copied or modified by each user. Unlike public domain software, Open Source software is licensed, generally under the GNU General Public Licence (GNU GPL or just GPL). Types of open source software include operating web browsers, databases and the Linux operating system.

8.5 Data Protection Legislation

Personal data is legitimately held by a number of institutions and agencies. People's detailed financial records may be held by a bank or financial lending institution with which they conduct business. Such records could include a person's monthly income, mortgage repayment details, schedules of loan repayments, overdraft requirements, credit rating, and savings and investments. Local authorities may have details on services to which an individual is entitled that could include payment records of local taxes and charges, dog licences, applications for planning permission, planning objections and appeals. Some of this information may be stored for public access. Sensitive medical records will be held by various agencies, such as health boards, general hospitals, local area clinics and general practitioners.

In each of the above cases, it is important to govern access to the information and the use to which the information is put. Data protection legislation exists to ensure that appropriate levels of privacy are safeguarded and the information is used only in an appropriate manner. In the Republic of Ireland, a Data Protection Act was passed on 13 July 1988 and came into force on 13 April 1989. It was amended in 2003.

The following is an extract from *IRELAND, The Data Protection Act, 1988, A Summary from the Data Protection Commissioner.*

> The Act gives a right to every individual, irrespective of nationality or residence, to establish the existence of personal data, to access any such data relating to him, and to have inaccurate data rectified or erased. It requires data controllers to make sure that the data they keep are collected fairly, are accurate and up-to-date, are kept for lawful purposes, and are not used or disclosed in any manner incompatible with those purposes. It also requires both data controllers and data processors to protect the data they keep, and imposes on them a special duty of care in relation to the individuals about whom they keep such data.

Similar legislation has been passed by other governments. You should contact the appropriate local authority regarding the legislation that applies in your own country.

Those who store or have access to data on individuals are under a legal obligation in most countries to protect this data. In the Republic of Ireland, according to the Data Protection Act 1988 & 2003, the protection of data can be basically summarised in eight rules. These rules require that those who store or have access to an individual's data must:

1. **Obtain and process the data fairly**: At the time when data is being collected, individuals must be made aware of who is collecting the data, what it will be used for, who the data will be disclosed to and what any future or secondary uses may be.

2. **Keep data only for a clear and lawful purpose**: The purpose of data collection must be specific, clear and legitimate.

3. **Process data only for the purposes for which it was originally gathered**: Data cannot be passed on to third parties or used for any other purpose than what was originally stated.

4. **Keep data safe and secure**: Data collectors are responsible for determining appropriate security measures, which may require upgrading security technology or providing security compliance training to staff.

5. **Keep data accurate and up to date**: Data must be reviewed periodically and kept updated whenever necessary so that an individual's details are current.

6. **Ensure that data is adequate, relevant and not excessive**: Data that is collected must fit the purpose for which it is collected and nothing more.

7. **Keep data no longer than is necessary for the purpose or purposes of collection**: At the time data is collected, it should be made clear how long the data will be kept and for what reason it will be kept. Also, data cannot be kept on the basis that it might be useful at some point in the future. Once data has been used for the purpose for which it was collected, it should be deleted.

8. **A copy of an individual's data must be provided to them upon their request**: Upon receiving a written request, a copy of the data must be given to that individual, including a description of the purpose as to why it was being held, a description of anyone that the data might have been disclosed to as well as the source of the data.

In most countries, data protection legislation not only requires data controllers to take on specific responsibilities, but also outlines the rights of individuals whose data is being held. One of the most common of these rights is that of an individual to request a copy of his or her data from any data controller. Making such a request usually requires a written letter or e-mail along with the payment of a small fee to compensate the data controller for the time needed to process the request.

Another common right of the individual under data protection legislation is the right to seek compensation in court for any damage caused to the individual by the mishandling of their data. An example of this particular right may be if an individual's credit rating was not kept up to date by a financial institution and that person was subsequently denied a loan for a mortgage. In this case, the affected individual could take the financial institution that was responsible to court and sue for damages.

There may be other rights provided to individuals under various data protection legislation, depending on the country. This information is often widely available on the internet or by contacting the appropriate authority. It is important to be aware of such rights as they provide security against identity theft or other types of damage caused by the mishandling of personal data.

In many countries, data protection legislation deals with direct marketing organisations that send unsolicited mail and e-mail, or make unsolicited phone calls to an individual to obtain data. In these cases, individuals have the right to request that their information be deleted from the data collector to ensure that no further mail or phone calls are received. There are circumstances in which this right may be limited, for example, in a legal situation, a person who is standing trial for a crime will not be able to request certain data from the police.

module **2**

Using the Computer and Managing Files

module 2
Using the Computer and Managing Files

Module Goals for Module 2

Using the Computer and Managing Files require the candidate to demonstrate competence in running and managing a personal computer.

The candidate shall be able to:

- Use the main features of the operating system including adjusting the main computer settings and using in-built help features.

- Operate effectively around the computer desktop and work effectively in a graphical user environment.

- Know about the main concepts of file management and be able to efficiently organise files and folders so that they are easy to identify and find.

- Use utility software to compress and extract large files and use antivirus software to protect against computer viruses.

- Demonstrate the ability to use simple text editing and print tools available within the operating system.

2

Section 1 ▶   Getting Started

1.1   Introduction

1.1.1   The Computer

This module starts from the very beginning – with how to turn on a computer. Various ways of working with the computer and managing and manipulating what you see on the screen will then be covered to give users confidence and a sense of control.

This module will provide the operational skills and knowledge needed to work effectively with the **Microsoft Windows 7 operating system**.

1.1.2   Files and Filing

The documents, pictures, etc. that are created using a computer are called **files**. They are stored on the computer in a structured way, and can be retrieved and presented easily the next time they are needed. They can also be sent to other people, copied onto other computers, etc.

This module covers how these files are stored and how this relates to the way paper files are stored in the 'real' world, enabling them to be organised and used efficiently.

1.2   First Steps

1.2.1   Starting the Computer

The illustration below shows a typical modern computer. Both the screen (**monitor**) and main 'box' (or **base unit**) need to be plugged in and switched on. Most of the other devices that might be connected to the computer take their power from the base unit, unless they are large devices, e.g. printers.

To turn on the base unit and monitor use the **power button** on each. There will be a button with a coloured light on both items. Although they could be in different places on different computers, they will all have the universal power button logo.

When the computer is started, text and pictures will appear and disappear on the screen for a while. Do not use the mouse or keyboard while this is happening, in case the **boot sequence** is interrupted by mistake.

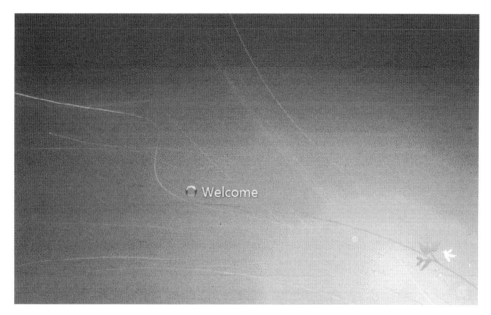

The Welcome Screen, shown above, is the default in Windows 7. The logon screen will appear when it is part of a **homegroup** or **workgroup** network. This means that the computer may be accessed by multiple users who have an account. When the **Welcome/Logon Screen** is displayed one of the listed account names must be clicked to continue. A different screen will be shown when a Windows 7 machine is part of a domain, managed by an administrator in an office or educational network.

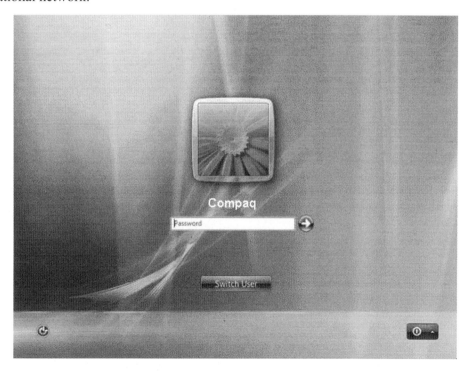

If the computer is part of a **Domain** or shared workgroup, as in the above illustration, a valid **password** must be entered to continue. This is known as **logging in**. The Welcome/logon screen may also display a username box in addition to the password box.

2

The Windows **desktop** will be displayed after a while, which should look similar to the illustration below. (The desktop is covered in Section 2 of this module.)

1.2.2   Restarting the Computer

To restart the computer, do the following:

- Click the Start button at the bottom left of the desktop.
- Move the mouse over the arrow besides the **Shut down** button to see a menu with further options.
- Select **Restart**.

1.2.3   Shutting Down a Non-Responding Application

A problem may arise where the computer appears to 'freeze', and doesn't respond to the mouse or keyboard. In this case, it is necessary to force the computer to end the task it is engaged in.

To shut down a non-responding application using Task Manager, do the following:

- Press the **CTRL**, **ALT** + **DEL** keys simultaneously.
  The **Task Manager** window opens.
- Applications that are currently open are listed on the **Applications** tab. Any that have stopped responding will have **Not Responding** in the Status column.
- Click the non-responding application to select it.
- Click **End Task** to terminate it.

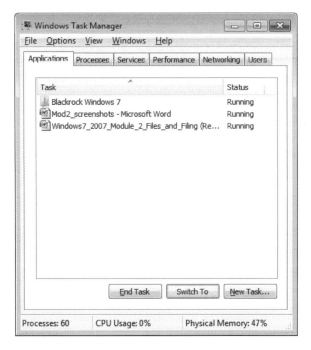

1.2.4   Shutting Down

When the computer is no longer being used, it should be **shut down**. If the computer is switched off without going through the shut down procedure, problems may arise the next time it is switched on. Any work that was not saved prior to switching off may also be lost.

To shut down the computer, do the following:
- Select the **Start** button.
- Click **Shut down**.

1.3 Getting Help

To get help with Windows 7, do the following:
- Click any empty area of the desktop.
- Press the F1 key.
  The Windows Help and Support window will open.
- Follow the instructions to choose a topic or type in a topic to search.

2

Section 2 ▶   The Desktop

2.1   The Start Menu

The **Start** button is located at the bottom left-hand corner of the screen on the **taskbar**.

Click here to
start

If the taskbar is not visible, it may be set to **auto-hide** (meaning it will disappear when not in use). If this is the case, then moving the cursor to the bottom of the screen will make the taskbar pop up.

When clicked, the Start button opens the **Start Menu**. This menu is the central point from which most applications can be started.

This has been 'pinned' to the Start menu

Internet

Commonly used applications

Account picture and account name (in this example, the account name is the computer name)

The left-hand side of the Start Menu displays **icons** for access to web browsing and e-mail, along with a list of commonly used applications. The Search box is located at the bottom of the Start menu. The right-hand side has a list of standard windows, e.g. Documents, Pictures and Music, enabling them to be opened quickly (these are called **Libraries**). It also has options for managing devices and printers and for opening the Windows 7 Help and Support window.

The **All Programs** item on the Start Menu will display a list of all or most installed applications on the computer.

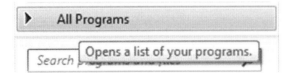

Some menu items have an arrow to the right, indicating that moving the cursor over the item will display a **sub-menu**.

To select a menu item, position the cursor on it and click the left mouse button once.

2.2 Working with the Desktop

The first thing displayed on the monitor after logging into Windows 7 is the **desktop**. It is the backdrop for all the things you can do when using Windows and is meant to be roughly equivalent in concept to an actual desk. Every desktop varies, depending on the version of Windows 7, the desktop theme being used, the applications installed, etc. However there are common elements to all desktops.

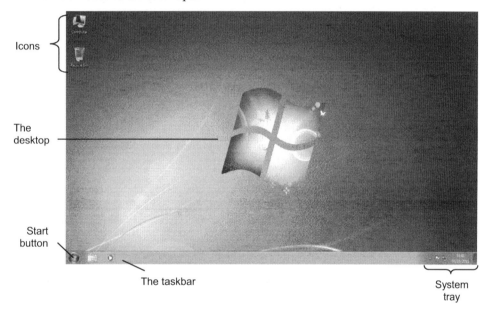

- **Icons** represent different applications, documents, accessories, etc. Double-click an icon to access the item it represents.

- The **Start Button** displays a menu providing access to all the applications installed on the computer, and many other items.

- The **Taskbar** displays a button for each application or window that is open. (See Section 1.5 of the BYB module).

- The **System Tray** contains items (such as the clock and small icons for **services**) that start automatically with windows and remain available at all times. An example of a service would be the real-time scanner of an anti-virus application.

2.2.1 Working with Desktop Icons

Each icon on the desktop represents an application, function, folder or document that can be opened and used. By moving the cursor over an icon on the desktop and double-clicking the left mouse button, the function it performs is activated.

The standard Windows 7 desktop has one icon, for the Recycle Bin, but icons will be added in due course through normal use. Below are examples of the some common types of icon.

An application icon, such as the Microsoft Word icon, can be used to start that application.

A folder icon can be clicked to open and view the folder contents
(the arrow denotes a shortcut to the desktop).

This document icon, **Team List.docx**, was created in Microsoft Word
2010. Double-clicking this icon will start Microsoft Word and display
the document.

Team
List.docx

This application icon will start the Firefox web browser.

Mozilla Firefox

This icon is for a movie file. Double-clicking the icon will play the
movie in a movie player application.

Holiday Movie.avi

2.2.2   Selecting and Moving Icons

The icons on the desktop are usually arranged in a vertical line down the left-hand side, but this
layout can be changed to suit user preference.

To **select** a desktop icon, do the following:
- Click the icon.

  The icon will be highlighted and a slight shading will appear around it.

To **move** an icon, do the following:
- Click the icon once with the left mouse button to select it.

- Holding down the left mouse button, drag the icon to another location on the desktop by
  moving the mouse.

2.2.3   Arranging Icons

In addition to moving individual icons on the desktop, they can also be arranged in a more
specific way.

To **arrange** icons, do the following:
- Right-click anywhere on a blank area of the desktop.

  A drop-down menu appears.

- Move the cursor over the **Sort by** menu option.

  A drop-down sub-menu appears.

  The sub-menu enables icons to be sorted on the
  desktop by Name, Size, Item Type or Date Modified.

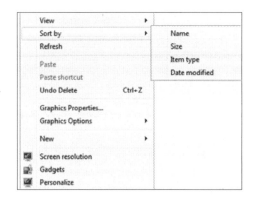

- Move the mouse arrow over the **View** menu option
  to see two important items:

  ▷ **Auto Arrange Icons** arranges the icons down
    the left-hand side of the screen.

  ▷ **Align Icons to Grid** means that when an icon
    is moved with the mouse, it will snap to the
    nearest point on an invisible grid on the screen
    when the mouse button is released.

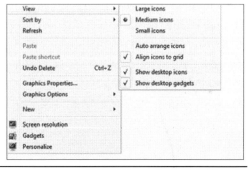

2.2.4   Creating and Removing a Shortcut Icon on the Desktop

It can be tedious to locate the menu item for a frequently used application every time it is needed. As an alternative, a desktop icon can be created as a **shortcut** to open the application more easily and quickly. A desktop shortcut can be removed if it is not used often or if it was created accidentally.

Creating a Desktop Shortcut
To create a desktop shortcut to the MS Paint application, do the following:
- Click **Start**.
- Select **All Programs**.
- Select the **Accessories** sub-menu.
- Move the cursor over the **Paint** menu item.
- Right-click and select **Send To** from the sub-menu that appears.
  A further sub-menu appears.

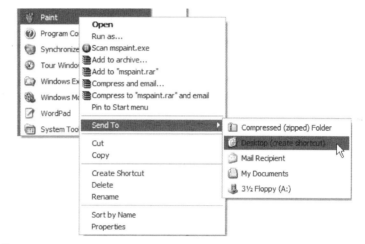

- Click **Desktop (create shortcut)** item.
  A shortcut for the Paint application will appear on the desktop.

Removing a Desktop Shortcut
To remove a desktop shortcut, do the following.
- Move the cursor over the shortcut icon and right click.
- In the pop-up menu, select **Delete**.
  The **Confirm File Delete** window opens, asking whether or not you want to delete the icon.
- Select **Yes** to delete the shortcut.
  The shortcut will disappear from the desktop.

2.2.5   Using an Icon to Open a File, Folder or Application

An application can be started, or a file or folder opened, using desktop icons.

To do this, do the following.
- Double-click the icon.
  The file, folder or application opens in a new window.
  If a file is being opened, it will open within the necessary application.

2.3   Using Windows

Everything that can be interacted with – individual applications, messages, prompts, files, folders, etc. – is displayed on the monitor in a rectangular area called a **window**. Windows have common features, such as title and menu bars.

2.3.1 Parts of a Window

The illustrations below show the **Explorer** window; the first screenshot displays the **Documents** library and the second screenshot displays the **Computer** window. To open the **Explorer** window, click the **Explorer** button ▦ on the taskbar.   Around the window there are various features that can be used to move and size the window effectively.

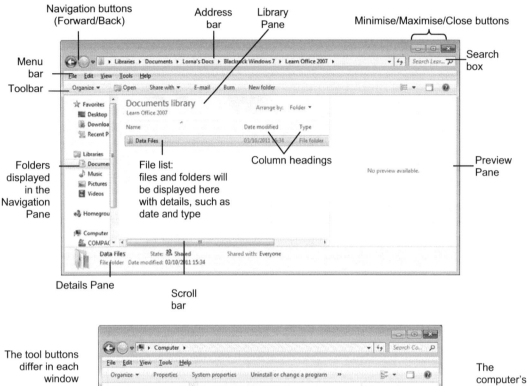

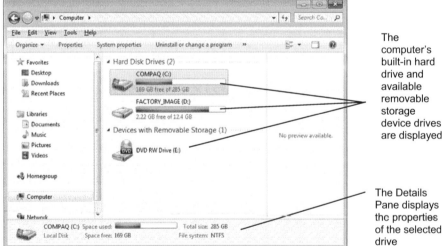

A **Border** surrounds the window and defines its boundary. The border can be dragged with the mouse to resize the window.

On the top right of the window, there are three buttons for changing the size of the window and for closing it. (See **Section 2.2.3** of this module for more information on these.)

The **Menu bar** contains drop-down menus that work in the same way as the Start Menu. A sub-menu arrow may appear alongside selected items enabling a further level of selection. The **Toolbar** contains buttons and drop-down lists. The buttons on the tool bar change depending on the type of file currently selected. For example, the buttons change to become more appropriate for picture files when a picture is selected.

Navigation Buttons enable the user to navigate backwards and forwards between folders and files. In the first illustration above, if the **Data Files** folder was double-clicked, the window would change to show the contents (files) stored in that sub-folder. At that point, clicking the **Back** button would display only the folder again. Clicking **Forward** would display the folder contents again.

The **Address bar** displays the current location, i.e. the folder that is being viewed. The Address field shows this location in a type of text notation called a **path**. When the computer is connected to the internet, entering a website address in the address field will display that website.

The **Details Pane** displays the amount of files within a folder, the name and type (i.e. file or folder) of the item displayed, the size of the file, the author's name and the date that the file/folder was last modified.

There are various actions that can be performed within a window, such as the following.

- **Search** for files and folders. Enter search criteria in the Search box and click the magnifying glass icon. A list of files matching the search criteria will be displayed.

- **Favorites** displays a list of favourite folders, files, web pages or saved searches.

To make it easier to find and access a frequently used location, such as a personal folder within a library, it can be saved to **Favorites**. This can be achieved by right clicking the **Favorites** option and selecting **Add current location to Favorites**.

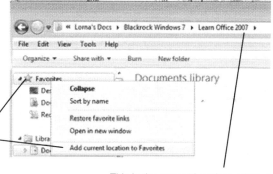

Right click Favorites and select **Add current location to Favorites**

This is the current location: a folder containing sub-folders within the Documents Library

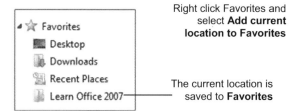

The current location is saved to **Favorites**

To remove an option from Favorites, right click and select **Remove**.

A **scroll bar** appears (as in the illustration on the right) when a window is too small to display all of its contents. There can be vertical or horizontal scroll bars, or both. Clicking the arrows at the ends of a scroll bar will shift the contents of window up or down or from side to side so that further items become visible. Holding the mouse button down on a scroll arrow at the end of the scroll bar gives continuous movement. The **slider** in the **scroll bar** gives a general indication as to which part of the window is presently displayed.

In the illustration on the right, the **slider bar** is at the top indicating that the top-most contents of the window are being displayed. The length of the slider bar relative to the height of the window also indicates how much of the full range of content is being displayed. In this case, almost all the contents are visible. The content that is not visible can be thought of as being 'off the bottom' of the window. Dragging the scroll bar downwards with the mouse would bring it into view.

Some windows also have a **Status bar** that appears at the bottom of the window.

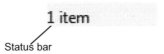

Status bar

The Status bar displays information about the contents of the window, such as how many items or objects it contains.

To display the Status bar for a particular window, do the following:
- Click the **View** menu.
- Select **Status Bar** to turn it on.

2.3.2   Viewing Windows

The contents of the main part of the window can be displayed in various ways to suit personal preferences.

To arrange icons within a window, do the following:
- Click the View menu to display a list of options.

The various options are:
- **Content**: If a file, such as a document or graphics-format file (i.e. a photo from a digital camera) or other file is selected, the content of the file is displayed. Content refers to the time and date that the file was created and the size of the file.

- **Tiles**: This displays large icons for each item in the folder in column format, along with summary details appropriate to the file type, such as the dimensions.

- **Icons**: This allows the user to view files as small, medium or large icons. This view is similar to Tiles but shows just the icon and name, in a row format.

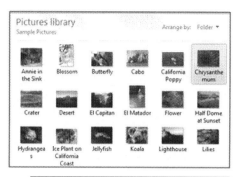

- **List:** This shows small icons for each folder item in a single column.

- **Details:** This is similar to List view but displays multiple columns of details about each item.

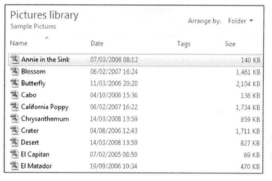

2.3.3   Manipulating Windows

Open windows can be manipulated to suit users' working requirements. It is useful when working between two or more windows to be able to move a window, change its size, minimise it or close it.

Moving Windows

To reposition a window on the desktop, do the following:

- Place the tip of the mouse arrow at the top of the window.

Point the mouse arrow at any part of the window above the Address Bar (be careful not click any of the Windows buttons) and drag

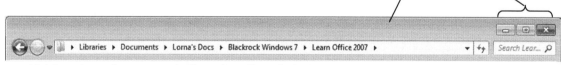

- Holding down the mouse button, drag the window.
  When the mouse button is released, the window assumes its new position.

Resizing Windows

The size of a window can also be changed. If multiple windows are open at the same time, it may be useful to have the principal window large enough to work in and the others smaller so all of them remain on the desktop with only some of their contents visible.

To resize a window, do the following.

- Move the arrow over the **Resize handle** in the bottom right corner of the window.

Resize handle

- When the mouse arrow changes to the double-headed resize arrow, click and drag diagonally to change the size of the window.
- When the mouse button is released, the window will remain at the size it was dragged to.

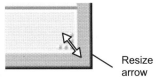

Resize arrow

It is possible to drag just one edge of a window in a similar way.

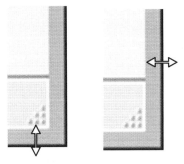

Sizing and Closing Windows

When a window is too small to display all of its contents, it can be enlarged or **maximised**, causing it to fill the whole desktop area. This is useful where scrolling would be tedious.

- Click **Maximise** at the top of the window to enlarge the window to full-screen size. When a window is maximised, the **Maximise** button becomes the **Restore** button.
- Click **Restore** to restore the window to its previous size.

If you want to temporarily remove a window from the desktop, it can be reduced or **minimised**. The window disappears from the desktop and is represented by a button on the taskbar.

- Click the **Minimise** button to temporarily close a window, reducing it to a button on the taskbar.

Click the button to open the window

To **redisplay** a minimised window, do the following:
- Click the button representing the window on the taskbar.

To **close** a window, do the following:
- Click the **Close X** button.

To minimise all open windows immediately and display the desktop, press the Windows key and the 'D' key together. The Windows key is to the left of the space bar and has the Windows logo.

2.3.4   Switching Between Open Windows

It is common to have several windows open on the desktop at once. Only one can be directly interacted with at a time using the mouse and keyboard, although processes can continue in the other windows. For example, a time-consuming mail-merge operation might be left running in one window (which is called '**running in the background**'), when another window is being used to edit a document. The window currently being used is referred to as having **focus** and is called the **active window**.

The **title bar** of the active window is usually a darker colour than inactive windows.

For example, the **Calculator** window example at the back is inactive and the WordPad window is active.

Clicking a window gives it **focus** and **brings it to the front**. In the illustration on the right, clicking the Calculator window would bring it forward, making it the active window, causing it to obscure part of the WordPad window.

Using the Taskbar

The taskbar, at the bottom of the desktop, displays a button for each open window. A window can be selected and made active by clicking the appropriate button.

When a window is active, its button is lighter than the buttons of the inactive windows.

When many windows are open, whether they are folders or applications, there will be many buttons on the taskbar and space may run out. If this happens, buttons representing windows belonging to the same application, or windows viewing folder contents, can be grouped together.

This will happen automatically, when this preference has been set (see below).

When buttons have been grouped you can display one of the windows (files) by doing the following:

- Move the mouse arrow over the grouped buttons on the Taskbar.
  A pop-up menu will appear listing all the files in the group.
- Left-click the required file to display its window again.

To **close all the files** in a button group, do the following:

- Right-click the grouped button on the Taskbar.
  A pop-up menu will appear listing options.
- Left-click **Close all Windows**.
  All the files in the group are closed.

To **set** this preference and ensure files are grouped together in this way, do the following:

- Right-click the **Taskbar**.
  A pop-up menu appears.
- Click **Properties**.

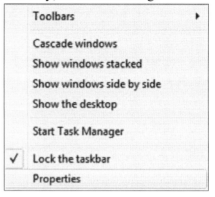

The **Taskbar and Start Menu Properties** window opens.
- Click the **Taskbar Buttons** menu and select **Always combine, hide labels**.
- Click **Apply**.

Click **Always combine, hide labels**

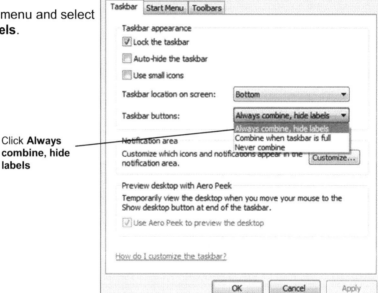

Using the Keyboard

The keyboard can also be used to cycle through open applications.
- Hold down the **Alt** key, and tap the **Tab** key.
- A task switcher window opens in front of all the other windows on the desktop with an icon for each open window.

- Still holding down the **Alt** key, repeatedly tap the **Tab** key and note that the selection rectangle moves to each icon in turn.
- When it surrounds the icon for the item to be switched to, release both keys and the selected window will be made active.

Section 3 ▶ Information and Settings

3.1   System Information

To obtain information about your computer, such as how much memory there is available, do the following:

- Right-click the **Computer** icon on the desktop.
- Select **Properties**.

The **System Properties** window opens.

Under **Windows edition:** the version of Windows 7 and its **Service Pack** level are displayed.

At the bottom, information about the computer itself is displayed.

Under the **Windows activation:** the name and company name of the registered user are shown, along with the Product ID number.

In the example on the right, under **System**, the processor is Pentium Dual Core CPU, it is running at 2.60GHz and there is 2GB of RAM installed.

3.2   Changing the Appearance of the Desktop

3.2.1   Themes

A **desktop theme** is a set of icons, fonts, colours, sounds, desktop background picture and other window elements that gives Windows 7 a distinctive look. The theme can be changed to suit different users or circumstances. A **color scheme** can then be applied to a theme to further customise the appearance of the desktop.

New themes can be created by modifying the elements of the default set of themes. These modified themes can be saved using a new theme name. The default theme in Windows 7 is the **Windows 7** theme with the **Default (Aero)** colour scheme (unless using Windows 7 Basic). To change the current theme, do the following.

- Right-click an empty area of the desktop.
  A pop-up menu appears.
- Select **Personalize**.
  The **Personalization** window opens.

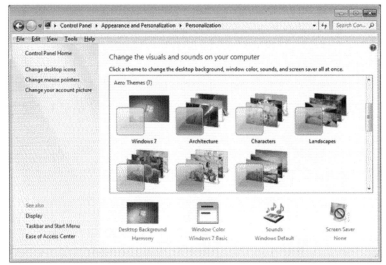

The overall appearance of Windows 7 is controlled by the selected Theme. There are several Windows 7 Aero themes (if using Home Premium or Professional) and also a Windows 7 Basic and Windows Classic Theme.

- Select a theme from the menu.

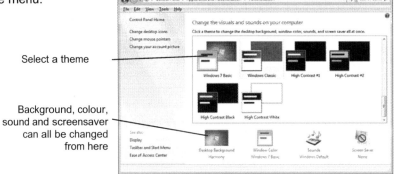

Select a theme

Background, colour, sound and screensaver can all be changed from here

The style of the windows, buttons, etc. changes to match the chosen theme.

The locations of items such as menus, close buttons and so on do not change.

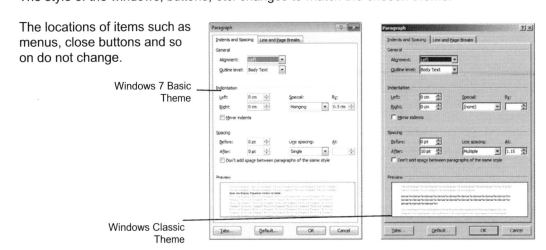

Windows 7 Basic Theme

Windows Classic Theme

- Open the **Personalize** window as before.
- Select the **Windows Color** option.

Windows Color

- Select an item to change (i.e. Desktop, Window, Menu, etc.).
- From the **Color** drop-down menu, select a colour.
- Click **Apply**.
  The color scheme will change.

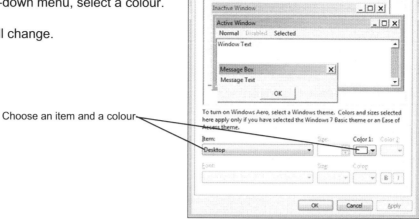

Choose an item and a colour

- A modified theme can be saved by right clicking a theme and selecting **Save Theme**.

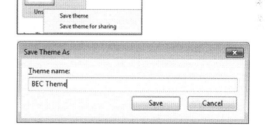

- Name the theme file, e.g. BEC theme.
- Click **Save**.
  It will then become available in the list of personal themes that can be chosen.

3.2.2 Changing the Desktop Background

The **Background** is what is displayed behind the icons on the desktop. It can be a plain colour or a picture and is part of the desktop theme.

To change the desktop background, do the following.
- Right-click an empty area of the desktop.
- A pop-up menu appears.
- Select **Personalize**.

The **Personalization** window opens.
- Select the **Desktop Background** option.
- To use a colour as the background, select **Solid Colors** from the **Picture Location** list.
- Choose a colour from the **Color** list.
- Click a colour from the palette or click **More** to see more colour options.
- Select **Save Changes**.

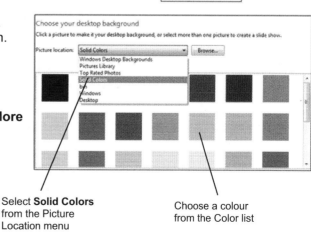

Select **Solid Colors** from the Picture Location menu

Choose a colour from the Color list

To use a picture as the background, do the following:
- Open the **Personalize** window and select the Desktop Background option.
- Select a Windows Desktop Backgrounds from the list.
- Select an image. Click **Save Changes**.

Use the **Browse** button to locate the picture

If the picture is not listed, or you would like to use a picture that you have loaded onto your computer, do the following:
- Click the **Browse** button.
The **Browse** window opens.
- Locate the picture using the **Look in:** box.

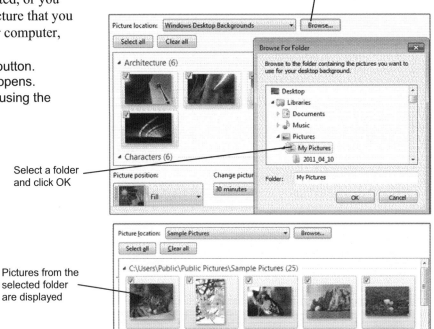

Select a folder and click OK

Pictures from the selected folder are displayed

Picture position can be changed here

- The **Position** drop-down menu is available when a background image has been selected, and the selection determines what will happen if the selected image is smaller than the desktop. The options are:

  ▷ **Center**: The image will be centred on the desktop. The rest of the desktop around the image will be shown in the colour that is selected in the **Color** drop-down menu.

  ▷ **Tile**: The image will be repeated in a tile pattern.

  ▷ **Stretch**: The image will be stretched to fill the available desktop space.

  ▷ **Fit**: The image will fit to the screen.

  ▷ **Fill**: The image will fill screen.

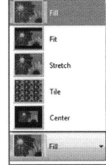

 A quick way of setting a picture stored on your computer as the desktop background is to right-click a picture and choose **Set as Background**.

3.2.3   Screen Resolution and Colour Quality

Screen Resolution

The image displayed on the monitor is made up of columns of tiny dots across and rows of tiny dots down, where each dot is capable of being any one of millions of colours. These dots are controlled by the computer to draw the images on the screen.

The number of dots across the display combined with the number of dots down is called the **resolution**. Common resolutions are 1024 across by 768 down, or 1152 across by 864 down. The higher the resolution numbers are, the more dots there are on the screen, which makes the images of the desktop, windows and icons appear more defined.

There are several reasons why it may not be possible to use high numbers to set the screen resolution:
- The computer will have a maximum resolution that it can handle.
- The monitor will have a maximum resolution that it can handle.
- The physical size of the monitor, the distance the user is from it and the user's eyesight are all factors, because while at higher resolutions more windows can be seen, and more icons and text will fit on the screen, everything will be smaller.
- Flat-screen monitors (LCD or plasma) have a **native resolution** which the computer should be set up to match. If not, the monitor will have to scale the images up or down, resulting in much poorer image quality.

Colour Quality

The colour quality, or colour depth, that Windows 7 is set to display determines the maximum number of colours that can be used for any image on the screen, including the desktop, icons, and windows, etc. All modern PCs are capable of using at least 32-bit colour, meaning that each individual dot on the monitor can be any one of 4,294,967,296 colours.

Changing Colour Quality and Screen Resolution

To change the screen resolution and colour quality, do the following.
- Right-click an empty area of the desktop.
- Select **Screen Resolution** from the pop-up menu that appears.

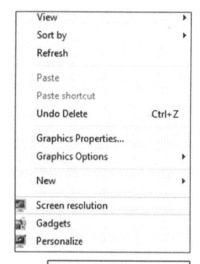

The **Screen Resolution** window opens.
- To adjust the resolution, select the **Resolution** menu.
- Drag the **Screen resolution** slider up or down to the desired setting.
- Click **Apply** to test the setting.
  If the setting is too high for the monitor to display, the screen will blank. If this happens, press the **Esc** key to restore the original settings.
- The **Color quality** can be set using the drop-down menu in **Advanced Settings**. Click this option.
- Select the **Monitor** tab.
- Select the **Colors** menu.
- Make a selection.
- Click **Apply**.
  It would be unusual to choose any setting other than **True Color (32-bit)**.

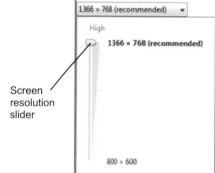

Screen resolution slider

Select the colour quality – True Color (32 bit) is the usual setting

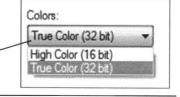

3.2.4 **Screensavers**

Screensavers automatically turn the screen blank or display a moving picture when the computer had been idle for a period of time. They are useful as a security mechanism as users can choose to require a password to be entered to turn off the screensaver and begin working again.

A screensaver, if enabled, will appear when there has been no activity from mouse or keyboard for a predetermined time. When a screensaver is active, pressing any key or moving the mouse will deactivate it and display the previous contents of the desktop. Windows 7 has many built-in screensavers.

To select a screensaver, do the following.
- Right-click on an empty area of the desktop.
- Select **Personalize** from the pop-up menu that appears.
  The **Personalization** window opens.

- Select the Screensaver option.

  A screensaver can be selected
  from the drop-down menu.

  The number of minutes that must elapse before
  the screensaver activates can also be specified.

  If the **On resume, logon screen**
  box is ticked, the Windows
  password must be entered to
  deactivate the screensaver.

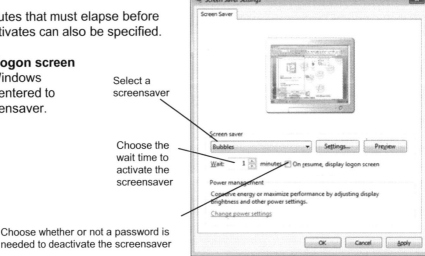

Select a
screensaver

Choose the
wait time to
activate the
screensaver

Choose whether or not a password is
needed to deactivate the screensaver

3.2.5 **The Control Panel**

Almost all changes that can be made to Windows 7 itself, from adding new applications to changing the time are done via the Control Panel.

To access the Control Panel, do the following:
- Click the **Start** button.
- From the **Start Menu**, select **Control Panel**.

Control Panel

The **Control Panel** can be displayed in either **Category View** as shown in the illustration on the right, or **Small icons** or **Large icons** as shown in the illustration below. Category View groups categories, such as hardware and sound, together. This text will assume that Small or Large icon view is being used.

Large icons   Small icons   Change **View** by

   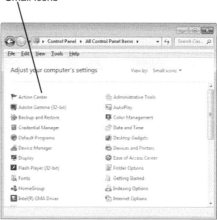

To change from Category View to Small or Large icons, do the following:

- Click the **View by** menu in the top right of the window and select an option.

Date and Time

Computers have an internal clock – displayed in the system tray at the right of the taskbar – that keeps track of the current date and time. This is important for many reasons.

- When a file is created or updated, it is stamped with the current date and time. This can be useful when searching for it later.
- The date and time can be easily inserted into Office documents.

To adjust the date and time, do the following.

- Click the **Start Button**.
- From the **Start Menu**, select **Control Panel**.
- Double-click the **Date and Time** icon.
  Alternatively, click the displayed date and time in the **System Tray** at the right of the taskbar.

The **Date and Time** window opens.

- Select the **Change Date and Time** button

  The year, month and day can be set using the controls on the left of the window.

  The time can be set by clicking the time field below the clock and typing new values, or using the up/down arrows.

- Click OK when finished.

- Select the **Change Time Zone** button. The **Time Zone** tab makes it possible to change the time zone that the computer is set to by choosing a zone from the drop-down list.

- The **Internet Time** tab enables Windows 7 to be configured to automatically obtain the correct time from a variety of atomic clocks connected to the internet.
- Select the **Change Settings** button to synchronize with an Internet time server.

Volume

Computers can have built-in or externally connected speakers so that sound from video clips, MP3 files etc can be heard.

To adjust the volume output from the computer, do the following.

- Click the **Start Button**.
- From the **Start Menu**, select **Control Panel**.
- Double-click the **Sound** icon. *Alternatively*, click the speaker icon in the **System Tray**.

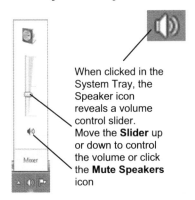

When clicked in the System Tray, the Speaker icon reveals a volume control slider. Move the **Slider** up or down to control the volume or click the **Mute Speakers** icon

- If selected from the Control Panel, select the speakers used and then click **Properties**.
- Select the **Levels** tab.
- Adjust the volume levels by moving the slider controls in the window.
- Click **OK** when finished.

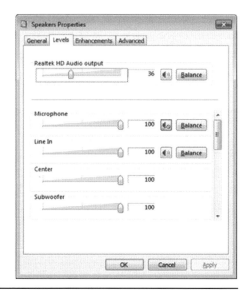

3.2.6   Changing the Keyboard Layout

The keyboard layout can be changed to suit the language that documents are being produced in. Each language has a default keyboard layout, but many languages have alternate layouts. Even if work is done mainly with one language, other layouts may be useful for typing letters with accents, etc.

To change the keyboard language, do the following.
- Click the **Start Button**.
- From the **Start Menu**, select **Control Panel**.
- Double-click the **Region and Language** icon.

The **Region and Language** window opens.
- Click the **Keyboard and Languages** tab.
- Click the **Change Keyboards** button.

Change Keyboards button

The **Text Services and Input Languages** window opens.

The current keyboard layout is displayed in the Default input language section.

Current keyboard layout

Add... button

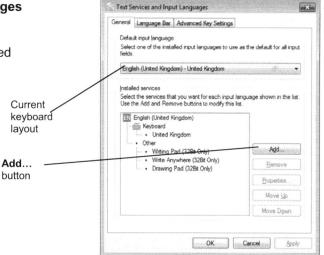

A different layout can be selected from the **Add Input Language** list. To add a new language, do the following:
- Click **Add** in the **Text Services and Input Languages window**.
  The **Add Input Language** window opens.
- Select a new language from the list.
- Click **OK**.

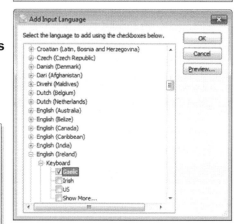

note   You can switch between different keyboard languages within the different programs that you use on your computer.

Hold down **Left Alt + Shift** to switch the keyboard to US format and **Alt Gr + Shift** to switch to UK format. The language changes are flagged in the status bar of the program you are using.

Section 4 ▶ Installing and Uninstalling Applications

2

4.1   Installing Applications

Applications can be added to or removed from Windows 7 to extend the range of functions available to users. Adding a new application is referred to as **installing** and removing an application is referred to as **uninstalling**.

Applications that are included with Windows 7 are called Windows Features and can be turned on or off using the Control Panel.

Other software that is not supplied as part of Windows usually comes with a special **installer** utility called **setup.exe** on the supplied CD, or as part of the download, as in the illustration on the right.

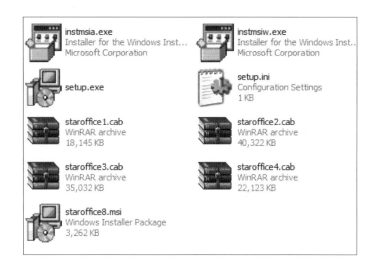

 note   In office or educational networks, users will often not have sufficient **permissions** on the computer to install or remove applications.

Running this installer will usually start a **wizard** – a series of simple steps that the user can follow to install the application.

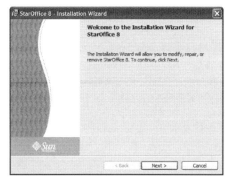

To turn on a new Windows Feature using the Control Panel, do the following:

- Click the **Start Button**.
- From the **Start Menu**, select **Control Panel**.
- Click the **Programs and Features** icon.

The **Programs and Features** window opens.

All the applications that are currently installed are listed here.

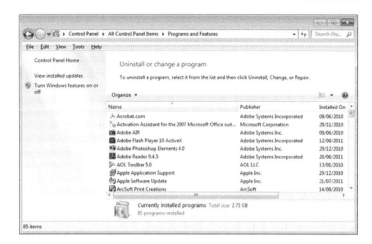

To turn on a new Windows Feature, do the following:
- Click the **Turn Windows features on or off** option on the left of the window.
- From this point, ticking an unticked item in the list and clicking the **OK** button will *turn on* the feature. Removing a tick will turn the feature *off*.

Tick or untick items

Click the expand button [+] to see further options for a particular feature

4.2 Uninstalling Applications

Sometimes it may be necessary to remove, or uninstall, an application.

To uninstall an application, do the following.
- Click the **Start Button**.
- From the **Start Menu**, select **Control Panel**.
- Click the **Programs and Features** icon.
  The **Programs and Features** window opens.
- Locate the required application in the list, and click it once to highlight it.

Click **Uninstall** to remove a program

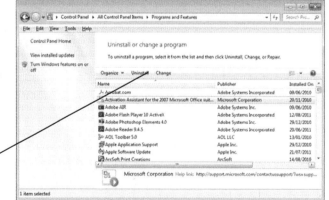

- Click **Uninstall**.
  A confirmation message will appear.
- Click **Yes** to uninstall the program.
  An uninstall wizard may open depending on the type of application being removed. If this is the case, follow the instructions in the wizard.

Section 5 ►   File Management

5.1   Main Concepts

A **file** is an organised collection of data that is stored on a computer and it can be identified as an individual entity having a file type and size. Examples include Microsoft Office documents, music files, etc. Applications, such as Microsoft Word and the Windows 7 operating system themselves, comprise many hundreds or thousands of individual files.

To do List.docx

A **folder** is a container in which files and other folders can be stored in an organised manner, in the same way that cardboard folders in an office filing cabinet might have letters, pictures and other folders inside them. The difference is that, on a computer, there is no restriction to the number of folders and files that can be put into other folders.

Empty folder

Containing files

5.1.1   Measuring Files

The size of a file is measured in **bytes** and determines how much memory is needed to store that file. One byte is the basic unit of measurement and is very small. The typical starting point for file measurement is a **Kilobyte (KB)**, which is equal to approximately 1,000 bytes. The next most common file measurement is a **Megabyte (MB)**. One MB is equal to 1 million bytes or 1,000 KB. The third most common file measurement is a **Gigabyte (GB)**. One GB is equal to 1 billion bytes or 1,000 MB. File sizes can increase beyond the measurement of GBs, but are not common and exist in specialist areas, such as computer generated special effects in films.

5.2   Storage Devices

All user-created files, files that comprise the installed applications and Windows 7 itself must be stored on a **storage device** so that they are retained safely and do not disappear when the computer is shut down.

There are two main categories of **file storage devices** for files. They devices are usually referred to as **drives**. For example, you put DVDs in a DVD drive, tapes in a tape drive, etc.

- **Non-Removable Storage Devices**: Windows 7 itself, applications and user-created files are generally stored on a **hard disk drive**.

- **Removable Storage Devices**: These devices, as the name suggests, are generally used for moving files from computer to computer, installing new software, archiving and creating backups.

Information on a computer is stored electronically. Because of this, there is always a possibility that it can be lost due to a malfunction in the system or through human error. To avoid total loss of data, it is important to have copies of all important files stored on disks or other removable media. These copies are called **backups**. Backups can be made in several ways. Copies can be made to tape, USB drive, external hard disks or burned onto a CD or DVD. The data from some files may also be kept as hard copy. These back-ups should be kept in a safe and secure place, e.g. locked away in fireproof containers or off the premises in a remote location.

5.2.1   Hard Disk Drive (Non-Removable or Removable)

The computer has a **non-removable hard disk** drive inside the **base unit**. At the time of writing, the average capacity of this drive would be over 100GB. It contains Windows 7 operating system, all the installed applications and user files.

More hard drives can be added to the computer if more **disk space** is required. These drives can be fitted internally or connected externally using a USB or FireWire cable.

Hard disk drives have one or more rotating **platters** on which data is stored magnetically. Information is read and written by a movable arm that flies slightly above the platters. The illustration shows a typical hard disk drive with its cover removed.

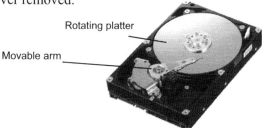

Rotating platter

Movable arm

Removable, or **external**, **hard disks** are the same as internal hard disks but are mounted in a tough casing and connect to the computer via the USB or similar port. They are typically used for archiving, moving large amounts of data between computers and backups. At the time of writing, 1TB (1,024GB) units are available.

5.2.2   USB Drives

USB drives are a convenient storage device that plug into the high-speed USB (universal serial bus) port that is available on most modern computers.

They use the same **flash memory** technology that is used in the memory cards of digital cameras and hand-held video games and are sometimes referred to as **flash drives**. They are small enough to fit on a keyring and, at the time of writing, typically have at least 512MB of storage space.

5.2.3   CDs (Compact Discs)

While hard disks are magnetic and USB drives use flash memory, CDs use a reflective coating that can be read using a laser, meaning that CD is a type of **optical storage**. A typical CD can hold 700MB of information. The CDs that are typically used to distribute copyrighted data, such as commercial software or music, are read-only – the information on these discs cannot be erased or added to – and they are more accurately called CD-ROMs.

Listed below are the two main types of **recordable** CD. The process of copying information to a CD is often called **burning**.
- **CD-R**: These can be written to once and read from multiple times.
- **CD-RW**: These can be written to and read from multiple times.

CDs are used in **CD drives**. This will have a front panel with a tray that can be opened to insert and remove the discs themselves. External CD drives are also available.

5.2.4   DVDs (Digital Versatile Discs)

DVDs have largely replaced the CD for optical storage use, and have displaced the videotape entirely in the consumer entertainment world.

DVDs look the same as CDs and use the same technology, but the capacity of a standard DVD disc is 4.7GB as opposed to 700MB for a CD. There are also dual-layer discs which can hold over 8GB. This is important in computer terms because as hard disk drive capacities increase, archival and backup media must keep pace.

In the entertainment world, the capacity of a dual-layer, or high-density, DVD is the only way to distribute films with high-quality pictures and sound. The DVDs that are typically used to distribute copyrighted data, such as commercial software or film, are read-only, referred to as DVD-ROM.

There are many types of recordable DVD disk which can be broadly broken down into the following two groups.

- **DVD-R** and **DVD+R**: These can be written to once and read from multiple times.

- **DVD-RW**, **DVD+RW** and **DVD-RAM**: These can be written to and read from multiple times.

DVDs are used in **DVD drives**, which are identical in appearance to CD drives. All DVD drives can read CDs, and most can write to them as well, meaning that drives that work with CDs only are effectively obsolete.

5.2.5   Network Drives

If a computer is part of a network, access storage can be used that is physically located on another computer. For example, a network server in an office may have several hard disks of huge capacity that are **shared**, and thus available to other computers on the network.

Users can transfer files to and from these shared locations in the same way as they would with the hard disks in their own **local** computers. The files are transmitted over **network cables** or via a **wireless network connection**.

In Windows 7, the icon for a normal folder on a local computer looks slightly different from that for a folder representing a network location.

5.2.6   High-Density DVDs

High-density DVDs are the successor to DVDs. Initially, there were two competing formats, namely **HD DVD** and **Blu-Ray**, but the latter emerged as the standard during 2008. The former could store up to 30GB, while Blu-Ray can store up to 50GB. High-density formats will eventually replace standard DVD.

5.2.7   Tapes

In computer networks, such as those found in most businesses, there are usually one or more **servers** (dedicated computers that provide centralised control and storage). The vitally important data on their hard drives is usually **backed up** using removable tape cartridges. These are then often removed from the premises and stored elsewhere as part of a **disaster recovery plan**. This type of storage is beginning to disappear as its traditional advantage of huge capacity at a relatively low cost is eroding in the face of inexpensive alternatives, such as hard disks, which are also more reliable.

5.2.8   Online File Storage

The mass availability of broadband internet access has brought about various types of **online storage**. This form of storage has been around since computers were first networked, but recent examples, such as Mozy (www.mozy.com), provide simple ways to use it. This type of storage is useful for transferring files, which might be too big to e-mail, and for off-site backups.

5.3   Storage Icons

Some Windows 7 icons representing different storage types are displayed below.

Hard drive   DVD drive   Removable drive,
                                                                e.g. USB drive

Zip drive   Network drive

5.4   Speed, Cost and Capacity of Storage Media

The following table gives an idea of the relative cost and capacity of different storage media in 2008.

Type	Capacity	Cost €/MB	Access Speed
Hard Disk	80GB -1TB	€0.00024	Up to 1.6Gb/sec
Tape (Sony AIT5)	400GB	€0.00009	192Mb/sec
USB Drive	Up to 64GB	€0.00943	Up to 240Mb/sec
Blu-Ray DVD	Up to 50GB	€0.0043	Up to 54Mb/sec
CD	Up to 700MB	€0.0014	Up to 62.4Mb/sec (at 52x)

5.5   Working with Files and Folders

5.5.1   How Windows 7 Organises Files and Folders

It is important that all the folders on a computer's hard disk are stored in a tidy and organised way, and that the basic structure is the same for every computer that uses the same operating system. This is called the **File System**, or sometimes the **Directory Structure**, 'directory' is another term for 'folder'.

Windows 7 is itself installed on an empty hard drive, normally by the computer manufacturer. This process creates a standard set of Windows 7 **system folders** that is the same on every Windows 7 computer. The contents of these folders should never be directly altered and access to them should be restricted.

When users are added in Windows 7, they each get their own personal folder plus some others. Normally, users can only see their own **user folder**. All user-created files, such as word processing documents, should be stored here.

All drives in Windows 7, except for network drives, are assigned a **drive letter** automatically. The main hard disk drive, upon which Windows 7 itself is installed, is given the letter **C**, and can be referred to as **C:** (pronounced **C colon**). Optical drives (CD and DVD drives) tend to be assigned to **D:** or **E:** but this can vary. Further drive letters are assigned to **removable drives** when they are connected. These drive letters disappear when the removable drive is disconnected.

The file system is structured like a tree. The **root** of the tree can contain files and folders. Those **sub-folders** can themselves contain more files and sub-folders, and so on.

5.5.2   Navigating to a Drive, File or Folder

Navigating through folders and sub-folders to find a particular location is a very common activity, especially when opening and saving files.

To explore the basic Windows 7 file system structure, do the following:

- Right-click the **Computer** icon on the desktop.
- Select **Open** from the pop-up menu that appears.
  Alternatively, double-click the icon.

Computer

> If the Computer icon is not visible, open the Start Menu and locate it. It can then be right-clicked from the Start Menu.

Navigating to a Drive

The **Computer** window opens.

Treeview showing contents of Desktop

This symbol ▷ indicates that the drive/folder contains further folders or files (click to expand)

Click this symbol ◢ to collapse

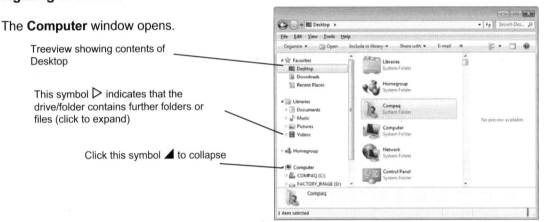

- In the navigation pane on the left, click the ▷ sign beside a drive, e.g. **Computer name (C:)**. The node will expand to show its contents of the **C: drive**.

  Any item with a ◢ beside it has been expanded. Click the ◢ to collapse the drive or folder and make the treeview more compact.

  Any drive or folder that has a ▷ sign beside it can be expanded.

Navigating to a File or Folder

To view the contents of a folder in the right-hand side of the window (navigation pane), do the following:

- Click the folder once to highlight it.
  Any sub-folders are displayed in the right-hand side of the window.
- Double-click a folder in the right-hand side of the window to open it.
  Double-clicking any file icon will start the application that it is associated with.

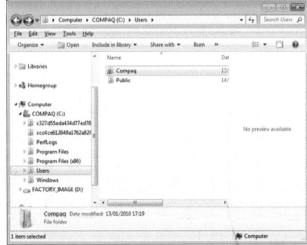

5.5.3   Creating a Folder and a Further Sub-Folder

A folder is a container in which files and other folders can be stored. Normally, files of a particular type or relating to a particular topic are kept together in the same folder.

Folders should be given recognisable names, such as **Finance** or **Novel**, to indicate their contents. It is also good practice for users to only create new folders underneath their own **home** folders – security settings in Windows 7 will not usually allow folders to be created in many other places anyway.

Creating a Folder

This sequence will describe how to create a folder called **Office** within your personal folder. If your personal folder is not visible on the desktop, do the following to show it.

- Open the **Start Menu** and locate your personal folder (it will be displayed as your username or account name)
  menu item.
- Right-click the personal folder menu item.
- Select **Show On Desktop** from the menu that is displayed.

Click **Show on Desktop**

To create a folder, do the following.

- On the **desktop**, double-click your personal folder to open it.
  A new window opens, with the contents of your personal folder displayed.
- Double-click the **My Documents** folder
- Right-click in an **empty** area of the main section of the **My Documents** window (on the right-hand side).
- Select **New** from the pop-up menu that appears.
- Select **Folder** from the pop-up menu that appears.
  Alternatively, click the **New folder** button on the command bar.

Compaq

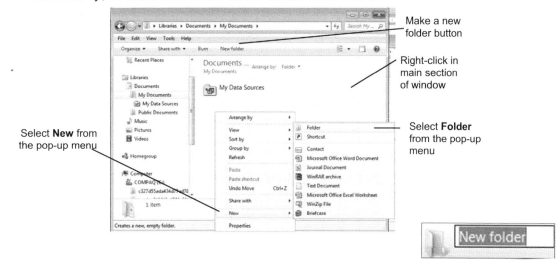

A new folder will appear. It will automatically be called **New Folder** and the name will be highlighted.

To give the folder a more meaningful name, start typing and press **Enter** when finished.

If the wrong name is entered, see **Section 5.7.3** for details on how to rename it.

Creating a Sub-Folder

To create a sub-folder, do the following:
* Double-click the newly created folder to open it.
  It will be empty.
* Repeat the same steps used to create a folder.
* When naming the sub-folder give it a different name to the main folder.

Creating a Folder from Within an Application

It is possible to create a new folder from inside an application itself, which can save time. As an example, we will create a document in a text editor and then save it to a new folder.

* From the **Start** menu, select **All Programs** and then **Accessories**.
* Select **WordPad**.
  The **WordPad** application opens.

Select **Accessories**

Select **WordPad**

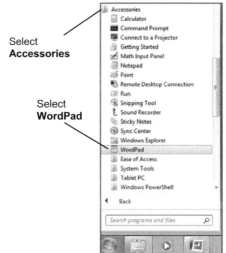

* Type some text into the blank document that appears.

To save the document in a folder that has not yet been created, do the following.

* From the **WordPad** menu button, move the mouse over the **Save As** menu option.
* Select **Rich Text document** (alternatively, click Save As to bypass the file format options)

The **Save As** window opens.
The cursor will be in the **File Name** field.
- Delete the contents of the **File Name** field and type the name for the file, e.g. **test.rtf**.

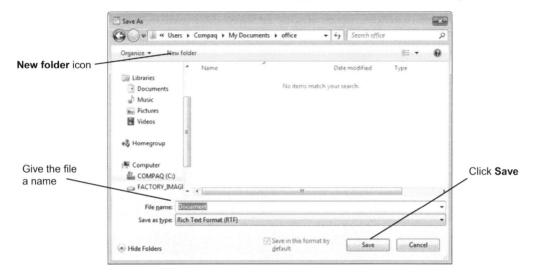

New folder icon

Give the file
a name

Click **Save**

- Click the **New Folder** button in the command bar at the top of the window.
- Give the new folder a name.
- Double-click the new folder in the main area of the window to open it.
- Click **Save** to save the new document in the newly created folder.
- Close the **WordPad** application.

5.5.4   Displaying Folder Properties

In Windows 7, every file or folder has **Properties**. These are pieces of information that describe that particular item.

To view the properties of a folder, do the following.
- Right-click any folder and select **Properties** from the pop-up menu.
- The **Properties** window opens.

Information about the folder, such as it's size
and the number of files it contains can be seen.
These figures also include any sub-folders and
their contents.

In addition, there are various tabs containing
other advanced options concerning security
and network sharing.

Number of files
and folders

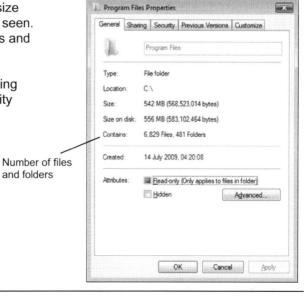

5.6 Working with Files

All files must have a **filename**. In Windows 7, this name can be up to 256 characters in length, containing upper case and lower case letters, numbers, spaces, punctuation marks and almost anything else that can be typed.

Most files have an **extension** to their name, which is a dot (full stop) followed by some additional characters. For example, the filename **My Novel.docx** has the extension **docx**, indicating that it was created using Microsoft Word 2010.

In Microsoft Windows, the file extension establishes the application a file was created in and the icon that is used to represent it – e.g. all Microsoft Word files have the same icon. When a file icon is double clicked, Microsoft Windows opens the file with the application dictated by its extension.

 note
> Filenames are **not case sensitive** in Windows. 'My Novel.docx', 'MY NOVEL.DOCX', etc. would refer to the same file.

5.6.1   Recognising Common File Types

Icons in Windows 7 make folders and particular types of file easy for users to identify. For example, when an application suite such as Microsoft Office is installed, it takes ownership of all files with particular extensions and tells Windows to use particular icons when displaying them.

Double-clicking a file which has the Microsoft Word icon and the extension **.docx** will automatically start Microsoft Word, if needed, and **open** the file within it. This mechanism is called **file association**.

Below are the icons for files created with Microsoft Office 2010.

My Novel.docx	Lottery Numbers.xlsx	Proposed Mars Mission.pptx
Microsoft Word	Microsoft Excel	Microsoft PowerPoint
Accounts.accdb	Expenses.xsn	Parish News.pub
Microsoft Access	Microsoft InfoPath	Microsoft Publisher

There can be many **formats** for some file types. For example, files containing image data can be **JPEG** format or **PNG** format or **GIF** format or **BMP** format, to name a few. The format describes a method for how the bits and bytes are structured inside the file. In the case of these image files, JPEG and PNG are more recent formats and are intended to enable large images to be stored in small files, though with some expense to image quality.

Different computers may have different applications installed to handle some file types.

For example, one computer might only have the standard Microsoft Paint application installed, in which case the icon for an image file in BMP format would be like the icon on the right.

Zapotec.bmp

On a computer with Adobe PhotoShop installed, it would probably look like the icon on the right.

Zapotec.bmp

File Type	Example Formats	Icon
Image Files	**.jpg** (JPEG - Joint Photographics Experts)	Boston.jpg
	.bmp (a bitmap format)	Zapotec.bmp
Sound Files	**.mp3** (MPEG Layer 3)	My Last Serenade.mp3
Video Files	**.mpeg** or **mpg** (Moving Picture Experts Group) **.avi** (Audio Video Interleaved file)	AVI
Portable document format Files	**.pdf**	PDF Adobe
Compressed Files	**.zip** (WinZip)	
Temporary Files	**.tmp** (temporary file – when Word is using autorecovery it often uses tmp files to temporarily save information)	

5.7   Saving Files

Work that is created on a computer using an application such as Microsoft Word needs to be saved, for example to the internal hard drive or a removable drive. This makes it available the next time the computer is turned on. If files are not saved, they will not exist after the application that has been used to create them is closed.

When saving files two things need to be decided – what the file should be called and where it should be saved.

5.7.1   Giving a File a Name

Files and folders should be given sensible and descriptive names. It might be easier and quicker at the time to create ten Microsoft Word files called **myfile1.docx**, **myfile2.docx**, etc., but later each would have to be opened individually to discover what they contained.

When collaborating with others, where many users are creating and editing the same files, a file naming **convention** should be adopted. This is a set of rules defining exactly how files should be named that everyone must follow and ensures that structure and control is maintained. For example, it might be decided that all files should have a project code followed by a name followed by a revision date – **0234-Green Valley Estate-05-06-08.docx**.

Take a similar approach to naming folders (file extensions do not apply here, of course). There is nothing to prevent users from putting all their documents into one documents folder, but it might make more sense to create sub-folders for particular projects or type of document. Planning beforehand and then following the plan can save a lot of time in locating files later.

5.7.2   **Where Files are Saved**

Any application that allows a file to be created by a user will provide a method of saving the file. This process can be initiated by the user clicking a menu option, or the user will be automatically prompted to save when they attempt to close the application with unsaved work.

When saving, the user will be prompted for a **filename** and a folder in which to place the file. If the file is one that already existed, and changes are being saved, then the filename will be present already. Almost all applications running under Windows 7 will use a variation of the same window to request this information. It will look similar to the illustration below.

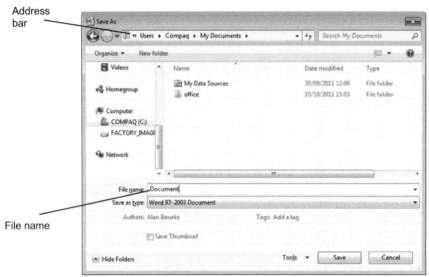

The two areas to note are the **Address bar** and **File name** fields.

The folder selected in the Address bar is where the file will be saved, and the current contents of that location are shown in the main part of the window. When a newly created file is being saved, this usually defaults to the Documents library, or a sub-folder within it such as My Music. This is intended as an 'easy' option for beginners.

If the file that is being saved already exists and has just been changed in the current session, the location in the Address bar will default to the folder where the file already resides.

To save your work in an organised way, folders should be created for the principal subject area.

> Saving everything in the **My Documents** folder is equivalent to saving all your work and documents in a single drawer in an office desk instead of using the filing cabinet. It may suffice for a few documents, but it will become chaotic very quickly as work accumulates. Create categorised sub-folders in the My Documents folder.

Practice Sequence

To practise naming and saving files, in the following sequence, you will create some folders and create a word-processing file to save in one of the folders.

Create some new folders to keep the file in.

1	Open the **My Documents** folder.	☐
2	Select the **New folder** button.	☐
3	Name the folder **Finance Department**.	☐

4   Open the Finance Department folder by double-clicking it. ☐

5   Create three new sub-folders called **Letters**, **Bank** and **Business**. ☐

6   Double-click the **Bank** folder to open it. ☐

7   Inside the **Bank** folder, create new sub-folders, called **National Bank**, **Finance Bank**, **Bahamas Bank** and **Equity Bank**. ☐

Next, create a new Microsoft Word document and save it in the Equity Bank folder.

8   From the Start menu, select the Microsoft Office sub-menu, and then Microsoft Word from the drop-down menu that appears. ☐

W| Microsoft Word 2010

Alternatively, double-click the Microsoft Word icon on the desktop.
The **Microsoft Word** application will start, with a blank document open called 'Document1.

9   Type some text into the blank document. ☐

10   To save this short document, click on the File menu within Microsoft Word and select **Save**, or press **Ctrl + S**. ☐

The **Save As** window opens, asking where the document should be saved.

In the Save As window, navigate to the **Equity Bank** folder that was created earlier.

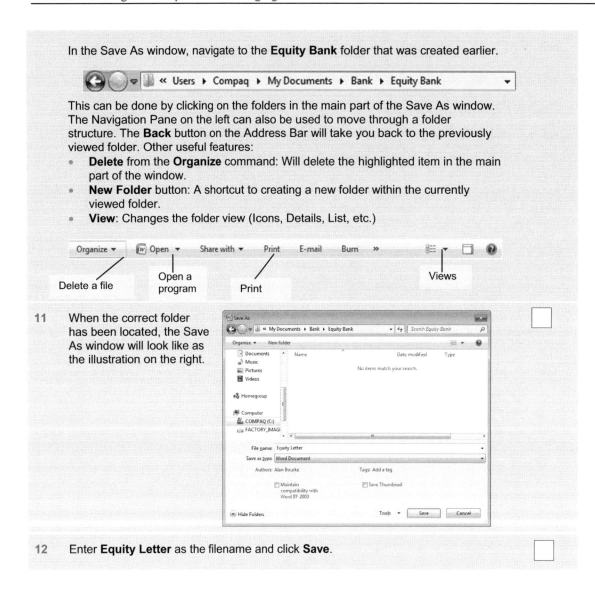

This can be done by clicking on the folders in the main part of the Save As window. The Navigation Pane on the left can also be used to move through a folder structure. The **Back** button on the Address Bar will take you back to the previously viewed folder. Other useful features:

*   **Delete** from the **Organize** command: Will delete the highlighted item in the main part of the window.
*   **New Folder** button: A shortcut to creating a new folder within the currently viewed folder.
*   **View**: Changes the folder view (Icons, Details, List, etc.)

11   When the correct folder has been located, the Save As window will look like as the illustration on the right.

12   Enter **Equity Letter** as the filename and click **Save**.

note   If the file already exists, an alert will appear and the existing file can be overwritten, or the save cancelled, or a new filename entered.

5.7.3   Renaming Files and Folders

A file or folder can be given a new name as long as that new name is not already being used by another file or folder in the same folder.

To rename a file, do the following.

*   Locate the file to be renamed and right-click it.
*   In the pop-up menu, select **Rename**.
    The main part of the filename will be highlighted.

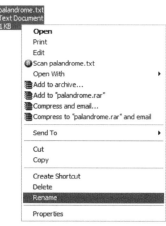

*   Type the new filename.
*   Press Enter.
*   To restore the original filename, press **Escape** instead of entering a new name.

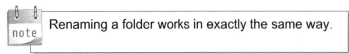

note   Renaming a folder works in exactly the same way.

5.8   Changing File Properties

A particular user's files are normally stored in their own Documents folder, which most other users set up on the computer cannot access. The exceptions are users with **Power User** or **Administrator** security rights.

Individual files can be made **read-only**, meaning that they can be opened and viewed but the contents cannot be changed. This is useful to prevent accidental deletion, for example.

To view and change the file read-only properties, do the following:
- Locate the file and right-click it.
- Select **Properties** from the menu.
  The **Properties** window opens.

  To make the file read-only, do the following:
- Tick the **Read-only** checkbox.
- Click **Apply**.
- Click **OK**.

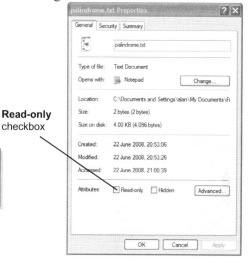

Read-only checkbox

 note

To make the file Read-write so that changes can be made to it, untick the Read-only checkbox.

5.9   Sorting Files

When viewing a list of files in a window, it can be useful to sort them in a particular way. For example, they could be sorted so that the largest appeared first to make it easier to delete large files to free up disk space.

To sort files by name, size, type or the date they were modified, do the following:
- Open the **My Documents** folder.
- Change the window to **Details** view by clicking the **View** command and selecting **Details**.

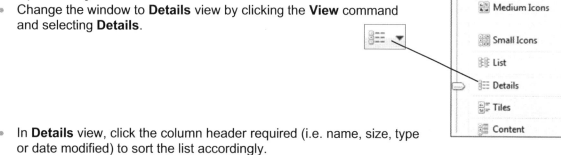

- In **Details** view, click the column header required (i.e. name, size, type or date modified) to sort the list accordingly.

Click triangle to change sort direction

The small triangle in the column header indicates the direction of the sort. Sorting can either be in ascending order (**A–Z**) or descending order (**Z–A**).

In the example on the right, the list is sorted in ascending name order. Therefore names beginning with **A** will be listed before those beginning with **B**. Click the column header again to change the sort direction.

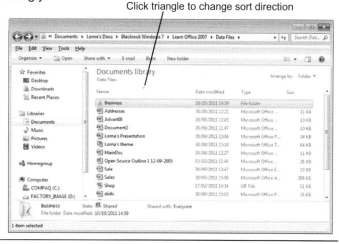

5.10   Copying and Moving Files and Folders

5.10.1   Selecting

Before an action can be performed on a file or folder, the file or folder must first be selected. This lets Windows 7 know that this is the item (or items) to be acted upon. Selecting a file or folder will cause its icon to change colour.

A single item or a group of items can be selected either on the desktop or in a file browser window. Actions such as dragging or deleting affect all the selected items.

- To select a single item, click it once.

Curriculum
Vitae.docx

When unselected, it is not highlighted

Curriculum
Vitae.docx

When selected, it is highlighted

- To select several items that are not located next to each other, hold down the **Ctrl** key and click each item once.

Curriculum   My Novel.docx   Loan
Vitae.docx   Application.docx

- To select a range of items, that are next to each other, hold down the **Shift** key, click the first item and click the last item. All the items in between these two will also be selected automatically.

Curriculum   My Novel.docx   Loan
Vitae.docx   Application.docx

- To select a group of items that are next to each other, click anywhere near the items on a blank area of desktop or window background, then with the right mouse button held down drag a selection rectangle (or marquee) around the items.

Curriculum   My Novel.docx   Loan
Vitae.docx   Application.docx

- To select multiple groups of items using a selection rectangle hold down the **Ctrl** key and then proceed to select each group.

- To select all the items in the active window, hold down **Ctrl** and press **A**.

5.10.2   Copying and Moving Files and Folders

Copying and moving files and folders is a common requirement, for example copying documents to a USB drive from time to time for backup purposes.

When a folder is copied or moved, everything contained within that folder (files and other folders) is also copied. It might be useful to check the size of the folder you are copying or moving first and the space available in the location you are copying or moving to to ensure there is enough space.

- Copying files or folders makes a copy of them in the new location and keeps the original file or folder in the original location
- Moving files or folders removes them from the original location and places them in the new location.

5.10.3 Copying Files and Folders Using the Menu and Keyboard Shortcuts

To copy files or folders using the menu and keyboard shortcuts, do the following:

* Locate the item to be copied in a window and **select** it by clicking on it once.
* Right-click the selected item and select **Copy** from the
  pop-up menu.
  Alternatively, press **CTRL + C** to copy the file or folder.

* Browse to the **target location** where the item is to be copied to.
  This can be done using the same window (because once the item is copied Windows 7 will remember what it is even if you browse to a different location, a different file window or the desktop).
* Right-click an empty area in the target location.
* Click **Paste**.
  Alternatively, press **CTRL + V** to paste the file or folder.
  The file or folder is copied to the new location.

note	If the item is pasted into the same location that it was copied from, Word will generate a new filename or folder name automatically as appropriate – this is normally the original file or folder name with **Copy of** at the beginning. This is because two items in the same location cannot have exactly the same name.

Copy of My
Novel.docx

5.10.4 Copying Files and Folders Using Drag and Drop

Rather than copying and pasting, selected items can also be copied by dragging and dropping them. For this method, both the location to copy from and the location to copy to must be visible at the same time.

* Ensure that both locations are visible.
  This could be two windows, a window and the desktop, etc.
* In the screenshot on the right, there are two windows open, and the copy is taking place from the left one (Samples) to the right one (Copy Of Samples).

 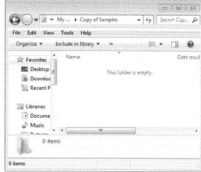

* Select the item or items to copy.
* When the items are selected, press and hold the **CTRL** key.

- Click the selected item (if there are more than one, click any selected item) and hold the mouse button down.
- Move the item to the target location with the mouse, still holding the **CTRL** key.

Notice that when the cursor is over the destination as in the illustration below, the tag includes a **+** to indicate a copy is taking place.

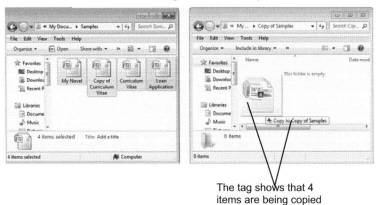

- Release the mouse button and the **CTRL** key to 'drop' the item(s) in the new location.

The tag shows that 4 items are being copied

5.10.5 Copying Files and Folders Using the Computer Window

From time to time you may need to make a copy of a file or folder. For example, you may want to copy an entire folder to back it up. If you copy a folder the entire contents of that folder and any sub-folders it contains are copied to the new location.

To copy a file/folder using the Computer window, do the following:

- Select the file or folder you wish to copy by clicking it.
- Click the **Edit** menu and then select **Copy to folder**. The **Copy Items** window opens.

- Select the folder, drive or sub-folder where the copied file/folder is to be stored and click **Copy**. If you want to create a new folder in which to store the copied file/folder, click the **Make New Folder** button.

When a file/folder is copied, the original remains where it is and a copy is placed in the new location. This means that there are now two copies of the file/folder available.

5.10.6 Copying Files and Folders Using any Window

In addition to copying files/folders using the Computer window, you can also **copy** files and folders using My Documents or any of the Documents, Music, Pictures or Games Libraries. If you copy a folder, the entire contents of that folder and any sub-folders it contains are copied to the new location.

To copy a file/folder using any window, do the following.

- Click the file or folder you wish to copy.
- Right-click the file/folder. A pop-up menu appears.
- Click **Copy** in the menu.
- Right click the drive, disk or folder where the file is to be copied to and then choose **Paste** from the menu that appears.

5.10.7　Moving Files or Folders Using the Menu and Keyboard Shortcuts

Moving files and folders using this method works in almost exactly the same way as copying them.

The differences are:

* When using the menu after right-clicking the item (or items) select **Cut** instead of **Copy**.

* When using the keyboard shortcuts, press **Ctrl + X** to cut rather than **Ctrl + C** to copy.

5.10.8　Moving Files and Folders Using Drag and Drop

This is almost the same procedure as copying files, which is described above. The difference is that the **CTRL** key is not held down when dragging.

Also, the cursor will not change to include a + symbol, which indicates a move is taking place.

5.10.9　Moving Files and Folders Using the Computer Window

There may be times when you wish to move a file or folder to a different location on your computer.

If you move a folder, the entire contents of that folder and any sub-folders it contains are moved to the new location.

To move a file/folder using the Computer window, do the following.
* Click the file or folder you wish to move.
* Select the **Edit** menu and then select **Move to Folder**.
  The **Move Items** window opens.

* Select the folder or sub-folder where the moved file/ folder is to be stored and click **Move**. If you want to create a new folder in which to store the moved file/ folder, click the **Make New Folder** button.

5.10.10　Moving Files and Folders Using any Window

In addition to moving files/folders using the Computer window, you can also **move** files and folders using My Documents or any of the Documents, Music, Pictures or Games Libraries. If you move a folder, the entire contents of that folder and any sub-folders it contains are moved to the new location.

To move a file/folder using any of the windows, do the following.

- Click the file or folder you wish to move.
- Right click the file/folder. A menu appears.
- Click **Cut** in the menu.
- Right-click the disk or folder where the file is to be moved to and then choose **Paste** from the menu that appears.

Practice Sequence

This sequence will copy a folder from one location to another.

1	Open the **My Documents** folder.	☐
2	In the file browser, double-click the **Finance Department** sub-folder to open it.	☐
3	Open the **Bank** sub-folder.	☐
4	Right-click the **Equity Bank** folder, and select **Copy** from the menu that appears.	☐
5	In the **Tree** on the left of the file browser window, select the **Letter** folder by clicking it.	☐
6	In the main part of the window, which should be empty, right-click anywhere and select **Paste** from the menu that appears.	☐
7	The folder will be copied.	☐
8	In the **Tree**, click back on the **Bank** sub-folder to verify that the original still exists, i.e. that the folder was copied and not moved.	☐

Try moving the Bahamas Bank sub-folder from the Bank folder into the Business folder. Remember that to move folders use cut rather than copy.

5.11   Deleting and Restoring Files and Folders

5.11.1   Deleting

If a file or folder is no longer required, it can be deleted. This might be done to free up space on the hard disk or just to keep files tidy and up to date.

Care should be taken when deleting — if the file or folder is important it is better to be safe, although Windows 7 makes it very difficult to delete something that would damage the operating system itself.

 An entire application such as Microsoft Word cannot be removed in the same way as files and folders. The application should instead be **uninstalled** as discussed in Section 4.2.

Deleting items from the **hard drive** does not remove them completely, but moves them to the **Recycle Bin** folder. It is important to remember that files deleted from a *removable storage device* are deleted permanently. The **Recycle Bin** is represented by an icon on the desktop.

Recycle Bin

The item will remain there and can be retrieved until the Recycle Bin is emptied. The deleted items still take up the same amount of disk space when in the Recycle Bin, so to free that disk space (and delete items permanently), the Recycle Bin must be emptied. When the Recycle Bin is emptied, as far as Windows 7 is concerned, the items in the Recycle Bin are gone.

note

Even if the Recycle Bin is emptied, the contents are *still* not necessarily gone forever. The Recycle Bin records that the space used by the files in the Trash is available again for other files to use, but does not necessarily remove the data that comprises the files themselves. There is **utility software** available that can then **undelete** these files. This software can be invaluable for retrieving important information, perhaps files deleted mistakenly or damaged as a result of a crash. It is also a security risk. If an old computer is sold or donated after all the files on the hard disk are deleted, it may still be possible for a third party to undelete them. There are still other utilities that will securely overwrite the space used by deleted files ensuring that they really are gone forever. This is a common requirement for computers used by the military and governments.

There are various ways to delete an item (or items).
- **Using Drag and Drop**: An item or items can be dragged and dropped into the Recycle Bin. Select an item or items and drag and drop the selection over the Recycle Bin icon.
- **Using the Menu**: To delete an item or items using a menu, select what is to be deleted, right-click the selection and choose **Delete** from the menu.
- **Using the Keyboard**: Select the item or items to be deleted and press the **Delete** key on the keyboard.
  A confirmation window will always appear as a precaution.
- Click **Yes** to confirm the deletion.

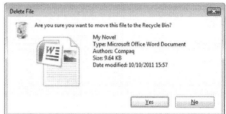

5.11.2 Retrieving Items
Deleting items moves them to the Recycle Bin. Items that are in the Recycle Bin folder can still be retrieved, or **undeleted**.

To retrieve an item, do the following:
- Double-click the Recycle Bin icon to view the contents in a window.

- Select the item or items to be restored from the **Recycle Bin**.
- Right-click on the selection.
- Select **Restore** from the pop-up menu that appears.

note

The item will automatically be restored to its last location before it was deleted.

5.11.3 Emptying the Recycle Bin
To remove items completely, the Recycle Bin must be emptied. Open the Recycle Bin first and double-check that it is safe to delete everything. Individual items in the Recycle Bin can be deleted or the entire folder can be emptied.

2

Deleting Individual Items

To delete an individual item in the Recycle Bin permanently, do the following:

- Open the **Recycle Bin** by double-clicking its icon.
- Select the item to be deleted.
- Right-click the selection.
- Select **Delete** from the pop-up menu that appears.

To Empty All Items from the Recycle Bin

To delete all items in Recycle Bin permanently, do the following:

- Right-click the Recycle Bin icon.
- Select **Empty Recycle Bin** from the pop-up menu that appears.

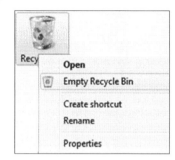

5.12   Searching

The Windows 7 Search tool enables various search criteria to be used to find files or folders. This is a vital ability as hard disk capacity increases and computers are used to store many thousands of files. It is available on the Start menu and on the toolbar within each open window.

- Click **Start** and enter the search words (criteria) into the Search box.

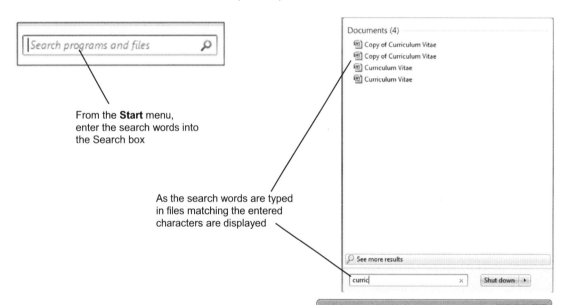

From the **Start** menu, enter the search words into the Search box

As the search words are typed in files matching the entered characters are displayed

- Select **See more results**.

    Results, if any, are displayed in the main section of the window.

    The files listed can be manipulated (copied, deleted, moved, etc.) in the normal way.

    The files in the search results may be located in different folders.

To open a file location, do the following:
- Right-click the file in the results list.
- Select **Open File Location** from the pop-up menu that appears.

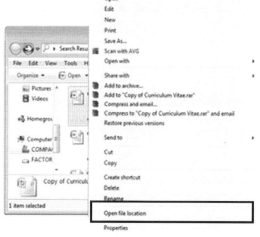

5.12.1 Searching for a File or Folder Using All or Part of Its Name

To search for a specific document or folder, at least part of its name must be known.
- Open the **Windows Explorer** window. Ensure that **Libraries** is displayed in the Address Bar.
- Click the cursor into the **Search** box.
  Recent search criteria will be displayed in the drop-down menu. More advanced searching can be performed from this menu.
- Search filters can be added, i.e. documents and files can be searched by the date they were last modified (saved), the type of file and the name of the file.
- Enter the name or part of the name after **Name:**
  As the search criterion is typed in, files and folders with file/folder names matching the entered characters will be displayed in the main part of the window (File List Pane).
- The search operation can be stopped using the x button.

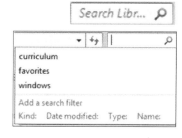

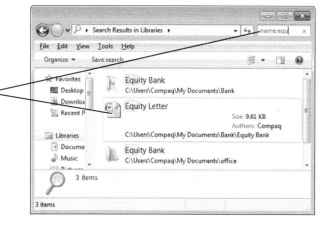

In this example, the characters *equ* are typed in the Search box. Files and folders with names containing those characters are displayed.

- Other search filters include **Date modified:**

  With this option you can select a date from the calendar or, if unsure about the exact date that the file was last modified, select from the following options:

  ▷ A long time ago
  ▷ Earlier this year
  ▷ Last week
  ▷ Earlier this week
  ▷ Yesterday

Practice Sequence

In this sequence the Search box will be used to find a file copied from one location to another on your computer.

1	Open the **Windows Explorer** window.	☐
2	Click into the **Search** box.	☐
3	Click the **Date modified** option from the drop down menu.	☐
4	Select the option **Earlier this week** to search for files that have been modified in the past seven days (or a date relevant to the last time the file was modified).	☐
5	Now click the **Name** filter. Type **equity** after **Name:**	☐
6	Press the **Enter** button.	☐
7	When search results are listed click the **x** button to end the search.	☐

5.12.2   Searching for Content

One of the main criteria used to search for files or folders is by content. In searching for all files relating to or mentioning ECDL, for example, the files would probably all have very different names. In this case searching file content, rather than filenames, would be more likely to locate all relevant files.

- Open the **Windows Explorer** window.
- Click into the **Search** box.
- Select the **Type** menu option and choose **Document**.
- Now select **Kind** and choose **.docx (the file extension for Microsoft Word 2010 documents)**.
- Type the text that will be searched for in the **Search box** (e.g. ECDL).
- Select any of the other search options if you wish to refine the search further.
- Click **x** to stop searching.

Practice Sequence

This sequence provides practice in using the Search box to find documents containing a particular word.

1	Open the Windows Explorer window and click in the **Search** box.	☐
2	Select the **Type** menu option and choose **Document**.	☐
3	Type a word or phrase to search for in the Search box.	☐
4	Click the **x** button at any time to end the search.	☐
5	Close the **Windows Explorer** window.	☐

5.12.3 Searching for Files by Date, Type and Size

Searching by Date Last Modified

When searching for documents, the date of last modification can be searched for using the **Date modified** option in the Search menu and then choosing a date option, as shown in the illustration on the right.

Searching by Date Created

When searching for documents, the date that the file was created can be searched for using **Date Created**.

- Open the **Windows Explorer** window.
- Click into the **Search** box.
- In the Search box, type in **Date Created:**
  A drop-down menu will appear with various date options from which to choose.

Searching by File Size

Files of a particular size can be searched for. For example, a user may want to find files that are **at least** or **at most** a particular size in **kilobytes (KB)**.

- Open the **Windows Explorer** window.
- Click into the **Search** box.
- In the Search box, click **Kind** and then **Document**.
- Type in **Size:**
- A drop-down menu will appear with various size options from which to choose.
- Make a selection from the available options.
  To search for a specific size, e.g. a file that is 25KB, enter this in the Search box after Size:
- To find files that are larger than a specified size, enter > and then the size (>25KB will find all files that are larger than 25KB). Use the < operator to find files smaller than a specified size.

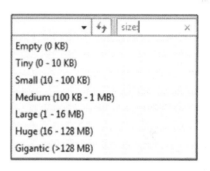

Searching by File Type

The file type to search for can be specified using the **Kind** and **Type** options.

- Click the cursor into the Search box and click **Kind**.
- Scroll through the available list and select the kind of file to search for (e.g. Document).
- To narrow the search further, click **Type**.
- Scroll through the available list and select the file type to search for.
- Select a file extension, e.g. .doc or .docx, or choose a specific program.

Choose a file extension associated with a particular file type or scroll down to choose a specific program

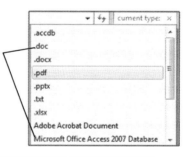

note The various methods discussed above can be combined to refine the search as much as possible, and ensure that it completes quickly.

5.12.5   Using Wildcards in Searches

A wildcard character is a keyboard character – such as an asterisk (*) or a question mark (?) – that can be used to represent one or more real characters in a name. It is a particularly useful tool when a filename cannot be remembered precisely.

Question Mark (?):

The question mark can be used as a substitute for a single character in a name. For example, if **hot** was entered, files such as Hot1 and Hots would be located, but not Hotel.

Asterisk (*):

You can use the asterisk as a substitute for zero or more characters. If you're looking for a file that you know starts with **hot** but you cannot remember the rest of the file name, type: **hot***. This will return all files (Word, Excel, Access, etc.) that begin with the letters **hot**.

If you know the file you are searching for is a Word file, adding the Word extension (.doc) will narrow the search to that file type, for example, entering **hot*.doc** will find all files that begin with **hot** and have the file extension **.doc**, such as **Hotel.doc** and **Hotspot.doc**.

To search for all files of a particular type, the * plus the **file extension** (.doc, .xls, .rtf) can be used. For example entering the search criteria ***.doc** will return all Word files, entering ***.xls** will return all Excel files, and so on.

5.12.6   Viewing Recently Used Files

The most recent documents used can be accessed by selecting the **File Menu** and then **Recent** and selecting a file from the **Recent Documents** list.

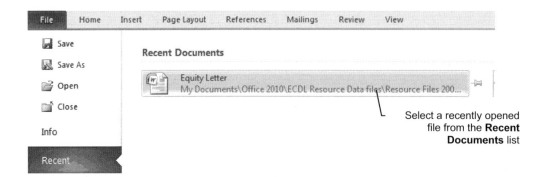

Select a recently opened file from the **Recent Documents** list

To change the number of documents listed in Recent Documents, do the following:

- Select File menu followed by **Options**.
- Select the **Advanced** button and scroll down to the **Display** section.
- Enter the number of recent documents that should display in the File menu.

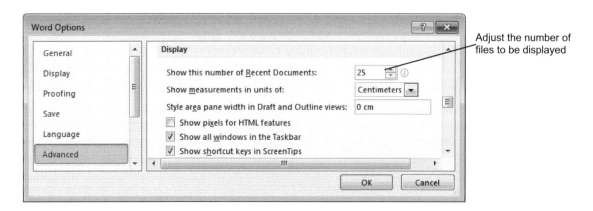

Adjust the number of files to be displayed

5.13   Compressing Files

5.13.1   What File Compression Means

It is possible to reduce the size of some files so that they take up less space on the computer or so they can be transferred across a network, including the internet, more efficiently. The process for doing this is referred to as compressing.

It is important to note that not all files can be compressed equally. Text files may be compressed by up to 90 per cent. Files produced by Microsoft Office 2010, such as .docx files, or graphic image file formats such .jpeg or .gif will not normally compress further except by very small amounts, because they are already compressed internally.

A large file attachment that is emailed to a recipient who does not have a fast internet connection can take a long time to download. If the file was compressed before it was sent, the number of bytes to be sent would be reduced and so the time taken to download would be less. The recipient would also need to be able to **extract** the original file from the compressed file using the relevant software.

A very simple example of one type of compression would be as follows.
A file contains the following text: **88888AAA2222222222**.

There are 18 characters present, taking up a certain amount of space. A program is used to **compress** the file, resulting in a **compressed** version containing the following: **8[5]A[3]2[10]**. That file obviously takes up less space – 13 characters. If that compressed file is processed by an **extraction** utility program, that utility knows for example that 2[10] should be expanded back to the original form, i.e. **2222222222**.

There are different methods that can be used to compress files, such as ZIP, RAR and LHA. The standard for compression in the Windows world is the **Zip** format. This format is a **standard**, in the same way as JPEG-format graphic files conform to that particular standard. As a result, there are many pieces of **utility** software such as ZipGenius and WinZip that can work with these .zip files. These utilities are **archivers** as well as **compressors**. In other words, they can be supplied with a list of files or folders and will compress each one individually before then rolling them all up into one compressed file. **Extracting** the contents of this file in another location or on another computer will then recreate all the files and folders archived within it. This makes the compression process even more useful for transferring files since it not only makes the overall size smaller, it can also bundle multiple files into one.

For example, this is a **zip file**.

**Finance
Department.zip**

Opening it with the WinRAR utility
shows that it contains compressed
files and folders.

Windows 7 has the built-in ability to work with Zip files. One advantage of this is that if Windows is allowed to handle zip files instead of a third-party utility, then those zip files work exactly like normal folders. Double-clicking one will open its contents in a normal window and the contents can be acted upon as with any window.

This manual will use this standard Windows 7 functionality in any examples.

5.13.2 Compressing a Single File

To compress a single file, do the following:

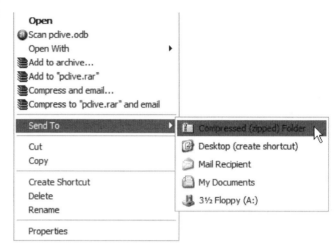

- Open a window and locate the item to be compressed.
- Right-click the item and click **Send To** on the pop-up menu that is displayed.
- Click the **Compressed (zipped) Folder** option on the sub-menu.

- If the file is large, the compression make take some time.
- If this is the case a progress window will be displayed.
- The compressed filename will be the name of the file but with a .zip extension.

5.13.3 Compressing a Single Folder

A single folder can be archived and compressed in exactly the same way as a single file. Note that this is a **recursive** procedure – in other words everything inside the folder and any sub-folders will be included.

5.13.4 Compressing Multiple Items

Multiple files and folders can be selected and compressed using the same method as single files and folders. See Section 5.13.2.

5.13.5 Viewing the Contents of Compressed Files

Double-clicking a compressed file will open it in a normal window, assuming a third-party utility, such as ZipGenius, has not been installed and is not associated with zip files.

5.13.6 Extracting Files and Folders

To use the files in a compressed file again, they must be extracted. Either everything in a compressed file or folder can be extracted or just selected items.

To extract the entire contents of the compressed file, do the following:
- Copy the compressed file to the location where the files are to be saved after extraction.
- Right-click the compressed file, select **Extract Here**.
  The contents will be extracted.
  If there are folders involved, the folder structure and contents will be recreated.

Extracting a single item from a compressed file, do the following:
- Double-click the compressed file to open it in a window.
- Locate the item in question.
- Copy or move the item out of the window in the normal way.
  The zip file will be updated automatically.

Section 6 ▶ Viruses

6.1   Viruses

A virus is a **malware** computer program written with the intention of secretly causing damage to the files on a computer, stealing information stored on a computer or network, or allowing the computer to be controlled remotely without the owner's knowledge.

The term **virus** refers to one particular type of **malware**, but is usually incorrectly used to describe a number of different types of program.

Antivirus, **Antispyware**, **Firewall** and similar software applications, are a vital requirement on any computer running Microsoft Windows. These functions are increasingly integrated into single products from individual software vendors.

6.2   Types of Malware

6.2.1   Viruses

Viruses attach themselves secretly to other programs. When the infected program is run by a user, the virus hides in the computer's memory. Then, when other programs are run by the user, the virus infects them, thus spreading. Some modern viruses also change themselves constantly to avoid detection. They are called viruses because their behaviour is exactly the same as a biological virus.

6.2.2   Trojans

A **Trojan horse**, or **Trojan**, works in the same way as the horse in the classical story. It is an application that, when run, appears to do something useful but will also secretly perform some sort of nefarious action. Modern Trojans usually create a **back door** allowing illegal remote access to the computer and its files if it is connected to the internet.

They rely on **social engineering** rather than virus-like infection to spread, for example, through e-mail attachments, seemingly coming from a familiar e-mail address.

6.2.3   Worms

Worms are similar to Trojans but spread across networks by exploiting security problems in operating systems and network equipment.

6.3   Using Antivirus Software

Antivirus software is used to detect and remove malware. The process of removing a problem file is called **disinfecting** or **cleaning**.

Because viruses modify legitimate files, it may or may not be possible to remove the infected part without damaging the original content. If it is not possible to remove the infection, and the file is a crucial part of the operating system, it could be necessary to reinstall the operating system.

Antivirus applications use **virus definition libraries** which are databases of all known malware programs to recognise problems. Modern antivirus applications usually have one or more of the following.

- A **resident scanner** which is loaded into memory when the computer starts up and monitors files as they are being read and written. If a file is infected, the user is notified and the file either deleted or moved to quarantine.
- **Quarantine**, a safe area where infected files are stored.
- An **on-demand** scanner. This will perform a **scan** of all infectable files on hard drives, and can usually be set to run automatically at a specified time.
- A **mail scanner**, which plugs into an e-mail client application and scans and disinfects e-mails as they arrive.

An example of a graphical antivirus application is Avast!. In the illustration below, the **on-demand scanner** section of Avast! is visible.

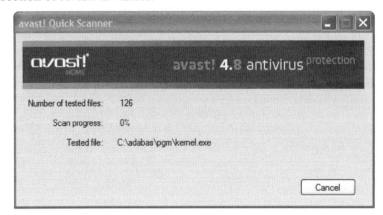

6.3.1   Keeping Antivirus Software Up to Date

New viruses, Trojans and other assorted undesirable programs are created every day, so it is important to keep the **database** that your antivirus software uses up to date. Antivirus software vendors maintain central databases which are updated regularly, and modern antivirus software will keep itself updated automatically via the internet.

Section 7 ▶ Print Management

2

7.1 Introduction

In the home, it is not uncommon to have a single printer attached to a single computer. However, in an office network multiple printers are usually available to each user's computer. For example, an office might have a black and white laser printer dedicated to large-volume printing and a colour printer restricted to lower volume documents, such as presentations, brochures, invitations or report covers.

Before any printer can be used, Windows 7 needs to know how to connect to it and communicate with it.

To enable the computer to operate a printer properly it is important that the appropriate **driver software** is installed. As part of the installation of the driver software, Windows 7 also needs to be informed as to how the printer is connected to the computer, for example through a USB port or across a network.

To view the printers that have been installed, do the following:
- From the **Start** menu, select **Devices and Printers.**

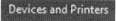

The **Devices and Printers** window opens. Icons for the printers that have been installed are displayed in the window.

Icons for the installed printers are displayed in the window

7.2 Changing the Default Printer

Many printers can be installed in Windows 7, but only one printer is designated as the default printer. The default printer is the one automatically used for printing unless another is specified in the print window when printing from applications, such as Microsoft Word.

The default printer is indicated with a tick in the **Devices and Printers** window.

A tick denotes the default printer

To change the default printer, do the following:
- From the **Start** menu, select **Devices and Printers**. The **Devices and Printers** window opens.
- Right-click the printer to be set as the default. A pop-up menu appears.
- Select **Set as default printer** from the menu and then, from the sub-menu, choose the printer name.

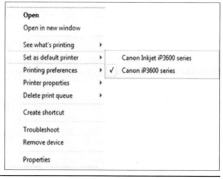

7.3   Installing a New Printer

When installing a new printer that is directly connected to the computer, the exact manufacturer and printer model must be known as it is very important that the correct driver is installed. If this doesn't happen, the printer may not work or may produce output of a lower quality than it is capable of.

Windows 7 comes with drivers for many common printers from many manufacturers, even older models. It is possible, though, that there isn't a driver available with Windows 7, especially for very new, very old or obscure devices. In this eventuality, the options are as follows.

- Check any CDs that came with the printer for a driver.
- Check the printer manufacturer's website for a driver.
- Read the documentation and see if any **generic** drivers will work.
- For example, almost all Hewlett Packard printers will print to some degree using a generic Hewlett Packard driver.
- Check the documentation and see what the printer **emulates**. Some printers can interpret data formulated for a different type of printer, if they are set to **emulate** or impersonate the other model.

The following sequence describes how to install a driver for a locally connected printer with a supplied Windows 7 driver. Installing a network printer is a somewhat more complex task and will probably be automated or performed by a network technician.

- Ensure the printer is connected to the computer. This could be via **parallel cable**, **USB**, **FireWire**, a **wireless connection**, etc.
- From the **Start** menu, open the **Devices and Printers** window.
- Click the **Add a Printer** command.

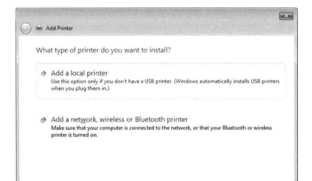

Add a printer

The **Add Printer** wizard will start.
- Click **Add a local printer**.

- On the next step, select the **Use an existing port** option button.
  Click **Next**.
- At the next step, select the correct printer (click **Windows Update** to see more models). If you have an installation CD, click **Have Disk**. Insert the CD and choose the correct folder/drive.
- Follow the instructions in the wizard, clicking **Next** as requested until the last step in the wizard.
- **Click Finish**.
  The new printer will be listed in the **Devices and Printer** window.

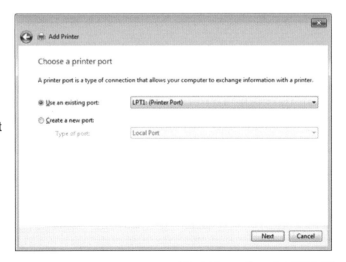

7.4   Printing from an Application

When printing from an application, a **print job** is created and placed in the **print queue** for the printer. The queue enables many print jobs to be lined up, printed and deleted in an orderly fashion, so that the one printing doesn't have to complete before another can be sent.

The **print driver** is then used to translate the job into a form that the particular printer will understand, and finally it is sent to the printer itself. Reports come back from the printer about the progress of the job until it is complete, at which point it is removed from the queue.

7.4.1   Printing From WordPad

Start **WordPad** from the **Accessories** menu (Open the Start menu, select All Programs, followed by Accessories and then Wordpad) and type in some text.

To print, do the following:
* Click the **Main Menu** button and select **Print** from the drop-down menu.
* The **Print** window opens, with the default printer already selected.
  A different printer can be selected from the list.
  The number of copies can be changed.
  The page(s), or range
  of pages to be printed
  can be changed.

Printer to be used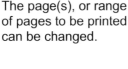

Pages to be printed

Number of copies to be printed

* When all the preferences have been set, click **Print**.

7.5   Viewing the Progress of Print Jobs

It is possible to check the progress of a print job when it has been sent to the printer. This can be useful in estimating the time remaining for a large print job to complete.

To check the progress of a print job, do the following:
* Print from an application as normal.
* Open the **Devices and Printers** window from the icon on the taskbar.
  Double-click the icon for the printer that the job was sent to (or select the printer and click the **See what's printing** command).

The printer queue contents will be shown in a window.
The current status can be seen,
along with the number of pages,
the size and other information.

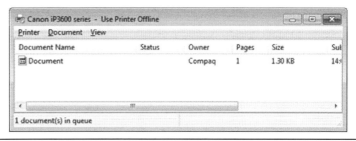

7.6   Managing Print Jobs

It is also possible to manage a print job after it has been submitted. This is useful, for example, when a job needs to be cancelled.

To manage a print job, do the following:
* Right-click the job in the printer queue window.

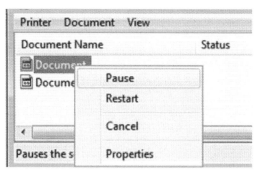

* Select one of the options available from the drop-down menu.
  * ▷ **Pause**: This pauses the selected job, which, for example, can be useful when more paper needs to be added to the printer. Select again to resume.
  * ▷ **Restart**: This will restart a job from scratch, for example, in case there was a paper jam.
  * ▷ **Cancel**: This will remove the job whether it is finished or not. Sometimes jobs get stuck in the queue and stop later jobs printing, this option can be useful in that situation to clear the traffic jam.

7.7   Capturing Images from the Screen

There may be occasions when it is useful to capture an image of the desktop or a particular window and then paste those contents into a file, such as a Microsoft Word document. For example, a user may want to send a colleague a sample of how to complete a particular screen within the Windows 7 environment. This can be achieved using the **keyboard print screen** facility.

To capture the contents of a screen or window, do the following:
* Press **Alt + Print Screen** to capture the contents of the active window only.
  Alternatively, press the **Print Screen** button to capture the entire screen as it appears on the monitor.

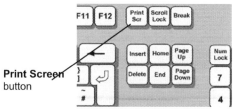

To paste the contents of the captured screen or window into a document, do the following:
* Ensure you are working in the document or file where the captured image should be inserted.
* From the **ribbon**, select the **Home** tab.
* Click **Paste**.

To edit the screen capture, an image editing application, such as **MS Paint**, can be used.

To access **Paint**, do the following:
* Click the **Start** menu and then click **All Programs**.
* Click the **Accessories** option and then choose **Paint**.
* From the **Edit** menu, click **Paste**.
* The screen shot will appear in the **Paint** window.

module **3**

Word
Processing

module 3
Word Processing

Module Goals for Module 3

Module 3 Word Processing requires the candidate to demonstrate an ability to use a word processing application to create everyday letters and documents.

The candidate shall be able to:

* Work with documents and save them in different file formats.
* Choose built-in options such as the Help function to enhance productivity.
* Create and edit small-sized word processing documents that will be ready to share and distribute.
* Apply different formats to documents to enhance them before distribution and recognise good practice in choosing the appropriate formatting options.
* Insert tables, images and drawn objects in documents.
* Prepare documents for mail merge operations.
* Adjust document page settings and check and correct spelling before finally printing documents.

3

Introduction

What is Word Processing?

Word processing refers to the creation of documents using word processing software, such as Microsoft Word. There are various types of document that can be created using a word processing application, such as the following:

* Letters
* Memos
* Agenda
* Minutes of meetings
* Posters
* Envelopes
* Mailshots (standard document merged with addresses)
* Newsletters
* Faxes
* Reports
* Flyers/adverts
* Business cards.

| **Company Name** |
| Address |
| Tel No |
| Date |
| Customer Name |
| Address |
| Dear _____ |
| Main body of the letter can be indented or fully blocked to the left. |
| Yours sincerely |
| Name |
| Status |

Word processing software enables the user to insert automatic fields into headers and/or footers (such as dates or filename fields) and formatting can be performed to enhance the overall appearance of the document using the application's formatting tools. Editing is performed easily within a word processing document, using overtyping, inserting and deleting text. The layout of the document can be managed by changing margins, orientation and paper size.

Section 1 ▶   Using the Application

An **application** refers to the software package that is used to perform a task. The application that will be used for this training manual is Microsoft Office Word 2010. This is a comprehensive word processing package, capable of creating a variety of documents.

1.1   Working with Documents

A word processed document may be a letter, memo, report, fax, agenda, poster or a variety of other documents. Word processed files may be saved in a variety of formats, such as template format or text or rich text format. Documents can also be saved in different versions so that they can be accessed in previous software versions.

In this section you will do the following:

- Open and close a word processing application.
- Open and close documents.
- Create a new document based on a default template or other available template, such as a memo, fax or agenda.
- Save a document to a location on a drive.
- Save a document under another name to a location on a drive.
- Save a document as another file type, such as text file, Rich Text Format, template, or a software specific file extension and version number.

1.1.1 Opening a Word Processing Application

Microsoft Word is a word processing package that comes as part of the Microsoft Office 2010 suite. This application will either be displayed as an icon on the desktop of your computer or found in the Start menu.

To open Word, do the following:

- Select the **Start** menu.
- Select **All Programs**.
- Select **Microsoft Office** and then select **Microsoft Word 2010**.

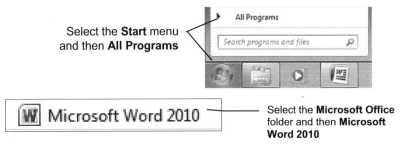

Select the **Start** menu and then **All Programs**

All Programs

Search programs and files

Select the **Microsoft Office** folder and then **Microsoft Word 2010**

Microsoft Word may be displayed as a shortcut icon on the desktop of your computer. If this is the case, double-click the shortcut to open it (or right-click the icon and select **Open** from the shortcut menu).

A **Microsoft Word 2010** window opens.

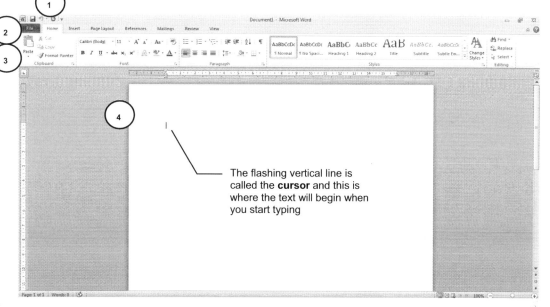

The screen layout will display the following:

① The Quick Access Toolbar.

② The **File** menu.

③ The ribbon.

④ A new, blank document.

1.1.2　Closing a Word Processing Application

To close Word, do the following:

- Select the **File** menu from the top left of the screen.

- Select **Exit**.
  The **Word** program closes.

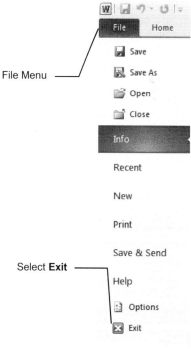

Alternatively, Select the **Close X** button in the top right corner of the Title Bar.

1.1.3　Opening a Document

To open an existing document, do the following:

- Open **Word**.

- Select the **File Menu**.

- Select **Open**.

File Menu

The **Open** window opens.

- Select the location of the file to be opened by selecting the drive and/or folder from the Navigation Pane (Folder pane). The selected drive and/or folder(s) will be displayed in the **Address Bar**.

- Select the file.

- Click **Open**.

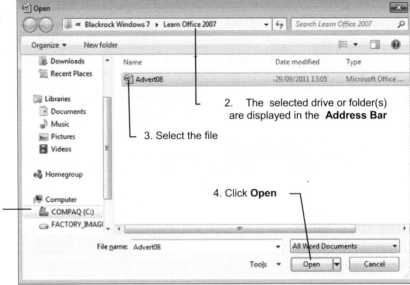

1. Folders and drives in which to save the file can be selected from the Navigation Pane

2. The selected drive or folder(s) are displayed in the **Address Bar**

3. Select the file

4. Click **Open**

note   To display the **Open** window using the keyboard, hold down the **CTRL** key on the keyboard and then click **O**.

Opening Recent Documents

Documents that have been opened recently can be accessed by selecting the **File Menu** and then selecting a file from the **Recent Documents** list.

Select a recently opened file from the **Recent Documents** list

Select a recently opened folder or drive from **Recent Places**

To change the number of documents listed in Recent Documents, do the following:

- Select the **File Menu** followed by **Options**.

- Select the **Advanced** command and scroll down to the **Display** section.

- Adjust the number of recent documents that should display in the File Menu.

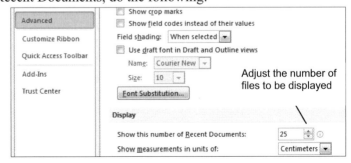

Adjust the number of files to be displayed

1.1.4 Closing a Document

To close a document, do the following:

- Select the **File Menu**.
- Select **Close**.

note

If changes have been made to the file, a message will appear asking if you want to save the file before closing.

- Click **Save** to save the file.
- Click **Don't Save** to close the file without saving.
- Click **Cancel** to cancel the message and return to the document.

1.1.5 Creating a New Document

A new document is based on the normal, default template. This template is created using default formatting and page layout settings. There are other templates available for use, such as memo, agenda, fax templates, among many other installed templates. A template is a document containing standard formatting/page layout that can be used repeatedly to create other documents.

To create a new document based on the normal, default template or on other available templates, do the following:

Default Template

- Select the **File Menu**.
- Select **New**.
  The **New Document** window opens.
- Select **Blank Document**.
- Select the **Create** button.

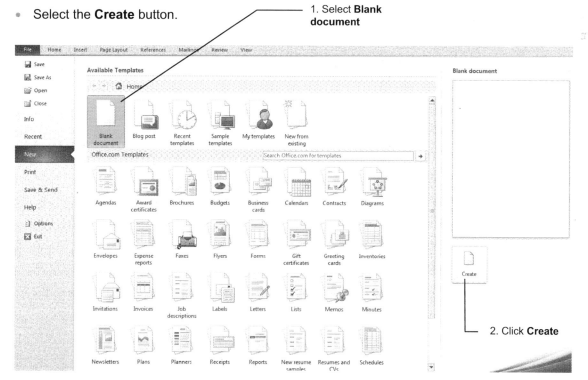

A new blank document appears.   **Title bar** displays the name of the document

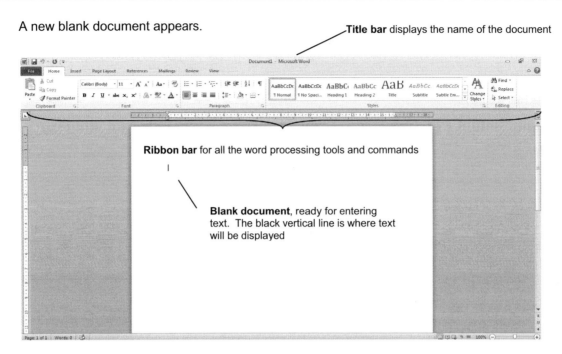

Ribbon bar for all the word processing tools and commands

Blank document, ready for entering
text. The black vertical line is where text
will be displayed

Sample Templates

- Select the **File Menu**.
- Select **New**.
  The **New Document** window opens
- From the **Templates** list, select **Sample Templates**.
- Select a template, e.g. letter, fax or report.
- Select the **Document** option button to create a document based on the template (select the
  Template option button to create a template).
- Click **Create**.
  A document will open, based on the chosen template.

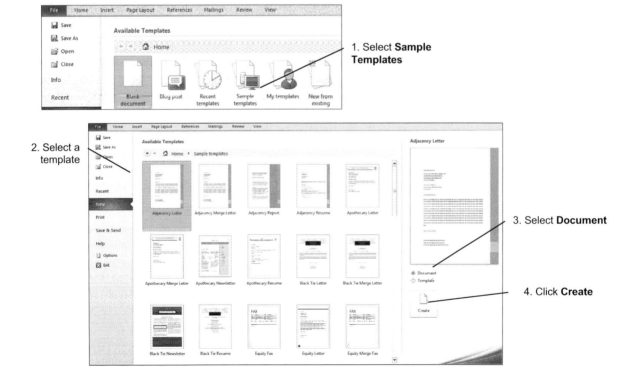

1. Select **Sample
Templates**

2. Select a
template

3. Select **Document**

4. Click **Create**

You can also select a template from **Microsoft Office Online**.

Click one of the template styles displayed in the Microsoft Office Online list of templates (Office.com), select a template and then select the **Download** button. You may have to validate your copy of Microsoft Office 2010 software before continuing the download.

1.1.6 Saving a Document to a Location on a Drive

To save a document for the first time, do the following:

- Select the **File Menu**.
- Select **Save**.

  The **Save As** window opens.

2. The Address bar will display the chosen drive and/or folder in which to save the file

1. Select the drive and/or folder(s) in which to save the file from the Navigation Pane

3. Enter a file name in the box. The default file name given to a document when saved for the first time is Doc1.

To hide the Navigation Pane click **Hide Folders**. To display the Navigation Pane, click **Browse Folders**

4. Click **Save**

- Select the correct drive and/or folder from the Navigation Pane (view the location in the **Address Bar**).
- Enter a name in the **File name** box.
- Click **Save**.

Click the **Save** button on the **Quick Access Toolbar** to save a file. The keyboard combination to save is **CTRL + S**.

1.1.7 Saving a Document Under Another Name

To save an existing document with a different name, do the following:

- Select the **File Menu**.
- Select the **Save As** menu option.

  The **Save As** window opens.

- Select the correct drive and/or folder from the Navigation Pane (view the current file location in the **Address Bar**).
- Enter a different name in the **File name** box.
- Select the **Word Document** menu option to save the document in the default file format
- Click **Save**.

note When saving a document for the first time, clicking **Save** or **Save As** from the File menu will result in the **Save As** window opening. Subsequent changes to a document can be saved by selecting the **Save** option from the **File Menu**. This will save the document with the same name and overwrite the original file.

1.1.8   Saving a Document as Another File Type

A document can be saved in a variety of different formats. This is useful if the document is being opened in another version of Word or a different word processing program. The different formats available are listed below.

Word Format	
• Document (.docx)	• Rich Text Format (*.rtf)
• Template (.dotx)	• Software specific file extension (e.g. *.doc or docx)
• Text (*.txt)	• Version number (Word 97-2003 Document)

To save a document in another file type, do the following:

Text Format (*.txt)

When a document is saved as a text file it loses all of its formatting features and graphics and saves in a format that enables it to be opened and viewed as text only.

- Click the **File Menu.**
- Select the **Save As** menu option.

The **Save As** windows opens.
- Select the correct drive/folder from the Navigation (Folder) Pane to display it in the **Address Bar**
- Enter a file name into the **File name** box.
- Click the **Save as type** arrow.
- Select **Plain Text (*.txt).**
- **Click Save**.

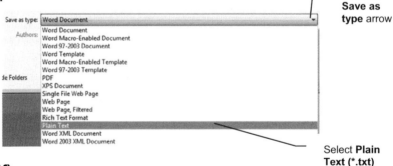

Click the **Save as type** arrow

Select **Plain Text (*.txt)**

Rich Text Format (*.rtf)

When a document is saved in Rich Text Format, it retains some of its formatting and enables the document to be opened in different applications, e.g. word processing or desktop publishing.
- Click the **File Menu**.
- Select the **Save As** menu option.
  The **Save As** windows opens.

- Select the correct drive/folder from the Navigation (Folder) Pane to display it in the **Address Bar**
- Enter a fil**e name** into the **File name** box and then click the **Save as type** arrow.
- Select **Rich Text Format (*.rtf)**.
- Click **Save**.

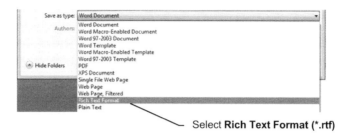

Select **Rich Text Format (*.rtf)**

Template

A template contains standard content that will appear on all pages in a document. A template can be used repeatedly to create other documents. This saves time and effort when creating a new document. Templates are saved with a **.dotx** file extension and, unless another location is specified, it saves in the following location:
C:\Users*username*\AppData\Roaming\Microsoft\Templates.

To save a document as a template, do the following:
- Click the **File Menu**.
- Select the **Save As** menu option.

The **Save As** windows opens.

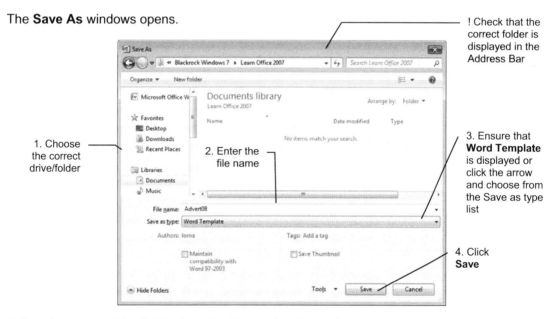

! Check that the correct folder is displayed in the Address Bar

1. Choose the correct drive/folder

2. Enter the file name

3. Ensure that **Word Template** is displayed or click the arrow and choose from the Save as type list

4. Click **Save**

- Select the correct drive/folder from the Navigation (Folder) Pane
- Enter a file name into the **File name** box and ensure that the **Save as type** box displays Word Template.
- Click **Save**.

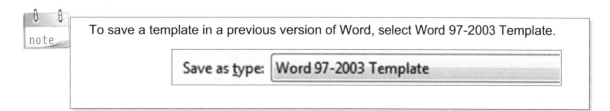

To save a template in a previous version of Word, select Word 97-2003 Template.

Save as type: Word 97-2003 Template

Version Number

Each version of Word has a different version number. If the document needs to be opened and viewed in a previous version of Word it can be saved with a different version number.
To check the version number of the software on your computer, do the following:

- Click the **File Menu**.
- Select **Help**.
- Read the **About Microsoft Word** section.
- This section provides information on the software version currently installed on your computer.

Information about currently installed software will be provided in this window

- Check the version number – it should be Microsoft Office Word **2010**.
- Click the **File** menu to close the menu.

To save the document with a different version number, do the following:

- Click the **File Menu**.
- Select the **Save As** menu command.
  The **Save As** windows opens.
- Select the correct drive/folder from the Navigation (Folder) Pane.
- Enter a file name into the **File name** box.
- Click the **Save as type** arrow.
  Note how the version is selected in the **Save As type** box (the default is Word Document).
  select the arrow and choose a version number.
- Click **Save**.

Word 97-2003 is an earlier version of the software

1.1.9 Switching between Open Documents

It is possible to have two or more documents open on your desktop. It is also possible to see two documents displayed together. Because they then both share the desktop, a much smaller part of each document is displayed. When you switch between open documents, you normally see them displayed full size on the desktop.

To switch between open documents, do the following:

- Select the **View** tab.
- In the **Windows** group, select the **Switch Windows** button.
  A tick will display beside the file name of the currently active document.
- Click another file name in the menu to make that the active document.

A tick beside the file name indicates that it is the active document, currently displayed on screen

You can also switch between open documents or other programs by using the taskbar.

● Open more than one document.

The documents (and any open windows) will be displayed as tabs on the taskbar at the bottom of the screen   which, when selected, will display a thumbnail of the document or window (in Windows 7 Basic only the file name will be displayed).

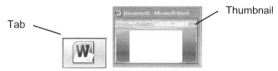

Tab ———

Thumbnail

● Click a thumbnail to open a document.

1.2   Enhancing Productivity

Productivity can be increased by setting user preferences, such as adding a user name and/or creating a default folder from which to open and in which to save all documents. Using the Help facility can also aid productivity by providing tips and advice on how to use the program effectively.

In this section you will do the following:

● Set basic options/preferences in the application: user name, default folder to open from, default folder to save documents to.

● Use available Help functions.

● Use magnification/zoom tools.

● Restore and minimise the ribbon.

1.2.1   Setting User Preferences

User preferences refer to the user name and the default location of opened and saved files. These can be changed as necessary so that the user name is different or so that files can be opened or saved in another location.

To set user preferences, do the following:

User Name

● Click the **File Menu**.

● Select **Options**.

The Word Options window opens.

● Select the **General** tab.

● In the **Personalize your copy of Microsoft Office** position the cursor in the User name box and delete the current user name.

● Enter the new user name.

● Click **OK**.

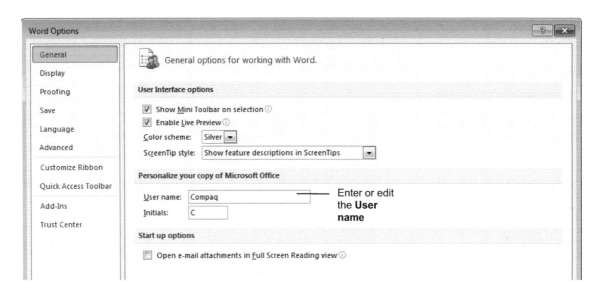

Default File Location to Open Files From and Save Files To

- Select the **File Menu**.
- Select **Options**.
  The **Word Options** window opens.
- Select the **Save** tab.
- In the **Default File Location** box, enter the required file location of opened and saved files (use the Browse... button to find the location if necessary).
- Click **OK**.

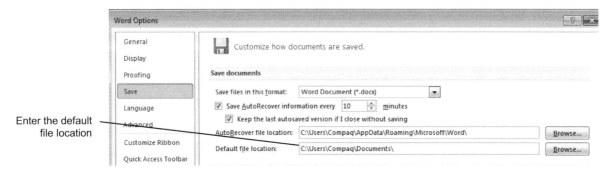

1.2.2 Using the Help Function

The Help function is available to give advice and help on aspects of the application you are using. This is useful when you are trying to perform an action and don't know how to proceed. Just ask the Help function a specific question and then select a relevant topic for the answer.

To use the Help function, do the following:
- Select the **Help** button or press the **F1** key.
  The **Word Help** window opens.
- Browse the help and how-to options
- Select a link to a relevant topic.
  A further set of links will appear that correspond with the selected topic.
- Select a relevant link to refine your search.
- Read the information on the chosen topic.
- Use the **Back** button to go back a step or the **Home** button to return to the first window of Word Help.

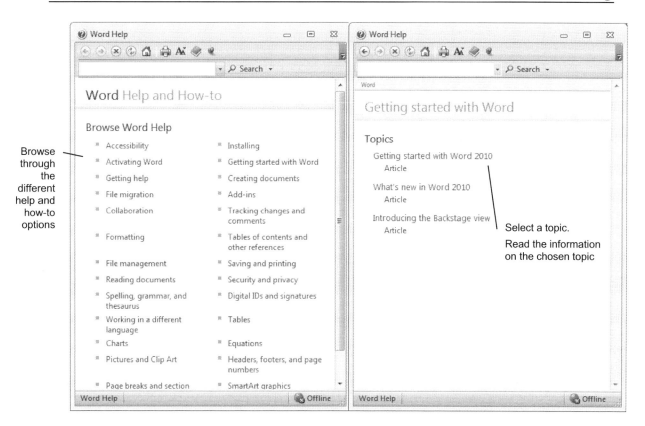

Browse through the different help and how-to options

Select a topic.

Read the information on the chosen topic

- Click **Print** to print a copy of the topic information.

You can also enter specific search criteria into the **Search** box to locate information on specific topics. To enter search criteria, do the following:

- Enter a question in the **Search** box.
- Click **Search**.

  A list of topic links relating to the search criteria will appear.

- Click a link to view the topic information.

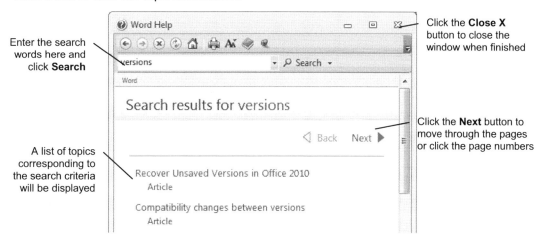

Enter the search words here and click **Search**

A list of topics corresponding to the search criteria will be displayed

Click the **Close X** button to close the window when finished

Click the **Next** button to move through the pages or click the page numbers

1.2.3 Using the Magnification (Zoom) Tools

The magnification tools are used to zoom in and out in a document.

To use the magification tools, do the following:

- Select the **View** tab.
- From the **Zoom** group, select the following:

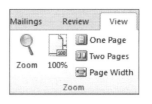

▶   **Zoom** to open the **Zoom** window.

  ▶   **100%** to zoom the window to full size.

  ▶   **One Page** to see one page at a time (in reduced view).

  ▶   **Two Pages** to see two pages at a time (side by side).

  ▶   **Page Width** so that the width of the page matches the width of the window.

●   Click the **Zoom** button.

  The **Zoom** window opens.

●   Select an option button to change the zoom percentage or change the amount or width of pages viewed or use the scroll wheels to increase or decrease the percentage in the **Percent** box.

●   Click **OK**.

Select a **Zoom to** option button or select **Custom** and enter a percentage by which to increase or decrease the magnification

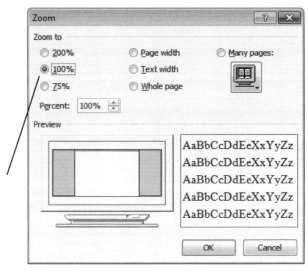

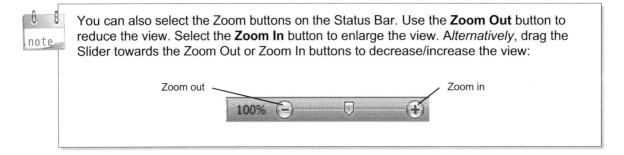

You can also select the Zoom buttons on the Status Bar. Use the **Zoom Out** button to reduce the view. Select the **Zoom In** button to enlarge the view. *Alternatively*, drag the Slider towards the Zoom Out or Zoom In buttons to decrease/increase the view:

Zoom out   Zoom in

1.2.4 Minimising and Restoring the Ribbon

The ribbon can be minimised and then restored if required.

To minimise and restore the ribbon, do the following;

Minimising the Ribbon

●   Right-click the ribbon bar.

●   Select **Minimize the Ribbon**.
   The ribbon is hidden.

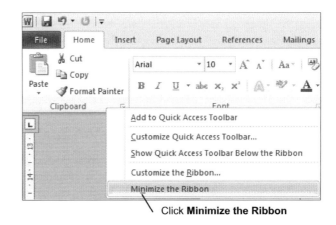

Click **Minimize the Ribbon**

Restoring the Ribbon

●   Right-click the bar containing the tabs.

- Click **Minimize the Ribbon** (note how a tick is displayed beside the menu command to indicate that it is active).

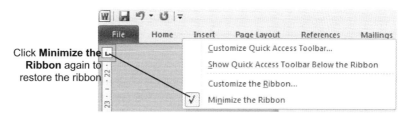

Click **Minimize the Ribbon** again to restore the ribbon

Practice Sequence

1	Open **Word** and create a new document.	☐
2	Save this document as **sale** in the default document format in a default folder location that you specify.	☐
3	Save another copy of the document in **Text** format with the filename **saleTXT**.	☐
4	Reopen **sale** and practise switching between the two documents.	☐
5	Zoom the **sale** document to **80%** and save.	☐
6	Close both documents.	☐
7	Use the **Help** function to find information on saving a document as a template.	☐
8	Open the **sale** document and save in template format (ensure that it saves in the correct drive/folder).	☐
9	Close the template file.	☐
10	Open a new document and save with the name **version** in Word 97-2003 format.	☐
11	Close all documents and exit Word.	☐

Section 2 ▶   Document Creation

Text is entered into a new document by using the keyboard (or voice recognition software if required). The text appears in the cursor position as it is entered. Words should be separated by one space; performed by pressing the space bar after each word is entered onto the page. The text will display along a line (the line length depends on the margins and indentation) and then, when it reaches the end of that line, it will wrap around to the next line. The **Enter** key (or carriage return) is used to create a new paragraph. One or two spaces should be entered after a full stop, and one space after a comma, semi-colon or other punctuation mark. When the text fills the page, a new page is automatically created for text to continue. A document may contain multiple pages. Microsoft Word uses WYSIWYG (what you see is what you get), so what you see on the screen is how it will appear on the printed output when viewed in Print Layout view.

2.1   Entering Text

Text refers to characters, words or symbols entered into a document using a keyboard. The page can be viewed in different modes, such as draft for entering text or print layout to view how the page will appear when printed.

In the next section, you will learn about the following:

- Switch between page view modes.
- Enter text into a document.
- Insert symbols or special characters like: ©, ®, ™.

2.1.1 Page Views

Page view refers to the way that the page is viewed on screen. The default page view is **Print Layout**. The page view buttons are displayed on the status bar and contain the following commands.

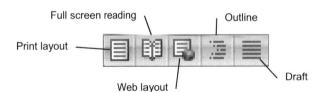

Print Layout	This enables you to see the page as it will look when it is printed.
Full Screen Reading	This enables you to see more than one page at a time (side by side) and increase text size for easier reading if required.
Web Layout	This enables you to see how the page will look when displayed as a web page.
Outline	This enables you to expand or collapse document titles and make changes to the document easily. This view also enables you to create sub-documents.
Draft	This was referred to as Normal View in previous versions of Word and enables you to see a draft of the document, along with page breaks. This view does not display images or page margins.

To change the page view, do the following:

- Select a page view command from the buttons displayed on the status bar.

  Alternatively, select the **View** tab and select a page view command from the **Document Views** group.

2.1.2 Entering Text in a Document

Text is entered at the cursor position. The cursor is the black vertical flashing line on the page. The mouse icon is called the **insertion point**. The **click and type** option enables the user to click the insertion point in the left, centre or right of the page and start typing from that position.

To see whether the click and type option is selected, do the following:

- Click the **File Menu.**
- Select **Options**.
- Select the **Advanced** tab.
- In the **Editing** section of the window, select the **Enable click and type** checkbox (this enters a tick in the box).
- Click **OK**.

  Practise moving the insertion point to the middle of the page (double click to position the insertion point in the required location), the right of the page and the left of the page

To enter text, do the following:

- Use the keyboard to enter text on the page:
- Hold down the **Shift** key on the keyboard and then press a letter for an initial capital at the beginning of a sentence. Release the **Shift** key when the letter has been entered and then continue typing the remainder of the word/sentence.
- Press the **Caps Lock** key to type in upper case (this is a *toggle* key which turns on/off each time it is pressed – look for the green light at the top of the keyboard to indicate whether the Caps Lock key is active).
- Press the full stop key to end a sentence.
- Press the **Space bar** to create a space between words as you type (one space between words and one or two after a full stop).
- Type until the text to 'wraps around' to the next line.
- Press the **Enter** key to create a new paragraph.
- To use keyboard characters which are displayed **above** other characters on keys, hold down the **Shift** key and press the key.
- Enter numbers by pressing the number keys on the top row of the keyboard or use the number pad (you may need to press the **Num Lock** key to make the number pad active).

2.1.3 Inserting Symbols and Special Characters

Symbols refer to the accented characters (e.g. é, ö, à, î) that are used in special characters. Special characters are the symbols (e.g. copyright or trademark symbols) or other characters (e.g. a telephone symbol before a telephone number).

To insert symbols and special characters, do the following.

Symbols:

- From the **Insert** tab and the **Symbols** group, select the **Symbol** arrow.
- Choose a symbol from the menu or select **More Symbols**.

  The **Symbols** window opens with the **Symbol** tab the active tab.

More symbols

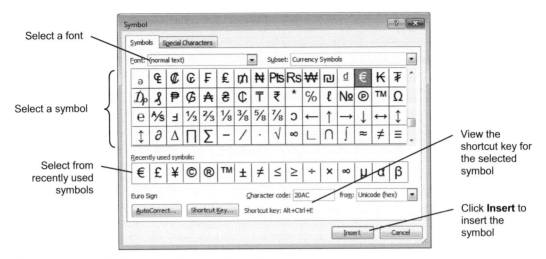

- Scroll through the list of symbols and select a symbol.
- Select **Insert**.
  Recently used symbols will display in the **Recently used symbols** section of the window.
  The shortcut key for the selected symbol will be displayed (e.g. **CTRL + '** and **e** for the **é** symbol).
- Click the **Font** arrow to see different fonts/symbols (**Wingdings** or **Webdings** are good fonts to use for pictorial symbols).
- Click **Close**.

Pictorial symbols can be selected from the **Wingdings** and **Webdings** font list. See examples below.

Wingdings	Webdings

Special Characters:

- From the **Insert** tab and the **Symbols** group, select the **Symbol** arrow.
- Select **More Symbols**.
  The **Symbol** window opens.
- Select the **Special Characters** tab.
- Select a special character, such as registered ®, copyright ©, trade mark™.
- Click **Insert**.
- Click **Close**.

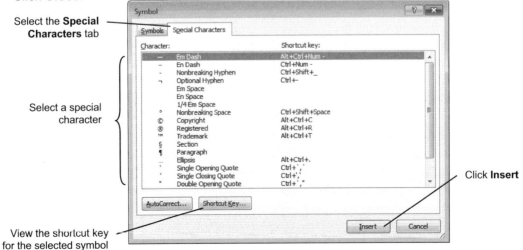

2.1.3 Moving Text Around

In order to edit text, you need to be able to move the insertion point within text and position the cursor wherever you need to insert or delete characters/words.

To move the cursor around text, do the following:

Mouse

- Move the mouse and observe the Insertion Point (I).
  Position the insertion point in the required position and click the left mouse button.
- The cursor will appear in the selected position.

Keyboard

- Use the directional arrow keys on the keyboard to move around text.

→	Moves the cursor one character to the right or **CTRL + →** moves the cursor a *word* at a time.
←	Moves the cursor one character to the left or **CTRL + ←** moves the cursor a *word* at a time.
↑	Moves the cursor one line above or **CTRL + ↑** moves the cursor to the beginning of the paragraph before.
↓	Moves the cursor one line below or **CTRL + ↓** moves the cursor to the beginning of the next paragraph.
HOME/ END	Select **HOME** to move to the beginning of a line (use **CTRL + Home** to move to top of document). Select **END** to move to the end of a line (use **CTRL + End** to move to end of document).

3

Practice Sequence

1	Open **Word** and then open the **sale** document.	☐
2	Switch to **Draft** view.	☐
3	Enter the text as shown below, inserting symbols and special characters where required.	☐
4	Switch to **Print Layout** view.	☐
5	Save and close the **sale** document.	☐

JUMBLE SALE

To be held at the Village Hall on Saturday, 16 August 2008, starting 12 noon

STALLS
Clothes · Toys · Bric a brac · Household goods · Shoes · Books

If you have any of the above items to donate, they will be gratefully received.
If you wish to volunteer to man one of the stalls, your help will be greatly appreciated.
Please contact Mary on: ☎ 01234 567890

All profits to go to the Community Hall Refurbishment Fund

ⓘ Please note that we cannot use the CHRF logo on our flyers because the trade mark ™ is owned by another company. Please also note that when downloading images and text from the internet for advertising literature, that the original author owns the copyright ©.

2.2   Selecting and Editing Text

In this section, you will learn about the following:

- Displaying and hiding non-printing formatting marks, such as spaces, paragraph marks, manual line break marks and tab characters.

- Selecting a character, word, line, sentence, paragraph or the entire body text.

- Editing content by entering and removing characters and words within existing text, by overtyping to replace existing text.

- Using a simple search command for a specific word or phrase.

- Using a simple replace command for a specific word or phrase.

- Copying and moving text within a document and between open documents.

- Deleting text.

- Using the undo and redo commands.

2.2.1   Non-Printing Formatting Marks

Non-printing formatting marks refer to marks such as spaces, paragraph marks, manual line breaks and tab characters. These marks do not display by default on screen, but they can be displayed if required. Displaying non-printing formatting marks can be useful to see where paragraphs have been made or tabs inserted.

To display and hide non-printing formatting marks, do the following:

- In the **Home** tab and **Paragraph** group, select the **Show/Hide** command (the keyboard shortcut is **CTRL + ***).

  The non-printing formatting marks will be displayed. This command is a *toggle* button which means that it is turned on/off each time it is selected.

- See the examples below of formatting marks within a document.

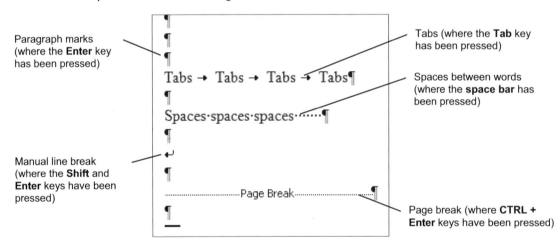

- A **paragraph** mark is displayed when the Enter key has been pressed to create a new paragraph.

- A **space** is displayed when the space bar is used.

- A **manual line break** is used to create a new line, but not a new paragraph (this is when you may want another line that does not perform like a paragraph by starting a new line with an initial capital letter or with a number or bullet before the text). The keyboard shortcut is Shift + Enter.

- A **tab** mark is displayed when the Tab key is pressed (tabs are used to create parallel columns of text).

- A **page break** mark is displayed when a new page is created. The keyboard shortcut is **CTRL + Enter**.

2.2.2 Selecting

Before text can be formatted or edited, it must first be selected. This can be done by using the mouse or by using the keyboard.

To select text, do the following:

Mouse
- Position the insertion point in front of the text to be selected.
- Hold down the left mouse button and drag over the text.
- Release the mouse button when you have selected all the required text.

To remove the selection, do the following:
- Click away from the selected area.

Other selection methods using the mouse are shown below

A word	Position insertion point before, after or within word to be selected. Double-click the left mouse button.
A line	Move the cursor (which becomes an arrow) into the left margin so that the arrow tip is pointing at the line to be selected. Click the left mouse button.
A sentence	Move the cursor to the left of the first character in the sentence. Left-click the mouse button. Holding down the mouse button, drag to the right until the sentence is highlighted. *Alternatively*, place the cursor within the sentence, hold down the CTRL key and left-click the mouse button.
A paragraph	Move the cursor (arrow) into the left margin so that the arrow tip is pointing at the paragraph to be selected. Double-click the left mouse button.
Whole document	Move the cursor (arrow) into the left margin so that the arrow tip is pointing at the paragraphs to be selected. Treble-click the left mouse button.

Keyboard
- Position the insertion point in front of the character to be selected. Hold down the **Shift** key + press a directional arrow key to select the character. Hold down **CTRL, Shift** + directional arrow key to select a *word* at a time.
- To select the remainder of text in a document from a specific point in the document, position the cursor in front of the text to be selected, hold down the **Shift** + **CTRL** keys and press **End**.
- To select the whole document, press **CTRL + A**.
- To remove the selection, use a directional arrow key to move away from the selected area.

Ribbon Bar
- To select all of the text in the document, click the **Select** arrow from the **Home** tab/**Editing** group and then choose **Select All**.

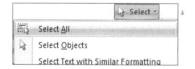

2.2.3 Editing Text

Characters and words can inserted to or deleted from text or text can be overtyped.

To edit text, do the following:

Inserting Text
- Position the cursor where the text should appear (position the insertion point in the correct place and then click to position the cursor).
- Enter text (note how existing text moves to accommodate the newly inserted text).
- Ensure that there is one space between words and a full stop at the end of a sentence. There may be one or two spaces after a full stop.

Overtyping

- Press the **Insert** key on the keyboard.
- Position the cursor where the text should start and start typing.
  Note how existing text is overwritten with the newly inserted text.
- To turn Overtype off, press the Insert key again.

Deleting Text

- Position the insertion point in the correct place within the text and then click to position the cursor.
- Press the **Delete** key on the keyboard to delete characters to the right of the cursor position or press **Backspace** to delete characters to the left of the cursor position.
- Hold down the **CTRL** key and press **Delete/Backspace** to delete whole *words* instead of characters.
- To delete blocks of text, first select the text and then press the **Delete** key.

2.2.4 Searching Text

Finding information in a document can be time consuming if it is a lengthy document containing lots of data. Using the Search command facilitates the process as it will find specific information throughout the document in one action.

To search for information, do the following:
- On the **Home** tab, click the **Find** arrow in the **Editing** group (or press **CTRL + F** to open the **Find** window). Select **Advanced Find**.
  The **Find** window opens.
- Enter the search word or phrase into the **Find what:** box.

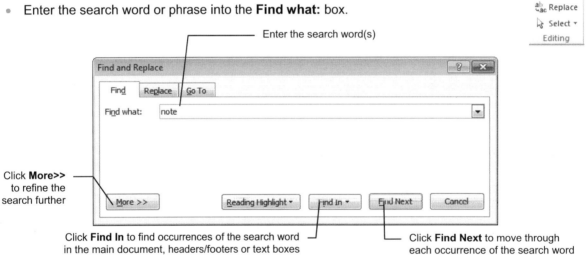

Enter the search word(s)

Click **More>>** to refine the search further

Click **Find In** to find occurrences of the search word in the main document, headers/footers or text boxes

Click **Find Next** to move through each occurrence of the search word

- Select the **More>>** button to refine the search further.
- In this section of the **Find** window, you can do the following:
  - Match case (to ensure that the search word matches the case, e.g. upper/lower case, typed in the Find what box).
  - Find whole words only (to ensure that only whole words are found, e.g. the word **note** is found but not bank**note**, **note**worthy, end**note**, foot**note**, etc.).
  - Use wildcards (to stand in place of characters if you don't know the full word, e.g. **n??e** will find do**nate**, volu**ntee**r and **note**).
  - Sounds like (to find words that sound similar (e.g. **nite** will find **note, night** and **neat**).
  - Find all word forms.
- Press **Find Next** to find each occurrence of the search word(s) in the document.

- When the **Find** facility has finished searching for all occurrences of the search word, a confirmation window opens.
- Click **OK**.
- Click **Cancel** to close the **Find** window.

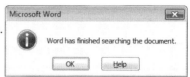

2.2.5 Replacing Text

It can be time consuming to replace each occurrence of an existing word or phrase throughout a document with another word/phrase. If the word to be replaced appears many times, it is easier to use the Replace command to change the existing word throughout the document.

To replace words, do the following:

- On the **Home** tab, click the **Replace** command from the **Editing** group (or press **CTRL + H** to open the **Replace** window).

  The **Replace** window opens.
- Enter the search word or phrase into the **Find what** box.
- Enter the replacement word in the **Replace with** box.

Enter the search word(s) in the **Find what** box

Enter the replacement word(s) in the **Replace with** box

Click **More>>** to refine the search further.

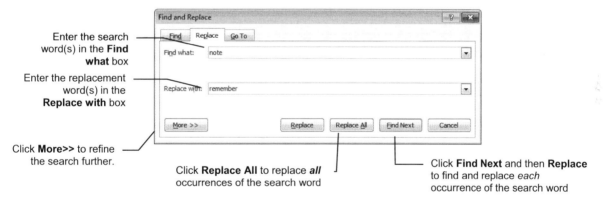

Click **Replace All** to replace *all* occurrences of the search word

Click **Find Next** and then **Replace** to find and replace *each* occurrence of the search word

- Select the **More>>** button to refine the search further.
- In this section of the **Find & Replace** window, you can do the following:
  - ▶ Match case (to ensure that the search word matches the case, e.g. upper/lower case, typed in the **Find what:** box).
  - ▶ Find whole words only (to ensure that only whole words are found, e.g. the word note is found but not bank***note***, ***note***worthy, end***note***, foot***note***, etc.).
  - ▶ Use wildcards (to stand in place of characters if you don't know the full word, e.g. **n??e** will find do***nate***, volu***nte***er and ***note***).
  - ▶ Sounds like (to find words that sound similar (e.g. **nite** will find **note, night** and **neat**).
  - ▶ Find all word forms.
- Press **Find Next** to find the first occurrence of the search word(s) and then press **Replace** or select **Replace All** to replace all occurrences of the search word(s) with the replacement word

Refine the search by matching the case or finding whole words only, etc.

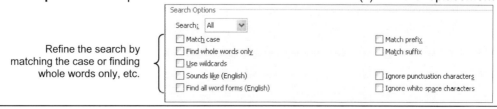

- When **Replace All** is selected, a confirmation window opens informing you of the number of replacements that have been made.
- Click **OK**.
- Click **Cancel** to close the **Replace** window.

Microsoft Word

ⓘ Word has completed its search of the document and has made 2 replacements.

OK   Help

2.2.6 Copying and Moving Text
Text can be moved within the same document or between open documents.

To copy and move text, do the following:

Within a Document
- To copy text within the same document, select the text and then, from the **Home** tab, select the **Copy** button from the **Clipboard** group (or press **CTRL + C**).
- Select a destination position within the document and then click the **Paste** button (or press **CTRL + V**).
- The duplicated text will appear in the new position.
- To *move* text, follow the procedure above but click the **Cut** button (scissors) from the **Clipboard** group at Step 1 (or press **CTRL + X**).

Paste   ✂ Cut
         ▤ Copy
         ✍ Format Painter
         Clipboard

Between Documents
- Open the required document files. Both files will be displayed as tabs on the taskbar at the bottom of the screen.
- Ensure that the document containing the text to be copied, is the active document.
- To copy text, select the text and then, from the **Home** tab, select the **Copy** button from the **Clipboard** group (or press **CTRL + C**).
- Click the other document on the taskbar or select the **View** tab and **Switch Windows**.
- Choose the other document from the list and ensure that the correct document is displayed.
- Position the mouse where you want the copied text to be placed.
- From the **Home** tab, in the **Clipboard** group, click the **Paste** button (or press **CTRL + V**).
- The text will be duplicated in the selected position within the document.
- To *move* text to another document, repeat the above procedure but click the **Cut** button at Step 3 (or press **CTRL + X**).

note

You can also copy, cut and paste text within and between documents by right clicking and selecting the **Cut**, **Copy**, **Paste** commands from the shortcut menu or by using the **Drag and Drop** method. The latter method uses the mouse to copy or move text to a different destination within the *same* document.

To move text, select the text to be moved, hold down the mouse button and drag to the new destination (or hold down the **CTRL** key whilst dragging to **copy** the text to the new destination).

2.2.8 Undoing and Redoing
If a mistake is made when entering, editing or deleting text, it can be corrected by using the undo button. To redo the action, the redo button is used.

To use undo and redo, do the following:
- To undo an action, click the **Undo** button from the **Quick Access Toolbar**. *Alternatively*, press **CTRL + Z** to undo.

Redo

Undo —

Arrow

To redo an action, click the **Redo** button from the **Quick Access Toolbar**. *Alternatively*, press **CTRL** + **Y** to redo.

- To see a list of actions, click the arrow between the buttons and select an action from the list. Any actions that exist before the selected action will also be undone.

The previous four actions (highlighted) will be undone from this list

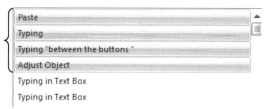

note

The Redo button displays as a repeat button, until the Undo button is utilised. When the Undo button is used, the Redo button becomes active.

Select the Undo arrow to see a list of actions

The Redo button displays as the **Repeat** button until the Undo command is used

Practice Sequence

1	Open Word and the document called **sale**.
2	Display the non-printing marks in the document (you should see where spaces and paragraphs have been created).
3	Hide the non-printing marks.
4	Select the word **Jumble.**
5	Remove the selection and select the final paragraph.
6	Remove the selection.
7	Select the whole document.
8	Remove the selection.
9	Edit the paragraph starting *If you wish to volunteer to man one of the stalls* so that it reads *If you wish to volunteer <u>to help on</u> one of the stalls*
10	Change the name **Mary** to **Deirdre**.
11	Using the search and replace facility, replace the word **note** with the word **remember** (there should be two replacements).
12	Move the text starting *If you have any of the above items to donate...* so that it displays after the telephone number (ensure there is a clear line space between the paragraphs).
13	Copy the text starting **Stalls** and ending **Books** into a new document.
14	Save this document as **stalls** and close.
15	Save and close the **sale** document.

Section 3 ▶ Formatting

Formatting refers to enhancing the appearance of text by changing fonts, sizes, colours and styles. Text can be further enhanced by changing the case to upper, lower or sentence case and by using hyphenation throughout the document to hyphenate long words at the end of a line of text. To ensure that a document is presented to a professional standard, text formatting should be consistent throughout a document and appropriate for the subject and content. For example, a legal document should appear professional, formal and consistent, without using colour, elaborate fonts or large font sizes throughout the document, whereas a poster should use all of these formatting features to grab attention.

3.1 Text

In this section you will learn about the following:

- Changing text formatting: font sizes, font types.
- Applying text formatting: bold, italic, underline.
- Applying text formatting: subscript, superscript.
- Applying different colours to text.
- Applying case changes to text.
- Applying automatic hyphenation.

3.1.1 Text Formatting

Text can be formatted with a variety of different fonts, both serif and sans serif. Serifs are the 'tails' on characters; sans serif fonts don't have these 'tails'. See the examples below.

TIMES NEW ROMAN
COURIER NEW
CAMBRIA

These are serif fonts. Note the serifs ('tails') on the characters, such as on the **T** in Times.

ARIAL
MYRIAD PRO
ST HUNTINGTON

These are sans serif fonts. Note there are no serifs ('tails') on the characters. ST Huntington is an informal font, ideal for posters but not formal business documentation.

Font size can also be increased or decreased to enhance text. It is important to ensure that font size is consistent throughout the document (e.g. all headings share the same font size, as do the sub-headings and body text). Headings should be displayed in a larger font size than sub-headings, which should in turn be a larger font size than the main body text. See some examples below:

This is in font size 8.

This is in font size 12.

This is in font size 18.

To change the font type, size, style and colour of cell contents, do the following:

Font Types
- Select the text to be formatted.
- From the **Home** tab and **Font** group, select the **Font** arrow.
- Select a font from the drop-down list.

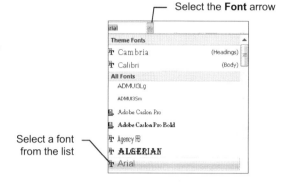

Select the **Font** arrow

Select a font from the list

Font Sizes
- Select the text to be formatted.
- From the **Home** tab and **Font** group, select the **Font Size** arrow.
- Select a size from the drop-down list.

  Alternatively, select the **Grow Font** or **Shrink Font** buttons to increase or decrease the font size (the font will grow/shrink by one point size each time the button is pressed).

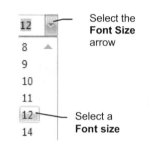

Select the **Font Size** arrow

Select a **Font size**

Grow font   Shrink font

Font Colours
- Select the text to be formatted.
- From the **Home** tab and **Font** group, select the **Font Color** arrow.
- Select a colour from the drop-down list or select **More Colors** to see the **Colors** window for further colour options.
- Select a colour from the palette.
- Click **OK**.

Select the **Font Color** arrow

Select a font colour

Select **More Colors** to see the **Colors** window

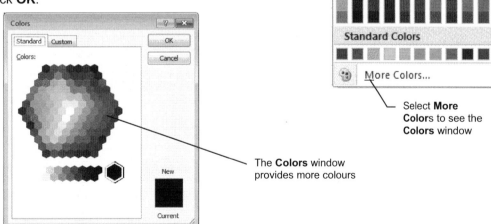

The **Colors** window provides more colours

Font Styles
- A font style refers mainly to **bold**, *italic* and <u>underline</u>.
- Select the text to be formatted.
- From the **Home** tab and **Font** group, select the required font style.

Bold

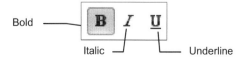

Italic

Underline

3.1.2 Subscript and Superscript

Superscript refers to text that appears above the normal line of text, as in ^{TM}. A subscript refers to text that displays below the normal line of text, such as H_2O.

To apply superscript and subscript, do the following:

Superscript

- Select the text to be made superscript.
- From the **Home** tab and the **Font** group, select the **Superscript** command.
  Alternatively, select the command first and then type in the superscript text.

> Superscript can also be applied by pressing the keyboard combination of **CTRL + Shift + =**.
> Superscript can be removed by selecting the text and pressing **CTRL + space bar**.

Subscript

- Select the text to be made subscript.
- From the **Home** tab and the **Font** group, select the **Subscript** command.
  Alternatively, select the command first and then type in the subscript text.

> Subscript can also be applied by pressing the keyboard combination of **CTRL + =**.
> Subscript can be removed by selecting the text and pressing **CTRL + space bar**.

3.1.3 Change Case

Case refers to UPPER CASE, lower case, Sentence case, tOGGLE cASE (the case of each character is reversed) and Title Case (each word is capitalised).

To change case, do the following:
- Select the text to be changed.
- From the **Home** tab and the **Font** group, select the **Change Case** command.
- Select a case from the menu.
  Alternatively, use the keyboard combination of **Shift + F3** to move through the different case options.

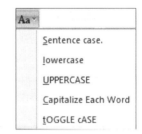

> All of the above formatting features are available in the Font window (select the Font window launcher icon).

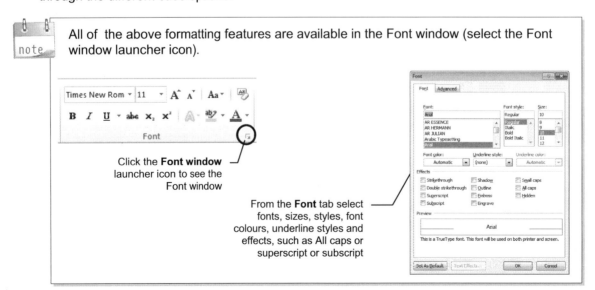

Click the **Font window** launcher icon to see the Font window

From the **Font** tab select fonts, sizes, styles, font colours, underline styles and effects, such as All caps or superscript or subscript

3.1.4 Automatic Hyphenation

Hyphenation refers to using hyphens to break up a word when it is too long to fit at the end of a line. See the example below.

This text uses hyphena-
tion so that words that
are too long to fit at the
end of a line are broken
with a hyphen

Note how the text is hyphenated at the end of the first line in this example.

This text uses no
hyphenation so words
that are too long to fit at
the end of a line are
carried on to the next line
of text

In this example, there is no hyphenation and instead the word is wrapped around to the next line of text.

To apply automatic hyphenation, do the following:

- From the **Page Layout** tab and the **Page Setup** group, select the **Hyphenation** arrow

- Choose a hyphenation option from the drop-down menu, such as **Automatic** to use automatic hyphenation in the whole document.

- Select **Hyphenation Options** to see further hyphenation features.

  ▹ Select the **Automatically hyphenate document** checkbox (to enter a tick in the box) to use hyphenation in the whole document.

  ▹ Select **Hyphenate words in CAPS** to use hyphenation on all upper case words in the document.

- Click **OK**.

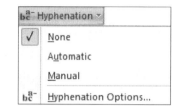

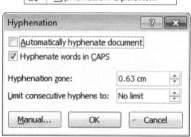

Practice Sequence

1	Open the **sale** document.	☐
2	Format the heading JUMBLE SALE with **Comic Sans MS** font, **24** font size, **dark blue** font colour, **bold** and <u>underlined</u>.	☐
3	Format the text **STALLS** in **Comic Sans MS** font, **18** font size, **dark blue** font colour, **bold** and *italics*.	☐
4	Change the case of the text STALLS to Sentence case.	☐
5	Format the text **Village Hall** in *italics*.	☐
6	Format the date and time of the jumble sale in **bold** and with a **red** font colour.	☐
7	Format the telephone symbol as **bold** with a **red** font colour (do not format the telephone number).	☐
8	The remainder of the text should display as Arial 12.	☐
9	Apply automatic hyphenation to the document.	☐
10	Apply superscript to the copyright © symbol.	☐
11	Save the **sale** document and close.	☐

3.2   Paragraphs

In this section you will learn about the following:

- Creating and merging paragraphs.
- Inserting and removing a soft carriage return (manual line break).
- Recognising good practice in aligning text. Using align, indent and tab tools rather than inserting spaces. Aligning text to the left, centre, and right and justify text.
- Indenting paragraphs: left, right and first line.
- Setting, removing and using tabs: left, centre, right and decimal.
- Recognising good practice in paragraph spacing. Applying spacing between paragraphs rather than using the Enter key.
- Applying spacing above and below paragraphs. Applying single, 1.5 lines and double line spacing within paragraphs.
- Adding and removing bullets and numbers in a single level list. Switching between standard bullet and number styles in a single level list.
- Adding a box border and shading/background colour to a paragraph.

3.2.1 Creating and Merging Paragraphs

A paragraph refers to one or more lines of text that are separated from previous or subsequent lines of text by a carriage return (press Enter).

To create and merge paragraphs, do the following:

Creating Paragraphs

- Position the cursor at the end of an existing paragraph or at the end of a sentence within a paragraph and then press the **Enter** key twice (to ensure that there is a clear line space between paragraphs).

Merging Paragraphs

- Position the cursor at the beginning of the second of the paragraphs to be merged and press the **Backspace** key twice to delete the line spaces between the paragraphs.
  Alternatively, position the cursor at the end of the first of the paragraphs to be merged and then press the **Delete** key twice.

3.2.2 Inserting and Removing Manual Line Breaks

Manual line breaks are also referred to as **soft carriage returns**. A line break moves the cursor to the next line without creating a paragraph break. This is useful if you want to create a new line in a list without a bullet or number appearing automatically before the list item.

To insert a line break, do the following:
- Position the cursor on the page and then press the following key combination: **Shift + Enter** The cursor will move to the next line.
- Click the **Show/Hide** button (**Home** tab/**Paragraph** group) to see the line break mark.   ↵

To delete a line break, do the following:
- Click the **Show/Hide** button.
- Position the cursor in front of the line break mark (or double click to select the mark).
- Press **Delete**.

3.3.3 Aligning Text

It is good practice to align text on a page by using the alignment tools, tabs or indents, rather than by entering spaces with the spacebar. This ensures that all text will line up accordingly and, when using indents and tabs, to a specific measurement on the page.

Text can be aligned horizontally to the left, right or centre of a page, or be displayed with fully justified alignment. See the examples below.

This text is left aligned with a ragged right margin and a justified left margin. This is the default alignment in Microsoft Word documents.	This text is right aligned with a justified right margin and ragged left margin.	This text is centred and neither of the margins are justified.	This text is justified with straight edges on both left and right margins. Justified text will stretch to reach the end of a line by creating spaces between words to ensure a straight edge on the right margin.

To align text, do the following:

- Select the text to be aligned.
- From the **Home** tab and **Alignment** group, select an alignment.

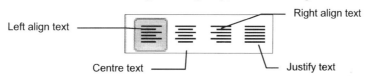

Left align text — ... Centre text — ... Right align text ... Justify text

The shortcut key combinations for alignment are:

CTRL + L = Left   **CTRL + R = Right**

CTRL + E = Centre   **CTRL + J = Justify**

3.2.4 Indenting Paragraphs

Paragraphs can be indented from the left and/or the right margins by a specified measurement.

> This is **indented** from the left by 9cm.

> This is a **first line indent** which will indent the first line of text by 1cm and then align the remainder of the paragraph to the left at 0cm. This type of indentation is used in some styles of letter writing and business documentation.

> This is a 1cm **hanging indent** which will indent a paragraph from the left margin by 1cm, but leave the first line at 0cm, allowing text/number/symbol to be entered at the left margin before each paragraph.

To indent text, do the following:

- Select the paragraph(s) to be indented.

- From the **Home** tab and the **Paragraph** group select the **Increase Indent** command to indent the selected paragraph(s) by the default measurement of 1cm. Click again to increase the indent further.

- Notice the indent marker on the **ruler bar** indicating the indent measurement.

The ruler bar displays the indent markers and indicates the indent measurement

To decrease the indent, do the following:

- Select the **Decrease Indent** command.

Decrease indent ——— Increase indent

The indent markers can be dragged to a specific measurement on the ruler bar to create different types of indent.

Drag the bottom indent to create a hanging indent

Drag the top indent to create a first line indent

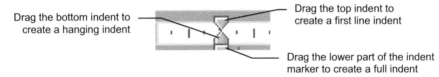

Drag the lower part of the indent marker to create a full indent

To enter a specific measurement for an indent, do the following:

- Select the **Paragraph** window launcher icon.

  The **Paragraph** window opens.

- In the **Indentation** section of the window, use the **Left** and/or **Right** scroll arrows to increase or decrease the current indent measurements (the upwards arrow increases the measurement and the downward arrow decreases the measurement).

- Select the **Special** arrow and choose an option, such as **Hanging** or **First Line**.

- Enter a measurement for the indent by selecting the **By** scroll arrow.

Use the scroll arrows to enter a measurement for the left and/or right indents

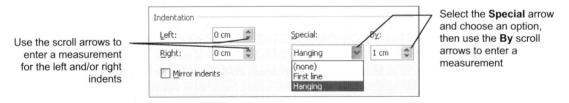

Select the **Special** arrow and choose an option, then use the **By** scroll arrows to enter a measurement

- Click **OK**.

3.2.5 Using Tabs

Tabs are used to position text in parallel columns to a specified position on the page. Tabs can be left, right, centre or decimal aligned. See the examples below:

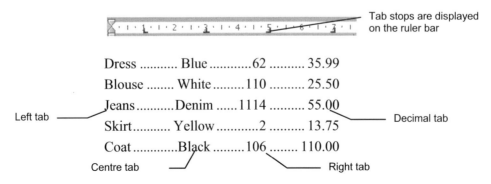

Tab stops are displayed on the ruler bar

Dress .... Blue .... 62 .... 35.99

Blouse .... White .... 110 .... 25.50

Jeans .... Denim ...... 1114 .... 55.00

Skirt .... Yellow .... 2 .... 13.75

Coat .... Black .... 106 .... 110.00

Left tab

Centre tab

Decimal tab

Right tab

The dots between the tab stop positions are called **leaders**.

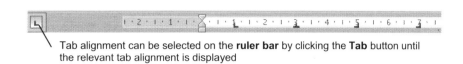

Tab alignment can be selected on the **ruler bar** by clicking the **Tab** button until the relevant tab alignment is displayed

To create tabs, do the following:

Ruler Bar

- Click the **Tab alignment** button on the **ruler bar** as shown above.
- Click the ruler bar to insert a **tab stop** in the specified position.
- Move a tab by dragging the tab stop along the ruler bar.
- Remove a tab by dragging the tab stop off the ruler bar.

Tabs Window

- Click the **Paragraph** window launcher icon.
  The **Paragraph** window opens.
- Select the **Tabs** button (at the bottom of the window).
  The **Tabs** window opens.
  The default tab stop position is displayed. This can be overridden by setting new tab stop positions.
- Enter a measurement for the first tab stop position.
- Select an alignment (use **Decimal** for numbers using decimal precision).
- Select a **Leader** if required.
- Select **Set**.
- Repeat this procedure to set further tabs.
- Click **OK**.

To remove a tab, do the following:

- Select the tab to be removed.
- Click **Clear** (or **Clear All** to clear all tab stops).
- Click **OK**.

3.2.6 Paragraph Spacing

Paragraph spacing refers to the space above and below a paragraph. Line spacing refers to the space between lines of text within a paragraph. It is good practice to use paragraph spacing rather than using the Enter key to apply spaces between paragraphs. Pressing the Enter key to create spaces between lines of text in a paragraph affects justified alignment. When the Enter key is used to create paragraph spacing above and below paragraphs, the spacing may take on the font size of the previous paragraph and so appear bigger than other spaces in the document. To ensure consistency throughout the document it is recommended that you use both paragraph and line spacing.

To apply paragraph and line spacing, do the following:

Paragraph Spacing

- Select the paragraphs to which spacing is to be applied.
- From the **Home** tab, click the **Paragraph** window launcher icon.
  The **Paragraph** window opens.

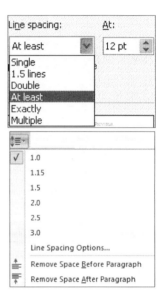

Select the **Before** and/or **After** scroll
arrows to increase the spacing before
and after paragraphs

- In the **Spacing** section use the **Before** and/or **After** scroll arrows to increase the spacing before and after paragraphs.
- Click **OK**.

Line Spacing

- Select the paragraphs to which spacing is to be applied.
- From the **Home** tab, click the **Paragraph** window launcher icon. The **Paragraph** window opens
- In the **Spacing** section select the **Line Spacing** arrow and choose a line spacing option from the menu.
- After selecting **Multiple, Exactly** or **At Least** use the **At** scroll arrows to select a measurement.
- Click **OK**.

Alternatively

- Select the paragraphs to which spacing is to be applied.
- Click the **Line Spacing** command from the **Paragraph** group.
- Choose a line spacing option from the drop-down menu or select **Line Spacing options** to see the **Paragraph** window.

3.2.7 Bullets and Numbering

Bullets and numbering are used to enhance the appearance and clarity of lists.

Bullets

- This is a bulleted list.
  - Bullets can be indented by a specific measurement from the left margin.
- The space between the bullet and the text can be altered.
- ❖ Bullets can be formatted to display with a different bullet symbol.
- ◆ Bullets can be formatted to display in a different font, size and colour.

Numbers

1. This is a numbered list.
   2. Numbered lists can be indented from the left margin.
3. The space between the number and the text can be altered.
A. Numbers can be formatted to display in a different format (a, b, c or i, ii, iii, etc.).
1. Numbers can be formatted to display in a different font, size and colour.

To apply bullets and numbering to lists, do the following:

- Select the text to which bullets or numbering are to be applied.
- From the **Home** tab and **Paragraph** group, click the **Bullets** or **Numbering** buttons to enter a standard bullet or number In front of text.

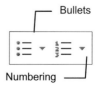

Bullets

Numbering

- Select the arrow to see the menu commands.

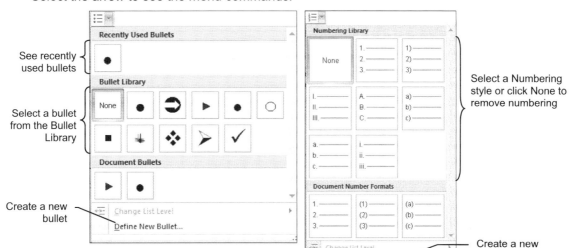

- Select a bullet or number from the Library options or select **Define New Bullet** or **Define New Number Format**

- From the **Define New Bullet** window, select the **Symbol** button and choose a symbol, or select **Picture** to select a saved image as a bullet. Select the **Font** button to change the font, size, style and colour. Click the Alignment arrow to select an alignment for the bullet. Click OK.

- From the **Define New Number Format** window, select the **Number Style** arrow and choose a number style from the list. Enter a **Number Format** into the box or retain the format provided for the chosen style and choose an alignment. Select the **Font** button to change the font, size, style and colour.

- Click **OK**.

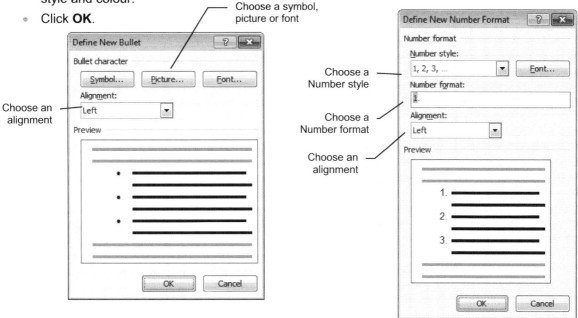

3.2.8 Borders and Shading

To apply borders and shading to a paragraph, do the following:

Borders

- Select the paragraph to which the border is to be applied.
- From the **Home** tab and **Paragraph** group, select the **Border** command.

3

- Select a border from the menu.

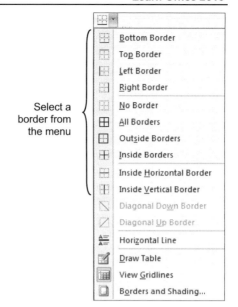

Select a border from the menu

Alternatively, select **Borders and Shading** from the **Border** menu.

The **Borders and Shading** window opens.

- Ensure that the **Borders** tab is selected and choose a **Setting**, such as **Box or Shadow**.

  Alternatively, select the **Border** buttons to apply borders to specific parts of the paragraph (top, bottom, left or right).

- Select a **Style** for the border, such as a dashed style or solid border.

- Select the **Color** arrow and choose a colour for the border.

- Select the **Width** arrow and choose a line width.

- Ensure that **Paragraph** is displayed in the **Apply to:** box.

- Click **OK**.

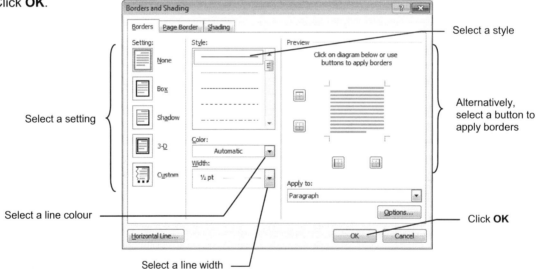

Shading

- Select the paragraph to which the shading is to be applied.

- From the **Home** tab and **Paragraph** group, select the **Shading** command.

- Select a shading colour from the menu.

- Select **More Colors** to see the colour palette.

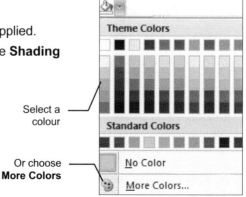

- Choose a colour.
- Click **OK**.

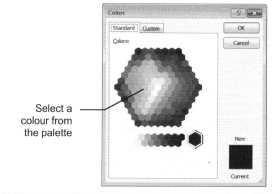

Select a
colour from
the palette

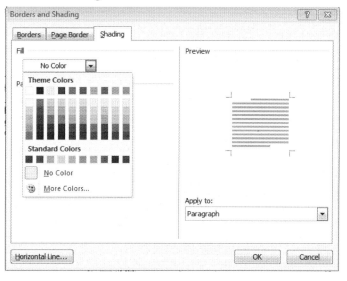

note

Shading can also be applied from the **Borders and Shading** window. Select the **Borders** button from the **Paragraph** group and then select the **Borders and Shading** tab. Select the **Shading** tab and then click the **Fill** arrow. Choose a colour from the menu or select **More Colors** to see the **Colors** window. Choose a colour from the palette and click **OK**. Click **OK** to close the **Borders and Shading** window.

Practice Sequence

1	Open the **sale** document.
2	In the final paragraph, create a new paragraph for the sentence beginning **Please also remember that when downloading images…**.
3	Merge the paragraph beginning **All profits to go…** with the previous paragraph. Ensure that there is a full stop and at least one space separating the two sentences where the new paragraph merges.
4	Insert a line break beneath the final list item Books.
5	Align the heading **Jumble Sale** in the centre of the page. Align the telephone number to the right of the page.
6	Justify the final three paragraphs, all other paragraphs should remain left aligned.
7	Indent the paragraph starting **If you would like to volunteer…** from the left and right by **2cm**.
8	Format the paragraph beginning **If you have any of the above items…** with a **2cm** First Line Indent.

9	Apply **6pt** spacing before and after the final three paragraphs. Apply 1.5 line spacing to the final three paragraphs.	☐
10	Add a black round bullet to the list of stalls. Ensure that the bullet is indented at 0cm and the bullet list is indented from the bullet symbol by 1cm.	☐
11	Add a box border and pale grey shading to the final paragraph.	☐
12	Delete the line break that you inserted at step 4.	☐
13	Insert the following text one clear line space beneath the final paragraph: **Profits from last jumble sale:**	☐
14	Insert the following tabs one clear line space beneath the newly entered text: 2cm left aligned tab, 5cm centre aligned tab, 8cm right aligned tab and a 10cm decimal aligned tab. Enter the tabulated text as shown below.	☐

Mary	Sales	Toys	80.00
Joan	Sales	Clothes	98.65
Deirdre	Refreshments	Teas	99.60
John	Sales	Books	60.20
David	Sales	Household	77.45
Jackie	Sales	Shoes	45.50

15	Save and close the **sale** document.	☐

3.3   Styles

In this section you will learn about the following:

- Applying an existing character style to one or more paragraphs.
- Applying an existing paragraph style to one or more paragraphs.
- Using the copy format tool.

3.3.1 Applying Styles

A style is a set of formatting features – such as fonts, sizes, colours, alignment, spacing, borders and shading – that can be applied to an entire document or selected areas of a document. Styles facilitate formatting by enabling more than one formatting characteristic, such as font, size and colour, to be applied in one action. Styles ensure consistency throughout a document.

A **Character style** contains formatting features (such as font, size, style, colour, borers and shading) that can be applied to text. Character styles do not contain formatting features that affect paragraphs, such as alignment or spacing.

A **Paragraph style** contains all of the formatting features of a character style, but also contains line spacing, alignments, indents and tabs.

To apply a style, do the following:

- Select the text to which the style is to be applied.
- From the Home tab, select the **Styles** window launcher icon.

Styles window launcher icon

- The **Styles** task pane opens, displaying default and created styles.
- Select a style from the task pane to apply it to the selected text.
- Close the window by clicking the **Close X** button.

Alternatively

- Select the text to which the style is to be applied.
- From the Home tab, select the **More** button in the **Styles** group.

- Select **Apply Styles**.
  The **Apply Styles** window opens.
- Select a style from the **Style Name** menu to apply it to selected text.
- Close the window by clicking the **Close X** button.

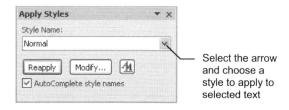

Select the arrow and choose a style to apply to selected text

3.3.2 Format Painter

Formatting can be copied by using the Format Painter tool. This tool enables you to copy formatting from selected text to another text item, line of text or paragraph.

To copy formatting, do the following:

- Select the text with the formatting that is to be copied.

- From the **Home** tab and **Clipboard** group, select the **Format Painter** button.
- Drag the mouse over the text which is to display the same formatting (note how the cursor changes to include a paintbrush icon).

> **note** Double-click the **Format Painter** to keep it on whilst you copy formatting to more than one item of text or paragraph. Click the Format Painter button to turn it off.

Practice Sequence

1	Open the **sale** document.	☐
2	Apply the **Heading 3** style to the telephone number (do not apply to the telephone symbol).	☐
3	Apply the **Heading 2** style to text **Profits from last jumble sale**.	☐
4	Copy the formatting of the telephone number to the paragraph beginning **Please also remember that when downloading...** (this paragraph should be formatted with a border and shading from the previous practice sequence).	☐
5	Save and close the **sale** document.	☐

Section 4 ▶   Objects

Objects refer to tables, images, pictures, diagrams, charts and drawn objects.

4.1   Table Creation

In this section you will learn about the following:

- Creating a table ready for data insertion.
- Inserting and editing data in a table.
- Selecting rows, columns, cells and an entire table.

4.1.1 Creating a Table

A table consists of rows and columns. The intersection between a row and a column is called a **cell**.

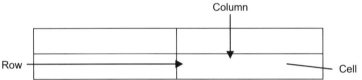

To create a table, do the following:

- From the **Insert** tab and the **Tables** group, select the **Table** arrow.
- There are two methods of creating a table:
  - ▷ Drag the mouse over the number or rows and columns required for the table and then release the mouse.
  - ▷ Select **Insert Table**.

  If method (b) is selected the **Insert Table** window will open.
- Use the scroll arrows to enter the number of columns and rows required to create the table.
- Click **OK**.

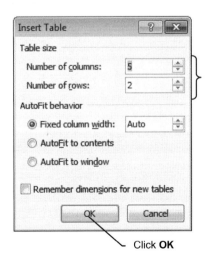

Use the scroll arrows to increase/decrease the number of rows and columns required

Click **OK**

4.1.2 Inserting and Editing Data in a Table

To insert and edit data in a table, do the following:

- Position the cursor within the relevant cell of the table and enter data as required.
- Use the **Tab** key, or the directional arrow key to move to the next cell in the row (or click the mouse into the next cell).
- Use **Shift + Tab** to move back a cell at a time or use the mouse to click in the required cell.
- If the cell is not wide enough to show all the data that has been entered on one line the data will wrap around within the cell.
- To edit table data, position the cursor within the cell and then do the following:
    - Delete a character at a time by pressing the **Delete** key – this will delete characters to the right of the cursor position within the cell.
    - Delete a character at a time by pressing the **Backspace** key – this will delete characters to the left of the cursor position within the cell.
    - To delete a whole word at a time, hold down the **CTRL** key and then press either **Delete** or **Backspace**, depending on the position of the cursor.
    - To select cell contents, position mouse within a word and double-click to select the word. Treble-click to select more than one line of data within a cell (data that is not separated by a carriage return).
    - To remove a selection, click away from the selected cell.
    - To delete all the contents of a cell, select cell contents by positioning the mouse arrow to the left of the cell contents. The mouse arrow turns into a black arrow pointing at the cell. Left-click the mouse button. Press **Delete**.
    - Overtype data by pressing the **Insert** key on the keyboard and then entering data into the cell in front of existing data. The new data will overwrite the existing data. Press the **Insert** key to turn **Overtype** mode *off*.
    - Enter new data within existing data by positioning the cursor within the text and then start typing. The existing data will move to accommodate the new text (if **Overtype** mode is *off*).

4.1.3 Selecting Cells, Rows, Columns and an Entire Table

Before the table, or individual rows/columns or cells, can be formatted or deleted, it must first be selected.

To select a cell, row, column or an entire table, do the following:

Cells

- Position the cursor near the cell you want to select.
- When a diagonal black arrow appears, left-click to select. *Alternatively,* make sure the cursor is in the cell to be selected.
- From the **Layout** tab, click **Select**, and then **Cell**.
- To select text in a cell, click within the cell and select the text using one of the usual text selection methods.

| apple |

Rows

- Move the cursor to the left of the row to be selected.
- Left-click the mouse to select.

Columns

- Move the cursor above the column to be selected.
- The insertion point turns into a black arrow.
- Left-click the mouse to select.

Table

- Move the cursor over the table to see a table tag.
- Left-click the tag to select.

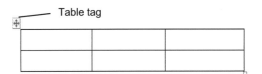

Table tag

 note This tag also enables you to move a table.

 note Tables, rows, columns and individual cells can be selected by using the **Select** command.

Click the mouse into a cell within the table, row or column to be selected and then, from the **Table Tools/Layout** tab and the **Table** group, select the **Select** command. Choose **Select Cell**, **Select Row**, **Select Column** or **Select Table**.

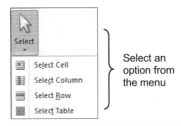

Select an option from the menu

4.1.4 Inserting and Deleting Rows and Columns

To insert rows and columns, do the following:

Inserting

- Position the cursor within the table and then, from the **Table Tools/Layout** tab and the **Rows & Columns** group, select an **Insert** command.
- Select an option to insert a row above or below the selected row or to insert a column to the left or right of the selected column.

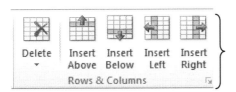

Select an option from the menu:
insert above/below for rows and
insert left/right for columns

 note If you select multiple rows or columns before inserting further rows/columns, then the same number of rows/columns will be inserted.

Deleting

- Select the row or column to be deleted.
- From the **Table Tools/Layout** tab and the **Rows & Columns** group, select a **Delete** option.

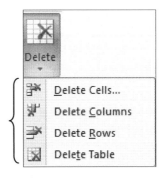

Select an option
from the menu

1   Open the **sale** document.   ☐

2   At the end of the document, beneath the tabulated data, enter the following title: ☐
     Helpers and format with the **Heading 3** style.

3   Beneath the title, enter a 2 column and 3 row table.   ☐

     Enter the data as shown below.   ☐

4

Mary Roberts	Teas
Bill Smith	Stalls
Deirdre Connor	Raffle

5   Edit the first cell in the table to read **Marie Robertson**.   ☐

6   Edit the cell in row 1, column 2 to read **Refreshments**.   ☐

7   Insert a new row above **Deirdre Connor** and insert the following data: **Neil**   ☐
     Brennan, Sales.

8   Delete the row for **Bill Smith**.   ☐

9   Save **sale** and close.   ☐

4.2   Table Formatting

In this section you will learn about the following:

- Modifying column width and row height.
- Modifying cell border line style, width and colour.
- Adding shading/background colour to cells.

4.2.1   Modifying Column Width and Row Height

Rows and columns can be adjusted by increasing or decreasing the row height and/or column width. A command on the ribbon bar enables both row, and columns to be adjusted to fit the contents of the cells, to fit the window or to display a specific measurement.

To adjust column widths and row heights, do the following:

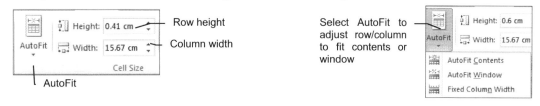

Column Width

- Select the column or columns to be adjusted.
- From the **Table Tools/Layout** tab and the **Cell Size** group, select the **Table Column Width** scroll arrows to increase/decrease the current width measurement.

  Alternatively, select the **Cell Size** window launcher icon to see the **Table Properties** window.

- Select the **Column** tab and then, from the **Size** section of the window, select the **Measure in** drop down menu to select a measurement type (percentage or centimetres).

- Use the **Preferred width** scroll arrows to increase or decrease the current column width measurement.
- Click **OK**.

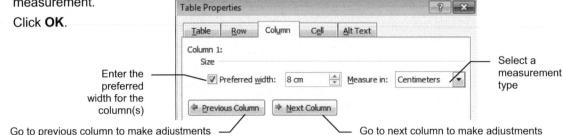

Enter the preferred width for the column(s)

Select a measurement type

Go to previous column to make adjustments — — Go to next column to make adjustments

Row Height

- Select the row or rows to be adjusted.
- From the **Table Tools/Layout** tab and the **Cell Size** group, select the **Table Row Height** scroll arrows to increase/decrease the current height measurement.

  Alternatively, select the **Cell Size** window launcher icon to see the **Table Properties** window.
- Select the **Row** tab and then, from the **Size** section of the window, select the **Specify height** checkbox (to enter a tick in the box). Use the scroll arrows to increase the row height measurement.
- Select the **Row height is** arrow and choose an option, such as **At least** or **Exactly**.
- From the **Options** section of the window, select whether to allow rows to break across pages by entering a tick in the box and/or select the **repeat as header row at the top of each page** (if the table will span more than one page it is useful to see the table headings at the top of the table on each page).
- Select **Previous Row** to adjust the previous row in the table or select **Next Row** to adjust the next row in the table.
- Click **OK**.

Select the Specify height tick box and enter a measurement

Select a row height option (Exactly or At least)

4.2.2 Border Line Styles

The default setting is for tables to display an outside and grid border. The existing border can be removed or formatted to display a different line style and line width and colour. To format cells within a table with borders and lines, do the following:

No Border

- Select the table or individual cells, rows or columns.
- From the **Table Tools/Design** tab and **Table Styles** group, select the **Border** arrow.
- Select **No Border**.

Select **No Border**

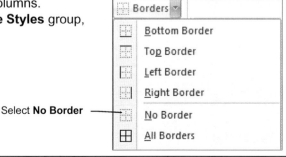

Gridlines

A table with no borders will display *gridlines*. Gridlines do not appear on a printout but are useful to display on screen to make it easier to enter data and edit and format a table.

To turn on/off gridlines, do the following:

- From the **Table Tools/Layout** tab and the **Table** group, select the **View Gridlines** command (this is a *toggle* button, which means that it is turned on/off each time it is selected).

Table displaying gridlines but no borders

Table displaying borders

Applying Borders

- Select the cell, row, column or table to be formatted.
- From the **Table Tools/Design** tab and **Table Styles** group, select the **Borders** arrow.
- Select a border from the menu or select **Borders and Shading** at the bottom of the menu.

  The **Borders and Shading** window opens, with the **Borders** tab selected.

- From the **Settings** section of the window, select a border setting, such as **Box**.
- From the **Style** section, scroll down the list of line styles and select a line style.
- Select the **Color** arrow and choose a line colour (the default line colour is black).
- Select the **Width** arrow and choose a line width (the default line width is ½ pt).
- Click the **Apply to** arrow and choose a page element to which to apply the border/lines (such as table or cell).

From the **Preview** section refine the border(s) by selecting top, bottom, left, right, middle or diagonal border buttons (these are *toggle* buttons which are turned on/off each time they are selected) to apply or remove a border.

- Click **OK**.

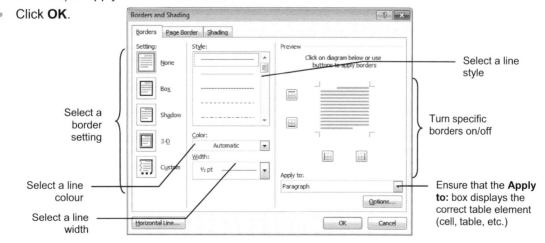

4.2.3 Shading

To format the background of a cell with colour, do the following:

- Select the cell, row, column or table to be formatted.
- From the **Table Tools/Design** tab and **Table Styles** group, select the **Shading** arrow.
- Choose a colour from the available **Theme Colors** or from **Standard Colors**.

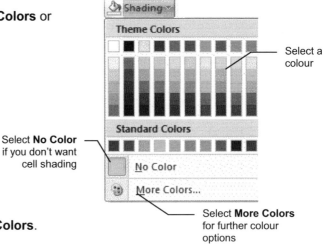

Select a colour

Select **No Color** if you don't want cell shading

Select **More Colors** for further colour options

- To see further colour choices, select **More Colors**. The **Colors** window opens.
- Select a colour.
- Click **OK**.

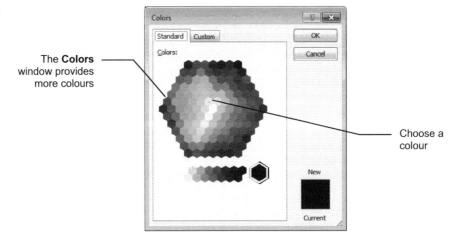

The **Colors** window provides more colours

Choose a colour

note

> You can also apply shading through the **Borders and Shading** window. Select the **Borders** arrow and then select **Borders and Shading**. Select the **Shading** tab. Select a colour and click OK.

4.3 Graphical Objects

A graphical object refers to a picture (from a stored location on a drive or in the Clip Art gallery), image, chart or drawn object.

In this section you will learn about the following:
- Inserting an object (picture, chart, drawn object) to a specified location in a document.
- Selecting an object.
- Copying, moving an object within a document and between open documents.
- Resizing and deleting an object.

4.3.1 Inserting an Object

Objects, such as pictures, images, shapes (drawn objects) and charts, can all be inserted from the **Insert** tab/**Illustrations** group. They are placed at the position of the cursor within a document.

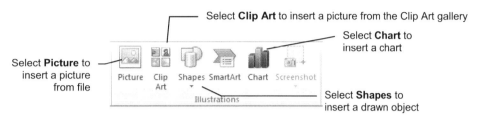

To insert an object, do the following:

Picture

- Position the cursor where the picture is to be inserted.
- From the **Insert** tab and the **Illustrations** group select the **Picture** command.
  The **Insert Picture** window opens.
- From the Navigation Pane, select the correct drive and/or folder in which the picture is stored.
- Select the picture file.
- Click **Insert**.
  The picture will be inserted into the cursor position in the document.

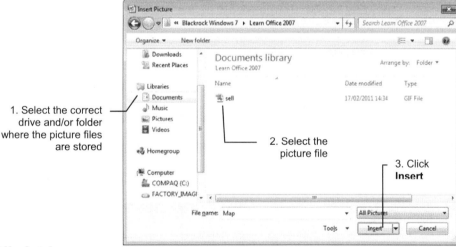

ClipArt Image

- Position the cursor where the image is to be inserted.
- From the **Insert** tab and the **Illustrations** group select the **ClipArt** command.
  The **ClipArt** task pane opens.
- Select the **Results should be** arrow and choose an option, such as **All media types** (to find images from the internet as well as from ClipArt collections), or **ClipArt**, **Photographs**, **Movies** or **Sounds**.
- Tick or un-tick the box to include Office.com content.
- Position the cursor in the **Search for** box and enter a search word (the name of the picture you wish to find, e.g. **computer** will find a variety of computer images).
- Click **Go**.
  A gallery of clip art images will display within the task pane.
- Move the mouse over an image to see a menu arrow.

- Click the arrow.
- Click **Insert**.

  Alternatively, just click an image to insert it in the cursor position).

- The picture will be inserted in the cursor position within the document.

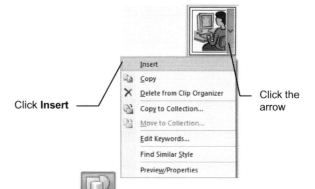

Click **Insert**

Click the arrow

Drawn Object

Drawn objects refer to *shapes*.

- From the **Insert** tab and the **Illustrations** group select the **Shapes** command.
- Select a shape from the menu.
- Move the cursor onto the page where the shape is to be inserted.

  The cursor turns into a black crosshair.

- Hold down the left mouse button and drag the mouse to create the shape.

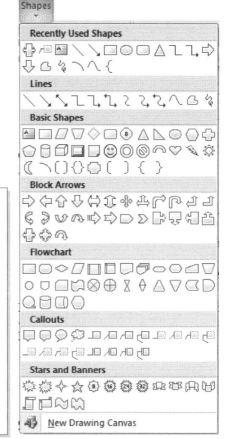

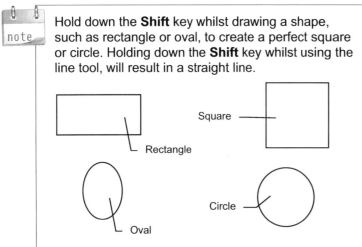

note

Hold down the **Shift** key whilst drawing a shape, such as rectangle or oval, to create a perfect square or circle. Holding down the **Shift** key whilst using the line tool, will result in a straight line.

Chart

A chart is created from data existing in a datasheet. There are a variety of chart types, such as a bar/column chart, a pie chart or a line chart, examples of which are given below.

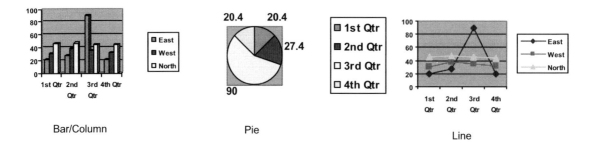

Bar/Column   Pie   Line

- From the **Insert** tab and the **Illustrations** group select the **Chart** command.

- The **Insert Chart** window opens.
- Select a chart type and click OK.

Select a chart type

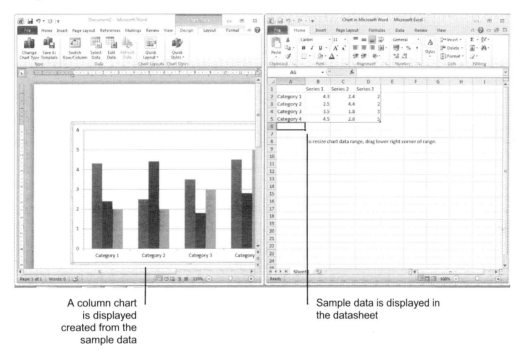

- A default column chart with a data sheet containing sample data will be displayed.
- Change the data in the sample datasheet.

A column chart is displayed created from the sample data

Sample data is displayed in the datasheet

- Close the spreadsheet by clicking the exit (X) button. The altered data will be reflected in the chart.

4.3.2 Selecting an Object

Before an object can be edited, formatted or manipulated, it must first be selected.

To select an object, do the following:

- Click an object (picture, chart or shape).
- The object will display with small blue squares (called handles) surrounding it.

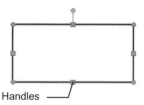

Handles

note

Charts are selected with one click, but they cannot be edited or formatted unless the **Chart Tools** are active. To do this, click the chart. The **Chart Tools** ribbon becomes active. From the **Chart Tools** (Design, Layout and Format tabs), you can change the chart type and select chart options, such as axis labels and titles.

4.3.3 Copying and Moving Objects

Objects can be copied or moved within a document or between open documents. The Clipboard group contains the copy, cut and paste tools.

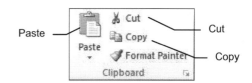

To copy or move an object, do the following:

Within a Document

- To **copy** an object, select the object and then, from the **Home** tab and the **Clipboard** group, select the **Copy** button (or use the keyboard shortcut **CTRL + C**).
- Move the cursor to the new location within the document.
- Select the **Paste** button (or press the keyboard shortcut **CTRL + V**).
- Objects can be **moved** by using the same procedure as above, but select the **Cut** button at step 1 (or the key combination **CTRL + X**).

Between Open Documents

- To **copy** an object between open documents, select the object and then, from the **Home** tab and the **Clipboard** group, select the **Copy** button (or use the keyboard shortcut **CTRL + C**).
  Open documents display on the taskbar at the bottom of the screen.
- Switch to the other document by clicking the tab on the taskbar (or select the **View** tab and then, from the **Window** group, select the **Switch Windows** command, then select the document by clicking the document name in the **Switch Windows** menu).
- Move the cursor to the new location where the object is to be copied within the second document.
- Select the **Paste** button (or press the keyboard shortcut **CTRL + V**).
- Objects can be **moved** by using the same procedure as above, but select the **Cut** button at step 1 (or the key combination **CTRL + X**).

You can also copy, cut and paste objects within and between documents by right-clicking and selecting the Cut, Copy, Paste commands from the shortcut menu or by using the Drag and Drop method. The latter method uses the mouse to copy or move objects to a different destination within the **same** document.

To move an object, select the object to be moved, hold down the mouse button and drag to the new destination (or hold down the **CTRL** key whilst dragging to **copy** an object to the new destination).

4.3.4 Resizing Objects

It is important that the original proportions of an object are retained when it is resized, otherwise it may appear distorted.

To resize an object, do the following:

Picture Tools

- Select the object and then, from the **Picture Tools/Format** tab and the **Size** group, use the **Height/Width** scroll arrows to increase or decrease the height and/or width of the object.
- Ensure that the object retains its original proportions by changing only the **Height** or the **Width**.

Format Picture Window

- Select the object and then, from the **Picture Tools/Format** tab, select the **Size** window launcher.

  The **Format Picture** window opens.

- Select the **Absolute** scroll arrows to increase or decrease the **Height** and/or **Width** measurements.

- To maintain the original proportions of the object, ensure that the **Lock Aspect Ratio** checkbox displays a tick and only change the height *or* the width (when the height is changed the width will alter proportionally).

- Click **OK**.

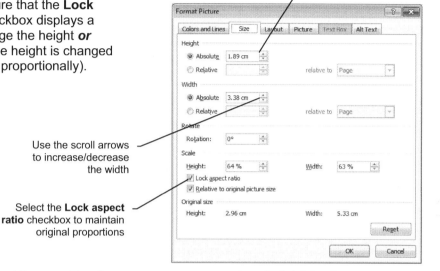

Use the scroll arrows to increase/decrease the height

Use the scroll arrows to increase/decrease the width

Select the **Lock aspect ratio** checkbox to maintain original proportions

Mouse

- Select the object and then position the cursor over a corner handle (resizing from a corner handle maintains original proportions and prevents distortion).

- The cursor turns into a black, double headed arrow when positioned over a handle. Hold down the left mouse button and drag inwards to reduce the size or outwards to increase the size.

- Release the mouse when the object is the required size.

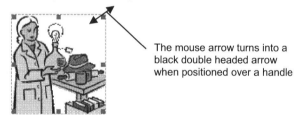

The mouse arrow turns into a black double headed arrow when positioned over a handle

4.3.5 Deleting Objects

To delete an object, do the following:

- Select the object and then press the **Delete** key on the keyboard.

	Practice Sequence	
1	Open the **sale** document.	☐
2	Position the cursor beneath the title **Jumble Sale** and insert the picture called **sell.gif** so that it displays beneath the title with centre alignment.	☐
3	Resize the **height** of the image to **2cm**.	☐
4	Using Clip Art, find a suitable image relating to one of the following: clothes, shoes, household goods, books or toys. Insert an appropriate image above the **Stalls** title.	☐
5	Resize the image if necessary, ensuring that the original proportions are maintained. Move the Clip Art image so that it is positioned on the right side of the **sell** image beneath the title **Jumble Sale**.	☐

6	Copy the **sell** image to a new document.	☐
7	Resize the height of the copied image to **4cm**.	☐
8	Save the new document as **Advert08** and close.	☐
9	Delete the Clip Art image (retain the **sell** picture in its current position).	☐
10	Create an arrow shape beside the bulleted list with the tip of the arrow towards the bulleted items.	☐
11	Resize the object with a height of 1.5cm and a width of 5.2cm.	☐
12	Save and close the **sale** document.	☐

3

Section 5 ▶   Mail Merge

The mail merge procedure facilitates the process of sending standard documents to customers by storing a data file of information (e.g. addresses), which can then be merged easily with any document, such as a mailshot document. (A mailshot is a document, such as a letter or flyer that is sent out to hundreds or thousands of addresses.)

To facilitate this procedure, a mail merge is performed by merging the names and addresses of existing or potential customers with the standard document. The individual items of data that are merged with the document are called **fields** (e.g Title, First Name and Last Name are all fields). Other fields may also be merged within the main body of the document.

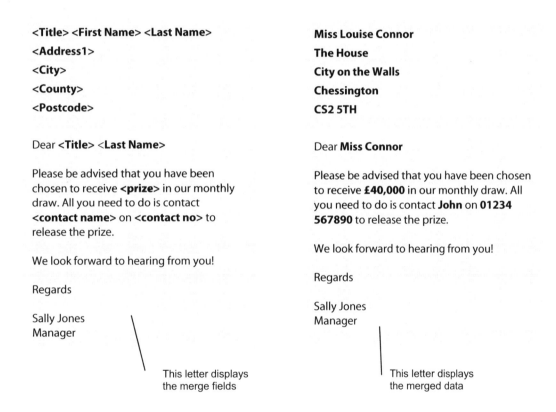

<Title> <First Name> <Last Name>

<Address1>

<City>

<County>

<Postcode>

Dear <Title> <Last Name>

Please be advised that you have been chosen to receive **<prize>** in our monthly draw. All you need to do is contact **<contact name>** on **<contact no>** to release the prize.

We look forward to hearing from you!

Regards

Sally Jones
Manager

This letter displays
the merge fields

Miss Louise Connor

The House

City on the Walls

Chessington

CS2 5TH

Dear **Miss Connor**

Please be advised that you have been chosen to receive **£40,000** in our monthly draw. All you need to do is contact **John** on **01234 567890** to release the prize.

We look forward to hearing from you!

Regards

Sally Jones
Manager

This letter displays
the merged data

A mail merge procedure can also be used to create mailing labels.

5.1   Preparation

In this section, you will learn about the following:

- Opening and preparing a document as a main document for a mail merge.
- Selecting a mailing list or other data file for use in a mail merge.
- Inserting data fields in a mail merge main document (letter, address labels).

5.1.1 Main Document

A main document is a standard document, such as a mailing letter, that is merged with a data file.

To create a main document, do the following:
- Create a new document.
- Select the **Mailings** tab and then, from the **Start Mail Merge** group, select the **Start Mail Merge** command.
- Select a document type from the menu, such as **Letters**.
- Enter the standard information into the document.
- Save the main document.

5.1.2 Mailing List

A mailing list is also referred to as a **data file**. The mailing list contains merge fields that can be merged with any main document, such as letter, labels, memo, agenda, minutes, flyer. A mailing list may be created in Word as a table or in another application, such as Microsoft Access or Excel.

To select a mailing list for use in a mail merge, do the following:
- Open the main document.
- From the **Mailings** tab and the **Start Mail Merge** group, select the **Select Recipients** command.
- From the menu, select **Use Existing List**.
- Select the correct drive and/or folder from the Navigation Pane.
- Select the data file.
- Click **Open**.

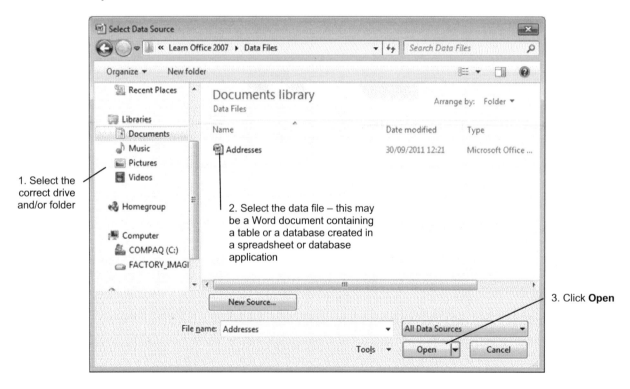

1. Select the correct drive and/or folder

2. Select the data file – this may be a Word document containing a table or a database created in a spreadsheet or database application

3. Click **Open**

- Save the main document.

5.1.3 Inserting Fields

Once the data source is attached to the main document, you can insert the mail merge fields.

To insert merge fields, do the following:

- Open the main document and esnure that the cursor is in the correct position for inserting the merge fields.
- From the **Mailings** tab and the **Write & Insert Fields** group, select the **Insert Merge Field** command.
- From the menu select the first merge field.
- Press the space bar to create a space between fields appearing on the same line, or press **Enter** to create a new paragraph for fields appearing on a separate line.
- Select the **Insert Merge Field** command and select the second merge field. Repeat this procedure to enter the remaining merge fields. (See the example below.)

«Title» «First_Name» «Last_Name» ——— Ensure that there is a space
«Address»   between fields that appear on the
«City»   same line or press Enter to insert
«Post_Code»   fields on a separate line

- Save the main document.

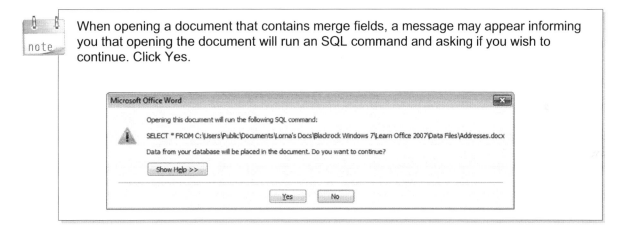

> **note** When opening a document that contains merge fields, a message may appear informing you that opening the document will run an SQL command and asking if you wish to continue. Click Yes.

5.1.4 Labels

In the previous section you learned how to perform a mail merge procedure to create a form letter. In addition to letters, mail merge can also be performed to create labels.

To create labels do the following:

- Open a new document.
- From the **Mailings** tab and the **Start Mail Merge** group, select the **Start Mail Merge** command.
- Select **Labels** from the menu.
  The **Label options** window opens.
- Select the **Label vendors** arrow and choose a name from the list, such as Microsoft or Avery.
- Select a **Product Number** and check the product information for the labels you have chosen.

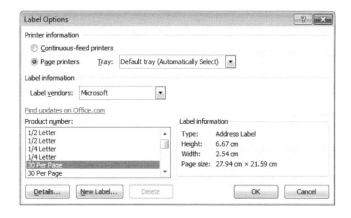

- Click **OK**.
- Select the **Select Recipients** command and choose **Use Existing List**.
- Locate the mailing list (data source).
- Click **Open**.
- Insert merge fields into the first label and then click the **Update Labels** command (each of the labels will display the merge fields).
- Save the labels and close.

5.1.6 Previewing Results and Finding Recipients

When merge fields have been inserted within a main document, they are displayed as fields and not actual data. For example, <<**First Name**>> will display rather than the data **Mary**. The merge fields can be previewed to see how they will look on printed output.

To preview the results of a mail merge procedure, do the following:

- From the **Mailings** tab and the **Preview Results** group, select the **Preview Results** command.

  The merge fields will be replaced by the data.

- Enter a number in the **Go To Record** box to go to a specific record or select the arrow to scroll through each record in the mailing list.

- Select the **Find Recipient** button.

  The **Find Entry** window opens.

- Enter the search word in the **Find** box.
- Click the **This field** arrow and choose the field.
- Click **Find Next**.
- Click **Close** to close the **Find Entry** window.

5.1.7 Using the Step-by-Step Mail Merge Wizard

The above steps can all be performed through the Mail Merge Wizard.

To use the Mail Merge wizard, do the following:

- Create a new document.
- Select the **Mailings** tab and then, from the **Start Mail Merge** group, select the **Step-by Step Mail Merge Wizard** command.
- Select a document type from the task pane, such as **Letters**.
- Click **Next: Starting document**.
- Select **Use the current document**.
- Click **Next: Select recipients**.
- Select **Use an existing list** and then click **Browse**.
- Locate the data file/mailing list from the correct drive/folder, select the file.
- Click **Open**.

  The **Mail Merge Recipients** window opens, displaying the records within the mailing list.

- Click **OK** to close the window and return to the main document.
- Select **Next: Write your letter.** Enter the standard information into the document.
- Position the cursor where the merge fields should appear in the document and then, from the **Mail Merge** task pane, select **More items**.

The **Insert Merge Fields** window opens.

- Select the first field and click **Insert**.

- Click **Close**.

- Insert a space with the space bar if the next field should appear on the same line or press **Enter** if the next field is to appear on a separate line. Reselect **More items** and choose another field – repeat the above procedure to insert each of the fields into the main document.

- Select **Next: Preview your letters**. Use the **Go to** arrows >> and << to scroll through the records in the mailing list or use the **Find a recipient** button to find a specific record (from this step of the Wizard, you can edit the recipient list or exclude specific records from the mail merge procedure).

- Select **Next: Complete the merge**.

- Select **Edit individual letters** to merge to a new document (alternatively, select **Print** to merge to printer without completing the mail merge procedure).

- Click **All**.

- Click **OK**.

- Save the document.

- Print the merged document, if you didn't perform this action at Step 6 of 6.

- Close the document.

Practice Sequence

1	Open the **activities** letter that is provided for this practice sequence.
2	Prepare the **activities** letter as a main document for a mail merge.
3	Select the **Address** mailing list for use in the mail merge.
4	Insert the merge fields in the letter where indicated (delete the existing text, e.g. <title> – these are not fields but are included as a guide only).
5	Preview the results and scroll through each record in the mailing list.
6	Save and close the **activities** document.
7	Create mailing labels, using the **Address** mailing list, with 30 Microsoft labels per page (use the second option in the **Product Number** list).
8	Update all of the labels to display the merge fields.
9	Preview the results and then save as **Labels**.
10	Close all open documents.

5.2   Outputs

Output refers to an onscreen or printed copy of a document.

In this section, you will learn about the following:

- Merging a mailing list with a letter or label document as a new file or printed output.
- Printing mail merge outputs: letters and labels.

5.2.1 Merge

The mail merge document will comprise an individual letter until the mail merge procedure is finalised. The merge procedure is not complete until the **Finish & Merge** command is used. This will merge each of the records in the mailing list with the main document. The resulting document will comprise many pages, subject to the amount of records that are merged with the main document. For example, if the original main document comprises one page and it is merged with a mailing list containing 5 addresses, the resulting merged document will comprise 5 pages.

To complete the mail merge procedure, do the following:
- Open the main document containing the merge fields.
- From the **Mailings** tab and the **Finish** group, select the **Finish & Merge** command.
- Select **Edit Individual Documents** to finalise the merge or select **Print Documents** to print the documents without completing the merge process.
- The **Merge to New Document** window opens (or the **Merge to Printer**, depending on the menu option selected).
- Select the **All** option button to merge all records with the main document.
- Click **OK**.

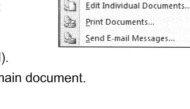

Select **All** to merge all records with the letter in a new document or choose specific records

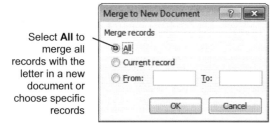

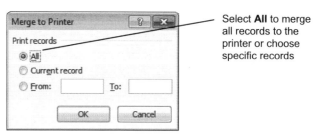

Select **All** to merge all records to the printer or choose specific records

 note

The number of pages will change on the status bar, when the **Merge to New Document** menu option is selected, to display a document for each of the records in the mailing list.

- If the **Merge to Document** menu option is selected, save the merged document with a different name to the main document (the main document can be used again with the same or different mailing list at a future date).
- If the **Merge to Printer** menu option is selected, without completing the mail merge procedure, save the document with the same name.

5.2.2 Printing a Mail Merge Document

To print a merged document (e.g. letter or labels), do the following:

- Open the merged letter or merged labels.
- From the **File Menu**, select the **Print** command (or press the keyboard combination of **CTRL + P**)..
- The **Print** properties opens.
- Select **Print** to print the mail merge outputs (letters and/or labels).

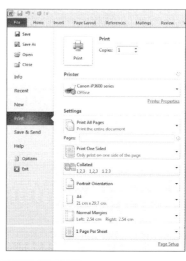

Practice Sequence

1	Open the **activities** document.	☐
2	Complete the mail merge process by merging the letter with all of the records in the mailing list to a new document.	☐
3	Save the merged document as **Activmerge.doc**.	☐
4	Print the merged **Activmerge** document and close.	☐
5	Open the **Labels** document and complete the mail merge process by merging to a new document.	☐
6	Save the merged labels as **Merged Labels**.	☐
7	Print the merged **Merged Labels** document.	☐
8	Close the document.	☐

3

Section 6 ▶   Preparing Outputs

6.1   Setup

Output refers to the way that a document is viewed, either on-screen or as printed hard copy. Both types of output require preparation by choosing an appropriate output format, such as changing orientation and margins or printing to a specific number of pages. It is good practice to check document text and correct any errors to ensure the finished document is presented to a professional standard.

In this section, you will learn about the following:

- Changing a document's orientation: portrait and landscape.
- Changing paper size of a document.
- Changing the margins of an entire document: top, bottom, left and right.
- Recognising good practice in adding new pages: inserting a page break rather than using the Enter key.
- Inserting and deleting a page break in a document.
- Adding and editing text in headers and footers.
- Add fields in headers and footers: date, page number information and file name.
- Apply automatic page numbering to a document.

6.1.1   Orientation

Orientation refers to the shape of the paper being used. It can be either Portrait or Landscape. The default orientation in Word is Portrait. Portrait orientation is taller than it is wide. Landscape orientation is wider than it is tall. You may need to change the orientation so that text and objects fit on the page. Changing the orientation of the document not only enhances the presentation of the printed output, it can also save paper. See the examples below.

This is
displayed
in portrait

This is displayed
in landscape

To change orientation, do the following:

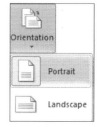

- From the **Page Layout** tab and the **Page Setup** group, select the **Orientation** command.
- Select the required orientation – Portrait or Landscape.

6.1.2   Paper Size

The default paper size is A4 (21cm x 29.7cm in portrait orientation). The paper size can be altered to another of your choice, such as A5, B3 or a variety of other sizes suitable for the intended printed output.

To change the paper size, do the following:

- From the **Page Layout** tab and the **Page Setup** group, select the **Size** command.

  A drop-down menu opens, displaying a variety of paper sizes.

- The default paper size is A4. Select the required paper size.

- To see further size options, select the **More Paper sizes** command at the bottom of the menu.

  The **Page Setup** window opens with the **Paper** tab the active tab.

- Select the **Paper size** arrow and choose a paper size from the list.

- Click **OK**.

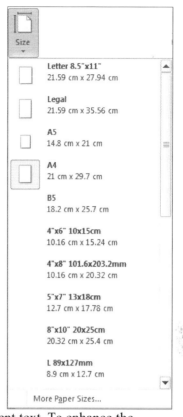

6.1.3 Margins

Margins are the space between the edge of the paper and the document text. To enhance the layout of the printed document the top, bottom, left and right margins can all be increased or decreased if required.

To change margins, do the following:

- From the **Page Layout** tab and the **Page Setup** group, select the **Margins** command.

  A drop-down menu opens.

- From this menu, you can select normal default margin settings, or select from the list of settings.

- To see further margin options, select **Custom Margins**.

  The **Page Setup** window opens with the **Margins** tab the active tab.

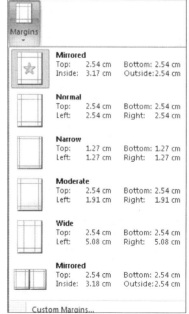

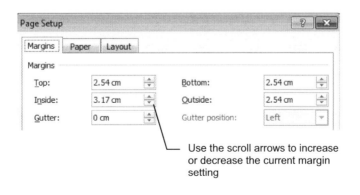

Use the scroll arrows to increase or decrease the current margin setting

- Use the scroll arrows to increase or decrease the current margin measurements for the Top, Bottom, Left and Right margins.

- Click **OK**.

6.1.4 Good Practice when Adding New Pages

It is good practice to use page breaks to create new pages within a document rather than using carriage returns (the Enter key). When the Enter key is pressed it creates a paragraph mark which can be formatted in the same way as text. If the paragraph marks are deleted then text beneath the paragraph marks will move up the page. If a page break is inserted, text and objects can be inserted, edited and formatted without affecting previous or subsequent pages in the document. A page break can be deleted if no longer required.

6.1.5 Inserting and Deleting Page Breaks

To insert and delete page breaks, do the following:

Inserting

- Position the cursor where the page break should be inserted.
- Select the **Insert** tab from the ribbon.
- Select **Page Break** from the **Pages** section.

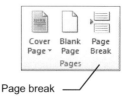

Page break

A page break will be inserted and the cursor will appear at the top of the new page.

Alternatively Position the cursor where the page break should be inserted and then hold down the **CTRL** key and press **Enter**.

Deleting

- Select the **Show/Hide** command from the **Home** tab/**Paragraph** group so that you can see the page breaks in the document.

- Position the cursor in front of the page break and press the **Delete** key.
- The page break is deleted.

6.1.6 Headers and Footers

Headers appear at the top of the page and footers appear at the bottom of the page. A header or footer can display information that you type in, such as your name or copyright information, or display page numbers or dates.

To create a header and a footer, do the following:

- From the **Insert** tab and the **Header & Footer** group, select the **Header** or **Footer** command.

- Select a built-in header/footer style or select **Edit Header** or **Edit Footer** to start entering the header or footer information.

  The **Header** or **Footer** area opens above your document, ready for you to enter the header/footer information.

- Press the **TAB** key once to align the cursor to the centre or twice to align the cursor to the right.

- Enter the required header text.

- The **Header & Footer Tools** contextual tab becomes active and displays the **Design** tab commands. From this ribbon bar, you can choose to insert page numbers, number of pages, date, time, file path (location) and file name.

- To switch between the header and footer area, select **Go to Footer** or **Go to Header**.

The **Header & Footer Tools**
become active on the ribbon

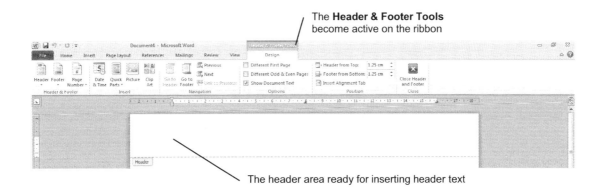

The header area ready for inserting header text

- To close the Header and Footer area, click away from the header/footer area into the main document.

Editing and Deleting a Header or Footer

To edit part of a header or footer, do the following:

- From the **Insert** tab and the **Header & Footer** group select the **Header** or the **Footer** command.
- Select **Edit Header** (or **Edit Footer**).
- Position the cursor within the header/footer text and make changes as required (header/footer text can be edited in the same way as ordinary document text).

To delete part of a header or footer, do the following:

- Select the header/footer text to be deleted.
- Press the **Delete** key on the keyboard.

To remove a header or footer, do the following:

- From the **Insert** tab and the **Header & Footer** group, select the **Header** or the **Footer** command.
- Select **Remove Header** or **Remove Footer**.
  This command removes the entire header or footer.
- To close the header and footer area, click away from the header/footer area into the main document.

6.1.7 Inserting Fields

Fields are items of header or footer data, such as dates and filename fields that update automatically.

To insert fields, do the following:

- From the **Insert** tab and the **Header & Footer** group select the **Header** or the **Footer** command.
- Select **Edit Header** (or **Edit Footer**).
  The **Header/Footer** area opens, ready for you to insert the field or fields.
- Press the **TAB** key once to align the cursor to the centre of the page or twice to align the cursor on the right of the page.
  The **Header & Footer Tools** contextual tab becomes active and displays the **Design** tab commands. From this ribbon bar, you can choose to insert page numbers and the date and time. From the Quick Parts menu, you can insert fields, such as, number of pages, date, time, file path (location) and file name.

- From the **Text** group, select **Quick Parts**.

Select **Page Number** to insert
page numbering information

Select **Date & Time** to insert
the current date/time

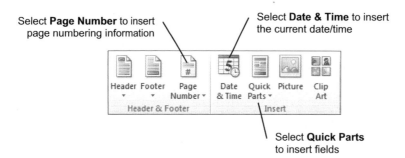

Select **Quick Parts**
to insert fields

- Select **Field….**

Select **Field...**

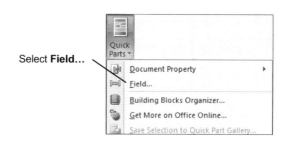

The **Field** window opens.

- Select a category from the **Categories** drop down menu (e.g. **Document Information** or **Date and Time**).
- Select a field name from the list of **Field names** (e.g. from the **Document Information** category, select **FileName** or **NumPages**, or from the **Date and Time** category, select **CreateDate**).
- Format the field if required in the **Field properties** section.
- Click **OK**.

File Name or Number of Pages

Select a category

Add path
(file location)

Select a field name,
such as **FileName**

Select **NumPages**
to insert the number
of pages in the
document

Change
properties

Date or Time

Select a category

Select a Field name

Select a date
and/or time
format

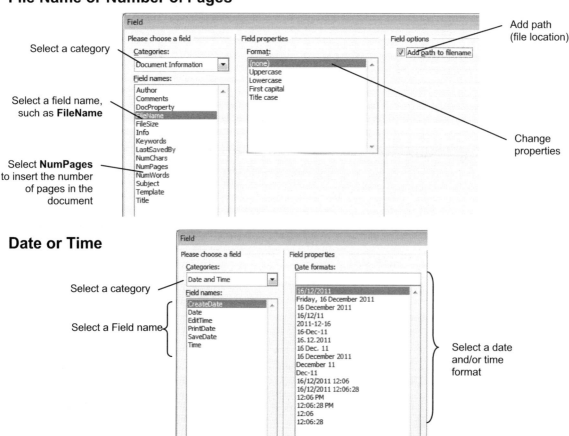

Example

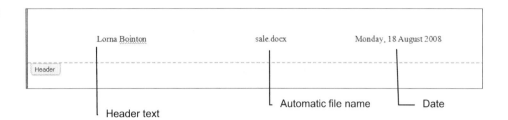

Lorna Bointon   sale.docx   Monday, 18 August 2008

Header

|___ Header text   └─ Automatic file name   └─ Date

Alternatively, to insert a date and/or time, select the **Date & Time** command.
The **Date and Time** window opens.
- Select a date format and a language.
- Ensure that the **Update automatically** checkbox is selected (there is a tick in the box).
- Click **OK**.

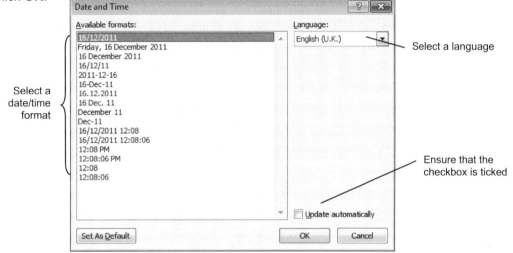

Select a date/time format

Select a language

Ensure that the checkbox is ticked

To switch between the header and footer area, do the following:
- Select **Go to Footer** or **Go to Header**.

To close the header/footer, do the following:
- Click away from the header/footer area into the main document.

6.1.8 Inserting Automatic Page Numbers

To insert automatic page numbers, do the following:
- From the **Insert** tab and the **Header & Footer** group, select **Page Number**.
- From the menu, select a page number option, such as **Top of Page**, **Bottom of Page** or **Current Position**.

  Each of these menu options will open a further sub-menu with page number formats displayed, such as simple number formats or **X of Y** (e.g. Page 1 of 3).
- Select a number format.
- Select **Format Page Numbers.**

  The **Page Number Format** window opens.
- Select the **Number Format** arrow and select a number format from the menu.
- In the **Page Numbering** section of the window, select the **Continue from previous section** option button to apply automatic numbering to each page in the document (alternatively, select the **Start at** option button if you want to start page numbering from a specific page).

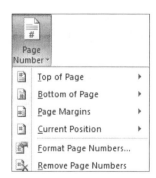

Page Number ▾
- Top of Page   ▶
- Bottom of Page   ▶
- Page Margins   ▶
- Current Position   ▶
- Format Page Numbers...
- Remove Page Numbers

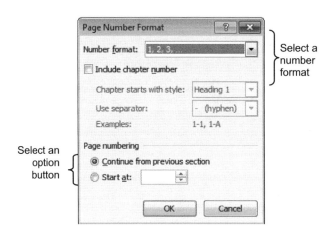

Select a number format

Select an option button

- Click **OK**.

Practice Sequence

1	Open the **sale** document.	☐
2	Change the top and bottom margins to 2cm and the left and right margins to 1.5cm.	☐
3	Check that the paper size is A4.	☐
4	Ensure that the orientation is Portrait.	☐
5	Create a new page after the final paragraph of shaded and bordered text (so that the heading **Profits from last jumble sale** and the tabulated text and the **Helpers** title and table appear on the second page).	☐
6	Enter a left aligned header with your name.	☐
7	Enter a centre aligned header with an automatically updating filename field (do not include the path).	☐
8	Enter a right aligned header with an automatically updating date field.	☐
9	Enter a centre aligned footer with a number of pages field.	☐
10	Edit the header by removing the date field.	☐
11	Edit the footer by inserting a left aligned date field and deleting the number of pages field.	☐
12	Apply centre aligned automatic page numbers.	☐
13	Save and close the **sale** document.	☐

6.2   Checking and Printing

In this section you will learn about the following:

- Spell checking a document and make changes: correcting spelling errors and deleting repeated words.
- Adding words to a built-in custom dictionary using a spell-checker.
- Previewing a document.
- Printing a document from an installed printer using output options: entire document, specific pages and number of copies.

6.2.1 Checking

It is important to check text within a document. Incorrect text appears unprofessional and affects the overall presentation of the document. It can also affect the understanding and assimilation of the subject matter if the text contains errors.

Therefore, you should do the following:

- Proofread the document text carefully for errors.
- Correct errors where necessary.
- Use the spell check facility to check spelling and grammar.

Checking Spelling

- From the **Review Tab** and the **Proofing** group, select the **Spelling & Grammar** command.

  The **Spelling and Grammar** window opens.

- Unrecognised words (words that are not in the Spelling dictionary) will be displayed and suggestions provided.

- Select a suggestion and then click **Change** if you want to change the spelling of a word to the suggested spelling.

- Select **Change All** to change all occurrences of the word throughout the document.

- Select **Ignore Once** if you know that the spelling is correct (such as proper names) or **Ignore All** if you want to ignore all occurrences of the word through the document.

- Repeated words are picked up within the document and displayed in the **Repeated word** box.

- Select **Delete** to delete repeated words (or click **Ignore Once** if you wish to keep the repeated word).

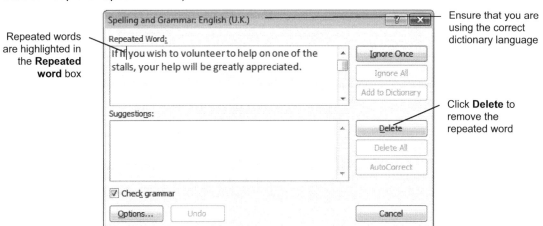

Repeated words are highlighted in the **Repeated word** box

Ensure that you are using the correct dictionary language

Click **Delete** to remove the repeated word

- When the **Spelling** tool has completed the spell check, a window will open.
- Click **OK**.

6.2.2 Adding Words to a Dictionary

The Spelling tool uses a built-in dictionary against which it matches words and provides suggestions. If the Spelling tool does not recognise the spelling of the word, it may provide unsuitable suggestions. Words can be added to the dictionary if required. This is useful if you use unfamiliar words, such as medical, technical or scientific terms within a document.

Words can be added to the dictionary through the **Spelling and Grammar** window or through the **File Menu** and **Word Options**.

If the spelling check is complete, you will be unable to reopen the **Spelling & Grammar** window and so will have to open **Options** from the **File Menu**.

To add words to a dictionary, do the following:

* From the **Spelling & Grammar** window, select the **Options** button (the **Proofing** tab is selected).

    Alternatively, from the **File Menu** select **Options**. In the **Word Options** window, select the **Proofing** tab.

* Select **Custom Dictionaries**.

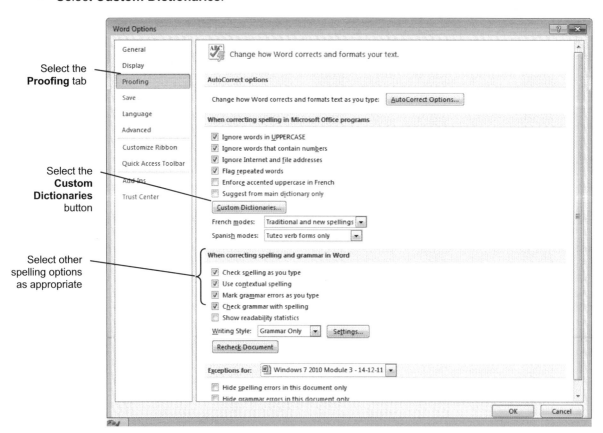

The **Custom Dictionaries** window opens.

* Click **Edit Word List**.

- Enter the word into the **Word(s)** box.
- Click **Add**.

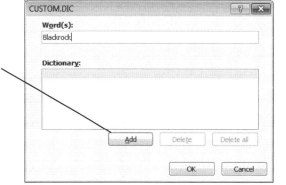

Select **Add** to
add the word to
the dictionary

- Click **OK** (three times to exit Word Options).

6.2.3 **Previewing a Document**

It is good practice to check the layout of a document before printing it.

To preview a document, do the following:

- From the **File Menu**, select **Print**.
  The document is displayed in the **Preview** pane.

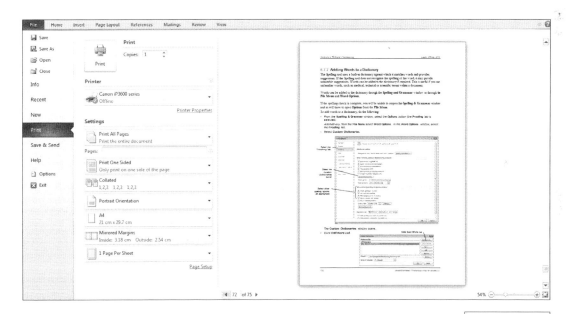

- Select the view arrows to view each page of the document.

- To zoom in and out, move the slider towards the + cross to zoom in and the - minus sign to zoom out.
- Close Print Preview by selecting the **File** menu.

6.2.4 **Printing**

There are various options that you can choose when printing. For example, you can print the entire document (which may contain multiple pages) or print specific pages and/or a specific number of copies. The default setting is for printing one copy.

To print, do the following:

- From the **File Menu**, select **Print**.
- From the print menu, select the **Print** button to print a document without changing settings or press the keyboard shortcut **CTRL + P**).
- Make changes to print settings before printing:

Entire Document

- Select the **Print All Pages** option

Specific Pages

- From the **Print** menu, enter page numbers in the **Pages** box.
- The page numbers should be separated by a comma if you want non-adjacent pages or separate with a hyphen if you want to print a page range (for example, **1, 4, 6** will print pages 1, 4 and 6 only and exclude pages 2, 3 and 5. However, if **1-6** is entered, pages **1 to 6** will be printed, including pages 2, 3 and 5).

Number of Copies

- From the **Print** menu, use the scroll arrows on the **Copies** list box to increase/decrease the required number of printed copies.

Practice Sequence	
1	Open the **sale** document.
2	Check the spelling of text within the document and correct any errors.
3	Add the word **Blackrock** to the custom dictionary.
4	Preview the document.
5	Print two copies of page 1 of the document.
6	Save and close the **sale** document.

module **4**

Spreadsheets

module 4
Spreadsheets

Module 4 Spreadsheets requires the candidate to understand the concept of spreadsheets and to demonstrate an ability to use a spreadsheet to produce accurate work outputs.

The candidate shall be able to:

- Work with spreadsheets and save them in different file formats.

- Choose built-in options such as the Help function within the application to enhance productivity.

- Enter data into cells and use good practice in creating lists. Select, sort and copy, move and delete data.

- Edit rows and columns in a worksheet. Copy, move, delete and appropriately rename worksheets.

- Create mathematical and logical formulas using standard spreadsheet functions. Use good practice in formula creation and recognise error values in formulas.

- Format numbers and text content in a spreadsheet.

- Choose, create and format charts to communicate information meaningfully.

- Adjust spreadsheet page settings and check and correct spreadsheet content before finally printing spreadsheet.

Introduction

What is a Spreadsheet?

A spreadsheet is used for mathematical calculations and analysis, such as to plot figures to find profits and losses based on income and expenditure, and for communicating information through charts and graphs. A spreadsheet consists of a grid containing rows and columns. Rows are numbered (e.g. **1**) and columns are lettered (e.g. **A**). The intersection between a row and a column is called a **cell**. Cells are named with the column letter and row number (e.g. **A1**). Cell names are referred to as **cell references**. A range of cell references (e.g. A1:A10) is called a **cell range**.

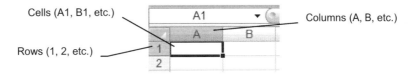

Spreadsheets use cell references in formulas and functions, rather than figures, which makes it easier to modify and update data in a spreadsheet. For example, =A1+B1 will total the contents of cells A1 and B1. When data is modified, or rows/columns deleted or inserted, formulas and functions will automatically update to reflect the modifications. Formulas can be copied (referred to as **replicating**) across or down over subsequent cells and the cell reference will change to match the cell to which the formula is replicated. A normal cell reference is called a **relative cell reference**, because it is relative to the cell to which the formula is being copied. Sometimes, an **absolute cell reference** may be required in a formula if the cell reference should not change during replication, but should remain constant. An example of this is in a spreadsheet which uses a cell, such as VAT which will remain constant. A formula using absolute cell references looks like this: =A1+$B$1. The relative cell reference A1 will change when copied downwards to cells A2 and A3, but the absolute cell will remain constant and refer to cell B1.

Spreadsheets should have relevant and appropriate row and column headings to identify data.

Section 1 ►   Using the Application

An **application** refers to the software package that is used to perform a task. The application that will be used for this training manual is Microsoft Office Excel 2010. This is a comprehensive spreadsheets package, capable of creating complex spreadsheets consisting of formulas, functions, charts and graphs.

1.1   Working with Spreadsheets

A spreadsheet is a grid consisting of rows and columns. Each spreadsheet file (also referred to as a *workbook*) can contain many worksheets. Spreadsheet files may be saved in a variety of formats, for use in different applications.

In this section, you will learn about the following.
- Opening and closing a spreadsheet application.
- Closing a spreadsheet.
- Creating a new spreadsheet.
- Switching between open spreadsheets.
- Saving a spreadsheet to a location on a drive and with a different name.
- Saving a spreadsheet in another format, such as template, text file, software specific file extension and version number.

1.1.1   Opening a Spreadsheet Application

Excel is a spreadsheet package that comes as part of the Microsoft Office 2010 suite. This application will either be displayed as an icon on the Desktop of your computer or found in the Start menu.

To open Excel, do the following:
- Select the **Start** menu.
- Select **All Programs**.
- Select **Microsoft Office** and then select **Microsoft Excel 2010**.

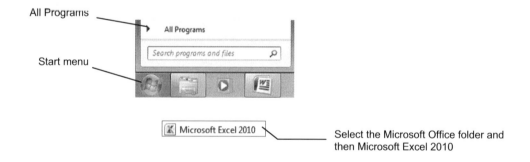

All Programs

Start menu

Microsoft Excel 2010   Select the Microsoft Office folder and then Microsoft Excel 2010

note   To keep the taskbar visible, point and right-click on the taskbar and, from the pop-up menu, click Properties. The Taskbar and Start Menu Properties window opens. Click the box to the left of 'Auto-hide the taskbar' to uncheck this option

Microsoft Excel 2010 opens.

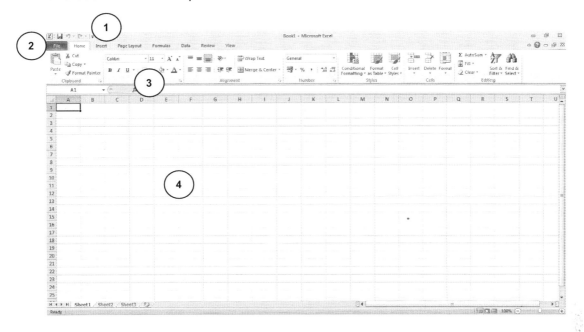

The screen layout will display the following:

①   The Quick Access Toolbar.

②   The File menu.

③   The ribbon.

④   A new, blank spreadsheet.

1.1.2   Closing a Spreadsheet Application

To close Excel, do the following:

- Select the **File menu**.
- Select **Exit**.

  The Excel program will close.

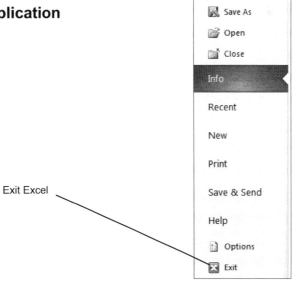

Exit Excel

Alternatively, select the **Close X** button in the top right corner of the title bar.

1.1.3   Opening a Spreadsheet

To open an existing spreadsheet, do the following:

- Open **Excel**.
- Select the **File menu**.
- Select **Open**.

File menu

The **Open** window opens.

- Select the location of the file by choosing a drive and/or folder from the Navigation Pane.
- Select the file.
- Click **Open**.

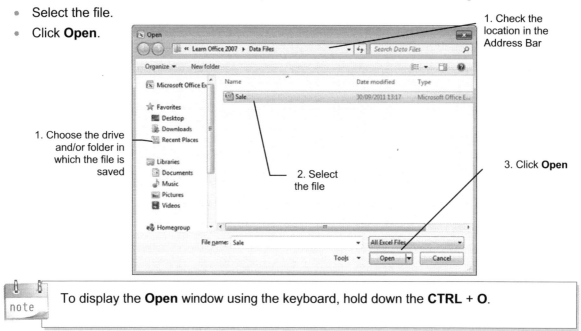

1. Choose the drive and/or folder in which the file is saved

2. Select the file

1. Check the location in the Address Bar

3. Click **Open**

note   To display the **Open** window using the keyboard, hold down the **CTRL + O**.

Opening Recent Documents

Documents that have been opened recently can be accessed by selecting the **File menu** and then **Recent** and then selecting a file from the Recent Documents list.

Select a recently opened file from the **Recent Documents** list

To change the number of documents listed in **Recent Documents**, select the **File menu** and then **Options**. Select the **Advanced** button and, in the **Display** section, enter the number of documents that you want to display.

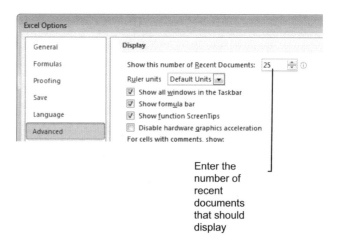

Enter the number of recent documents that should display

1.1.4 Closing a Spreadsheet

To close a spreadsheet, do the following:

- Select the **File menu**.
- Select **Close**.

> **note** If changes have been made to the file, a message will appear asking if you want to save the file before closing.
>
> - Click **Save** to save the file.
> - Click **Don't Save** to close the file without saving.
> - Click **Cancel** to cancel the message and return to the spreadsheet.

1.1.5 Creating a New Spreadsheet

To create a new spreadsheet, do the following:

- Select the **File menu**.
- Select **New**.
  Select **Blank Workbook**.
- Click **Create**.

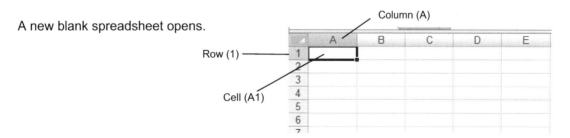

Select **Blank Workbook**

Click
Create

A new blank spreadsheet opens.

Column (A)

Row (1)

Cell (A1)

1.1.6 Saving a Spreadsheet to a Location on a Drive

To save a spreadsheet for the first time, do the following:

- Select the **File menu**.
- Select **Save**.
  The **Save As** window opens.
- Select the correct drive and/or folder from the **Navigation (Folder) Pane**.
- Enter a name in the **File name** box.
- Click **Save**.

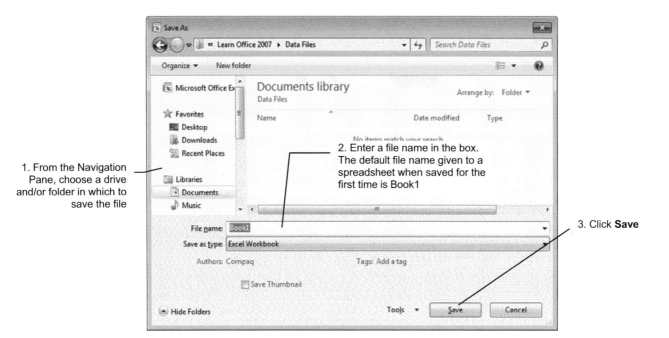

1. From the Navigation Pane, choose a drive and/or folder in which to save the file

2. Enter a file name in the box. The default file name given to a spreadsheet when saved for the first time is Book1

3. Click **Save**

 note

Click the **Save** button on the **Quick Access Toolbar** to save a file.

The keyboard combination to save is **CTRL + S**.

1.1.7 Saving a Spreadsheet with Another Name

To save an existing spreadsheet with a different name, do the following:

- Select the **File menu**.
- Select the **Save As** menu option.
- The **Save As** window opens.
- Select the correct drive and/or folder from the Navigation Pane.
- Ensure that the **Save as type** box displays **Excel Workbook**.
- Enter a name in the **File name** box.
- Click **Save**.

 note

When saving a spreadsheet for the first time, clicking **Save** or **Save As** from the **File** menu will result in the **Save As** window opening. Subsequent changes to a spreadsheet can be saved by selecting the **Save** option from the **File** menu. This will save the spreadsheet with the same name and overwrite the original file.

1.1.8 Saving a Spreadsheet as Another File Type

A spreadsheet can be saved in a variety of different formats. This is useful if the spreadsheet is being opened in another version of Excel or a different spreadsheet program. Some of the common formats are listed below.

Excel Format	
• Spreadsheet (.xlsx)	• Version number (Excel 95-2003 Workbook)
• Text (*.txt)	• Software specific file extension (e.g. *.xls or xlsx)
• Template (.xltx)	

To save the spreadsheet in another file type, do the following:

Text Format (Tab Delimited)

When a spreadsheet is saved as a text file, it loses all of its formatting features and saves in a format that enables it to be opened and viewed as text and values only. Columns of data are separated by tabs and each row ends in a carriage return (Enter).

To save a file in text format, do the following:
- Select the **File menu**.
- Select the **Save As** menu option.
- The **Save As** windows opens.
- Select the **correct** drive and/or folder from the Navigation Pane.
- Enter a file name into the **File name** box.
- Click the **Save as type** arrow.
- Select **Text (Tab Delimited) (*.txt)**.
- Click **Save**.

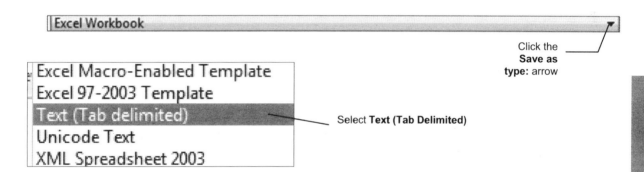

Click the
**Save as
type:** arrow

Select **Text (Tab Delimited)**

Other text formats include **Formatted Text (Space Delimited)** which loses all formatting and in which columns are separated by commas and end with carriage returns; **Text (Unicode)** which can be read in Windows NT Notepad; and **Comma Separated Value** (.csv) which displays text and values as they appear in the active worksheet and converts cells containing formula to text values. Columns of data are separated by commas and rows end in a carriage return. Again, with this format, all formatting is lost but it is a useful format for importing data between applications.

Template

A template contains standard content/formulas that will appear on all sheets in a spreadsheet. A template can be used repeatedly with other spreadsheets. This saves time and effort when creating a new spreadsheet. Templates are saved with a **.xltx** file extension and, unless another location is specified, will automatically save in the following location: **C:\Users\ *user name* \AppData\Roaming\Microsoft\Templates**

To save a spreadsheet as a template, do the following:
- Select the **File menu**.
- Select the **Save As** menu option.
  The **Save As** windows opens.

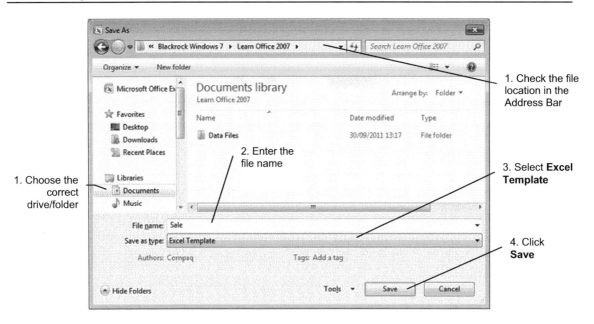

- Select the correct drive and/or folder from the Navigation Pane.
- Enter a file name into the **File name** box.
- Click the **Save as type** arrow.
- Select **Excel Template**.
- Click **Save**.

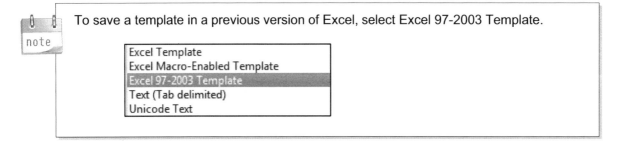

To save a template in a previous version of Excel, select Excel 97-2003 Template.

Excel Template
Excel Macro-Enabled Template
Excel 97-2003 Template
Text (Tab delimited)
Unicode Text

Version Number

Each version of Excel has a different version number. If the spreadsheet needs to be opened and viewed in a previous version of Excel it can be saved with a different version number.

To check the version number of the software on your computer, do the following:

- Select the **File menu** and select **Help**.
- Read the version details in the **About Microsoft Excel** section.

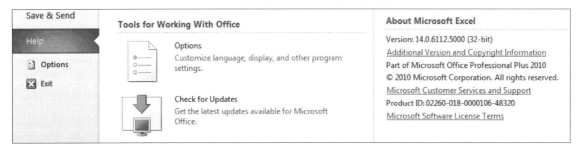

- Check the version – it should be **Microsoft Excel® 2010**.
- Click the **File** menu to close the menu.

To save the spreadsheet with a different version number, do the following:

- Select the **File menu**.
- Select the **Save As** menu command.
  The **Save As** windows opens.
- Select the correct drive and /or folder from the Navigation Pane.
- Enter a file name into the **File name** box.
- Click the **Save as type** arrow.
- Select **Excel 97-2003 Spreadsheet** to save a copy of the spreadsheet that is fully compatible with Excel 97-2003.
- Click **Save**.

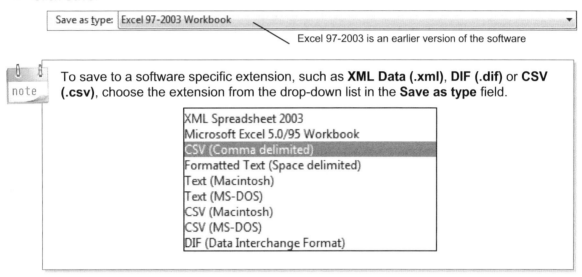

Save as type: Excel 97-2003 Workbook

Excel 97-2003 is an earlier version of the software

note To save to a software specific extension, such as **XML Data (.xml)**, **DIF (.dif)** or **CSV (.csv)**, choose the extension from the drop-down list in the **Save as type** field.

```
XML Spreadsheet 2003
Microsoft Excel 5.0/95 Workbook
CSV (Comma delimited)
Formatted Text (Space delimited)
Text (Macintosh)
Text (MS-DOS)
CSV (Macintosh)
CSV (MS-DOS)
DIF (Data Interchange Format)
```

1.1.9 Switching between Open Spreadsheets

Open spreadsheets will be displayed as tabs on the task bar.

To switch between open spreadsheets, do the following:

- To switch between different spreadsheets within Excel, select the **View** tab.
- In the **Windows** group, select the **Switch Windows** button.
- A tick will display beside the file name of the currently active spreadsheet.
- Click another file name in the menu to make that the active spreadsheet.

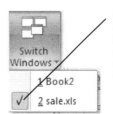

A tick beside the file name indicates that it is the active spreadsheet, currently displayed on screen

note You can also switch between open worksheets or other programs by using the taskbar.

- Open more than one spreadsheet.
- The spreadsheets will be displayed as tabs on the taskbar at the bottom of the screen. When the mouse arrow is hovered over a tab, a thumbnail of the file is displayed (unless using Windows 7 Basic).
- Click a tab and then click the thumbnail to open that spreadsheet.

To switch between open spreadsheets using the keyboard hold down the **ALT** key and press **TAB**.

1.2   Enhancing Productivity

Productivity can be increased by setting user preferences, such as adding a user name and/or creating a default folder from which to open and in which to save all spreadsheets. Using the Help facility can also aid productivity by providing tips and advice on how to use the program effectively.

In this section, you will learn about the following:

- Setting user preferences.
- Using available Help functions.
- Using magnification/zoom tools.
- Restoring and minimising the ribbon.

1.2.1   Setting User Preferences

User preferences refer to the user name and the default location from where opened files are saved to. These can be changed as appropriate so that the user name is different or so that files can be opened or saved in another location.

To set user preferences, do the following:

User Name

- Select the **File menu**.
- Select **Options**.
- Select the **General** command.
- In the **Personalize your copy of Microsoft Office**, position the cursor in the User name box and delete the current user name.
- Enter the new user name.
- Click **OK**.

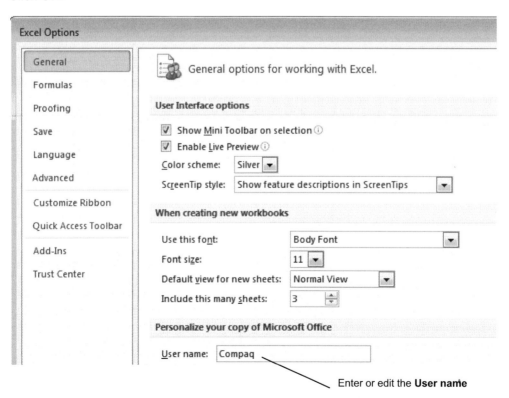

Enter or edit the **User name**

Default File Location

- Select the **File menu**.
- Select **Options**.
- Select the **Save** tab.
- In the **Default File Location** box, enter the required file location from where files will be opened from and saved to.
- Click **OK**.

Enter the file location

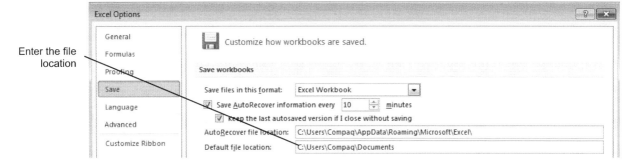

1.2.2 Using the Help Function

The Help function is available to give advice and help on aspects of the software that you are using. This is useful when you are trying to perform an action and don't know how to proceed further. Just ask the Help function a specific question and then select a relevant topic for the answer.

To use the Help function, do the following:

- Select the **Help** button or press the **F1** key.
  The **Excel Help** window opens.

- Select a link to a relevant topic.
  A further set of links will appear that correspond with the selected topic.
- Select a relevant link to refine your search.
- Read the information on the chosen topic.
- Use the **Back** button to go back a step or the **Home** button to return to the first window of Excel Help.

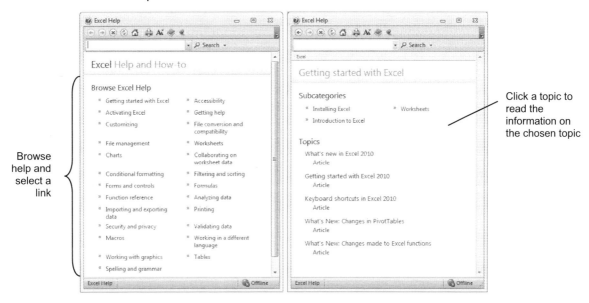

Browse help and select a link

Click a topic to read the information on the chosen topic

- Select **Print** to print a copy of the topic information.

You can also enter specific search criteria into the **Search** box to locate information on specific topics.

To enter search criteria, do the following:
- Enter a question in the **Search** box.
- Click **Search**.

  A list of topic links relating to the search criteria will appear.
- Click a link to view the topic information.

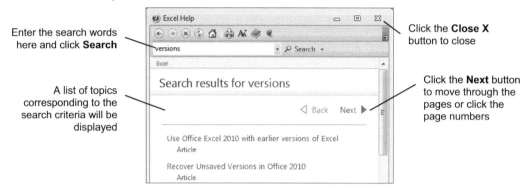

Enter the search words here and click **Search**

A list of topics corresponding to the search criteria will be displayed

Click the **Close X** button to close

Click the **Next** button to move through the pages or click the page numbers

1.2.3 Using Magnification (Zoom)

The magnification tools are used to zoom in and out in a spreadsheet.

To use the magification tools, do the following:
- Select the **View** tab.
- In the **Zoom** group, click the **Zoom** button.

  The **Zoom** window opens.
- Select an option button to change the magnification or type a custom percentage in the **Custom** box.
- Click **OK**.

Select a **Zoom to** option button or select **Custom** and enter a percentage by which to increase or decrease the magnification

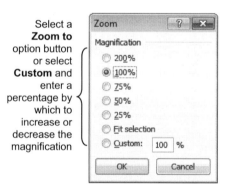

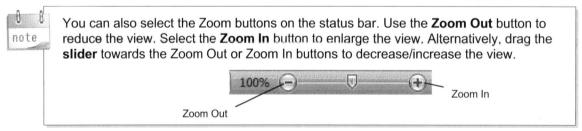

You can also select the Zoom buttons on the status bar. Use the **Zoom Out** button to reduce the view. Select the **Zoom In** button to enlarge the view. Alternatively, drag the **slider** towards the Zoom Out or Zoom In buttons to decrease/increase the view.

Zoom Out

Zoom In

1.2.4 Minimising and Restoring the Ribbon

The ribbon bar can be minimised and then restored if required.

To minimise and restore the ribbon, do the following;

Minimising the Ribbon

- Right-click the ribbon bar.
- Select **Minimize the Ribbon**.

  The ribbon is hidden.

Click **Minimize the Ribbon**

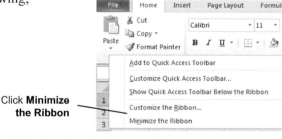

Restoring the Ribbon

- Right-click the bar containing the tabs.
- Click **Minimize the Ribbon** (note how a tick is displayed beside the menu command to indicate that it is active).

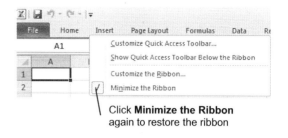

Click **Minimize the Ribbon** again to restore the ribbon

The ribbon is restored and is visible again.

Practice Sequence

1	Open Excel and create a new spreadsheet.	☐
2	Save this spreadsheet as **sale** in the default spreadsheet format in a default folder location that you specify.	☐
3	Save another copy of the spreadsheet in **Text** format with the filename **saleTXT**.	☐
4	Reopen **Sale** and practise switching between the two spreadsheets.	☐
5	Zoom the **Sale** spreadsheet to **80%** and save.	☐
6	Close both spreadsheets.	☐
7	Use the **Help** function to find information on saving a spreadsheet as a template.	☐
8	Open the **Sale** spreadsheet and save in template format (ensure that it saves in the correct drive/folder).	☐
9	Close the template file.	☐
10	Open a new spreadsheet and save with the name **version** in **Excel 97-2003** format.	☐
11	Close all spreadsheets and exit Excel.	☐

4

Section 2 ► Cells

A spreadsheet is a grid comprising rows and columns. The intersection between a row and a column is called a **cell**. Cells are named with the grid reference referring to its location; this is called a **cell reference**. For example, the cell named A1 refers to the cell positioned in column A and row 1. Multiple cells are referred to as a **cell range**. An example of a cell range is A1:A12 (a cell range is separated by a colon).

2.1 Inserting and Selecting Data

Data refers to text, dates and numerical figures. Each of these data items can be entered into a cell and then selected so that editing or formatting can be performed.

> In this section, you will learn about the following:
>
> - Understanding that a cell in a worksheet should contain only one element of data (for example, first name detail in one cell, surname detail in adjacent cell).
>
> - Recognising good practice in creating lists: avoiding blank rows and columns in the main body of the list, inserting a blank row before the Total row and ensuring cells bordering list are blank.
>
> - Entering a number, date or text in a cell.
>
> - Selecting a cell, range of adjacent cells, range of non-adjacent cells or an entire worksheet.

2.1.1 Good Practice

A cell should only contain one element of data, such as a first name in one cell and a last name in an adjacent cell. This enables the user to edit or format cell elements individually, e.g. with different fonts, sizes and styles, or sort columns in a specified order.

	A	B
1	First Name	Last Name
2	Anne	Jones
3	Bill	Smith

When creating numerical lists, it is good practice to avoid creating blank rows and columns in the main body of the list. This is because a blank row or column can affect formula results. However, to enhance clarity, it is good practice to insert a blank row before a Total row to separate the main list from the formula result. Any cells bordering a numerical list used in a calculation should remain blank. This ensures that the data and the results are clearly defined and can be easily identified and understood.

JUMBLE SALE	
ITEM	PRICE
Dress	£2.99
Vase	£1.50
Decanter set	£3.45
TOTAL	£7.94

2.1.2 Entering Data

The default position for text within a cell is left aligned. The default position for numbers and dates is right aligned. Numbers will not display decimal precision unless formatted to a specific number of places. For example, when you enter 1.50, it will display as 1.5.

To enter text, numbers or dates into a cell, do the following:

- Click a cell to select it and then enter text or a number directly into the cell.
- Press **Enter** to complete the entry.

  Alternatively, position the cursor in the **Formula bar** and enter the data.

  Press **Enter** to complete the entry.

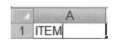

2.1.3 Selecting Cells

A cell must be selected before data can be entered, edited or formatted. This may entail selecting a single cell or a range of adjacent or non-adjacent cells.

To select a cell or cells, do the following:

Single Cell

- Click a cell to select it. A dark border displays around a selected cell.

Adjacent Cell Range

- Select the first cell and then, holding down the left mouse button, drag over the cells to be selected and release. The first cell in the selected range appears to be unselected.

ITEM	PRICE	
Dress	£2.99	
Vase	£1.50	
Decanter Set	£3.45	

Non-Adjacent Cell Range

- Select the first cell or range of cells and, holding down the **CTRL** key, click the cell or drag over the cells to be selected and release.

	A	B	C
1	ITEM	PRICE	DONATED BY:
2	Dress	£2.99	Mrs Jones
3	Vase	£1.50	Mr Brown
4	Decanter Set	£3.45	Miss Smith

Entire Worksheet

- Select the button on the top left of the spreadsheet (above row number 1 and to the left of column A). All cells in the worksheet will be selected.
  Alternatively, press **CTRL + A**.

Click away from a cell range to remove the selection.

Practice Sequence

A spreadsheet containing the data shown below is also provided on CD for your use. Note that the spreadsheet refers to profits from Jumble Sales.

1   Open Excel and then open the **sale** spreadsheet.   ☐

     Check the data on the right has been inserted in the correct columns and rows (don't worry if the data overlaps; you will adjust column widths later).   ☐

2

	A	B
1	PROFITS 1ST QTR 2008	
2	EXPENDITURE	
3	Transport costs	15
4	Venue hire	50
5	Refreshment Costs	20
6	Other expenses	50
7	Total Expenditure	
8	SALES	
9	Entrance Fees	50
10	Sales of goods	650
11	Refreshment Sales	60
12	Total Sales	

3   Select cells A1 and cell B3.   ☐

4   Select the cell range A1:B12.   ☐

5   Remove the selection.   ☐

6   Close the **sales** spreadsheet.   ☐

2.2   Editing and Sorting

In this section, you will learn about the following:

- Editing cell content and modify existing cell content.
- Using the undo and redo commands.
- Using the search command for specific content in a worksheet.
- Using the replace command for specific content in a worksheet.
- Sorting a cell range by one criterion in ascending or descending numeric order and ascending or descending alphabetic order.

2.2.1   Editing Cells

Cell content can be edited or modified by positioning the cursor within a cell and making modifications, such as entering characters or deleting characters, or by selecting a cell and editing the contents in the Formula Bar.

To edit or modify cell content, do the following:

- Double-click a cell to position the cursor within the cell (the cursor will appear wherever the insertion point is positioned when you double-click).

  Alternatively, select a cell and then position the cursor on the Formula Bar either in front, in the middle or behind the cell contents.

- Delete characters by positioning the cursor in front of a character and pressing **Delete** (the **Delete** key deletes characters to the right of the current cursor position) or by positioning the cursor behind a character and pressing **Backspace** (the **Backspace** key deletes characters to the left of the current cursor position).

- Enter characters by positioning the cursor in the correct position and then typing.

- To replace the whole contents of a cell, select the cell and type over existing contents.

2.2.2   Using the Undo and Redo Commands

If a mistake is made when entering, editing or deleting data, it can be corrected by using the undo button. To redo the action, the redo button can be used.

To use undo and redo, do the following:

- To undo an action, click the **Undo** button from the **Quick Access Toolbar** (or press **CTRL + Z**).

- To see a list of actions, click the arrow and select an action from the list. Any actions that exist before the selected action will also be undone.

The **Redo** button displays as the **Repeat** button until the Undo command is used

Select the Undo arrow to see a list of actions

Clear

Typing

Cancel

- To redo an action, click the **Redo** button from the **Quick Access Toolbar** (or press **CTRL + Y**).

 note   The Redo button displays as a repeat button, until the Undo button is utilised. When the Undo button is used, the Redo button becomes active.

Undo   Redo

2.2.3 Searching

Finding information in a spreadsheet can be time consuming if it is a lengthy spreadsheet containing lots of data. Using the Search command facilitates the process as it will find specific information throughout the spreadsheet in one action.

To search for information, do the following:

- On the **Home** tab, click the **Find & Select** command from the **Editing** group (or press **CTRL + F** to open the **Find** window).
- Select **Find** from the menu.
  The **Find** window opens.
- Enter the search word or phrase into the **Find what** box.

Enter the search word(s) here

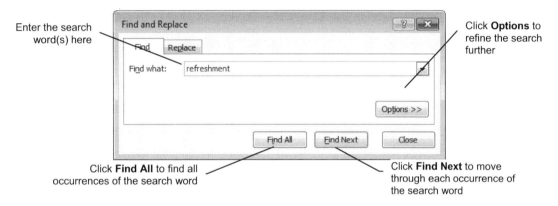

Click **Options** to refine the search further

Click **Find All** to find all occurrences of the search word

Click **Find Next** to move through each occurrence of the search word

- Select the **Options>>** button to refine the search further.
  - In this section of the **Find** window, you can do the following:
  - Search within a sheet or a workbook (if the workbook contains many sheets).
  - Search by rows or columns.
  - Look in formulas, values or comments.
  - Match the case of search word (upper/lower case)
  - Match entire cell contents or only part of a cell (e.g. if you select this checkbox and enter **Refreshment** as the search word it will find cells containing the word **Refreshment** but will not find **Refreshment Costs** or **Refreshment Sales**).

Choose to match case or match entire cell contents or part of a cell

Refine the search by looking within a sheet or a workbook. Search by rows or columns. Look in Formulas, values or comments

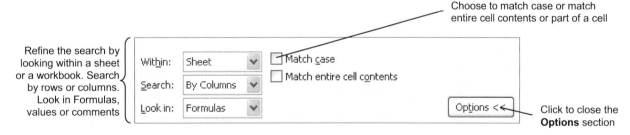

Click to close the **Options** section

- Press **Find Next** to find the first occurrence of the search word(s) or **Find All** to find all occurrences of the search word(s).

Find All will list all occurrences of the search word in the sheet (or workbook if this option is selected)

- Click **Close** to close the **Find** window.

2.2.4 **Replacing**

It can be time consuming to replace the contents of multiple cells with another value if the spreadsheet is lengthy and contains many rows and columns of data. If the search word appears many times, it is easier to use the Replace command to replace the contents of the cell with a specified value throughout the spreadsheet.

To replace the contents of cells, do the following:

- On the **Home** tab, click the **Find & Select** command from the **Editing** group (or press **CTRL + H** to open the **Replace** window).
- Select **Replace** from the menu.
  The **Replace** window opens.

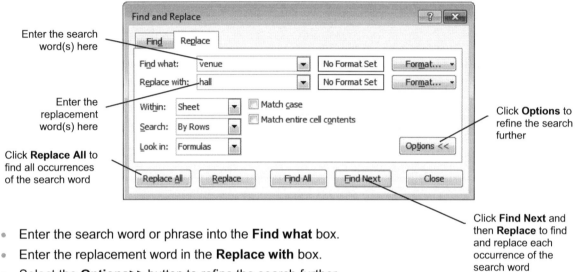

- Enter the search word or phrase into the **Find what** box.
- Enter the replacement word in the **Replace with** box.
- Select the **Options>>** button to refine the search further.
- In this section of the **Find** window, you can do the following:
  - ▷ Search within a sheet or a workbook (if the workbook contains many sheets).
  - ▷ Search by rows or columns.
  - ▷ Look in formulas, values or comments.
  - ▷ Match the case of the entered replacement word (upper/lower case).
  - ▷ Match entire cell contents or only part of a cell (e.g. if you select this checkbox and enter **Refreshment** as the search word it will find and replace cells containing only the word **Refreshment** but will not find and replace the cells containing **Refreshment Costs** or **Refreshment Sales**).

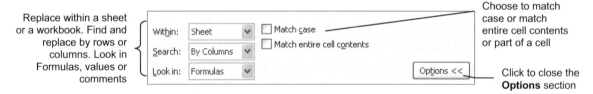

- Press **Find Next** to find the first occurrence of the search word(s) and then press **Replace** or select **Replace All** to replace all occurrences of the search word(s) with the replacement word.
- When **Replace All** is selected, a message window opens informing you of the number of replacements that have been made.
- Click **OK**.
- Click **Close** to close the **Replace** window.

2.2.5 Sorting

Data can be sorted to display in ascending or descending order in either numerical or alphabetical order. See the examples below.

Alphabetical (Ascending, A–Z)

Clothes
Ornaments
Shoes
Toys

Alphabetical (Descending, Z–A)

Toys
Shoes
Ornaments
Clothes

Numerical (Ascending, smallest–largest)

£1.99
£2.50
£2.99
£3.00
£3.50

Numerical (Descending, largest–smallest)

£3.50
£3.00
£2.99
£2.50
£1.99

To sort data, do the following:

Numerical Order

- Select the numerical data to be sorted (you must also include adjacent cells in the selection if these cells are to be sorted alongside the numerical data).
- From the **Home** tab. click **Sort & Filter** from the **Editing** group.
- Select **Sort Smallest to Largest** for ascending order or **Sort Largest to Smallest** for descending order.

Alphabetical Order

- Select the text to be sorted (you must also include adjacent cells in the selection if these cells are to be sorted alongside the text).
- From the **Home** tab, click **Sort & Filter** from the **Editing** group.
- Select **Sort A to Z** for ascending order or **Sort Z to A** for descending order.

Practice Sequence

1	Open Excel and the spreadsheet called **sale**.	☐
2	Edit the title in cell A1 so that it reads **PROFIT 1ˢᵗ QTR JAN – MAR 2008**.	☐
3	Modify cell A8 to read **INCOME**.	☐
4	Using the Search and Replace command, find all occurrences of the word **Venue** and replace with the word **Hall**. Ensure that the case is matched.	☐
5	Select the cell range A3:B6 (start the selection from B6 and drag backwards up to A3 so that the Sort command identifies that it is the numerical data that should be sorted).	☐
6	Sort this cell range in descending order (largest–smallest).	☐
7	Select the cell range A9:B11 (start the selection from cell A9 so that the Sort command identifies that the sort should be performed on the text).	☐
8	Sort this cell range in ascending order (A–Z).	☐
9	Save and close the **sale** spreadsheet.	☐

2.3   Copying, Moving and Deleting

The contents of a single cell or a range of cells can be duplicated or moved within a worksheet or between open worksheets. Values in cells can be copied to other cells or, if sequential numbers or months, days or dates, are required these can be incremented by using the AutoFill tool (for example, if you type in Monday and then copy this across or down other cells, the data entry will be incremented to display as Tuesday, Wednesday, etc).

Cells containing formula, that use cell references, can be replicated across other cells. Spreadsheet data can be updated by deleting outdated cell contents.

In this section, you will learn about the following:

- Copying the content of a cell and a cell range within a worksheet, between worksheets and between open spreadsheets.

- Using the AutoFill tool/copy handle tool to copy and increment data entries.

- Moving the contents of a cell and a cell range within a worksheet, between worksheets and between open spreadsheets.

- Deleting cell contents.

2.3.1   Copying and Moving Cell Contents

To copy or move cell contents within or between worksheets, do the following:

Within a Worksheet

- To **copy** the contents of a cell, select the cell (or range of cells) and then, from the **Home** tab, click **Copy** from the **Clipboard** group (or press **CTRL + C**).

- Select the destination cell within the worksheet and click **Paste** (or press **CTRL + V**).

   The duplicated cell contents will appear in the new position.

- To *move* cell contents, follow the procedure above but click **Cut** (scissors) from the **Clipboard** group at Step 1 (or press **CTRL + X**).

note
Cell contents can be copied or moved **between** worksheets by following the procedure above, but open a new worksheet by clicking a **Sheet tab**, before pasting the contents in the new destination.

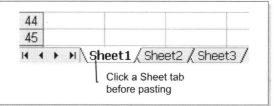

Click a Sheet tab before pasting

Between Spreadsheets

- Open the required spreadsheet files. Both files will be displayed as tabs on the taskbar at the bottom of the screen.

- Ensure that the spreadsheet containing the cell contents to be copied, is the active spreadsheet.

- To **copy** cell contents, select the cell or cell range and then, from the **Home** tab, click **Copy** from the **Clipboard** group.

- Click the other spreadsheet on the taskbar or select the **View** tab and **Switch Windows**.

- Choose the other spreadsheet from the list and ensure that the correct worksheet is displayed.

- Click the mouse in the destination cell.

- From the **Home** tab, in the **Clipboard** group, click **Paste**.

   The cell contents will be duplicated in the selected position within the spreadsheet.

- To *move* cell contents to another spreadsheet, repeat the above procedure but click Cut (scissors) at Step 3.

---

note You can also copy, cut and paste cell contents within and between spreadsheets by right-clicking and selecting a command from the shortcut menu or by using the Drag and Drop method. The latter method uses the mouse to copy or move cell contents to a different destination within the *same* worksheet. Point at the border of a cell or cell range containing the contents to be copied or moved, hold down the mouse button and drag to the destination cell to move the contents or hold down the **CTRL** key whilst dragging to copy the cell contents.

2.3.2 Using the AutoFill Tool

The AutoFill tool or Copy Handle replicates formulas, or increments data entries over other cells within the spreadsheet.

To use the AutoFill tool, do the following:

- Position the mouse over the **fill handle** (this is the small black square in the lower right corner of a cell) and then hold down the left mouse button.

  The cursor becomes a black cross.   ┼

- With the mouse button depressed, drag over subsequent cells to increment entries.

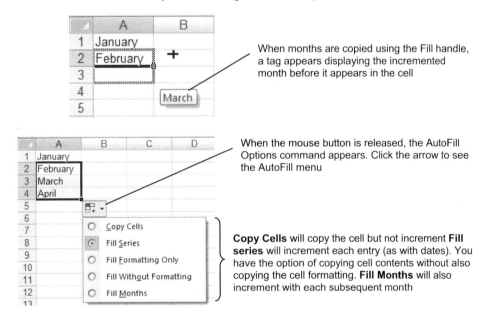

When months are copied using the Fill handle, a tag appears displaying the incremented month before it appears in the cell

When the mouse button is released, the AutoFill Options command appears. Click the arrow to see the AutoFill menu

Copy Cells will copy the cell but not increment **Fill series** will increment each entry (as with dates). You have the option of copying cell contents without also copying the cell formatting. **Fill Months** will also increment with each subsequent month

Alternatively, enter the first number or date and then select the cells into which you want the incremented numbers/dates/months to appear.

- From the **Home** tab and the **Editing** group, select the **Fill** arrow.

- Select a **Fill** option from the drop down menu – select **Down**, **Right**, **Left** or **Up** to copy a value without incrementing the value.

- Select **Series** for further incremental options, such as AutoFill for months or Linear for numbers.

- Click **OK**.

2.3.3 Deleting Cell Contents

To delete cell contents, do the following:

- Select the cell or cell range containing the content to be deleted.
- Press the **Delete** key on the keyboard or select the **Delete** button from the **Home** tab/**Cells** group.

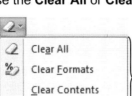

Alternatively, from the **Home** tab and the **Editing** group, select the **Clear** arrow and then choose the **Clear All** or **Clear Contents** commands from the drop down menu.

Selecting **Clear All** deletes the contents of the selected cell, along with the formatting and any comments. To only delete the cell contents, select **Clear Contents**

Practice Sequence

1	Open the **sale** spreadsheet.
2	Copy the contents of cell A2 to cell A1 in Sheet2.
3	Ensure that you are on Sheet1. Move the title in cell A1 to cell F1.
4	Move the title from cell F1 back to its original position in cell A1.
5	Copy the cell range A1:B12 to a new worksheet.
6	Edit the title to read **PROFITS 2ND QTR APR – JUN 2008**.
7	Delete the contents of the cell range **B3:B11**.
8	Save the spreadsheet with the name **sales 2nd Qtr 2008** and close.
9	Save the **sale** spreadsheet and close.
10	Create a new spreadsheet and enter **January** into cell A1.
11	Copy this down over cells **A2:A12** so that the data entries increment with each month (you should end up with 12 months Jan–Dec).
12	In cell **B1** enter the number **1**.
13	Highlight the cell range **B1:B12** and then select the **Fill** command (from the **Home** tab/**Editing** group). Ensure that the numbers will increment in a linear series from 1-12.
14	In cell **C1** enter **=B1+2**.
15	Copy this formula down over the cell range **C2:C12**.
16	In cell **D1** enter **Monday**. Highlight the cell range **D1:D7** and then use the AutoFill command to increment the days (Monday–Sunday).
17	In cell **E1** enter **Monday** and fill down the cell range E2:E7 without incrementing.
18	Save the spreadsheet as **AutoFill** and close.

Section 3 ▶   Managing Worksheets

A spreadsheet is also referred to as a **workbook**. In the same way that a book has many pages, a workbook can have many **worksheets**. A new spreadsheet or workbook contains three default worksheets. The worksheet name is displayed on a sheet tab at the bottom of the screen, such as Sheet1, Sheet2, Sheet3. Worksheets contain many rows and columns that can be deleted, or modified with a different column width/row height or frozen to make it easier to scroll through multiple rows/columns of data without losing sight of the spreadsheet titles. In addition to inserting new rows/columns, you can also insert new worksheets and rename and rearrange the order of worksheet tabs. Worksheets can also be copied or moved within a spreadsheet.

3.1   Rows and Columns

Rows and columns can be selected, whether adjacent or non-adjacent, so that editing and formatting can be performed. It is useful to freeze spreadsheet titles so that they remain in the same position when you scroll through the remainder of the spreadsheet. Sometimes row height or column widths need to be modified to accommodate cell contents; this can be achieved through dragging the row/column to the required height/width or by entering a specific measurement for the row/column.

In this section, you will learn about the following:

- Selecting a row, range of adjacent rows and range of non-adjacent rows.
- Selecting a column, range of adjacent columns and range of non-adjacent columns.
- Inserting and deleting rows and columns.
- Modifying column widths and row heights to a specified value and to the optimal width or height.
- Freezing and unfreezing row and/or column titles.

3.1.1   Selecting Rows

To select a single row, a range of adjacent rows or a range of non-adjacent rows do the following:

Single Row

- Position the mouse icon on the row selector for the row that you want to select.
  The mouse icon displays as a black arrow.
- Click the left mouse button to select the row.

The mouse icon turns into a black arrow
when positioned over a row selector

	A	B	C	D	E
1	PROFITS 1ST QTR JAN - MAR 2008				
2	EXPENDITURE				
3	Hall hire	50			

Range of Adjacent Rows

- Position the mouse icon on the row selector for the first row that you want to select.
  The mouse icon displays as a black arrow.
- Click the left mouse button to select the row.
- Hold down the left mouse button and drag the mouse over the required rows. Note the tag that appears as you drag the mouse. This will indicate the number of rows that have been selected.

The tag indicates the
number of rows that have
been selected

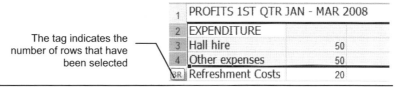

1 PROFITS 1ST QTR JAN - MAR 2008	
2 EXPENDITURE	
3 Hall hire	50
4 Other expenses	50
5R Refreshment Costs	20

Range of Non-Adjacent Rows

- Position the mouse icon on the row selector for the first row that you want to select. The mouse icon displays as a black arrow.
- Click the left mouse button to select the row.
- Hold down the **CTRL** key on the keyboard and then select more rows as required (by clicking the row selector).
- Release the **CTRL** key when you have finished selecting the rows.

3.1.2 Selecting Columns (4.3.1.2)

To select a single column, a range of adjacent columns or a range of non-adjacent columns, do the following:

Single Column

- Position the mouse icon on the column selector for the column that you want to select The mouse icon displays as a black arrow.
- Click the left mouse button to select the column.

	A	B	C
1	PROFITS 1ST QTR JAN - MAR 2008		
2	EXPENDITURE		
3	Hall hire	50	
4	Other expenses	50	
5	Refreshment Costs	20	
6	Transport costs	15	
7	Total Expenditure		
8	INCOME		
9	Entrance Fees	50	
10	Refreshment Sales	60	
11	Sales of goods	650	
12	Total Sales		

Range of Adjacent Columns

- Position the mouse icon on the column selector for the column that you want to select.
- The mouse icon displays as a black arrow.
- Click the left mouse button to select the column.
- Hold down the left mouse button and drag over adjacent columns to select them.
- Release the mouse when all columns have been selected. Note the tag indicating the number of columns that have been selected as you drag.

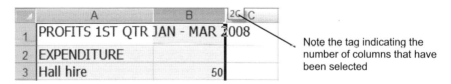

Note the tag indicating the number of columns that have been selected

Range of Non-Adjacent Columns

- Position the mouse icon on the column selector for the first column that you want to select. The mouse icon displays as a black arrow.
- Click the left mouse button to select the column.
- Hold down the **CTRL** key on the keyboard and then select more columns as required (by clicking the column selectors).
- Release the **CTRL** key when you have finished selecting the columns.

3.1.3 Inserting and Deleting Rows and Columns (4.3.1.3)

Rows and columns can be inserted in a specified position within a worksheet.

To insert and delete rows and columns, do the following:

Inserting Rows

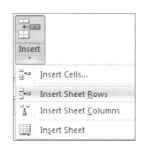

- Select the row below where the new row is to be inserted (the row will be inserted above the selected row).
- From the **Home** tab and the **Editing** group, select the **Insert** arrow and then select **Insert Sheet Rows**.
- A new row will be inserted *above* the currently selected row.

Inserting Columns

- Select the column to the *right* of where the new column is to be inserted (the column will be inserted to the *left* of the selected column).
- From the **Home** tab and the **Editing** group, select the **Insert** arrow and then select **Insert Sheet Columns**.
- A new column will be inserted to the *left* of the currently selected column.

Deleting Rows and Columns

- Select the row(s) or column(s) to be deleted.
- From the **Home** tab and the **Editing** group, select the **Delete** arrow and then select **Delete Sheet Rows** or **Delete Sheet Columns**.
- This will delete the whole row or column and all of the data within the row/column.

3.1.4 Modifying Column Widths and Row Heights (4.3.1.4)

Column widths and row heights can be modified to accommodate cell contents by increasing or decreasing their size.

To modify row height or column width, do the following:

Column Width

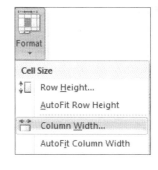

- Select the column to be modified.
- From the **Home** tab and the **Cells** group, select the **Format** button.
- Select **Column Width**.
  The **Column Width** window opens.
- Enter a new measurement into the box.
- Click **OK**.

Enter a new column width measurement

Row Height

- Select the row to be modified.
- From the **Home** tab and the **Cells** group, select the **Format** button.
- Select **Row Height**.
  The **Row Height** window opens.
- Enter a new measurement into the box.
- Click **OK**.

Enter a new row height measurement

note

Column widths and row heights can also be modified by dragging a row/column to increase or reduce size. Position the mouse over the column or row border and the mouse icon turns into a black cross. Hold down the mouse button and drag to the right to widen a column or drag down to resize a row. Note the column width and row height indicators as you drag. This provides the current measurement as you resize the row or column.

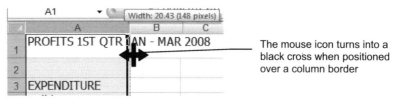

The mouse icon turns into a black cross when positioned over a column border

Cells in a worksheet can be automatically adjusted to a size that best fits the data.

To use adjust cells to an optimal size, do the following:

- Click the **Select All** button to select the cells.
  *Alternatively, s*elect individual columns or rows.
- From the Home tab, click the **Format** button in the **Cells** group.
- Select **AutoFit Column Width** from the drop-down menu.
- Select **AutoFit Row Height** from the drop-down menu.

The row height and column width of the selected cells adjusts to the optimal size for the data within them.

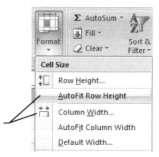

Select **AutoFit Row Height** and **AutoFit Column Width**

3.1.5 Freezing and Unfreezing Row and/or Column Titles (4.3.1.5)

To ensure that spreadsheet titles can be viewed whilst scrolling through a spreadsheet, the row and/or column titles should be frozen.

To freeze and unfreeze rows and columns, do the following:

Freezing

- Select the cell, row or column to freeze (for example, select cell B2 to freeze both column A and row 1).
- From the **View** tab and the **Window** group, select **Freeze Panes**.
- From the menu, select a command:
  - ▷ Select **Freeze Panes** if you want to freeze panes based on your current selection.
  - ▷ Select **Freeze Top Row** to keep the top row visible whilst you scroll through the remainder of the spreadsheet.
  - ▷ Select **Freeze First Column** to keep the first column visible whilst you scroll through the remainder of the spreadsheet.

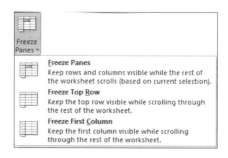

Unfreezing

- Select the cell, row or column to unfreeze.
- From the **View** tab and the **Window** group, select **Freeze Panes**.
- From the menu, select **Unfreeze Panes**.

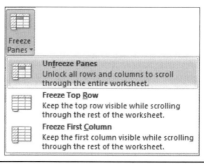

1	Open the **sale** spreadsheet and practise selecting rows and columns: • Select Row 1. • Select Row 1 and Row 3. • Select Rows 1 to 5. • Select Column A. • Select Column A and Column C.	☐
2	Insert a new column between Columns A and B.	☐
3	In the **Expenditure** section of the spreadsheet, insert a row before the **Expenditure** row (to become Row 8).	☐
4	Insert a row after the title **Profits 1ST QTR JAN - MAR 2008**.	☐
5	In the **Income** section of the spreadsheet, insert a row before the **Total Sales** row (to become Row 15).	☐
6	Insert a row above the **INCOME** row (to become Row 10).	☐
7	Delete Column B.	☐
8	Modify Column A to display with a column width of **25**.	☐
9	Modify Row 1 to display with a row height of **22**.	☐
10	Freeze Column A and Row 1 (select B2), to keep this column and row visible when scrolling down or across the remainder of the spreadsheet.	☐
11	Scroll down and across the spreadsheet to test that the panes are frozen as specified.	☐
12	Unfreeze panes in the spreadsheet.	☐
13	Save the **sale** spreadsheet and close.	☐

4

3.2 Worksheets

In the previous section you practised editing a worksheet by inserting, deleting and freezing rows and columns within a worksheet. In addition to working with rows and columns, you can also edit the worksheet by renaming it, inserting a new worksheet or deleting worksheets.

In this section, you will learn about the following:

• Switching between worksheets.

• Inserting a new worksheet and delete a worksheet.

• Recognising good practice in naming worksheets: using meaningful worksheet names rather than accepting default names.

• Copying, moving and renaming a worksheet within a spreadsheet.

3.2.1 Switching between Worksheets

The default number of worksheets in a workbook is three. You may wish to work on more than one worksheet within a workbook. To do this you need to switch between sheets.

To switch between worksheets, do the following:

- The example below displays the currently active worksheet tab as Sheet1.
- Select a different sheet tab to make it the active worksheet.

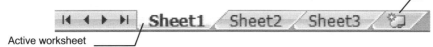

3.2.2 Inserting a New Worksheet

You can add more worksheets to a workbook if required. It will be inserted to the left of a selected sheet. Therefore, select a sheet tab to the right of where you want to insert the new worksheet.

To insert a new worksheet, do the following:

- Select a sheet tab to the right of where the new worksheet is to be inserted.
- From the **Home** tab and the **Cells** group, select the **Insert** arrow.
- From the menu select **Insert Sheet**.
  Alternatively, select the **Insert New Sheet** button on the tab bar.

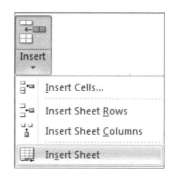

 note Press **Shift** and **F11** to insert a new worksheet or right-click a sheet tab and choose **Insert**. Select **Worksheet** and click **OK**.

3.2.3 Deleting a Worksheet

A worksheet can be deleted if required, but please note that all data is lost in a deleted worksheet, so be careful to delete the correct worksheet.

To delete a worksheet, do the following:

- Select the sheet tab to be deleted.
- From the **Home** tab and the **Cells** group, select the **Delete** arrow.
- From the menu select **Delete Sheet**.
- If the worksheet contains data, the following message will appear.

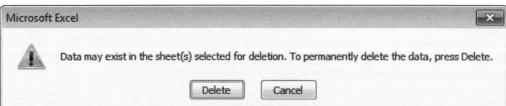

- Click **Delete** to complete deletion of the worksheet.

3.2.4 Naming Worksheets – Good Practice

Worksheets should be renamed with meaningful names, appropriate to the worksheet subject, such as **sales2011** or **QTR1sales**, etc. It is good practice to use appropriate names that are easily identifiable. Using **Sheet1** and **Sheet2**, etc., makes it harder to differentiate between different worksheets and more meaningful names should be used to facilitate locating and identifying relevant worksheets within a workbook.

3.2.5 Renaming Worksheets

To rename a worksheet, do the following:

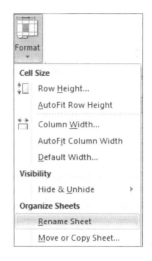

- Select the worksheet tab to be renamed.
- From the **Home** tab and **Cells** group, select the **Format** arrow.
- Select **Rename Sheet**.

  The tab name will be selected, ready for you to type over the existing tab name.

- Enter a meaningful name for the worksheet.
- Press **Enter**.

Example of a renamed worksheet

3.2.6 Copying and Moving Worksheets

To copy a worksheet, do the following:

- Select the worksheet tab to be copied.
- Holding down the left mouse button and the **CTRL** key, drag the worksheet tab to the required position.

  The mouse icon changes to a white arrow with a cross at its tip.

- The copied worksheet will display with (2) after the worksheet name e.g. **Qtr1 (2)**

To move a worksheet, do the following:

- Select the worksheet tab to be moved.
- Holding down the left mouse button, drag the worksheet tab to the required position.

  The mouse icon changes to a white arrow with a blank sheet of paper at its tip. Watch for the downwards facing black arrow that moves with the mouse and indicates where the worksheet will be positioned when the mouse is released.

Alternatively, do the following:

- Select the worksheet to be copied or moved, and then, from the **Home** tab and **Cells** group, select the **Format** command.
- Select **Move or Copy Sheet** from the menu.
- The **Move or Copy** window opens.
- Ensure that the correct workbook is selected from the **To book** menu.
- Choose the location of the moved or copied worksheet from the **Before sheet** list of sheets or **Move to end**.
- Select the **Create a copy** checkbox if you want to copy the worksheet rather than move it.
- Click **OK**.

An alternative method to insert, delete, rename, move or copy a worksheet, is to right-click the worksheet tab and then select the relevant menu command.

Practice Sequence

1	Open the **sale** spreadsheet.	☐
2	Insert a new worksheet before **Sheet1**.	☐
3	Rename the new worksheet as **practise**.	☐
4	Move the **practise** worksheet so that it is at the end of the other worksheets within the spreadsheet.	☐
5	Rename Sheet1 as **Qtr1**.	☐
6	Delete the **Practise** worksheet.	☐
7	Save and close the **sale** spreadsheet.	☐

4

Section 4 ▶   Formulas and Functions

Formulas and functions are used to create calculations and find results. Arithmetic formulas use arithmetic operators, such as + (addition), - (subtraction), * (multiplication) and / (division).

Functions are used to find totals, averages, minimum and maximum figures, to count numbers and text entries and to round figures up or down. A logical function is used to find a result if a value corresponds with specified criteria. For example, **if** a salesman makes over £10,000, he will get a bonus, if the amount earned is below £10,000 he will not get the bonus. Logical functions use comparison operators, such as = (equals), < (less than) and > (greater than).

It is good practice in creating formulas and functions to use cell references rather than inputting numbers into the formula. This makes it easier to update the formula/function when the worksheet is edited or new data is added.

4.1   Arithmetic Formulas

Arithmetic formulas use arithmetic operators:

+ (addition) - (subtraction) * (multiplication) / (division)

It is important to understand and remember the principles of BODMAS when using arithmetic operators. BODMAS stands for:

(B)rackets

(O)rder

(D)ivision

(M)ultiplication

(A)ddition

(S)ubtraction

When creating a formula, you need to be aware that numbers will be divided before multiplication, addition or subtraction takes place, which can alter the results of a formula. See the example below.

=30+3*10/2   This formula should yield 165 as the answer, but will actually yield 45.
                   This is because the formula divides 30 by 2 and then multiplies 3 by 10.

=(30+3)*(10/2)   This formula yields 165 due to the brackets used in the formula. The brackets force
                   the first part of the formula to be performed first,
                   regardless of the BODMAS principle.

In this section, you will learn about the following:

- Recognising good practice in formula creation: referring to cell references rather than type numbers into formulas.

- Creating formulas using cell references and arithmetic operators (addition, subtraction, multiplication and division).

- Identifying and understanding standard error values associated with using formulas: #NAME?, #DIV/0! and #REF!.

- Understanding and using relative and absolute cell referencing in formulas.

4.1.1 Formula Creation – Good Practice

When creating formulas, always use cell references rather than numbers.

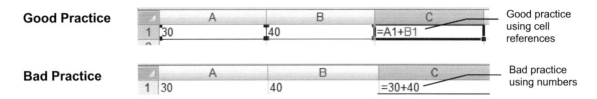

Both of the examples above will yield the same result (70). However, in the above good practice example, the formula result will change if data is edited in either cell A1 or B1. In the bad practice example, if the figures are changed in cells A1 or B1, the formula result will remain the same.

Using cell references also means that you can copy (replicate) a formula to other cells and insert/delete cells, rows and columns and the formula result will update accordingly.

4.1.2 Arithmetic Operators

To create a formula using arithmetic operators, do the following:

To **add** the contents of cells together:
* Enter the following formula (changing the cell references as appropriate): **=A1+B1**.

To **subtract** the content of one cell from another cell:
* Enter the following formula (changing the cell references as appropriate): **=A1-B1**.

To **divide** the contents of one cell by the contents of another cell:
* Enter the following formula (changing the cell references as appropriate): **=A1/B1**.

To **multiply** the contents of one cell by the contents of another cell:
* Enter the following formula (changing the cell references as appropriate): **=A1*B1**.

> Remember BODMAS principles when using arithmetic operators and use brackets if you want an arithmetic operator to perform in a certain order (Tip: the BODMAS order is Divide, Multiply, Add and Subtract.)

4.1.3 Error Values

Error values sometimes occur when you are creating formulas in a spreadsheet. To identify error values associated with using formulas, see the table below.

Error Value	Error	Solution
######	Column is too narrow to display data.	Widen the column to accommodate all of the data.
#NAME?	Excel does not recognise text in a formula.	Check that you have typed the function name correctly.
#DIV/0	Division by 0 or a cell with no value.	Ensure that the cell reference is correct and does not contain a null value or 0.
#REF!	Cell reference is not valid.	Check the cell references used in the formula.

When an error occurs in a formula, a green triangle appears in the top left of the cell containing the error. When this is clicked, the **Error Checking** button appears.

Click the arrow to see the menu options.

Select **Help on this error** if you need help in resolving the error

Select **Error Checking Options** to see further options in resolving formula errors

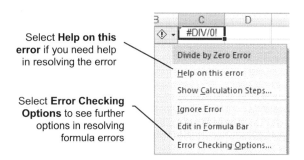

note: If you don't see the green triangle error indicator, select the **File** menu and then **Options**. Select the **Formulas** tab and then select the **Enable background error checking** checkbox. Click **OK**.

To change the colour of the error indicator, do the following:

- Select the **File menu** and then **Options**.
- Select the **Formula** tab.
- From the **Error Checking** section of the window, select **Indicate errors using this color:**.
- Select a colour from the palette.
- Click **OK**.

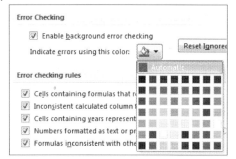

4.1.4 Cell Referencing

Spreadsheets use cell references in formulas and functions, rather than figures, which makes it easier to modify and update data in a spreadsheet. For example, =A1+B1 will total the contents of cells A1 and B1.

When data is modified, or rows/columns deleted or inserted, formulas and functions will automatically update to reflect the modifications. Formulas can be copied (referred to as **replicating**) across or down over subsequent cells and the cell reference will change to match the cell to which the formula is copied.

A normal cell reference is called a **relative cell reference**, because it is relative to the cell to which the formula is being copied. Sometimes an **absolute cell reference** may be required in a formula if the cell reference should not change during replication, but should remain constant. An example of this is in a spreadsheet which uses a cell, such as VAT which will remain constant.

A formula using absolute cell references looks like this: =A1+$B$1. The relative cell reference A1 will change when copied downwards to cells A2 and A3 (i.e. =A2+$B$1, =A3+$B$1) but the absolute cell will remain constant and refer to cell B1.

Relative Cell References
- Select the cell that is to contain the formula.
- Enter the cell reference, e.g. A1 or B3 , or click the cell containing the contents to be used in the calculation.

Absolute Cell References
- Select the cell which is to contain the formula.
- Enter the cell reference, e.g. $A$1 or $B$3 using the dollar sign before the column and before the row.

  Alternatively, enter the cell reference e.g. A1 or B3, or click the cell, and then press **F4** to make the cell reference absolute.

Practice Sequence

1   Open the **sale** spreadsheet.

2   In cell **B9** enter a formula to find the total expenditure for the **1st Qtr Jan–Mar 2008**. (Tip: use cell references and the arithmetic operator **+**.)

3   In cell **B16** find the total sales by entering a formula that uses cell references and arithmetic operators.

4   In cell A18 enter the title **PROFITS**.

5   In cell A19 enter a formula that will find the profits for the **1st QTR Jan–Mar 2008**. (Tip: subtract total expenditure from the total sales.)

6   In cell A20 enter **PROJECTED PROFIT 2008**.

7   In cell A21 enter a formula to find the profit for the whole year, based on the profits for the 1st QTR (tip: multiply the Profits for the 1st QTR by 4 to get a projected profit for the whole year).

8   In cell A22 enter **AVERAGE SALES**.

9   In cell A23 enter a formula to find the monthly profit. (Tip: divide the profit for the 1st QTR by 3).

10 Save the spreadsheet as **Arithmetic** and close.

11 Create a new spreadsheet and, starting in cell A1, enter the following data:

	A	B	C
1	COURSES 2008/2009		
2			
3	*Sept Increase*	1.02	
4			
5	COURSE NAME	PRICE	PRICE INCREASE
6	Word Processing	45	
7	Databases	52	
8	Spreadsheets	50	
9	Presentations	42	
10	Internet and Email	40	
11	File Management	35	

12 In cell C6 multiply the price for Word Processing by the Sept Increase figure (in cell B3). You will need to use an absolute cell reference for the Sept Increase.

13 Copy (replicate) this formula over the cell range C7:C11.

14 Save the spreadsheet as **absolute** and close.

4.2   Functions

In this section, you will learn about the following:

- Using SUM, AVERAGE, MINIMUM, MAXIMUM, COUNT, COUNTA, COUNTBLANK and ROUND functions.
- Using the logical function IF (yielding one of two specific values) with comparison operator: =, > and <.

4.2.1 Using Functions

- The **SUM** function is used to find the total of a specified cell range.
- The **AVERAGE** function is used to find the average value in a specified cell range.
- The **MINIMUM** and **MAXIMUM** functions are used to find smallest and largest values in a specified cell range.
- The **COUNT, COUNTA** and **COUNTBLANK** functions are used to count the number of entries in a specified cell range.
- The **ROUND** function is used to round figures up or down (towards or away from zero).

To create a function, do the following:

Sum
- All formulas and functions begin with the equals sign (**=**).
- After the equals sign, enter the function **SUM**.
- As you enter the function name, a menu appears with alternative SUM function options. Double-click the SUM option or do the following:
  - Enter an open round bracket (**.**
  - Enter the cell range, e.g. **=SUM(A1:A12**.
  - Close the bracket, e.g. **=SUM(A1:A12)**.

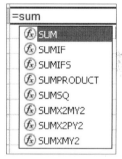

Alternatively, after the open bracket, drag the mouse over the cell range to select it and press Enter. This will find the total of the specified cell range.

Average
- All formulas and functions begin with the equals sign (**=**).
- After the equals sign, enter the function **AVERAGE**.
- As you enter the function name a menu appears with alternative AVERAGE function options. Double-click the AVERAGE option or do the following:
  - Enter an open round bracket (**.**
  - Enter the cell range, e.g. **=AVERAGE(A1:A12**.
  - Close the bracket, e.g. **=AVERAGE(A1:A12)**.

Alternatively, after the open bracket, drag the mouse over the cell range to select it and press Enter. This will find the average of the specified cell range.

Minimum
- All formulas and functions begin with the equals sign (**=**).
- After the equals sign, enter the function **MIN**.
- As you enter the function name a menu appears with alternative MIN function options. Double-click the MIN option or do the following:
  - Enter an open round bracket (**.**
  - Enter the cell range, e.g. **=MIN(A1:A12**.
  - Close the bracket, e.g. **=MIN(A1:A12)**.

Alternatively, after the open bracket, drag the mouse over the cell range to select it and press Enter. This will find the smallest number or minimum value in the specified cell range.

Maximum

- All formulas and functions begin with the equals sign (=)
- After the equals sign, enter the function **MAX**.
- As you enter the function name a menu appears with alternative MAX function options. Double-click the MAX option or do the following:
  ▷ Enter an open round bracket **(**.
  ▷ Enter the cell range, e.g. **=MAX(A1:A12**.
  ▷ Close the bracket, e.g. **=MAX(A1:A12)**.

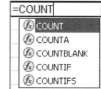

Alternatively, after the open bracket, drag the mouse over the cell range to select it and press Enter. This will find the largest number or maximum value in the specified cell range.

COUNT

The COUNT function counts the number of cells in a range of cells that contain numbers.

- All formulas and functions begin with the equals sign (**=**).
- After the equals sign, enter the function **COUNT**.
- As you enter the function name a menu appears with alternative COUNT function options. Double-click the COUNT option or do the following:
  ▷ Enter an open round bracket **(**.
  ▷ Enter the cell range, e.g. **=COUNT(A1:A12**.
  ▷ Close the bracket, e.g. **=COUNT(A1:A12)**.

Alternatively, after the open bracket, drag the mouse over the cell range to select it and press Enter. This will count the number of cells containing numbers in the specified cell range.

COUNT A

The COUNTA function counts the number of cells in a range that are not empty (will count cells containing numbers and text).

- All formulas and functions begin with the equals sign (=).
- After the equals sign, enter the function **COUNTA**.
- As you enter the function name a menu appears. Double-click the COUNTA option or do the following:
  ▷ Enter an open round bracket **(**.
  ▷ Enter the cell range, e.g. **=COUNTA(A1:A12**.
  ▷ Close the bracket, e.g. **=COUNTA(A1:A12)**.

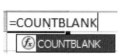

Alternatively, after the open bracket, drag the mouse over the cell range to select it and press Enter. This will find the number of cells in the specified cell range that are not blank.

COUNTBLANK

The COUNTBLANK function counts the number of cells in a range that are empty (will count cells containing no numbers or text).

- All formulas and functions begin with the equals sign (=).
- After the equals sign, enter the function **COUNTBLANK**.
- As you enter the function name a menu appears. Double-click the COUNTBLANK option or do the following:
  ▷ Enter an open round bracket **(**.
  ▷ Enter the cell range, e.g. **=COUNTBLANK(A1:A12**.
  ▷ Close the bracket, e.g. **=COUNTBLANK(A1:A12)**.

Alternatively, after the open bracket, drag the mouse over the cell range to select it and press Enter. This will find the number of cells in the specified cell range that are blank.

ROUND

The ROUND function rounds figures up or down to a specified number of digits. Rounddown rounds figures down to zero (0). Roundup rounds figures up away from zero (0).

- All formulas and functions begin with the equals sign (**=**).
- After the equals sign, enter the function **ROUND** to round figures to a specified number of digits, **ROUNDDOWN** to round a figure down towards zero or **ROUNDUP** to round a figure up away from zero.
- As you enter the function name a menu appears. Double-click an option or do the following:
  - ▶ Enter an open round bracket **(**.
  - ▶ Enter the cell, e.g. **=ROUND(A1**.
  - ▶ Enter a comma followed by the number of digits by which you want to round down or up. Close the bracket, e.g. **=ROUND(A1,0)**.

  Alternatively, after the open bracket, drag the mouse over the cell range to select it and press Enter.

  For example typing =ROUND(B4,2) will round the number in cell B4 rounded to 2 decimal places.

> Numbers in a range of cells can also be rounded. For example, typing =ROUND(A1:C5,3) will round the numbers in the range A1 to C5 to 3 decimal places.
>
> When rounding numbers in a range of cells hold down **CTRL** before pressing **Enter**. This ensures that all the numbers in the range are rounded and not just the first one.

4.2.2 Using Logical Functions

The **IF** function is called a **logical function** and it checks whether or not a condition has been met, returning one value if **TRUE** and another value if **FALSE**. The IF function uses comparison operators to find values equal to, greater than or less than a specified amount.

=	equal to
>	greater than
<	less than
>=	greater than and equal to
<=	less than and equal to

- All formulas and functions begin with the equals sign (**=**).
- After the equals sign, enter the function **IF**.
- As you enter the function name a menu appears.
- Double-click the IF function or do the following:

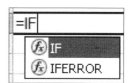

  - ▶ Enter an open round bracket **(**.
  - ▶ Enter the condition e.g. **=IF(A1>10000**.
  - ▶ This means: **If the figure in cell A1 is greater than 10000...**
  - ▶ Enter a comma to separate the condition from the values that should be returned subject to the condition being met, e.g. **=IF(A1>10000,**.
  - ▶ Enter the TRUE value that should appear when the condition is met, e.g. **=IF(A1>10000, "Yes"**.

Text values that will be returned subject to condition being met should be enclosed in quotation marks. You can use cell references as TRUE or FALSE values so that a specific cell is referenced if the condition is met or not.

▷ Enter a comma to separate the TRUE value from the FALSE value.

▷ Enter the value that should be returned if the condition is not met, e.g. **=IF(A1>10000, "Yes", "No"**.

▷ Close the bracket e.g. **=IF(A1>10000, "Yes", "No")**.

If the condition is met (the contents of cell A1 is greater than 10000), then the value **Yes** will be returned; if the condition is not met (the contents of cell A1 is 10000 or below), then the value **No** will be returned.

You can also insert functions by doing one of three methods shown below.

1. From the **Home** tab and **Editing** group, select the **AutoSum** arrow and then choose a function from the list or click **More Functions** to see the **Insert Function** window.

2. Select the **fx** function button on the Formula Bar to see the **Insert Function** window.

The **Functions Argument** window opens. This window enables you to add values and/or conditions.

Type a function name and click **Go**

Or select a function

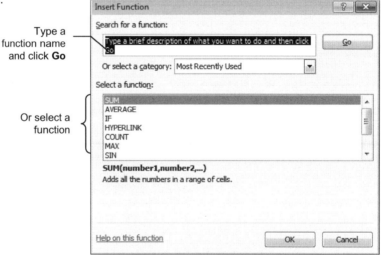

3. From the **Formulas** tab, select functions from the **Function Library** group.

Practice Sequence

1   Open the **sale** spreadsheet. ☐

2   In cell B9 use the SUM function to find the total expenditure. ☐

3   In cell B16 use the SUM function to find the total sales. ☐

4   In cell A18 enter **PROFITS**. In cell B18 enter a formula to find the profits (subtract B9 from B16). ☐

5   In cell A19 enter **AVG EXPENSE**. In cell B19 enter a function to find the average expenditure cost ☐

6   In cell A20 enter **MIN EXPENSE**. In cell B20 enter a function to find the minimum expenditure cost. ☐

7   In cell A21 enter **MAX EXPENSE**. In cell B21 enter a function to find the maximum expenditure cost. ☐

8   In cell A22 enter **AVG ROUND DOWN**. In cell B22 enter a function to round down the Average result in B19 to 0 digits. ☐

9   In cell A23 enter REFRESHMENTS VIABLE?. ☐

10   In cell B23 enter a logical function to test whether or not it is viable to sell refreshments at the jumble sales. If the Refreshment Costs are less than the Refreshment Sales, then the cell should display **Yes**, otherwise **No**. ☐

11   In cell A24 enter **COUNT OF EXPENDITURE**. In cell B24 enter a function to count the number of Expenditure items (you may use **COUNTA** to count the Labels, or **COUNT** to count the numeric cells). ☐

12   Save and close the **sale** spreadsheet. ☐

4

Section 5 ▶ Formatting

Formatting can be applied to text, dates and numbers.

- Text can be formatted to display with different fonts, sizes, styles, colours and alignment.
- Dates can be formatted to display in different formats: 10/10/2008, 10-Oct-08, 10 October 2008.
- Numbers can be formatted to display as percentages or with or without currency symbols or decimal places. Numbers can also be formatted to display with a thousand separator, e.g. **10000** can be formatted to display as **10,000**.
- Cell contents can be aligned to display on the left, right or centre of a cell and also vertically aligned or orientated by an amount of specified degrees.
- Titles can be merged across cells and centred.
- Border effects and shading further enhances cell appearance.

5.1 Numbers and Dates

In this section you will learn about the following:

- Formatting cells to display numbers to a specific number of decimal places and to display numbers with or without a separator to indicate thousands.
- Formatting cells to display a date style and to display a currency symbol.
- Formatting cells to display numbers as percentages.

5.1.1 Format Numbers

When numbers are first entered into a new, unformatted worksheet, they display without decimal precision or currency symbols, e.g. 1.50 will display as 1.5 and 1.00 will display as 1.

To format numbers, do the following:

Decimal Places

- Select the cell or cell range containing the numerical data to be formatted.
- From the **Home** tab and the **Cells** group, select the **Format** arrow.
- Select **Format Cells**.
- In the **Format Cells** window and the **Number** tab, select **Number** from the list of categories.
- Use the **Decimal Places** scroll arrows to increase or decrease the number of decimal places. A preview of the selected format is provided in the Sample box.
- Click **OK**.

Percentages

- Select the cell or cell range containing the numerical data to be formatted.
- From the **Home** tab and the **Cells** group, select the **Format** arrow.
- Select **Format Cells**.
  The **Format Cells** window opens.

- In the **Number** tab, select **Percentage** from the list of categories.
- Use the **Decimal Places** scroll arrows to increase or decrease the number of decimal places. A preview of the selected format is provided in the Sample box.
- Click **OK**.

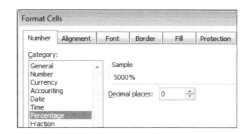

Currency

- Select the cell or cell range containing the numerical data to be formatted.
- From the **Home** tab and the **Cells** group, select the **Format** arrow.
- Select **Format Cells**.
- In the **Format Cells** window and the **Number** tab, select **Currency** from the list of categories.
- Use the **Decimal Places** scroll arrows to increase or decrease the number of decimal places.
- Select the **Symbol** arrow to select a currency symbol. A preview of the selected format is provided in the Sample box.
- Click **OK**.

Thousand Operator

- Select the cell or cell range containing the numerical data to be formatted.
- From the **Home** tab and the **Cells** group, select the **Format** arrow.
- Select **Format Cells**.
- In the **Format Cells** window and the **Number** tab, select **Number** from the list of categories.
- Use the **Decimal Places** scroll arrows to increase or decrease the number of decimal places.
- Select the **Use 1000 Separator** (,) checkbox (place a tick in the box). A preview of the selected format is provided in the Sample box.
- Click **OK**.

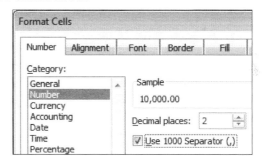

5.1.2 Format Dates

Dates can be formatted to display in different styles, e.g. long date, short date or medium date format.

To format a date, do the following:
- Select the cell or cell range containing the date(s).
- From the **Home** tab and the **Cells** group, select the **Format** arrow.
- Select **Format Cells**.
- In the **Format Cells** window and the **Number** tab, select **Date** from the list of categories.
- Select a date type from the **Type** list.
- Select the **Locale (Location)** arrow to choose a location (this may affect the date style, e.g. US dates display the month before the day).
- Click **OK**.

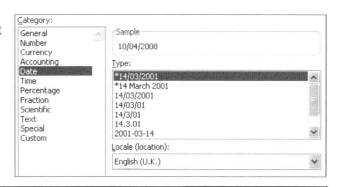

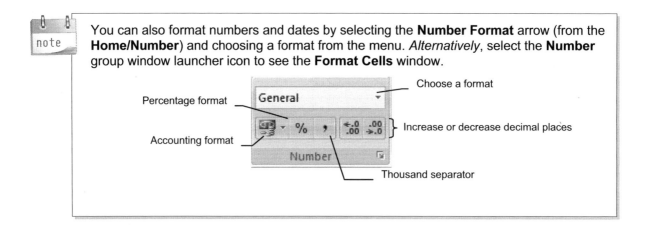

You can also format numbers and dates by selecting the **Number Format** arrow (from the **Home/Number**) and choosing a format from the menu. *Alternatively*, select the **Number** group window launcher icon to see the **Format Cells** window.

Practice Sequence

1	Open the **sale** spreadsheet.
2	Format the cell range B4:B16 to display with a currency symbol and 2 decimal places.
3	Format the cell B18 to display with 2 decimal places but no currency symbol.
4	Enter today's date in cell C2.
5	Format the date in long date format (e.g. 07 August 2008).
6	In cell D2 enter **Our current target for the year is:**.
7	In cell D3 enter **2500**.
8	Format the number in cell D3 to display with 2 decimal places and a thousand separator.
9	In cell D4 enter **The increase for next year is:**.
10	In cell D5 enter **0.05**.
11	Format this number to display as a percentage with 1 decimal place.
12	Save and close the **sale** spreadsheet.

5.2   Cell Content

The appearance of cell content can be enhanced by formatting, such as changing fonts, sizes, styles, colours, alignment, orientation, shading and borders.

In this section, you will cover the following:

- Changing cell content appearance: font size and font type.
- Applying formatting to cell contents: bold, italic, underline or double underline.
- Applying different colours to cell content and cell background.
- Copying the formatting from a cell, cell range to another cell or a cell range.

5.2.1 Fonts

To change the font type, size, style and colour of cell contents and background, do the following:

Font Types

- Select the cell or cell range to be formatted.
- From the **Home** tab and **Font** group, select the **Font** arrow.
- Select a font from the drop-down list.

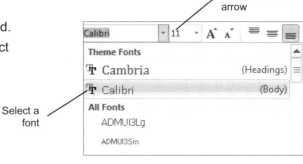

Select the **Font** arrow

Select a font

Font Sizes

- Select the cell or cell range to be formatted and then, from the **Home** tab and **Font** group, select the **Font Size** arrow.
- Select a size from the drop-down list.

  Alternatively, select the **Increase** or **Decrease Font Size** buttons.

Increase font size

Decrease font size

Select the **Font size** arrow

Select a font size

Font Colours

- Select the cell or cell range to be formatted and then, from the **Home** tab and **Font** group, select the **Font Color** arrow.
- Select a colour from the drop down list or select **More Colors** to see further colour options.
- Select a colour from the palette.
- Click **OK**.

The **Colors** window provides more colours

Select the **Font Color** arrow

Select a font colour

Select **More Colors** to see the palette

Chose a colour and click **OK**

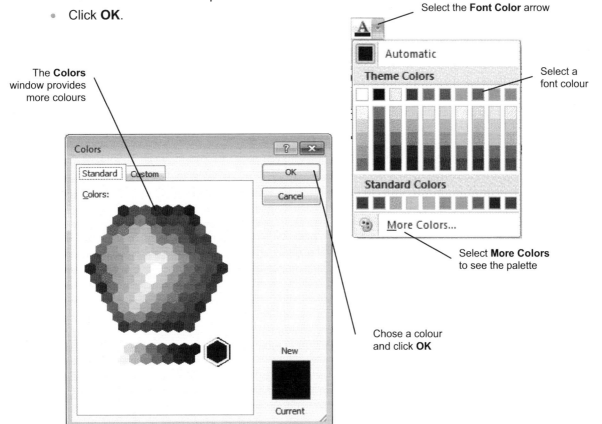

Font Styles

- Font style refers to **bold**, *italic* and <u>underline</u>.
- Select the cell or cell range to be formatted and then, from the **Home** tab and **Font** group, select the required font style.

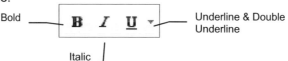

Bold — | **B** *I* <u>U</u> ⌄ | — Underline & Double Underline

Italic ⌋

Double Underline

- Select the cell or range of cells to be formatted.
- From the **Home** tab and **Font** group, select the **U** arrow and choose **Double Underline**.
- Alternatively, from the **Home** tab and **Font** group, select the **Borders** button.
- Select **Bottom Double Border** to apply a double underline at the bottom of selected cells.
- Select **Top and Double Bottom Border** to apply a double underline to the top and bottom of selected cells.

Select **Bottom Double Border** to apply a double underline effect to the bottom of the selected cell(s)

Format Cell Background

- Select the cell or range of cells to be formatted.
- From the **Home** tab and **Font** group, select the **Shading** arrow (this is sometimes called the Fill Color arrow).
- Choose a colour from the available **Theme Colors** or from **Standard Colors**.
- To see further colour choices, select **More Colors**.
  The **Colors** window opens.
- Select a colour.
- Click **OK**.

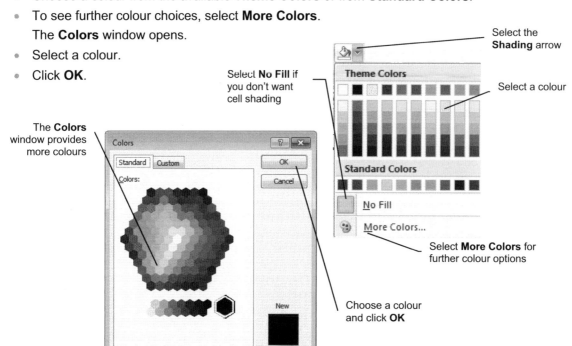

The **Colors** window provides more colours

Select **No Fill** if you don't want cell shading

Select the **Shading** arrow

Select a colour

Select **More Colors** for further colour options

Choose a colour and click **OK**

note   You can open the **Font** window by selecting the **Font** window launcher icon. The **Font** tab contains all of the formatting options listed above.

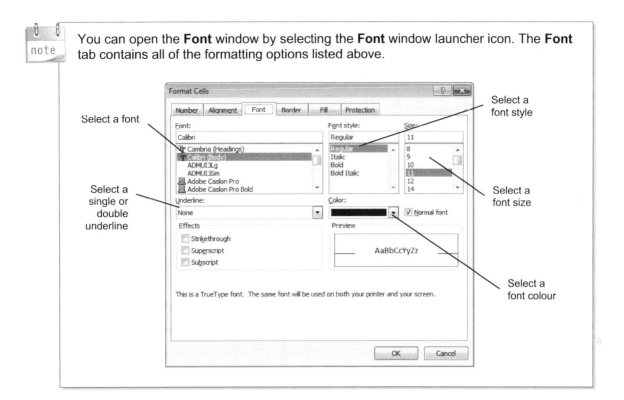

5.2.2 Copy Formatting

Formatting can be copied by using the Format Painter. This tool enables you to copy formatting from one cell or range of cells to another cell or range of cells.

To copy formatting, do the following:

- Select the formatted cell or range of cells to be copied.
- From the **Home** tab and **Clipboard** group, select the **Format Painter** button.
- Drag the mouse over the cell or range of cells which are to display the same formatting (note how the cursor changes to include a paintbrush icon).

note   Double-click the **Format Painter** to keep it on whilst you copy formatting to more than one cell/range of cells. Click the Format Painter button to turn it off.

Practice Sequence

1	Open the **sale** spreadsheet.
2	Format the title in cell A1 with **Comic Sans MS** font type, **Dark Blue** font colour, **Bold, Italic** font style and font size **14**.
3	Format cell A1 with a pale blue background.
4	Format the cell **A3** (Expenditure) with **Comic Sans MS** font type, **Dark Blue** font colour, **Italic** font style and font size **12**.
5	Copy this formatting to cells A9 (Total Expenditure), A11 (Income) and A16 (Total Sales).
6	Format cell B9 with a double underline.

7	Copy this formatting to cell B16.	☐
8	Format the cell range A18:B24 as **Times New Roman**, **12**, **Red**.	☐
9	Format the date as dark blue and bold.	☐
10	Format cell D2 as **Times New Roman**, **14**, **Red**.	☐
11	Copy this formatting to cell D4.	☐
12	Format the cell range D2:D5 in italics.	☐
13	Save and close the **sale** spreadsheet.	☐

5.3   Alignment and Border Effects

In this section, you will cover the following:

- Applying text wrapping to contents within a cell and a cell range.
- Aligning cell contents both horizontally and vertically. Adjusting cell content orientation.
- Merging cells and centre a title in a merged cell.
- Adding border effects to a cell and a cell range, including lines and colours.

5.3.1   Text Wrapping

To wrap text within a cell, do the following:

- Select the cell or cell range to be formatted.
- From the **Home** tab and **Alignment** group, select the **Wrap Text** button.
- Adjust the column width and row height if necessary.

5.3.2   Alignment

Cell contents can be aligned horizontally and/or vertically.

To align cell contents, do the following:

Horizontally

- Select the cell or cell range to be aligned.
- From the **Home** tab and **Alignment** group, select an alignment:

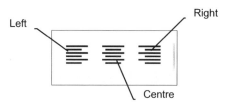

Vertically

- Select the cell or cell range to be aligned.
- From the **Home** tab and **Alignment** group, select an alignment:

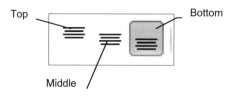

5.3.3 Adjusting Cell Orientation

To change the orientation of a cell's contents, do the following:

- Select the cell or cell range to be formatted.
- From the **Home** tab and **Alignment** group, select the **Orientation** arrow.

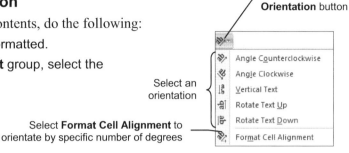

Select the **Orientation** button

Select an orientation

Select **Format Cell Alignment** to orientate by specific number of degrees

- Select an orientation or select **Format Cell Alignment**.
  The **Format Cells** window opens with the **Alignment** tab the active tab.
- Select an orientation by dragging the **Text** orientation slider in the required direction or use the **Degrees** scroll arrows to select a specific number of degrees.

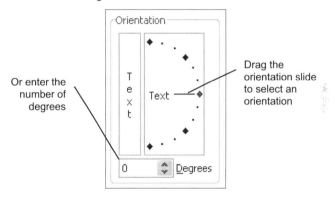

Or enter the number of degrees

Drag the orientation slide to select an orientation

- Choose the direction of the orientation by selecting the **Text Direction** arrow and then choosing a direction.

Select the **Text direction** arrow and choose a direction for the orientation

5.3.4 Merging Cells

To merge cells, do the following:

- Select the cell range to be merged.
- From the **Home** tab and **Alignment** group, select the **Merge Cells** arrow.
- Choose a merge option from the menu.

Select the **Merge** arrow

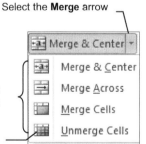

Select an option from the menu

Select **Unmerge Cells** to undo the merge (the relevant cells should be selected first)

Alternatively, select the **Alignment** group window launcher icon to open the **Format Cells** window and ensure that the **Alignment** tab is the active tab.

- Under **Text Control**, select the **Merge Cells** checkbox (click to enter a tick in the box).
- Click **OK**.

5.3.5 Border Effects

To format cells with borders and lines, do the following:

- Select the cell or cell range to be formatted.
- From the **Home** tab and **Font** group, select the **Border** arrow.
- Select a border from the menu or select **More Borders** at the bottom of the menu.

  The **Format Cells** window opens with the **Borders** tab selected.
- From the **Line** section of the window, select a line **Style** and/or a line **Colour**.
- From the **Presets** section, select the type of border you require.
- From the **Border** section refine the border by selecting top, bottom, left, right, middle or diagonal border buttons (these are *toggle* buttons which are turned on/off each time they are selected) to apply or remove a border.
- Click **OK**.

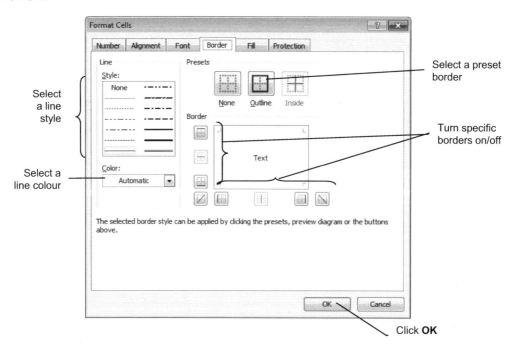

Practice Sequence

1	Open the **sale** spreadsheet.	☐
2	Merge and centre the title in cell A1 across the cell range A1:D1.	☐
3	Format cell A3 to be vertically aligned with **Centre Alignment**.	☐
4	Copy this formatting to cells A9, A11 and A16.	☐
5	Right align the contents of cells A9 and A16.	☐
6	Centre the date in cell C2.	☐

7	Wrap the contents in cells A23 and A24 (Refreshments Viable? and Count of Expenditure) so that the content in each of the cells display on two lines (you may need to adjust column width/row height).	☐
8	Format cells A9 and A16 to be orientated by -10^0 degrees (Text Direction - Context).	☐
9	Apply a thick black outline border to cells A1:D1.	☐
10	Apply a dark blue, dashed border to cells A3 and cell A11.	☐
11	Apply an inside and outline black border to the cell range A4:A7.	☐
12	Repeat this formatting for cell range A12:B14.	☐
13	Apply a double, dark blue, outline border to the cell range D2:D5.	☐
14	Repeat this formatting for the cell range A18:A24.	☐
15	Save and close **sale**.	☐

4

Section 6 ▶   Charts

Charts are visual graphical representations of numerical data, making it easier to see results 'at a glance'. Charts can be displayed in different formats, such as pie, bar/column and line, and can be formatted with colour and fonts, size and styles.

To use charts you need to input data in a spreadsheet. This data is then displayed in chart format in the chart type that you specify. The chart can be modified if required to display a different chart type. Chart titles can also be added or removed as required. The chart data is described by the data labels that are applied. For example, the following chart is meaningless without the data labels, but makes sense once data labels are applied:

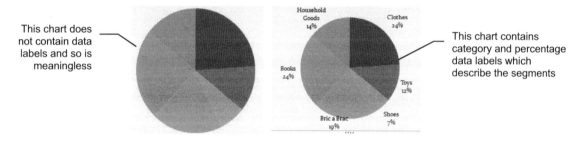

This chart does not contain data labels and so is meaningless

This chart contains category and percentage data labels which describe the segments

6.1 Creating Charts

In this section, you will learn about the following:

- Creating different types of charts from spreadsheet data: column chart, bar chart, line chart and pie chart.
- Selecting a chart.
- Changing the chart type.
- Moving, resizing and deleting a chart.

6.1.1 Chart Types

Charts can be displayed in a variety of types, such as a bar chart, column chart, line chart or pie chart. The type of chart that you choose should be suitable for the data being represented.

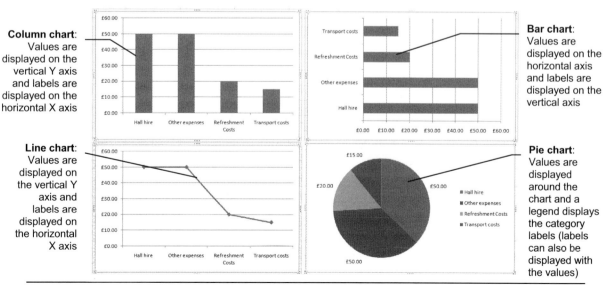

Column chart: Values are displayed on the vertical Y axis and labels are displayed on the horizontal X axis

Bar chart: Values are displayed on the horizontal axis and labels are displayed on the vertical axis

Line chart: Values are displayed on the vertical Y axis and labels are displayed on the horizontal X axis

Pie chart: Values are displayed around the chart and a legend displays the category labels (labels can also be displayed with the values)

6.1.2 Creating a Chart

To create a chart, do the following:

Column Chart

- Select the spreadsheet data.
- From the **Insert** tab and **Charts** group, select the **Column** command.
- A list opens, displaying different column chart sub-types.
- Select a sub-type from the list or select **All Chart Types**.
- The **Insert Chart** window opens.
- Select a column sub-type or select a different chart type if required.
- Click **OK**.

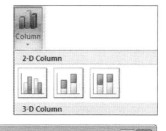

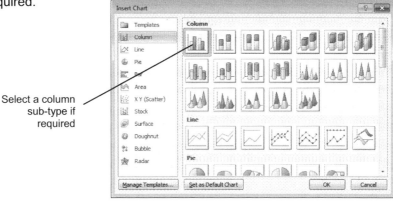

Select a column sub-type if required

 note

Bar charts are created in exactly the same way – just select the **Bar** command from the **Charts** group.

Line Chart

- Select the spreadsheet data.
- From the **Insert** tab and **Charts** group, select the **Line** command.
  A list opens, displaying different Line chart sub-types.
- Select a sub-type from the list or select **All Chart Types**.
  The **Insert Chart** window opens.
- Select a Line sub-type or select a different chart type if required.
- Click **OK**.

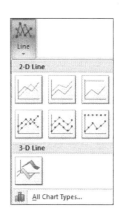

Pie Chart

- Select the spreadsheet data.
- From the **Insert** tab and **Charts** group, select the **Pie** command.
  A list opens, displaying different Pie chart sub-types.
- Select a sub-type from the list or select **All Chart Types**.
  The **Insert Chart** window opens.
- Select a Pie sub-type or select a different chart type if required.
- Click **OK**.

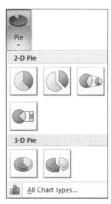

6.1.3 Selecting a Chart

Before a chart can be edited, resized, moved, deleted or formatted it first needs to be selected.

To select a chart, do the following:

- Click the chart to select it.

  A border appears around the chart with small dots in the middle and corners of the surrounding border.

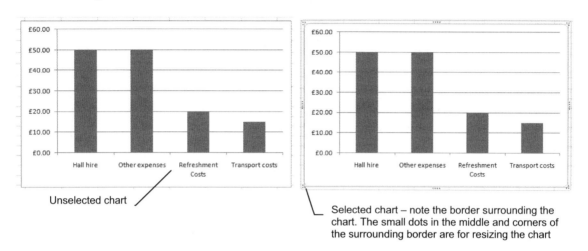

Unselected chart

Selected chart – note the border surrounding the chart. The small dots in the middle and corners of the surrounding border are for resizing the chart

Alternatively, do the following:

- From the **Home** tab and **Editing** group, select the **Find & Select** command.
- Select the **Selection Pane** command from the menu.
- Select objects from the task pane that opens (click the 'eye' icon to hide/unhide objects on the worksheet).

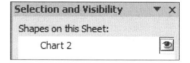

6.1.4 Changing the Chart Type

The chart can be altered, if required, to another type.

To change the chart type of a selected chart, do the following:

- Select the chart.
- From the **Chart Tools/Design** tab and the **Type** group, select **Change Chart Type**.

  The **Change Chart Type** window opens.
- Select a different chart type and a chart sub-type.
- Click **OK**.

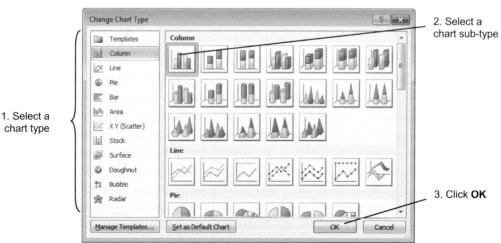

1. Select a chart type

2. Select a chart sub-type

3. Click **OK**

6.1.5 Moving, Resizing and Deleting a Chart

A chart can be moved to a different position on the same worksheet or moved to another worksheet or spreadsheet. If a chart overlaps or obscures spreadsheet data, it should be moved to a new position. A chart can also be resized to make it bigger or smaller. When a chart is no longer required it can be deleted.

To move, resize and delete a chart, do the following:

Moving a Chart (Within a Worksheet)

- Select the chart and then, holding down the left mouse button, drag to the new location within the worksheet (note how the mouse arrow changes to the black cross icon when moving the chart).

  Alternatively, select the chart and then, from the **Home** tab and **Clipboard** group, select the **Cut** button. Select the cell where the chart is to be positioned within the worksheet, and select the **Paste** button.

 The keyboard shortcuts are: **CTRL** + **C** (copy), **CTRL** + **X** (cut) and **CTRL** + **V** (paste).

Moving a Chart (Between Worksheets)

- Select the chart.
- From the **Home** tab and **Clipboard** group, click **Cut**.
- Select a new sheet tab.
- Select the cell where the chart is to be positioned within the worksheet.
- Click **Paste**.

  Alternatively, from the **Chart Tools/Design** tab and **Location** group, select **Move Chart**.

  The **Move Chart** window opens.

  Select the **New sheet** button if you want the chart to be moved to a new sheet.

- Enter a new name for the sheet if required.
- Select **Object in** if you want the chart to be positioned as an object in an existing sheet.
- Choose the sheet from the **Object in:** menu.
- Click **OK**.

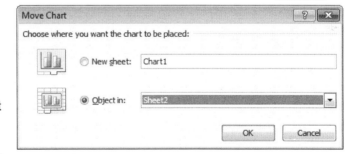

Resizing a Chart (Using the Mouse)

- Select the chart.
- Point the cursor at a corner of the chart (containing small dots).

  The cursor turns into a double-headed black arrow when positioned over the resizing handles.

- Hold down the left mouse button and drag in the required direction to increase/decrease the size (note how the double-headed black arrow turns into a black crosshair whilst resizing).
- Release the mouse button when the chart is the required size.

 When using the mouse to resize a chart, always drag from a corner resizing handle to maintain the original chart proportions.

Resizing a Chart (Using Chart Tools)

- Select the chart.

- From the **Chart Tools/Format** tab and the **Size** group, select a specific size for the height and/or width of the chart by selecting the **Shape Height** and/or **Shape Width** scroll arrows.

  Alternatively, select the **Size** window launcher icon to see the **Size and Properties** window.

- Change the size of the chart by increasing/ decreasing the measurements in the **Height** and/or **Width** boxes.

- Select the **Lock aspect ratio** option button before selecting a height to ensure that the width alters proportionally to the height (or vice versa).

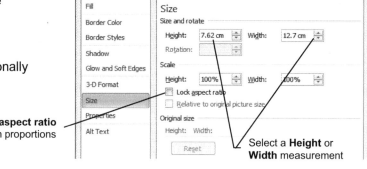

Select **Lock aspect ratio** to maintain proportions

Select a **Height** or **Width** measurement

Deleting a Chart

- Select the chart.

- Press **Delete** on the keyboard or right-click the chart and select **Delete** from the shortcut menu.

	Practice Sequence	
1	Open the **sale** spreadsheet.	☐
2	Copy the cell range A4:B7 to Sheet2 and position in cell A3 (beneath the EXPENDITURE title that you copied in an earlier task.	☐
3	Rename Sheet2 as Expenditure.	☐
4	In the Expenditure sheet, create a bar chart from the cell range A3:B6.	☐
5	Move the chart so that it is positioned beneath the spreadsheet data, starting in cell A12 (approximately).	☐
6	Resize the chart to have a height of 8cm and a width of 14cm.	☐
7	Using the same cell range, create a pie chart.	☐
8	Position this chart on the right hand side of the spreadsheet data in cell D1 (approx).	☐
9	Resize the pie chart as Height: 5.5 and Width 9.5.	☐
10	Using the same cell range, create a line chart	☐
11	Position this chart beneath the pie chart (to the right of the bar chart).	☐
12	Resize the line chart to Height: 6.5 and width 11.	☐
13	Change the chart type of the bar chart to a column chart.	☐
14	Delete the line chart.	☐
15	Save and close the **sale** spreadsheet.	☐

6.2   Editing Charts

In this section, you will learn about the following:

- Adding, removing and editing a chart title.
- Adding data labels to a chart: values/numbers and percentages.
- Changing chart area background colour and legend fill colour.
- Changing the column, bar, line or pie slice colours in a chart.
- Changing the font size and colour of chart title, chart axes and chart legend text.

6.2.1   Adding, Removing and Editing a Chart Title

To add, remove or edit a chart title, do the following:

Adding a Chart Title

- From the **Chart Tools/Layout** tab and the **Labels** group, select the **Chart Title** command.
- From the **Chart Title** list, select a position, such as **Above Chart**.
  A **Chart Title** box appears on the chart in the selected position.
- Position the cursor within this box and delete the existing text.
- Enter the chart title.

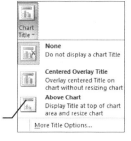

Select a position for the title

Editing a Chart Title

- Position the cursor within the chart title box and delete or enter text as required.

Deleting a Chart Title

- Select the chart title box and press **Delete** on the keyboard.
  Alternatively, select the **Chart Tools/Layout** tab.
- Select the **Chart Title** command.
- Select **None**.

note

Other chart elements can also be deleted by selecting the chart element and pressing **Delete**. To select different parts of a chart, do one of the following:

- Click the chart element to select it or, from the **Chart Tools/Format** tab and the **Current Selection** group, select the **Chart Elements** arrow.
- Select a chart element from the menu.

6.2.2   Adding Data Labels

Data labels help to identify the X and Y axes data in the chart.

To add data labels, do the following:

- Select the chart.
- From the **Chart Tools/Layout** tab and the **Labels** group, select the **Data Labels** command.

- Select a position for the data labels.

  Alternatively, select **More Data Label options** to open the **Format Data Labels** window.

Select a position for the data labels

Select **More Data Label Options...**

- Select a label type such as **Value**.
- Select a label position, such as **Outside End**.
- Select **Include legend key in label** if you want the category labels to display as a legend.
- Click **Close**.

The options shown in this illustration are for **bar**, **column** and **line** charts

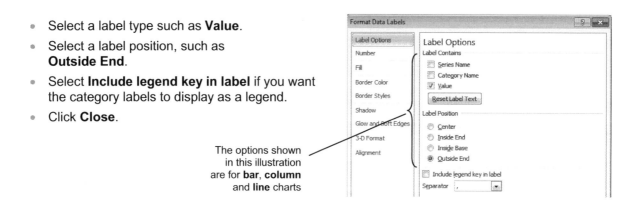

note

When using **pie charts**, the options for data labels are different.

The options shown in this illustration are for **pie** charts

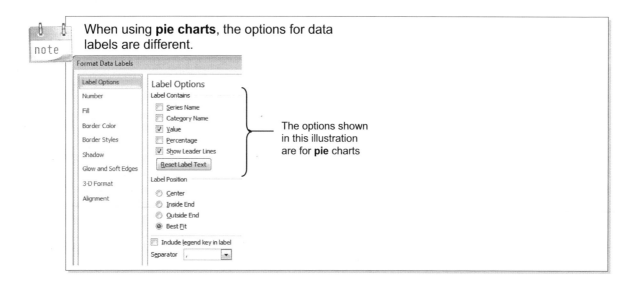

6.2.3 Changing the Chart Area and Legend Background

The background of the chart and the background of the legend can be formatted to display with a solid fill colour.

To change the chart area and legend background, do the following:

- Select the chart element to be formatted (**Chart Area** or **Legend**) by clicking the chart element to select it.

  Alternatively, select the **Chart Element** arrow from the **Chart Tools/Format** tab and the **Current Selection** group, and select the chart element from the list.

Chart Area
Chart Area
Chart Title
Legend
Plot Area
Series 1

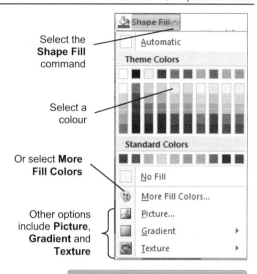

- From the **Chart Tools/Format** tab and the **Shape Styles** group, select the **Shape Fill** command.

- Select a colour from the menu or choose **More Fill Colors** to see the colour palette.

Select the **Shape Fill** command

Select a colour

Or select **More Fill Colors**

Other options include **Picture**, **Gradient** and **Texture**

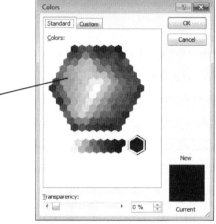

- Choose a colour from the palette.
- Click **OK**.

Select a colour from the palette

6.2.4 Changing Column, Bar, Line or Pie Slice Colours

The lines, bars, columns or pie slices of a chart can be formatted with a different colour if required.

To change the colour of a bar, column, line or pie slice, do the following:
- Select the column/bar/line/pie slice for the series to be formatted (by double-clicking to select or by selecting the **Chart Element** arrow from the **Chart Tools/Format** tab and the **Current Selection** group, and selecting the chart element from the list, such as Series1 or Series2).

- From the **Chart Tools/Format** tab and the **Shape Styles** group, select the **Shape Fill** command.

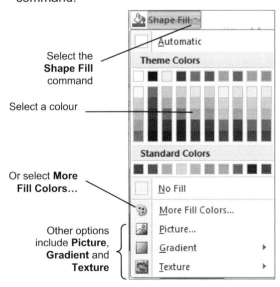

Select the **Shape Fill** command

Select a colour

Or select **More Fill Colors...**

Other options include **Picture**, **Gradient** and **Texture**

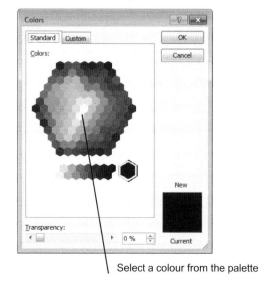

Select a colour from the palette

6.2.5 Formatting a Chart

The font type, size and colour of the chart title, legend or axis labels can all be changed if required.

To format a chart element, do the following:
- Click the chart element (chart title, legend or axis labels).

  Alternatively, select the **Chart Element** arrow from the **Chart Tools/Format** tab and the **Current Selection** group, and select the chart element from the list.

- From the **Home** tab and the **Font** group, select a font type, font size or font colour.

  Alternatively, select the **Font** window launcher icon to see the **Font** window. Select font type, font size and font colour as required. Click **OK**.

Select a font, size and colour or click the window launcher to open the **Font** window

Select a font type, font size, font style and font colour

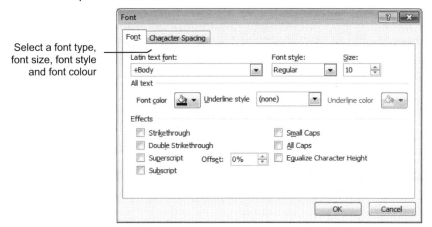

Practice Sequence		
1	Open the **sale** spreadsheet and the Expenditure sheet.	
2	Add a chart title to the pie chart as follows: **1st QTR 2008**.	
3	Edit the chart title to read **1st QTR Expenditure 2008**.	
4	Add a chart title to the column chart as follows: **Expenditure 2008**.	
5	Add data labels to the pie chart as percentages (ensure that the pie chart displays a legend).	
6	Change the pie chart area background to a pale blue colour.	
7	Change the pie chart legend colour to a darker blue (darker than the background colour of the chart area).	
8	Format the pie slice colours as follows: Refreshment costs=yellow; Transport Costs=Red; Hall Hire=green; Other Expenses=orange.	
9	Format the chart title on the pie chart to be **Comic Sans Serif**, **14** and **dark blue**.	
10	Delete the chart title from the column chart.	
11	Move the column chart to a new sheet called **Column**.	
12	Save and close the **sale** spreadsheet.	

Section 7 ▶   Preparing Outputs

Output refers to the way that the spreadsheet is viewed, either on screen or as printed hard copy. Both types of output require preparation by choosing an appropriate output format, such as displaying gridlines, row and column headings, or printing to a specific number of pages. It is good practice to check spreadsheet calculations and text and correct any errors to ensure the finished spreadsheet is presented to a professional standard. The layout of a spreadsheet can be altered so that it displays in a different orientation and paper size.

7.1   Setup

In this section, you will learn about the following:

- Changing worksheet margins: top, bottom, left and right.
- Changing worksheet orientation: portrait, landscape.
- Changing the paper size.
- Adjusting page setup to fit worksheet contents on a specified number of pages.
- Adding, editing and deleting text in headers and footers in a worksheet.
- Inserting and deleting fields: page numbering information, date, time, file name and worksheet name into headers and footers.

7.1.1   Margins

Margins are the space between the edge of the paper and the spreadsheet data. To enhance the layout of the printed spreadsheet the top, bottom, left and right margins can all be increased or decreased if required.

To change margins, do the following:

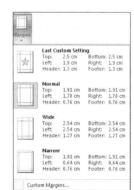

- From the **Page Layout** tab and the **Page Setup** group, select the **Margins** command.
- From the drop-down menu, select the last custom margin setting used, select normal default margin settings or select wide or narrow settings.
- To see further margin options, select **Custom Margins**.
- The **Page Setup** window opens with **Margins** tab active.
- Use the scroll arrows to increase or decrease the current margin measurements for the **Top**, **Bottom**, **Left** and **Right** margins.
- Click **OK**.

Use the scroll arrows to increase or decrease the current margin measurement for each margin

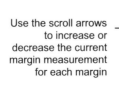

The spreadsheet can be centred on the page, horizontally and/or vertically

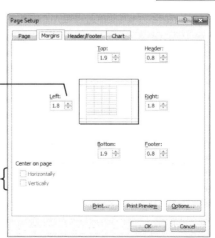

7.1.2 Orientation

Orientation refers to Portrait and Landscape. The default orientation in Excel is Portrait.

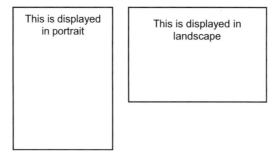

You may need to change the orientation so that the data fits on the page. For example, a spreadsheet containing many columns but few rows (a wide spreadsheet), may display better in landscape orientation. Likewise, a spreadsheet with many rows and few columns (a long, narrow spreadsheet) may display better in portrait orientation. Changing the orientation of the spreadsheet not only enhances the presentation of the printed output, it can also save paper usage.

To change orientation, do the following:

- From the **Page Layout** tab and the **Page Setup** group, select the **Orientation** command.

- Select the required orientation – Portrait or Landscape.

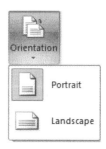

7.1.3 Paper Size

The default paper size is A4 (210mm x 297mm for portrait orientation). The paper size can be altered to another of your choice, such as A5, B3 or a variety of other sizes suitable for the intended printed output.

To change the paper size, do the following:

- From the **Page Layout** tab and the **Page Setup** group, select the **Size** arrow.
  A drop-down menu opens, displaying a variety of paper sizes. The default paper size is A4.

- Select the required paper size.

- To see further size options, select the **More Paper sizes** command at the bottom of the menu.
  The **Page Setup** window opens with **Page** the active tab.

- Select the **Paper size** arrow and choose a paper size from the list.

- Select a **Print quality**.

- Select **OK**.

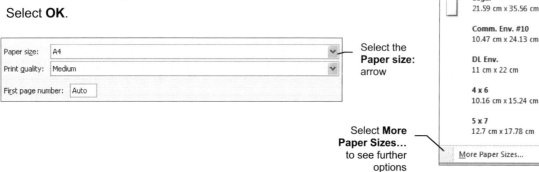

7.1.4 Fitting to a Specified Number of Pages

You may want to fit the spreadsheet to a certain number of pages; for example, to reduce paper wastage or to enhance clarity of the spreadsheet by ensuring that data fits on one sheet.

The default scale of an Excel spreadsheet is 100%. This scale alters depending upon which **Width** (to shrink the width of printed output to fit a maximum number of pages) or **Height** (to shrink the height of printed output to fit a maximum number of pages) option is selected.

To ensure that the spreadsheet fits to a specified number of pages, do the following:

- From the **Page Layout** tab and the **Scale to Fit** group, select the **Width** or **Height** arrow.
- From the drop-down menu, choose how many pages to which to fit the spreadsheet.
- To see further page options, select **More Pages**.
  The **Page Setup** window opens.
- Select the **Fit** option button and then use the scroll arrows to choose the number of pages to which to fit the spreadsheet.
- Click **OK**.

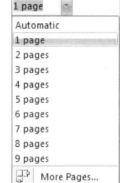

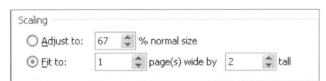

7.1.5 Headers and Footers

Headers appear at the top of the page and footers appear at the bottom of the page. A header or footer can display information that you type in, such as your name or copyright information, or display page numbers or dates.

Creating a Header or Footer

To create a header and a footer, do the following:

- From the **Insert** tab and the **Text** group, select **Header & Footer**.
  The **Header** area opens above your spreadsheet, ready for you to enter the header information.
- Use the **Tab** key to align the cursor to the right or **Shift + Tab** to move the cursor back a step to the left.
- The **Header & Footer Tools** contextual tab becomes active and displays the **Design** tab commands. From this ribbon bar, you can choose to insert a preset header or footer by selecting the **Header** or the **Footer** arrow. Further header or footer elements include: page numbers, number of pages, date, time, file path (location), file name and sheet name.
- To switch between the header and footer area, select **Go to Footer**.

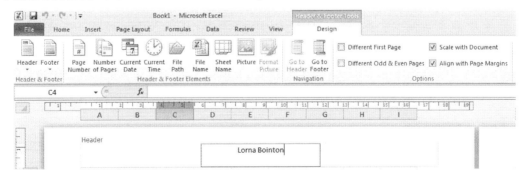

- To close the header and footer area, click away from the header/footer area into the main spreadsheet.

All of the above commands can also be accessed through the **Page Setup** window. To open this window, click the **Page Setup** group window launcher icon. Select the relevant tab.

Editing a Header

To edit a header, do the following:

- From the **Insert** tab and the **Text** group, select **Header & Footer**.

- The **Header & Footer Tools** tab becomes active.

- Click in the header and select the text to be edited.

- Click the **Home** tab and apply the desired formatting.

- Click away from the **Header** to view the changes.

Footers are edited in the same way as Headers. Click inside the Footer to select the text before formatting.

Deleting a Header or Footer

- Click the header or footer area and then click the header/footer to be deleted.
- Press **Delete**.

7.1.6 Inserting Fields

Fields are items of header or footer data, such as dates, time, worksheet name and filename fields that update automatically.

To insert fields, do the following:

- From the **Insert** tab and the **Text** group, select **Header & Footer**.

  The **Header** area opens above your spreadsheet, ready for you to insert the field or fields.

- Use the **Tab** key to align the cursor to the right or **Shift** + **Tab** to move the cursor back a step to the left.

- The **Header & Footer Tools** contextual tab becomes active and displays the **Design** tab commands. From this ribbon bar, you can choose to insert page numbers, number of pages, date, time, file path (location), file name and sheet name.

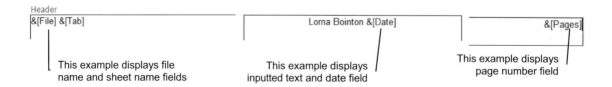

- To switch between the header and footer area, select **Go to Footer**.

- To close the header/footer, click away from the header/footer area into the main spreadsheet.

7.1.7 Deleting Fields

- Click the header or footer area.
- Select the field to be deleted.
- Press **Delete**.

Practice Sequence

1	Open the **sale** spreadsheet and the **QTR1** sheet.	☐
2	Change the top and bottom margins to 1.5 cm and the left and right margins to 2cm.	☐
3	Check that the paper size is A4.	☐
4	Ensure that the orientation is portrait.	☐
5	Move the cell range A18:B24 to start in cell F2.	☐
6	Adjust page setup so that the page fits to 1 page wide by 1 page tall.	☐
7	Enter a centre aligned header with your name and a date field.	☐
8	Enter a left aligned header with a file path field.	☐
9	Enter a right aligned header with a page number field.	☐
10	Enter a centred footer with a number of pages field.	☐
11	Edit the header by removing the file path field and replacing with a filename and sheet name field.	☐
12	Edit the footer by deleting the number of pages field and inserting a left aligned time field.	☐
13	Open the **Expenditure** sheet and change the orientation to landscape.	☐
14	Save and close the **sale** spreadsheet.	☐

7.2 Checking and Printing

In this section, you will learn about the following:

- Checking and correcting spreadsheet calculations and text.
- Turning on and off the display of gridlines and the display of row and column headings for printing purposes.
- Applying automatic title row(s) printing on every page of a printed worksheet.
- Previewing a worksheet.
- Printing a selected cell range from a worksheet, an entire worksheet, a number of copies of a worksheet, the entire spreadsheet and a selected chart.

7.2.1 Checking

It is important to check both the text and the calculations within a spreadsheet. Incorrect text appears unprofessional and affects the overall presentation of the spreadsheet. It can also affect the understanding and assimilation of numerical data if the row/column headings are incorrect. If numerical data is incorrect, this could affect calculations and charts based on that data, and may also affect linked calculations on different sheets. Incorrect data and calculations appear unprofessional and may make a spreadsheet unworkable. Therefore, you should do the following.

- Proofread the spreadsheet data carefully for errors (numerical and textual).
- Correct errors where necessary.
- Check calculations – comparison/arithmetic operators, functions, cell references and brackets.

Checking Spelling

- From the **Review Tab** and the **Proofing** group, select the **Spelling** command.

  The **Spelling** window opens.

- Unrecognised words (words that are not in the Spelling dictionary) will be displayed and suggestions to correct them provided.

- Select a suggestion and then click **Change** if you want to change the spelling of a word to the suggested spelling.

- Select **Change All** to change all occurrences of the word throughout the spreadsheet.

- Select **Ignore Once** if you know that the spelling is correct (such as proper names).

- Select **Ignore All** if you want to ignore all occurrences of the word through the spreadsheet.

- When the **Spelling** tool has completed the spell check, a confirmation window opens.

- Click **OK**.

Checking Calculations

- From the **Formulas Tab** and the **Formula Auditing** group, select the **Error Checking** command.

  If errors have been made in the calculations the **Error Checking** window opens..

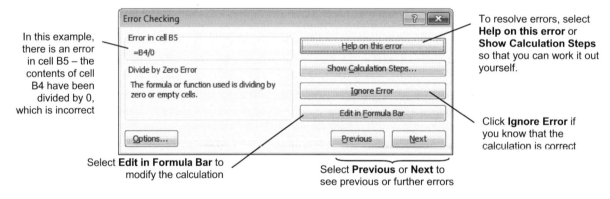

In this example, there is an error in cell B5 – the contents of cell B4 have been divided by 0, which is incorrect

To resolve errors, select **Help on this error** or **Show Calculation Steps** so that you can work it out yourself.

Click **Ignore Error** if you know that the calculation is correct

Select **Edit in Formula Bar** to modify the calculation

Select **Previous** or **Next** to see previous or further errors

- When error checking is complete, a confirmation window opens.

- Click **OK**.

7.2.2 Gridlines

Printed spreadsheets can be displayed with or without gridlines. The default setting is to **view** the gridlines on screen, but to **print** without gridlines.

To display gridlines on printed output, do the following:
- From the **Page Layout** tab and the **Sheet Options** group, in the **Gridlines section**, select the **Print** checkbox (to enter a tick in the box).

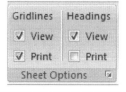

- Select the **Sheet Options** window launcher to see the **Page Setup** window.
- The **Sheet** tab should be the active tab in the **Page Setup** window.
- In the **Print** section, ensure that the **Gridlines** tick box is selected.
- Click **OK**.

7.2.3 Row and Column Headings

Spreadsheets can be printed with or without the row and column headings displayed. The default setting is to print without row and column headings. The row and column headings refer to the row numbers and the column letters. Viewing row and column headings on printed output can help a reader to locate data on the spreadsheet by supplying visual grid references.

To display row and column headings on printed output, do the following:
- From the **Page Layout** tab and the **Sheet Options** group, select the **Print** checkbox (enter a tick in the box) in the **Headings** section.

Alternatively, select the **Sheets Options** window launcher icon and, in the **Print** section, select the **Row and Column Headings** checkbox (enter a tick in the box).
- Click **OK**.

7.2.4 Automatic Title Rows

Automatic row titles can be set to print on every page of a printed spreadsheet.

To apply automatic row titles, do the following:
- From the **Page Layout** tab and the **Page Setup** group, select the **Print Titles** command.

  The **Page Setup** window opens with the **Sheet** tab the active tab.
- In the **Print Titles** section of the window, select the **Rows to repeat at top** button.

Click here

- Select the row titles on the spreadsheet and then click the **Rows to repeat at top** button.

Click here

- Check the row reference is correct.
- Click **OK**.

7.2.5 Previewing a Worksheet

It is good practice to check the layout of a spreadsheet before printing. To preview a spreadsheet, do the following (there are two methods shown below):

Method 1

- From the **File menu**, select **Print**. The spreadsheet will be displayed in the right hand section of the menu.
- Close **Print Preview** by selecting the **File** menu.

Method 2

- From the **Page Layout** tab and the **Page Setup** group, select the **Page Setup** window launcher icon.

  The **Page Setup** window opens.
- Select **Print Preview**.

  The **Print** menu opens, displaying the spreadsheet.
- Close **Print Preview** by selecting the **File** menu.

Print Preview

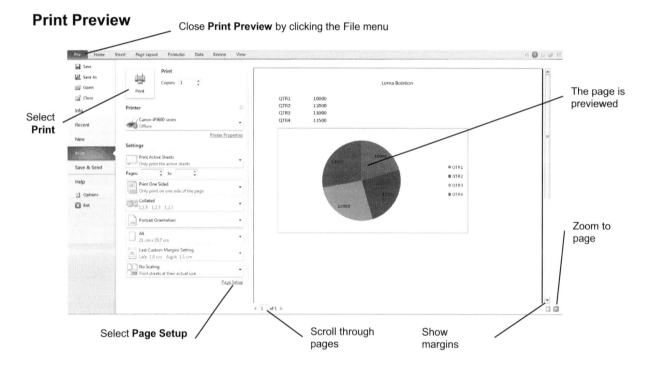

Close **Print Preview** by clicking the File menu

Select **Print**

The page is previewed

Zoom to page

Select **Page Setup**

Scroll through pages

Show margins

note   To preview a chart, select it first before using one of the methods described above.

7.2.6 Printing

There are various options that you can choose when printing. For example, you can print the entire worksheet or the entire spreadsheet (which may contain multiple worksheets), a selected area of a spreadsheet, a chart and also a specific number of copies. The default setting is for printing active worksheets.

To print, do the following:

- From the **File menu**, select **Print**.
- Select the **Print** command to print a worksheet without changing settings or press the keyboard combination of **CTRL + P**).

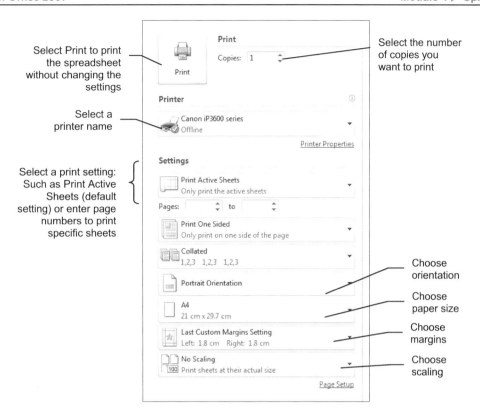

Entire Spreadsheet

- Click the **Settings** arrow.
- Select the **Print Entire Workbook** option.
- Click **Print**.

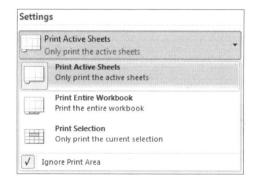

Entire Worksheet

- Select the **Print Active Sheets** option from the **Settings** drop down menu.
- Click **Print**.

Selected Range

- Select the cell range to be printed on the worksheet.
- From the **File menu**, select **Print**.
- From the **Settings** drop down menu, select the **Print Selection** option.
- Click **Print**.

  Alternatively:

  ▷ Select the cell range to be printed on the worksheet.
  ▷ From the **Page Layout** tab and the **Page Setup** group, select the **Print Area** command.
  ▷ Select **Set Print Area** from the drop down menu.
  ▷ From the **File** menu, select **Print**.
  ▷ Ensure that **Print Active Sheets** is displayed in the **Settings** drop down menu.
  ▷ Click **Print**.
  ▷ To ignore the print area, select the Settings drop down menu and choose **Ignore Print Area**.
  ▷ To remove the print area, from the **Page Layout** tab and the **Page Setup** group, select the **Print Area** command and select **Ignore Print Area**.

Chart

- Click the chart to select it (if displayed as an object within a worksheet).
- From the **Print** menu, select the **Print Selected Chart** option from the **Settings** drop down menu.
- Click **Print**.

Number of Copies

- From the **Print** menu, use the scroll arrows on the **Number of Copies** list box to increase/decrease the required number of printed copies.
- Click **Print**.

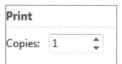

	Practice Sequence	
1	Open the **sale** spreadsheet and the **QTR1** sheet.	☐
2	Check the spelling of text within the spreadsheet and correct any errors.	☐
3	Check the calculations in the spreadsheet and correct any errors.	☐
4	Turn on gridlines and row and column headings for printing.	☐
5	Preview the worksheet.	☐
6	Print one copy of the cell range **A3:B7**.	☐
7	Print one copy of the entire **QTR1** worksheet.	☐
8	On the **Expenditure** sheet, print the pie chart.	☐
9	Save and close the **sale** spreadsheet.	☐
10	Open **Skills.xls** and apply automatic row titles that will print on every page of the **Profit** worksheet (Row 5).	☐
11	Save and close the **Skills** spreadsheet.	☐

Databases

module 5
Databases

Module Goals for Module 5

Databases requires the candidate to understand the concept of a database and demonstrate competence in using a database.

The candidate shall be able to:

- Understand what a database is and how it is organised and operated.
- Create a simple database and view the database content in various modes.
- Create a table, definite and modify fields and their properties; enter and edit data in a table.
- Sort and filter a table or form; create, modify and run queries to retrieve specific information from a database.
- Understand what a form is and create a form to enter, modify and delete records and data in records.
- Create routine reports and prepare outputs ready for distribution.

5

Section 1 ►   Database Theory

1.1   What is a Database?

A database, like a word processing document or spreadsheet, is a file containing information that is kept on some form of electronic storage medium. Database files differ from other files, such as word processing documents, in that information in a database is added and retrieved in a controlled way and is stored in a structured manner.

Databases speed up many processes, particularly the retrieval of information. For example a car tax database used by a government would enable details on individual vehicles to be retrieved quickly, and would enable the automation of certain processes such as the mailing of renewal notices.

The accounts for a small business could be kept in a series of spreadsheet files, for example. But entering information into spreadsheets in an uncontrolled manner would be error-prone. It would be difficult to prepare a balance sheet, next to impossible to produce any level of reporting and difficult to search for information. In contrast, a software application designed for small business accounting would use a database to store the accounts data. Users would enter invoices and so on via on-screen forms, governed by certain rules. Reports could be designed and run, using database queries to retrieve the required information. All the data could be searched quickly with the use of indexes.

1.2   Common Uses of Databases

It might not be immediately apparent, but most people use databases of one sort or another every day, either directly or indirectly.

Some examples are:
- The Apple iTunes music library.
- Airline booking system.
- Accounts and payroll application software used by businesses.
- The contacts list on a mobile phone.
- A list of an electorate and other government records.
- Bank account records.
- Hospital patient records.

These can be compact databases that can be used on portable devices or databases housed in secure facilities and managed by mainframe computers.

1.3   Data and Information

The terms **data** and **information** are often used interchangeably but actually have different meanings.

Data is the raw low-level binary information that a computer can store on a disk or in memory, down to the level where a tiny magnetised area on a disk represents a '1' and a non-magnetised area a '0'. The letter 'A', for example, can be stored as the binary number '01000001' using this approach . That binary number equates to 65 in the normal decimal system, and character number 65 in the standard ASCII character set is the letter 'A'.

Computers and computer software know how to take this raw data and turn it into **information** that is understandable to a user. In the case of a database application, the files that comprise the database consist of nothing but binary '1' and '0', yet the computer operating system and the database software can represent all this as **human-readable** information. Database users should only come in contact with the information that the data in the file represents, not the underlying data itself.

1.4   Microsoft Access

This module will use **Microsoft Office Access 2010**, a straightforward **desktop database application.** Since it is included in the Microsoft Office suite it is very popular and is commonly used. Microsoft Access has database design, reporting and query tools that are closely integrated with its **JET database engine**, all under the umbrella of a single application. As such, it is a good learning tool.

It is useful for creating small databases that can be simultaneously accessed by a small number of users, but it does not scale to many users accessing large databases using a network and is slow when used in this way. In these situations, **professional databases** such as MySQL, PostgreSQL and SQL Server are used. While they are much more powerful, they also require more professional expertise to design and maintain them. The letters **SQL** in these names stand for **Structured Query Language**, a standard language used for retrieving data from and adding data to databases. Microsoft Access can also use this language.

1.5   Database Design and Administration

Professional, large-scale database systems are designed and created by groups of people with specialised skills. The structure of the database might be designed by one group of specialists, the data entry forms and reports designed by programmers and the maintenance of the database performed by a **database administrator (DBA)**. However, over time, these distinctions have often become blurred. Database design and report creation tools have become easier to use, and it often now falls to programmers to implement all aspects of the creation and design of a database through to the **user interface (UI)** that database users see on their screens. Database users enter data into the database, change and update existing data, and retrieve information from the database. The users of a professional database are often the general employees of a company and might not necessarily be aware of how a database actually works. The role of the database administrator is still essentially to ensure that the database is available to users at all times.

The typical duties of a DBA include:
- Choosing the physical hardware and operating systems used for hosting the database.
- Overseeing security, for example determining the levels of access that individual users have to parts of the database.
- Optimising performance by analysing the design of the database and the capacity of the hardware.
- Implementing a database backup strategy and recovering databases after system crashes or other catastrophic failures.

1.6   Database Overview

1.6.1 The Components of a Database

Microsoft Access is a **relational database management system** (RDBMS). It enables the creation of **databases** that contains **tables**, each of which, in turn, stores information on a particular topic. **Relationships** can then be defined to bring all the information together. Data relating to unique subjects is stored in **tables**.

In a database created to manage a club, there might be individual tables as follows:
- **Members**: Name and address details for club members.
- **Fees**: Details of fees paid and due.
- **Competitions**: Competition results for members.

Note that each table is concerned only with one distinct subject – there is no **Fees And Competitions** table, for example.

A table is the 'primary structure' in a database that stores fields and records.

- A **field** is a single item of data, like a person's first name.
- A **record** is a collection of fields, such as a person's first name, surname, address and phone number.

Fields and records make up other database objects, such as forms, reports and queries.

In a database, it is possible to store many different types of data, but care must be taken when the database is being organised. A field should contain only one element of data. For example, a field might contain a person's first name. That same field should not contain any other elements of data, such as the person's surname or title.

In Access, there are different types of fields, depending on what type of data they hold. The most common types of field are text fields and number fields.

- **Text fields** contain letters, such as a name, or combinations of letters and numbers, such as an address.
- **Number fields** contain data used in mathematical calculations.

The other types of field include: **Yes/No** fields, **Memo** fields, used for long entries of text, **Currency** fields, used for numbers that represent money, and **Date/Time** fields, used for numbers that represent a date or time.

1.6.2 A Note on Terminology

The terms **field** and **column**, **record** and **row** can be seen throughout Microsoft Access. The terms **column** and **row** are used when referring to the visual representation of a table in grid form within DataSheet View. When discussing the structure of the data, **record** is used instead of **row**, and **field** instead of **column**.

In the illustration, the table called **Members** has fields called **Forename**, **Surname** and **Age**.

The table must naturally be able to store information on more than one member. Each unique member in the **Members** table would be stored as a **record** or **row**. The illustration shows the table with four records, each containing data describing a different member.

Note that the fields are repeated in each record. This means that each individual item of data can be changed or retrieved if the record number is known. The value of the **Surname** field in record 3 is 'Gupta', for example.

Records and fields can be thought of as being organised in the same way as rows and columns in a spreadsheet. Microsoft Access uses the terms 'rows' and 'columns', 'records and 'fields' interchangeably.

1.6.3 Field Types

When a table is created each field in that table is given a name and a data type, which determines the type of data it can hold.

The types available in Microsoft Access 2010 are, in alphabetical order, as follows.

Type	Used For	Notes
Attachment	Attaching any type of file	The Attachment type is used to attach many types of file to a record. For example, an image file containing a photograph and a word processing document containing employment details could be attached to each employee's record in a personnel database. In the example below, the first record has two attachments. Double-clicking the field will open an Attachments window, from where attachments can be opened, added and deleted.
AutoNumber	Unique identifiers	A type used primarily for **primary key** indexes. When a new record is added to a table, Access will automatically enter a numeric value which is one greater than the previous record, making every record uniquely numbered. In the example here, the ID field is an AutoNumber field. If a new record were added, Access would automatically place the number 4 in the ID field for that new record. Users cannot overwrite the value in an AutoNumber field.
Currency	Currency values	Stores numeric data to 4 decimal places, and Access will include a currency symbol and commas when the data is displayed on a form or report, as appropriate for the regional settings of the database. Gross Pay: €120,229.23
Date/Time	Dates and times	Using this type of field for dates and times means that when a date is inputted it can be easily validated to be in a particular format, such as American or British, incorrect dates can be rejected. Access will also provide a **date picker** beside the field when it is displayed on a form.
Hyperlink	Web hyperlinks	This stores a **hyperlink** to a web location, which is displayed as such on forms and can be clicked to launch a web browser. Homepage: www.bec.ie http://www.bec.ie

Lookup	Predefined lists	A Lookup field displays a list of items to choose from. The items in the list can be fixed or can come from another table in the database.	
Number	Numeric data	This field is used to store numbers of varying types. The most common are: **Long integer**, which can store numbers with no decimal place from 2,147,483,648 to 2,147,483,647 **Double**, which can store decimal numbers from 4.94×10^{-324} to $1.79769313486231 \times 10^{308}$	
OLE Object	Embedding documents from other applications	Microsoft Word documents, graphics, sounds and many other types of file can be stored inside the Access database using this type of field. It has been superseded in Access 2010 by the **Attachment** type, but remains so that databases created by earlier versions of Access can still be used.	
Text	Text data	One of the most common field types, used for names, etc. Can also include a combination of letters and numbers, as in an address.	
Yes/No	'True or false' values or similar	By default, fields of this type are displayed as **checkboxes** when data is being entered.	

1.6.4 Field Properties

In addition to defining the **type** of a field, various other **properties** can also be set, and these are determined by their type.

The properties of a Text-type field are shown in the illustration below.

Some important properties are:
- **Field size**: This is the maximum number of letters and/or numbers that can be entered into this field.
- **Required**: This means that this field cannot be left empty when a new record has been created and data is being entered.
- **Indexed**: Whether or not an index is present for this field.
- **Format**: Format relates to how data in a field is displayed, e.g. a format might specific the Times New Roman font, size 10 pt.

General	Lookup	
Field Size		255
Format		
Input Mask		
Caption		
Default Value		
Validation Rule		
Validation Text		
Required		No
Allow Zero Length		Yes
Indexed		No
Unicode Compression		Yes
IME Mode		No Control
IME Sentence Mode		None
Smart Tags		

The properties of a number-type field look like the illustration below (note that some properties are the same as text-type fields):

Some important properties are:
- **Field size**: The most common sizes for number fields are Long Integer if no decimals are required, and Double if decimals are required. Other types such as byte and decimal can be also specified.

General	Lookup	
Field Size		Long Integer
Format		
Decimal Places		Auto
Input Mask		
Caption		
Default Value		
Validation Rule		
Validation Text		
Required		No
Indexed		No
Smart Tags		
Text Align		General

- **Decimal places**: When the Field Size is set to one of the decimalised types, then decimal places can be changed as required.
- **Format**: Format relates to how data in a field is displayed, e.g. a format might specific the Times New Roman font, size 10 pt.

Field properties should be set appropriately with sizes defined so that they are large enough to hold any data that is likely to be entered, but not so large that most of the capacity is wasted. A record in a table takes up an amount of storage on disk that is determined by the field properties as shown on the previous page. If all the text-type fields in a table are of Field Size = 255 when this capacity is not needed, then disk space will be wasted. As tables grow larger, this, in turn, has an impact on the speed of searches.

1.6.5 Setting a Default Value

Default Value is another field property. If it is defined for a field, then the field will automatically be set to this value when a new record is created. The value can then be changed or removed if required. This saves time in data entry, and also to help ensure data integrity. Default Values can be applied to Text, Memo, Number, Date/Time, Currency, Yes/No and Hyperlink fields.

Setting a **Yes/No** field to the default value of **Yes** will ensure it always displays a ticked checkbox when a new record is created.

Entering a number in the Default Value for a Currency field will display that value when a new record is created.

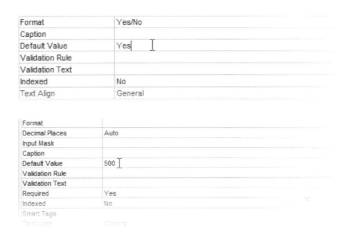

The effect of these settings on a new record can be seen in the following illustration.

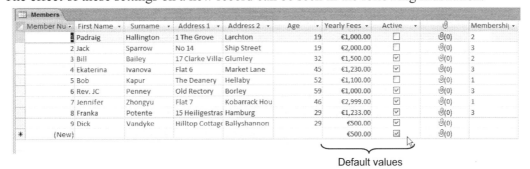

Default values

1.6.6 Changing Field Dimensions and Properties

Field sizes and properties can be changed when there is data in the table. However, reducing the size or changing the type of a field may result in the loss of data in some records.

For example, changing a Number field of type Double to type Integer would cause a number like 45.12 to be rounded to 45. If the field type were to be changed back to Double at a later stage, the table would contain 45.00, not the original value of 45.12. Similarly, reducing the field size of a Text field might truncate the text in some records. The removed data cannot be retrieved.

Access will display a warning before allowing these changes to happen.

1.6.7 Indexes

There are two ways to find a number in a phone book. One is to start at the beginning and read every entry until the number is found. This is obviously a hugely inefficient approach. A far more efficient approach is to utilise the fact that the phone numbers are **indexed** using the surnames of their owners. It is then possible to locate the required number very quickly by searching using the surname.

A similar approach is used within database tables. As part of the design process, fields that will be used to search frequently should have indexes defined for them.

An index can involve one or more fields. For example, in a table containing orders for a company's products, an index could be created on the order number and product code.

1.6.8 Primary Key Indexes

A primary key is a field or fields used for uniquely identifying each row in a table, e.g. a member number in a table containing information about club members. A field such as member number is a good choice for a primary key because it is unique to each member, it should never be empty and the values in it will never change. Fields of the AutoNumber type (see Section 1.6.3) are also a good choice. A name or address field is a bad choice because the information in these may change over time.

A primary key should be created for every table, and an index defined for it. If there are no likely candidates, create an autonumber-type field called 'ID' and specify this as the primary key. Otherwise, there will be no easy way of uniquely identifying each record.

When a table is created in Microsoft Access 2010 datasheet view, a primary key field called **ID** and associated index are created automatically.

In the illustration on the right, the Member Number field is a primary key as indicated by the key icon beside it.

Primary Key icon

1.6.9 What should Fields Hold?

Each field in a table should contain a single item of data.

It would be possible but incorrect to define a table like the one illustrated below.

Combining information in one field is bad practice. Each field should contain only one piece of data

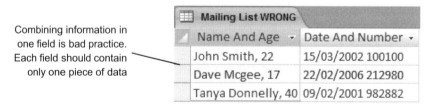

In this example, Names and Ages are contained in one field called **Name And Age**, and Date Joined and Member Number in another called **Date And Number**. This design would make searching and reporting on the data extremely difficult and is bad design practice.

The correct approach would be as follows.

Each field should contain only one piece of data

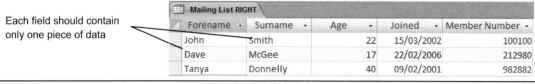

It is now possible to search easily for data based on surname, name, age, for example, or any combination of these fields.

1.6.10 What should Tables Hold?

At the table level, good database design dictates that each subject has its own table.

It would be possible to store information about fees due and fees paid in the same table as the member names and addresses. However, since each member will have many sets of fees applied to them over a period of time, this would cause repetition of data.

Databases should avoid needless repetition of data

The **Fee Payment History** table in the illustration above has been created to store information about fees due to be paid by club members.

A new record has been created in the table each time yearly fees are due for members. Since the fees information has been stored in the same table as the member details, the member name, surname, age and so on are needlessly repeated.

For example, taking the two records where Forename is **John**, and Surname is **Smith**, it is evident from examining the **Fee Due** and **Fee Paid** fields in those records that the fees due on 01/01/2009 are not paid, and the fees that were due on 01/01/2008 have been paid. If this table should only store information about fees, then the rest of the fields, those that contain name and address data, should not be present and also are storing needlessly repeated information.

1.6.11 Relationships

As discussed, the example in Section 1.6.10 is poor database design. Member name and address information has been mixed together in one table with fees information, whereas each of these individual subjects should have their own table.

In other words, there should be a table containing just information about members, such as their name, address and member number.

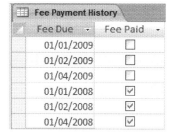

There should be a separate table containing dates on which fees are due from each member.

However, although good practice, separating data in this way creates a problem. The Fee Payment History table contains the dates on which fees are due, and an indication of whether they have been paid, but no way of **relating** this information to which member each record belongs to.

To get around this problem, a **relationship** must be established between the two tables. Relationships are based on a field or fields that are common between the two tables.

In the current example, the member number is the ideal candidate, as it is the primary key in the Member Numbers table. The Fee Payment History table does not contain a member number field, so it must be added, and it must be of the same type and size as the member number field in the Members table.

A field should be added that is common to both tables – this creates a relationship between them and gives context to the data

The common field should be the same type and size in both tables

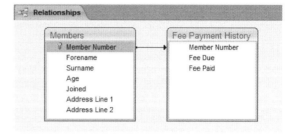

With this in place, a relationship can now be defined between the Members and Fee Payment History tables, and is indicated by the arrow in the diagram on the right. Details of how to create and define a relationship are covered in Section 2.7.

This is a **one-to-many** relationship. Member numbers are unique, so for every individual record in the Members table on the left there may be no fee payment records on the right, or one fee payment record, or many fee payment records.

The diagram below shows this relationship using the current example data:

The tables are related on the Member Number field, which is common to each. Member 100100 in the Members table has two related records in the Fee Payment History table, indicating the two separate dates on which fees for this member were due and whether or not the fees have been paid.

This relationship would be useful when designing queries, reports and forms, as fields from both tables can be used easily without having to worry about defining how the tables relate to each other at the time of designing the report or query.

1.6.12 Maintaining Integrity

The main use of relationships is to maintain **referential integrity** between tables. In the example in Section 1.2.10, if the relationship was not in place and a member was deleted from the Members table, this would result in **orphaned records** in the Fee Payment History table. These records would have a member number that matched them to a member who no longer existed.

A rule can be created against the relationship to ensure that if a member is deleted from the Members table, then any records belonging to that member in the Fee Payment History table are **automatically** deleted. This maintains integrity and ensures that there are no orphaned records.

1.7   Queries

Queries are requests for data to be returned from a database, based on certain rules. The results of a query can be used as a source of data for reports or forms. They can also be used in the opposite direction – to send data into a database.

Microsoft Access, and most other databases, use a special language for performing queries called **Structured Query Language (SQL)**.

An example of an SQL query is to return the First Name, Surname and Member Number field for all members whose age is greater than 18 from the Members table.

> SELECT Members. [First Name], Members.[Surname], Members.[Age], Members.[Member Number]
> FROM Members
> WHERE (((Members.[Age])>18));

In Access, queries can be created by entering the SQL directly, or by using a point-and-click Wizard. See Section 2.5 for more information and practice with Queries.

1.8   Forms

1.8.1   Definition

A **form** uses some or all of the data contained in an existing table and displays it in a user-friendly layout. You can use a form to easily display records in a database. For example, the **Golf Club** database table contains all the data about members of the golf club, including a complete list of names, addresses and membership numbers. If certain information is required from this table, such as a list of membership numbers, but not addresses, a form is used to filter this information from the table.

Using a form, it is also possible to maintain records, to enter new records and change existing records in a database.

note | Any changes made to data in a form will be updated in the table.

1.8.2   Using Forms for Data Entry

Almost all applications that use databases only allow users to enter data via a **form**. Even something as simple as a contact list on a mobile phone will have a simple **user interface layer** providing a form for controlled data entry.

Data can be entered into any table in **Datasheet View**.

Field Name	Data Type
Purchase Order ID	AutoNumber
Supplier ID	Number
Created By	Number
Submitted Date	Date/Time
Creation Date	Date/Time
Status ID	Number
Expected Date	Date/Time
Shipping Fee	Currency
Taxes	Currency
Payment Date	Date/Time
Payment Amount	Currency
Payment Method	Text
Notes	Memo
Approved By	Number
Approved Date	Date/Time
Submitted By	Number

The table can also be displayed in **DataSheet View**, which presents the data in a tabular format and allows data entry and navigation.

It is possible to enter data directly into the tables that make up the database using **DataSheet View** in Microsoft Access.

However, this is rarely allowed for anything other than direct manipulation of the tables by an administrator, for three main reasons.

- The interface is not particularly user-friendly.
- There are fewer opportunities to control and limit what users are entering.
- A form may ultimately update a variety of tables almost simultaneously, and this would be difficult to achieve by entering data directly.

Microsoft Access has a sample database application called Northwind Traders. It contains a form specially designed for entering Purchase Orders, and this is the interface that end users of the database see.

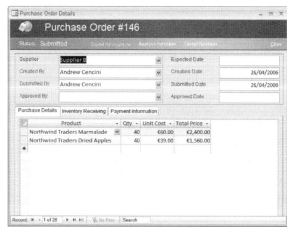

1.9   Reports

There is not much point in having data in a database if it cannot be extracted and used when needed. Reports are a vital part of almost all applications that use databases and are used to print selected information from a table or query.

A payroll application that uses a database to store employee and pay information would have a range of reports available, such as:

- Employee lists.
- Tax records.
- The payslips that are sent out to employees.

Microsoft Access contains a built-in report writing tool, and the options for outputting reports include being previewed to screen, printed and exported to Microsoft Excel. See Section 2.9 for more information and practice with reports.

1.10 Switching Between View Modes

Database objects such as tables, forms, queries and reports all have different view options. Each view option enables you to carry out a variety of functions. The most common views are listed below.

- **Tables** have a DataSheet View, where the data is displayed and can be manipulated in a variety of ways, and a Design View.
- **Forms** have Form View, Layout View and Design View
- **Reports** have Report View, Layout View, Design View and a Print Preview.

To change between views, do the following:
- Open the table, form or report.
- Select the **Home** tab on the ribbon.
- In the **Views** section, click the **View** button.
- Select the required view (these will be different, as listed above, depending on what is open).

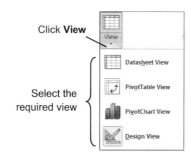

Click **View**

Select the required view

Alternatively

- ▷ Right-click the table, form or report name in the **Navigation Pane** at the left of the Access window.
- ▷ Select **Open** from the menu to open the table in **Datasheet View**.
- ▷ *Alternatively*, double-click the table name to open it in **Datasheet View**.
- ▷ Select **Design View** from the menu to open the table in **Design View**.

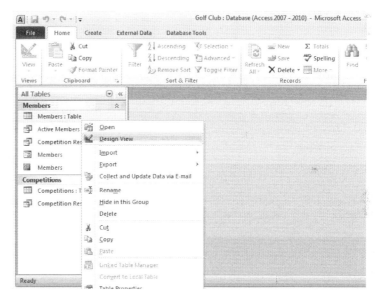

The View options for tables, forms and reports are covered in detail in later sections.

Section 2 ▶   Practice

Because of the integrated nature of databases, the remainder of this module will look at the creation and manipulation of a database called **Golf Club.accdb**, using a single set of data in Microsoft Access 2010.

2.1   Basic Operations

2.1.1   Opening and Closing a Database Application

Opening

There are several ways to open Microsoft Access, the database application being used in this module. Depending on the particular PC setup, the icon to start Microsoft Access 2010 may be present in one or more locations.

- If the Access icon is visible on the desktop or within a folder, double-clicking it will start the application.

- The icon may also be visible in the favourites area of the **Start menu** or within the **Microsoft Office** folder.

Access 2010 menu option (pinned to Start Menu in Favourites area)

- Access can be opened using the Start menu.
  - ▷ Click the **Start** button.
  - ▷ Select **All Programs**.
  - ▷ Select **Microsoft Office**.
  - ▷ Select **Microsoft Access 2010** from the sub-menu that appears.

- Double-clicking any **Microsoft Access database file** in Windows will open the file within the application.

Closing

Microsoft Access can be closed in the same way as any other application.

To close Access, do the following:
- Click the **Close X** button at the top right of its window.

Alternatively
▷ Click the **File menu** at the top left of the window.
▷ Click **Exit** on the menu that appears.

File menu

Exit Access

2.1.2 Opening and Closing a Database

Opening

A database can be opened easily by double-clicking its icon from within Windows, as mentioned in Section 2.1.1. Doing this will automatically start Microsoft Access and open the database.

To open an existing database from within Microsoft Access, do the following:
- Click the **File menu**.
- Click **Open** in the drop-down menu that appears.

File menu

Open

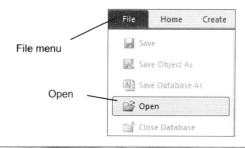

- The **Open** window opens.
- Locate the database.
- Select it by clicking it.
- Click **Open**.

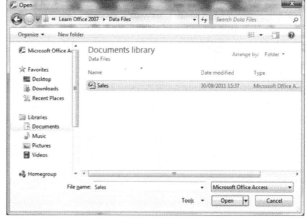

Alternatively, click **Recent** in the **File** menu and then click the database name in the **Recent Databases** list

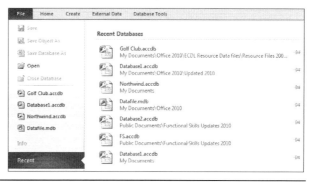

Closing

To close a database, do the following:

- Click the **File menu**.
- Select **Close Database** from the drop-down menu.

Close Database —— Close Database

2.1.3 Using Help

As with any Windows application, Help is readily available by pressing the F1 key, or clicking on the Help icon at the top right of the Access window.

See Section 7 in the BYB for more information on Help.

2.1.4 The Ribbon

The ribbon made its debut in Office 2007 and acts as the main application menu in all the Office applications, including Access. It is displayed at the top of the Access window and contains buttons and menus for all the most commonly performed tasks, grouped into tabs.

Clicking the title text of a tab will change the ribbon to display that group of commands, as in the two examples below.

Home tab

Create tab

In addition there is a **Quick Access Toolbar**. By default, this is shown at the top of the window, above the File menu.
Clicking the arrow icon at the right of the toolbar will display a customisation menu.

Click arrow to display the **Quick Access Toolbar** menu

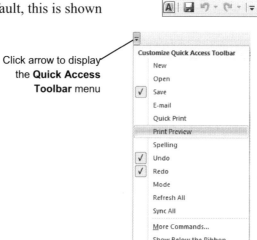

Ticking items on this menu will add that command to the
Quick Access Toolbar. In the illustration on the right, the
Quick Print and **Print Preview** commands have been added.

2.1.5 Minimising and Restoring the Ribbon

The ribbon can also be minimised or hidden. When minimised, only the titles of the various
ribbon tabs (Home, Create, etc.) are visible. Clicking any of these will cause the ribbon to pop up
and display that tab.

Minimising the Ribbon

To minimise the ribbon, do the following:
- Right-click anywhere on the ribbon.
  A drop-down menu is displayed.
- Select **Minimize the Ribbon**.

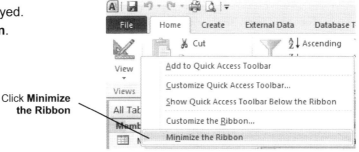

Click **Minimize the Ribbon**

The ribbon will now be displayed as in the illustration below.

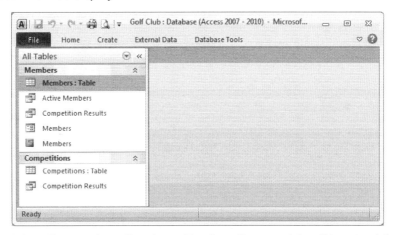

- Clicking a tab heading, such as **Database Tools**, will expand the ribbon enabling an option
  from that tab to be selected.

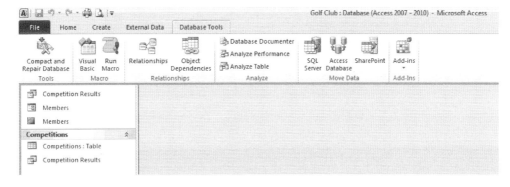

- Selecting an option will hide the ribbon again.

Restoring the Ribbon

To restore the ribbon, do the following:

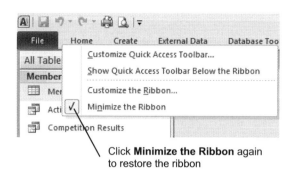

- Right-click the bar containing the tabs.

- Click **Minimize the Ribbon**.

- Note how a tick is displayed beside the menu command to indicate that it is active.

- Select the option again to restore the ribbon to its normal appearance.

Click **Minimize the Ribbon** again to restore the ribbon

2.2   First Steps with Databases

From this point onwards the text will take the form of the step-by-step creation of a new database, with an associated data entry form and report.

Follow each step and complete the Practice Sequences.

2.2.1   Creating and Saving a New Database

Creating a New Database

To create a new database, do the following:

- Start **Microsoft Access** using any of the methods detailed in Section 2.1.1.

  Initially, the **File** menu is open with **New** database options displayed.

- Click **Blank Database**.

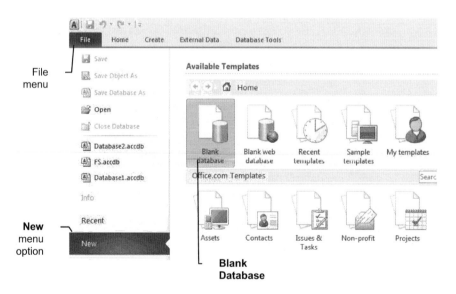

- The default file name for a new database is **Database1**. Click into the File Name box and enter a relevant name for the database.

- To create a database within the default file location, click the **Create** button; otherwise follow the instructions for **Saving a New Database** below.

Saving a New Database

The default location in which the **.accdb** database file will be saved is displayed below the File Name textbox.

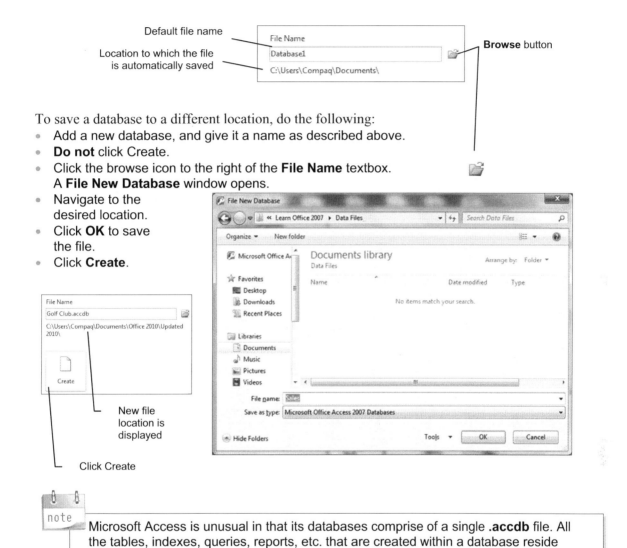

Default file name

Location to which the file is automatically saved

Browse button

New file location is displayed

Click Create

To save a database to a different location, do the following:
- Add a new database, and give it a name as described above.
- **Do not** click Create.
- Click the browse icon to the right of the **File Name** textbox.
  A **File New Database** window opens.
- Navigate to the desired location.
- Click **OK** to save the file.
- Click **Create**.

> **note** Microsoft Access is unusual in that its databases comprise of a single **.accdb** file. All the tables, indexes, queries, reports, etc. that are created within a database reside within the file. This has the advantage of making it very easy to move an entire database to a different location if needed.

2.3 Tables

2.3.1 Creating a Table

When a new database has been created, a new table called **Table1** will be created automatically and presented in **Datasheet View**. An AutoNumber field called **ID** has also been created automatically and marked as the primary key, to provide a unique identifier for each record.

- This table will be used to hold personal details and a unique membership number for each member.

These personal details are contained in fields (represented by columns in the table (and different types of data – e.g. text, number, date/time or yes/no – are kept in separate fields. See Section 2.3.4 for more on creating fields.

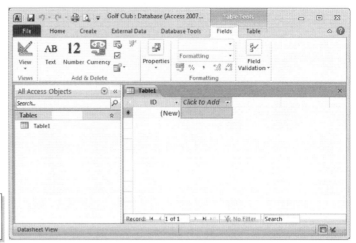

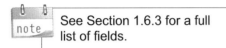 See Section 1.6.3 for a full list of fields.

- Right-click the ID field and choose **Rename Field** from the pop-up menu.

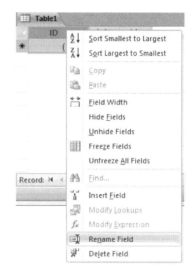

The cursor will move to the field heading.
- Overtype the word **ID** with the words **Member Numbers**.
- Click into the field beneath the field heading to accept the change.

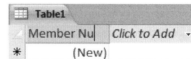

At this stage, the table should be saved.

2.3.2 Saving a Table
To save the table, do the following:

- Click the **Save** icon above the File menu at the top left of the Access window.

If this is the first time the table has been saved, a window will open prompting for a name.

- Enter a name for the table.
- Click **OK** to save.

2.3.3 Other Actions with Tables

Opening a Table
The standard way to open a table is as follows:

- Start **Microsoft Access**.
- Open the required database (see Section 2.1.2).
  The objects comprising the database are listed in the **Navigation Pane**.
  Tables are displayed with **: Table** after their name,
  e.g. **Members : Table** and **Competitions : Table** in
  the illustration on the right.
- Double-click the desired table to open it in DataSheet
  View.

Alternatively, right-click the table name and select
Design View to open it in that mode.

Closing a Table

To close a table, do the following:

- Click the **Close X** button at the right of the table.

Close X button

Reopening a Table

To reopen a table or other Access object (e.g. form, query, etc.), do the following:

- Double-click it in the
  Navigation Pane.
  The table will open in a tab in
  the middle part of the Access
  window. Multiple tables and
  other Access objects can be
  open simultaneously on
  different
  tabs.

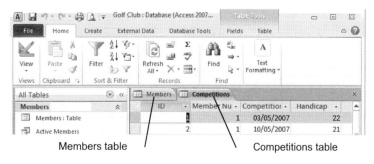

Members table   Competitions table

Deleting a Table

To delete a table or other Access object (e.g. form, query, report), do the following:

- Ensure it is not open.
- Right-click the name of the table (or form, query or report) in the **Navigation Pane**.
- Select **Delete** from the pop-up menu that appears.
  A confirmation window opens.
- Click **Yes** to delete.
- Click **Cancel** to keep the table.

2.3.4 Creating Fields and Applying Field Properties

To define new fields, it is more convenient to use **Design View**. This mode is specifically intended for this purpose.

To switch to Design view, do the following:

- Right-click the title tab of the table.
- Select **Design View** from the pop-up menu that appears.

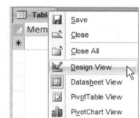

Design View lists the table fields and their types at the top of the window, and the properties associated with the currently highlighted field at the bottom.

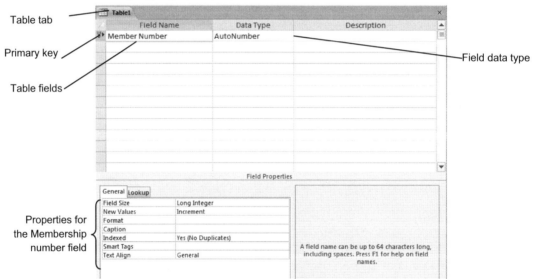

In Design View, the Data Type of a field can be changed as follows:

- Click in the **Data Type** column in the list of fields.
- Select the required **Data Type** from the drop-down list.

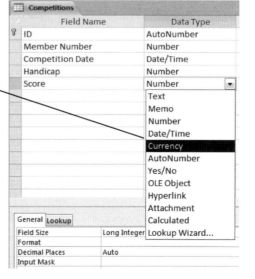

Select the data type from the drop-down list

Changing the data type of a field when the database already contains data can result in data loss. For example, changing a Memo-type field to a Text-type field will result in only the first 255 characters being retained. This is because the Text data type can only store this many characters.

Properties of a Text Field

After Membership Number, the next field that is required is for the members' first names.

- Click in the **Field Name** column, in the row below the existing **Member Number** row.
- Enter **First Name** as the field name.
- Press the Enter key.
  The default **Data Type** of **Text** is correct and so doesn't need to be changed.

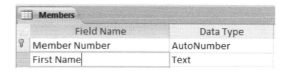

The maximum length of the **First Name** field should be specified.

- Ensure the **First Name** row is highlighted in the top of the screen.
- In the **Field Properties** section, click in the cell to the right of the **Field Size** property.
- Enter the value **30**.

Field size

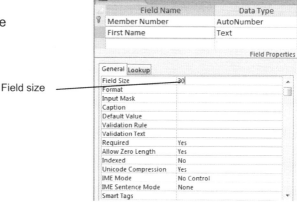

The First Name field is a required field – it should not be possible for a new record to be saved with no First Name entered.

To set the Required field property, do the following:

- Move the mouse cursor over the **Required** field property.
- Click the arrow.
- Select **Yes** from the drop-down list.

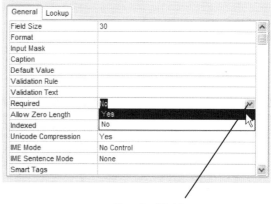

Required field arrow

Properties of a Number Field

The properties available for a number field are shown in the illustration below.

- **Field Size**: determines the type of numbers that will be stored. The two most common types are **Long Integer**, where decimals are not needed and **Double** where decimals are needed. There are various other types such as **byte**. For potentially large databases careful consideration should be given to the type, as some types take more storage space and result in slower processing.
- **Decimal Places**: controls the number of decimal places if extra precision is needed.
- **Format**: Format relates to how data in a field is displayed, e.g. a format might specific the Times New Roman font, size 10 pt.

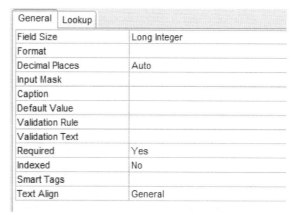

Properties of a Date/Time Field

The properties available for a Date/Time field are shown in the illustration on the right.

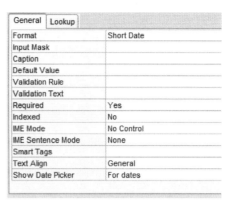

- **Format**: Format determines whether a Date and Time, or Date or Time are stored and how they are displayed.

Properties of a Yes/No Field

The properties available for a Yes/No field are shown in the illustration on the right.

- **Default Value**: Setting the Default Value to Yes will ensure it always displays a tick checkbox when a new record is created. See Section 1.6.5 for more on Default Values.

- **Format**: Format controls what is actually displayed for the field. This can be one of the three options on the right. The field will contain a **0** for **False/No/Off** and a **1** for **True/Yes/On**.

Practice Sequence

Create a table called **Members** with the following fields and listed properties.

Field Name	Data Type	Field Size	Properties
Member Number	[created automatically]	[created automatically]	[created automatically]
First Name	Text	30	Required: **Yes**
Surname	Text	50	Required: **Yes**
Address 1	Text	50	Required: **Yes**
Address 2	Text	50	
Age	Number	Long Integer	Required: **Yes**
Yearly Fees	Number	Currency	Default Value: **500.00** Required: **Yes**
Date Joined	Date/Time	Short Date	Required: **Yes**
Active	Yes/No	[not applicable]	Default Value: **Yes**
Photo	Attachment	[not applicable]	

2.3.4 Creating a New Table
Another table is needed to hold details of competitions that the member has played in.

To add a new table, do the following:
- Click the **Create** tab on the ribbon.
- Click **Table** in the list of commands.

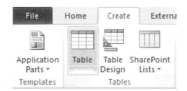

A new table, also called **Table1**, will be created.
- Change the view to Design View.
- Name the table **Competitions** and save it.
- Add the fields shown in the list below.

Field Name	Data Type	Properties
ID [created automatically]	AutoNumber	Set automatically
Member Number	Number	Field size: **Long Integer** Required: **Yes**
Competition Date	Date/Time	Format: **Short Date** Required: **Yes**
Handicap	Number	Field Size: **Long Integer** Required: **Yes**
Score	Number	Field Size: **Long Integer** Required: **Yes**

note   A Primary Key field called ID is automatically created. The ID field will provide a unique identifier for each row in the Competitions table.

Lookup Wizard
The last field to be added is a **Lookup Wizard** field. In this database, it is used to indicate whether or not the member is a Gold, Silver or Bronze member.

This field will be a Text-type field, but the values will come from a predefined list. This is set up as follows:
- Add a new field with the name **Membership Level**.
- Set the data type to **Text** in the normal way.
- Open the **Data Type** list for the field again, but this time select **Lookup Wizard**.
- Select the second option **I will type in the values that I want**.
- Click **Next**.

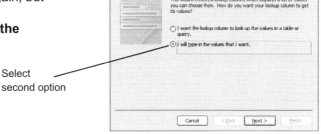

Select second option

In the next window, like the example on the right:
- Change the number of columns to 2.
- Click in the table list.
- Enter data as follows:
  1 Gold
  2 Silver
  3 Bronze
- Click **Finish**.

Select number of columns

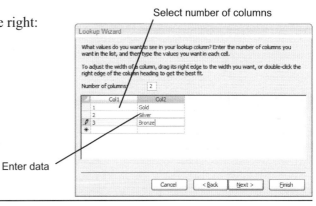

Enter data

The finished list of fields should look like the example on the right.

Field Name	Data Type
Member Number	AutoNumber
First Name	Text
Surname	Text
Address 1	Text
Address 2	Text
Age	Number
Date Joined	Date/Time
Yearly Fees	Currency
Active	Yes/No
Photo	Attachment
Membership Level	Text

2.3.5 Validation Rules

In addition to the properties already set, such as Required and Default Value, additional **Validation Rules** can be applied to fields to further control what can be entered. In our Golf Club, club rules state that members must be at least 18. It is also unlikely that any will join past the age of 100. Therefore, a rule can be applied to limit the ages entered to this range.

Number Fields

To set limits – validation rules – on what data can be entered in a number field, do the following:
- In **Design View**, click on the **Age** field in the field list at the top of the screen.
- The Validation Rule and Validation Text is one of the field properties at the bottom of the screen.
- Enter the following text next to **Validation Rule**:
  - ▶ **>=18 And <=100**
- Enter the following text next to **Validation Text**:
  - **Age must be between 18 and 100.**

Validation Rule	>=18 And <=100
Validation Text	Age must be between 18 and 100.

- If a value less than 18 or greater than 100 is entered into the field (in DataSheet View or via a form, or any other method), then an error message using the Validation Text will occur.

  This rule will be applied when adding a new record, or editing an existing record and modifying the value in the **Age** field.

Text Fields

Validation rules can be applied to Text-type fields in a similar way.

To prevent the use of the surname **Ahern**, do the following:
- Open the Members table in Design View.
- Select the **Surname** field in the field list.
- Enter the following text against **Validation Rule** in the properties list: **<>"Ahern"**.

Enter text in the **Validation Rule** field property

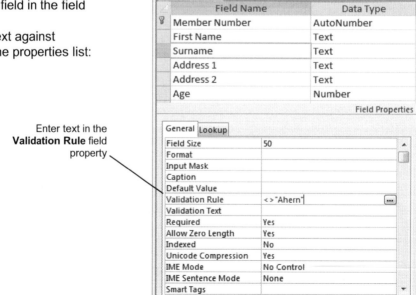

- When the table is saved a prompt will appear to confirm the change.

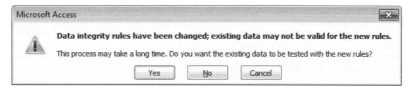

Currency Fields

To configure the Yearly Fees field to only accept values between 100 and 3000, do the following:
- Open the **Members** table in **Design View**.
- Select the **Yearly Fees** field in the field list.
- Enter the following text against **Validation Rule** in the properties list: **>100 and <3000**.
- Enter **Fees must be between 100 and 3000.** against the **Validation Text** property.
- When the table is saved a prompt will appear to confirm the change.

Enter text in the **Validation Rule** field property and **Validation Text** field property

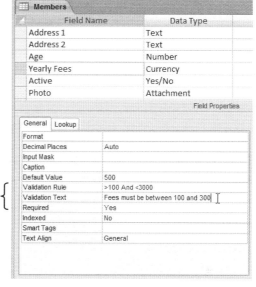

Date/Time Fields

The Golf Club was founded on 13 April 1960. It is therefore impossible that any member participated in a competition before this date.

To add a rule to the **Competitions** table preventing dates before the founding date being used, do the following:
- Open the **Competitions** table in Design View.
- Highlight the **Competition Date** field in the field list.
- Enter the following text against the **Validation Rule** property:
  >= #13/04/1960#
- Enter **Date must be on or after April 13th 1960** against the **Validation Text** property.
- When the table is saved a prompt will appear to confirm the change.

Enter text in the **Validation Rule** field property and **Validation Text** field property

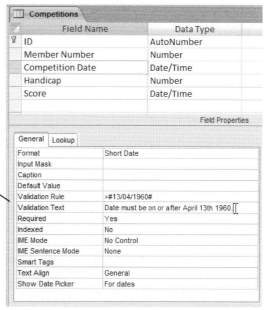

 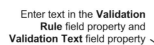 A date can be entered into the validation rule in the following format: #January 23, 1982#. It will then be converted to a short date format appropriate for the region.

2.3.6 Setting a Field as a Primary Key

A **primary key** is a field or fields used for uniquely identifying each row in a table, for example a member number in a table containing information about club members. A primary key should be created for every table, and an index defined for it.

To set a field as a primary key, do the following:
- Open the **Members** table in **Design View**.
- In the field list, highlight the **Member Number** field.
- Right-click in the area to the left of the field name.
- Select **Primary Key** from the menu.

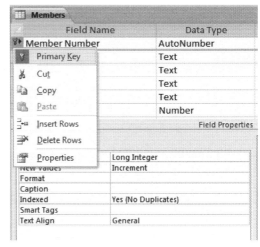

note | The key icon is displayed beside the field name.

2.3.7 Creating an Index

Fields that will be used to search should have indexes defined for them. An index can involve one or more fields. For example, in a table containing orders for a company's products, an index could be created on the order number and product code.

To create an index, perform the following steps:
- Open the **Members** table in **Design View**.
- Select the **Age** field in the field list.
- Click the **Indexed** property in the Field Properties list.
- As there can be multiple members with the same age, therefore, select **Yes (Duplicates OK)** from the menu that is displayed.

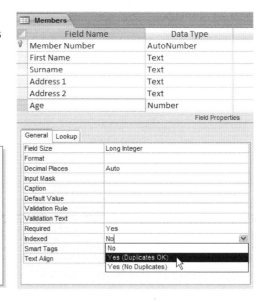

 note | Click **Yes (Duplicates OK)** if more than one record can have the same data in this field, e.g. there may be several members with the same last name.

Click **Yes (No Duplicates)** to ensure that no two records are the same, e.g. giving stock items a unique name.

In the **Members** table it would be useful to be able to search on the Member's full name, but the name is stored in two fields – **First Name** and **Surname**.

It is possible to create an index involving multiple fields, as follows:
- Open the **Members** table in **Design View**.
- On the ribbon, click the **Indexes** option.

The **Indexes** window opens.

- In the **Index Name** column, define a new index name by entering **Full Name** in the first empty cell.

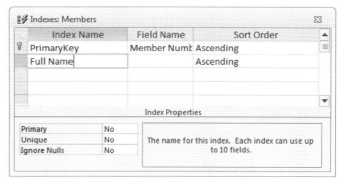

- Click the **Field Name** cell to the right and select **First Name** from the drop-down menu.

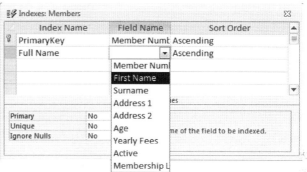

- Add the **Surname** field below the **First Name** field in the same way.

- Close the **Indexes** window with the **Close X** button at the top right to save the changes.

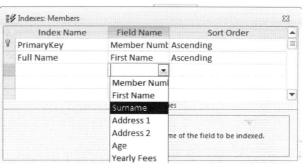

Practice Sequence

1	Add a validation rule to the **Yearly Fees** field, to check that the fees are between 100 and 3000.
2	Add appropriate **Validation Text**.
3	Change the Primary Key (right-click the existing key and select **Primary Key** from the menu that appears).
4	Ensure the **Primary Key** stays as the **Member Number** field.
5	An index must be added to the **Surname** field because users will often search on this field.
6	Still in **Design View**, click the **Surname** field in the field list at the top to display the properties at the bottom of the screen.
7	Click the **Indexed** property to display a menu with the following options.

- **No**: No index is present on this field.
- **Yes (Duplicates OK)**: No checking for duplicates will be done as records are added.
- **Yes (No Duplicates)**: When a record is added, all existing records will be checked to see if any have the same value in this field. If one already exists, the addition of the record will be disallowed and a message displayed.

In this case, there could be many members with the same surname, therefore, duplicates should be allowed.

8   Click **Yes (Duplicates OK)**.

2.3.8 Adding, Deleting and Modifying Data in a Record

It may be necessary to add, change or delete data, such as a change of address or telephone number. This is most easily done in DataSheet View.

- To add data, select the required field and type in the new data.
- To change or update data, select the required field and type in the new data.
- To delete data, select the data and use the Delete command in the Edit menu.

When you change or delete data, Access automatically saves the updates.

2.3.9 Changing the Width of Columns in a Table

The basic structure of a datasheet is columns and rows. When you enter information, you may find that the data is obscured because the column is not wide enough. Columns are also referred to as **fields**.

In order to widen the columns, do the following:
- Right-click the column to be widened.
- Select **Field Width** from the menu
- A dialog box will open enabling a precise width to be specified.
- Click the **Best Fit** button to automatically size the column to the size of the widest entry in the field (or field title).

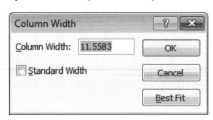

Alternatively, the width can also be altered interactively by clicking and dragging with the mouse.
- In datasheet view, position the mouse cursor at the right edge of the field title.
- The arrow cursor will change to a resize cursor.
- Click and hold down the left mouse button.
- Move the mouse left or right to resize the column.

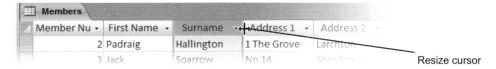

Resize cursor

2.3.10 Navigating Records in a Table

Records can be selected by clicking on any field within the record. The currently highlighted record is then displayed with a darker background.

In addition a navigation toolbar is displayed at the bottom of the screen.

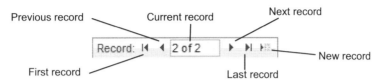

2.3.11 Adding a Field to an Existing Table

New fields can be added to existing tables in exactly the same way as they are added to a new table.

To add a new Yes/No field called **Deceased** to the Members table, do the following:

- Open the **Members** table in Design View.
- In the field list, enter **Deceased** in the first empty cell in the **Field Name** column.
- Change the Data Type to **Yes/No**.
- Save the table.

2.3.12 Adding Records to a Table

To create a new record, do the following:
- Click the **New Record** button on the **Navigation** toolbar. *Alternatively*, click the record marked with the asterisk.

- Enter, delete or modify data in the normal way as necessary to include all the necessary data for the record.
  Fields of some data types, such as Yes/No, will have checkboxes or other types of **control** as appropriate.
  A new attachment can be added to the record by double-clicking on the **Photo** field.
  The contents of the **Member Number** field are filled automatically and cannot be changed.
  The **Membership Type** can be selected from a drop-down list, as it is a **Lookup Wizard** field.

When all the data has been entered into the record, it should be saved.

To save a record, do the following:
- Navigate to another record.
  Alternatively, close the table.

To abandon changes to a field, do the following:
- Press the **Escape** key.
This will restore the original value of the field, prior to any changes.

2.3.13 Deleting Records in a Table

To delete a record, do the following:

- Select the entire record by clicking the **Select All** button to the left of the first field.

Select All button

- Right-click anywhere on the record.
- Select **Delete Record** from the menu that appears.

Practice Sequence

| 1 | Open the **Members** and **Competitions** tables. | ☐ |
| 2 | Using the information in sections 2.3.6–2.3.10, add a few records similar to those in the illustrations and experiment with resizing columns and deleting rows. | ☐ |

2.3.14 Applying a Filter to and Removing a Filter from a Table

Data can also be **filtered** in DataSheet View. This can be useful for limiting the number of records that a user has to view or deal with, or that field searches have to cover. Filters can be applied to more than one field at the same time.

To filter the Members table so that only Members with an age greater than 30 are included, do the following:

- In **DataSheet View** or **Form View**, click in the **Age** field of any record.
- Select the **Filter** command in the **Sort & Filter** section of the ribbon.

- In the menu that opens, click the **Number Filters** option.
- Select **Greater Than** from the sub-menu that opens.

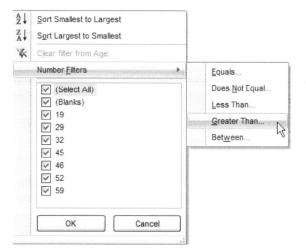

- In the **Custom Filter** window, enter the value **30**.
- Click **OK**.
  Only records where the Age field is greater than 30 are now available. This applies both to DataSheet View and Form View.

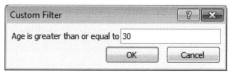

The **Navigation Bar** changes to indicate that the table is filtered.

To remove the filter, do the following:
- Click in the **Age** field.
- Click the **Filter** icon.
- Select **Clear Filter From Age**.
  The filter is removed and all records are, once again, available to view.

2.4   Forms

As discussed in Section 1.5, almost all user data entry into databases is done via **forms**.

These provide a clear and controlled interface for data maintenance across one or more tables, and are more appropriate for end users than DataSheet view. Microsoft Access can create forms automatically based on the fields in a table.

2.4.1   Creating a Form

To create a data entry form for the Members table, do the following:
- In the **Navigation Pane**, ensure the **Members** table is highlighted by clicking it.
- On the ribbon, click the **Create** tab.
- In the **Forms** section, click the **Form** command.

A new form is created, and the first record in the table is displayed.

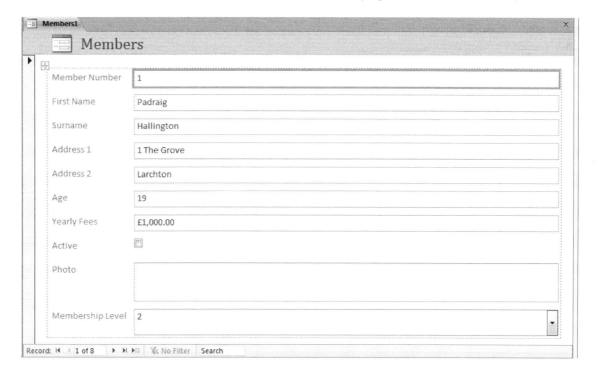

- The form is in **Layout View**, which is intended for defining the placement of elements.
- Data can be viewed but not added or modified in **Layout View**, enabling elements to be positioned and resized by clicking them and dragging with the mouse.

- The layout consists of **labels**, which display the name of each field, and **controls** which are used for data entry.
- A label/control pair is generated automatically for each field in the Members table.
- The type of control is dictated by the type of the underlying field. So the name and address fields use **TextBox** controls. The Active field uses a **CheckBox** control and the Membership Level uses a **ComboBox**.
- Data can be viewed but not added or altered in **Design View**.
- In a real-world application, the form might act as a **front end** for more than one table, and may or may not have controls for all available fields, as dictated by the person who designed it.

 note | The same navigation toolbar that was seen in table **DataSheet View** is again present at the bottom of the screen and can be used to move between the records in the underlying table.

2.4.2 Form Design View

The contents of a form are actually defined using Design View.

To change to this view, do the following:
- Right-click the form in the **Navigation Pane**.
- Select **Design View**.

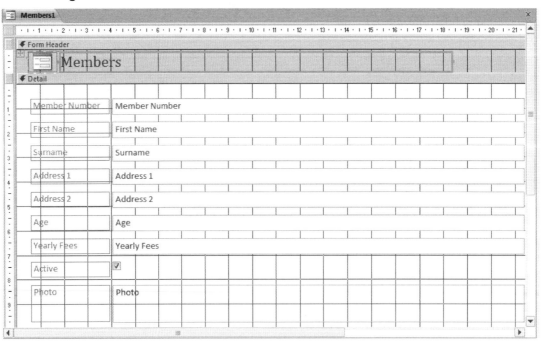

The process of automatically creating a form as described above generates a view similar to that in the above illustration. Using this view, controls for field labels and fields can be added and edited.

2.4.3 Naming and Saving a Form

To save a form, do the following:
- Click the **Save** icon, above the File menu, at the top left of the Access window.

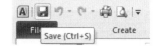

If this is the first time the Form has been saved, a window will open prompting for a name.
- Enter a relevant name.
- Click **OK** to save.

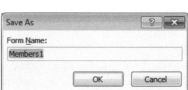

2.4.4 Opening and Closing a Form

Opening a Form

To open a form, do the following:

- Start **Microsoft Access**.
- Open the required database (see Section 2.1.1).
- The objects comprising the database are listed in the **Navigation Pane**.

> **note** Each database object has a different icon. Forms are displayed like this:

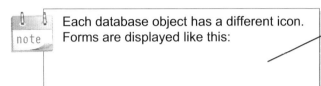

- Double-click the desired Form to open it in **Form View.**

  Alternatively, right-click the Form name and select **Design View** or **Layout View** to open in in that mode.

Closing a Form

To close a form do the following:

- Click the **Close X** button at the top right of the form

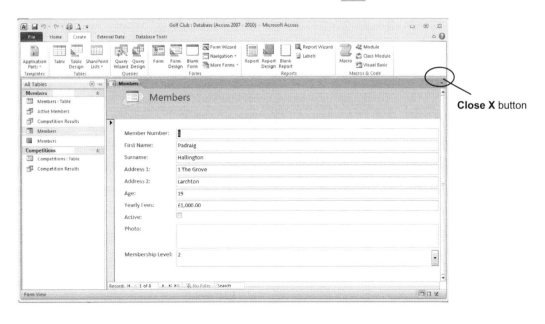

Close X button

2.4.5 Navigating Records in Form View

When viewing a form in **Form View**, the standard navigation toolbar is displayed at the bottom of the screen. Clicking on the different sections of the toolbar will change the form to display another record.

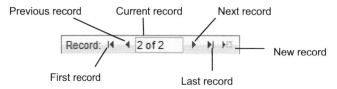

2.4.6 Headers and Footers in a Form

New items, such as the date and time, can be added to the form header or footer.

To add new items, do the following:
- Open the form in **Design View**.
- In the **Header / Footer** section on the ribbon, click the **Date and Time** button.

Date and Time button

- The **Date and Time** window opens
- Choose option buttons for the date and/or time format and click OK.
- New controls for the **Date and Time** are added to the form header area.

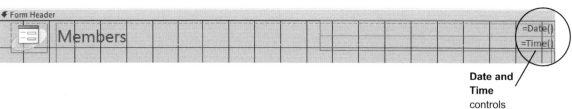

Date and Time controls

- Position the mouse cursor at the bottom edge of the **Form Footer** bar.
- The cursor changes to a resize cursor.
- Click and drag the footer edge downwards to resize the footer area Click the **Label** button on the ribbon.

  The cursor changes to a label cursor.

- Click anywhere in the **Form Footer**.
- Type some text into the new label control.
- Save and close the form, then reopen it in Form View.
  Note the date and time in the header and the text in the footer.

2.4.7 Inserting New Records Using a Form

To use the form for data entry and to insert new records, do the following:
- Double-click the form in the **Navigation Pane**.
  This activates **Form View**.

- To add a new record, click the **New Record** button on the navigation toolbar.

Alternatively, click the Home tab on the Ribbon, and then click the **New** command from the **Records** section.

A blank record will be added, and the form will reflect this by displaying empty fields.

- When data entry is complete, click the **Save** button in the **Records** section of the ribbon to save the new record.
- Notice that the record count on the Navigation Toolbar is increased by one.

2.4.8 Deleting Records in Form View

To delete a record, do the following:
- Navigate to the record using the **Navigation Toolbar**.
- Click the **Home** tab on the ribbon.
- In the **Records** section of the ribbon, click the arrow at the right of the **Delete** button.
- Select the **Delete Record** option.

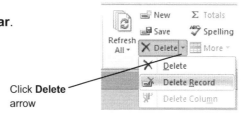

Click **Delete** arrow

A confirmation window opens to check you want to delete the record.
- Click **Yes** to delete the record.

2.4.9 Using the Search Command

To search for a specific word, number or date, enter the search term in the search section of the Navigation toolbar. The contents of each field will be searched as text is entered, and any matches will be highlighted.

note

This search is across all records. If a match is found in a record different to the one selected in DataSheet View or Form View, then the focus will change to the record with the matching text.

Searching for a Word

In this examle, the word **Grove** has been entered in the Search field of the Members table and the first match is highlighted.

Searching for a Number

In this example, the number 19 has been entered in the search field of the Members table, and the first match in **DataSheet View** is highlighted.

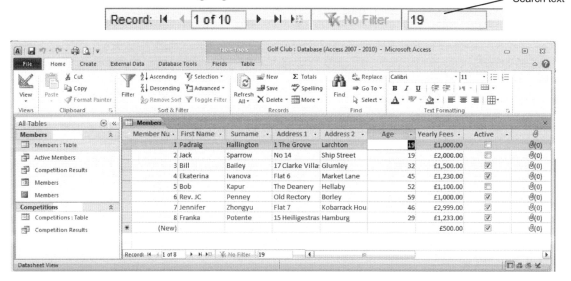

Searching for a Date

In this example, the date 17 May 2007 has been entered in the search field in the Competitions table and is highlighted in **DataSheet View**.

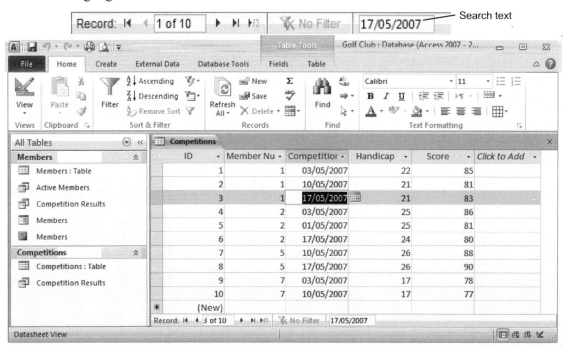

Using Find and Replace

The search function above is useful for quick searches, but sometimes a more thorough search is needed and the **Find and Replace** facility should be used. This can be accessed using the **Find** icon in the **Home** tab of the ribbon.

To search the Members table for the name **Sparrow**, do the following:

- Open the **Golf Club** database.
- Double-click the **Members** table to open it in **DataSheet View**.
- Click the **Find** icon on the ribbon.
  The **Find and Replace** window opens.
- Enter **sparrow** into the **Find What** textbox.
- Use the drop-down list arrow to select **Current Document** in the **Look In** list, if it is not already selected.
- Click the **Find Next** button.
- When the record has been found, click **Cancel** to close the **Find and Replace** window.

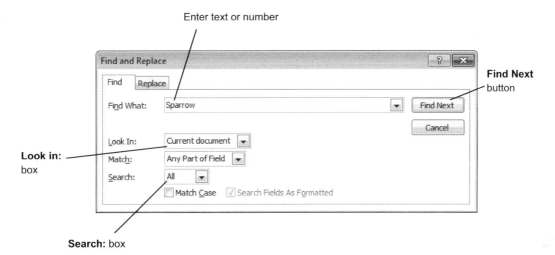

The **Find and Replace** option may be used to narrow down or widen out the search. For example, to search for the number 11 in the address 11 River Road, there are two options to locate the number.

First you may select **Any Part of Field** in the **Match:** box. Should the number 11 appear anywhere in a field, it will be located no matter what other text is there.

Selecting **Start of Field** will locate the number 11 only where it occurs at the very beginning of a field. Should the number be preceded by a currency label, it won't be recognised.

Choosing **Whole Field** will locate the number 11 only where the number itself is the entire field entry. Numbers with currency symbols will not be recognised with this option.

If you select the **Find Next** button, the computer will continue to search until the last instance of the criteria specified has been found, then an information window will display. Clicking **OK**, terminates the search.

The following table explains the different options displayed in the Find window.

Option	Choice	Action
Look In	Table Specific Field	Searches the complete table. Searches the specific field.
Match	Any Part of Field Whole Field Start of Field	Don will find **Don**caster or Lon**don**. **London** finds London, not Londonontario. **Caster** finds Casterbridge, not Doncaster.
Search	All Up Down	Searches all of the table. Searches towards the first record. Searches from the first record.
Match Case	If selected If deselected	Will only look for the case arrangement as it is specified in the Find what box. Will not be case sensitive.
Search Fields As Formatted	If selected If deselected	Data found will be in the same format as that in the Find what box. For example, a date stored as 1/3/9 but searched for in the format 01-Mar-91 will not be found. When deselected, the accepted formats can be matched across one another.

2.4.10 Applying and Removing a Filter to a Form
A filter can be applied when viewing in **Form View** in the same way as for a table in DataSheet View. See Section 2.3.14.

2.4.11 Sorting Data
It is useful to be able to sort data in a table or form. For example, it might make sense to view the data in the Members database in surname order, even though this is not the order that data will have been entered.

Data in a table, a form or a query can be sorted into numeric or alphabetical order. The A–Z button sorts selected text from A to Z and selected numbers from 1 to 10. The Z–A button sorts selected text from Z to A and selected numbers from 10 to 1.

To sort data, do the following:

Sort by Number
To sort on a number, e.g. members' age, do the following:
- Open the **Members** table in **DataSheet View**.
- Right-click the **Age** field.
- Select **Sort Smallest To Largest** from the menu that is displayed.
- The order of the records will change in **DataSheet View**, with the youngest members listed first.

Sort by Date
To sort on a date, e.g. a competition date, do the following:
- Open the **Competitions** table in DataSheet view.
- Right-click on the **Competition Date** field.
- Select **Sort Newest To Oldest** from the menu that is displayed.

The order of the records will change to place the most recent
competition dates first.

Sort by Text

To sort on text, e.g. members' surnames, do the following:

* Open the Members table in **DataSheet View**.
* Right-click in the **Surname** field.
* Select **Sort A to Z** from the pop-up menu that appears
  to sort by surname in ascending order.
  The order of the records will change.
  This is most obvious in **DataSheet View**.
* Navigating through the records will confirm that they are
  in surname order.

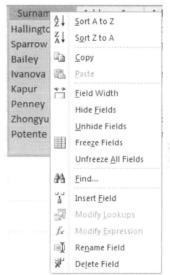

> The Member Numbers are no longer in sequence.
> This does not matter as long as they are unique.

Multiple Filters

Multiple filters can be active at the same time.

In the Competitions table, if a filter is applied to the Competition Date field first, and then applied
to the Score field, the sorting would be by date first, and then score within that.

Most types of field can be sorted:

* Number, Currency, AutoNumber.
* Text, Memo, Hyperlink.
* Yes/No.
* Date/Time.

The wording of the **Sort** menu will change depending on the
field type. For example, sorting on the Age field will give the
menu on the right. The sorting is saved when the table is
closed and reapplied when it is reopened.

To clear all sorting that is active on a table, do the following:

* Click the **Remove Sort** command button in the **Sort & Filter**
  section of the ribbon.

2.4.12 Using Forms to Add, Modify and Delete Data in a Record

It is possible to add, change or delete data, such as a change of address, when the data is being displayed in a form.

- Open the form and select the record whose data is to be modified or deleted or to which text is to be added.
- Select the field to be changed.
- Make the necessary changes, as follows:
  - ▶ Select the text and type to replace text.
  - ▶ Press **Delete** to delete the text.
  - ▶ Position the cursor where text is to be added and type.

As soon as the changes have been made and the cursor is clicked outside the field, the changes are accepted and saved.

Practice Sequence

1   Using the form that has been created for the Members table, add and amend records as necessary to produce the following list of members.

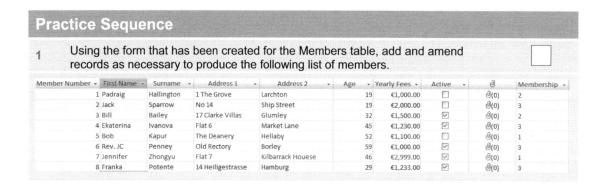

Deleting Records

If there is already data in the Members table, it may be necessary to delete the existing records.
- Open the table in DataSheet View.
- Click the **Select All** button at the top left of the grid of records.

Select All button

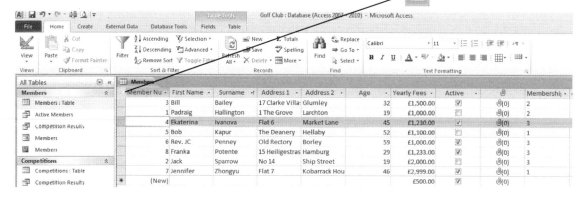

This will select all the records in the table.

- Press **Delete**.
  A confirmation window opens.
- Click **Yes** to delete the records.

Resetting the AutoNumber Field

The act of deleting all the existing entries in the Members table does not restart the numbering of the Member Number field. Therefore, it is necessary to open the Members **table** and use **Design View** to delete the Member Number field and then re-add it as an AutoNumber field and set it as the Primary Key. This will have the effect of restarting the Member Numbers from 1.

To reset the AutoNumber field, do the following:
- Open the **Members** table in **Design View**.
- Right-click the **Member Number** field in the field list.
- Select **Delete Rows** from the menu.

A confirmation window opens.
- Click **Yes**.

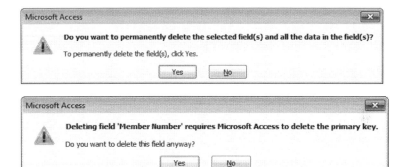

As the **Member Number** field is a **Primary Key**, a second confirmation window opens.

- Click **Yes**.
  The **First Name** field should now be the first in the list.
- Click in the **First Name** field to select it.
- Click the **Insert Rows** button on the ribbon to add a new field.
  A new entry is created in the field list, with the cursor in the **Field Name**.

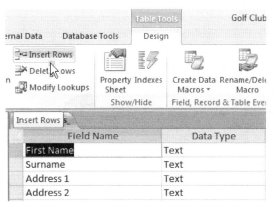

- Enter **Member Number** as the field name.
- Select **AutoNumber** from the Data Type list.
- Close **Design** View.
- Save the table when prompted.

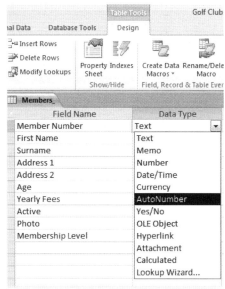

2.4.13 Adding Attachments to Records

Attachments can be added to attachment-type fields. This is useful for storing a graphic file, e.g. a member's photograph, with the member's record.

- Opens the **Members** table in Design View. A field name **Photo** and field type **Attachment** should have been added earlier.
  If not add it here.

Field Name	Data Type
Member Number	AutoNumber
First Name	Text
Surname	Text
Address 1	Text
Address 2	Text
Age	Number
Yearly Fees	Currency
Active	Yes/No
Photo	Attachment
Membership Level	Text

To attach a file to a record, do the following:
- Ensure that the Members table is open in **DataSheet View**.
- Double-click the **Photo** field of the record to which the photograph is to be attached.

Member Nu ▾	First Name ▾	Surname ▾	Address 1 ▾	Address 2 ▾	Age ▾	Yearly Fees ▾	Active ▾	◎	Membershi ▾
1	Padraig	Hallington	1 The Grove	Larchton	19	€1,000.00	☐	(0)	2
2	Jack	Sparrow	No 14	Ship Street	19	€2,000.00	☐	(0)	3

The **Attachments** window opens.
- Click **Add**.

The **Choose File** window opens.
- Browse to locate the required photograph.
- Click **Open**.
  The selected graphics file will appear in the **Attachments** window.

- Click **OK** to attach the file to the record.

Member Nu ▾	First Name ▾	Surname ▾	Address 1 ▾	Address 2 ▾	Age ▾	Yearly Fees ▾	Active ▾	◎	Membershi ▾
1	Padraig	Hallington	1 The Grove	Larchton	19	€1,000.00	☐	(1)	2
2	Jack	Sparrow	No 14	Ship Street	19	€2,000.00	☐	(0)	3

2.5 Queries

Queries are the cornerstone of database work. They are requests for data to be returned from a database, based on certain rules. The results of a query can be used as a source of data for reports or forms.

2.5.1 Opening, Closing and Saving a Query

Opening a Query

To open a query, do the following:
- Start **Microsoft Access**.
- Open the required database file.
- The objects comprising the database are listed in the **Navigation Pane**.

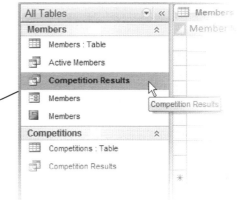

- Double-click the desired query to open it in **DataSheet View**.
  Alternatively, right-click the query name and select **Design View** to open it in that mode.

To save a query, do the following:
- Click the **Save** icon above the File menu.

If this is the first time the query has been saved, a window will be displayed prompting for a name.
- Enter the name.
- Click **OK** to save.

The query is then added to the Navigation Pane alongside the Members table and form.

Closing a Query

To close a query, do the following:

- Click the **Close X** button at the right of the query results.

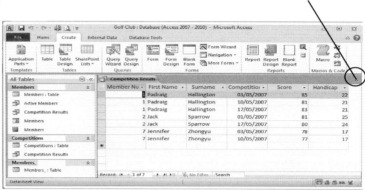

Close **X** button

2.5.2 Creating a Simple Query

To create a query, which will return all active members from the Members table, do the following:

- Select the **Create** tab on the ribbon.
- In the **Queries** section, click the **Query Design** command button.

A new query, called **Query1**, is created and is displayed, with a **Show Table** window in the foreground.

- Select the **Members** table.
- Click **Add**.
- Click **Close**.

The table (and its fields) is added to the table list at the top of the query designer.

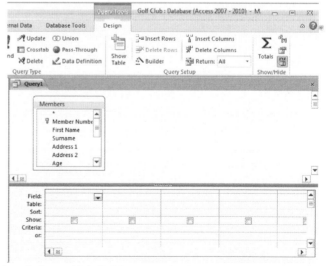

Below the table list is a grid. This is used to define which fields are to be included in the query and to sort criteria for inclusion.

Within each column, a field name can be chosen from the **Field:** drop-down list.

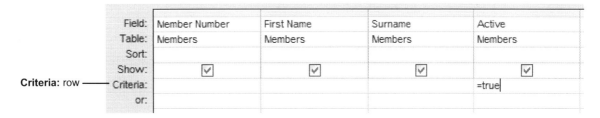

- Add the Member Number, First Name, Surname and Active fields as shown above.
- Ensure that the **Show:** checkbox is ticked for each.
- Save the table.

As only active members should be returned by this query, a criterion must be added to select only relevant records.

2.5.3 Adding Criteria to a Query

It is possible to specify precisely the information that a query needs to return by adding **criteria**.

In adding criteria to queries, you can more precisely specify the information you require. Operators such as **less than**, **greater than** or a combination of these are commonly used to define criteria. Specific mathematical symbols are used to express these criteria.

>	Greater than	<	Less than
>=	Greater than and equal to	<=	Less than and equal to
=	Equal to	<>	Not equal to

And	Returns records matching all criteria listed (can involve two or more criteria).
Or	Returns records matching any listed criterion (can involve two or more criteria)
Not	Returns records not matching listed criteria.

In addition, the logical operators **And**, **Or** and **Not** can be used to refine searches in queries.

To add a criterion to the query for the Members table, do the following:
- In the column for the **Active** field, enter **=true** in the **Criteria**: cell.

	Member Number	First Name	Surname	Active
Field:	Member Number	First Name	Surname	Active
Table:	Members	Members	Members	Members
Sort:				
Show:	☑	☑	☑	☑
Criteria: row ——— **Criteria:**				=true
or:				

To test the query, do the following:
- Click the **View** command button in the **Results** section of the ribbon.

Member Number ▾	First Name ▾	Surname ▾	Active ▾
3	Bill	Bailey	☑
4	Ekaterina	Ivanova	☑
6	Rev. JC	Penney	☑
7	Jennifer	Zhongyu	☑
8	Franka	Potente	☑

> Only the fields listed in the query (see Section 2.5.2) are included in the results. The results only contain active members.

The **Competition Results** query needs to be amended and criteria added to only return records where the score is between 75 and 85.

To add criteria to a query, do the following:
- Right-click the query entry in the Navigation Pane.
- Select **Design View** from the menu.
  The criteria to be added apply to the score field.
- Click in the Criteria cell in the Score column.
- Enter the criteria **>=75 AND <=85**.

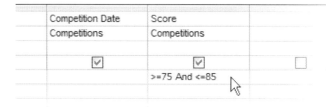

Competition Date	Score	
Competitions	Competitions	
☑	☑	☐
	>=75 And <=85	

- Save and run the query.
- Verify that the scores returned are in the correct range.

Competition Results

Member Nu ▾	First Name ▾	Surname ▾	Competition ▾	Score ▾
1	Padraig	Hallington	03/05/2007	85
1	Padraig	Hallington	10/05/2007	81
1	Padraig	Hallington	17/05/2007	83
2	Jack	Sparrow	01/05/2007	81
2	Jack	Sparrow	17/05/2007	80
7	Jennifer	Zhongyu	03/05/2007	78
7	Jennifer	Zhongyu	10/05/2007	77

2.5.4 Running a Query
To run the query, do the following:
- Click the **Run** button.
  A **DataSheet View** of the query results will be shown.

2.5.5 Creating a Two-Tabled Query
It is also possible to create a query to return data from more than one table, where the results are **joined** into a single result table.

In our example, competition details will be returned. The Competitions table does not hold the names of members. It does, however, contain the member number for each individual competition result, and this field will be used to link to the Members table.

To create a two-tabled query, do the following:

- Select the **Create** tab on the ribbon.
- In the **Queries** section, click the **Query Design** command button.
  A new query, called **Query1**, is created and is displayed, with a **Show Table** window in the foreground.
- In the **Show Table** window, highlight the **Competitions** table.
- Click **Add**.
- Highlight the **Members** table.
- Click **Add**.
- Click **Close**.
  The table list area in the query designer should look like the illustration on the right.

  Fields can be added to the query in the same manner as outlined in Section 2.5.1. Note that the drop-down lists contain the fields from both tables.

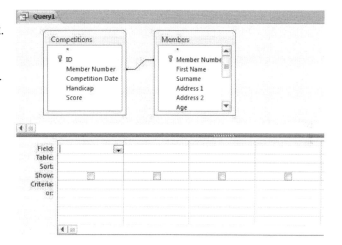

 The tables are **joined** using the Member Number fields. Since both tables contain this field and it is of the same data type in both tables, Access has created the join automatically. It can also be created manually.

 As both tables can and do contain fields with the same name, a method of specifying which table to take the field from is needed. This is done by using the notation **tablename.fieldname**, etc.

- Add the following fields to the query:
  - ▷ Competitions.Member Number
  - ▷ Members.First Name
  - ▷ Members.Surname
  - ▷ Competitions.Competition Date
  - ▷ Competitions.Score

To test the query, do the following:

- Click the **View** button in the **Results** section of the ribbon.
- The results are presented as if they are a single table.
- They can be used in this way in forms and reports.
- The results can be navigated using the **Navigation Toolbar** in the same way as tables and forms.
- Save the query, calling it **Competition Results**.

Member Nu ▾	First Name ▾	Surname ▾	Competitio ▾	Score ▾
1	Padraig	Hallington	03/05/2007	85
1	Padraig	Hallington	10/05/2007	81
1	Padraig	Hallington	17/05/2007	83
2	Jack	Sparrow	03/05/2007	86
2	Jack	Sparrow	10/05/2007	81
2	Jack	Sparrow	17/05/2007	80
5	Bob	Kapur	10/05/2007	88
5	Bob	Kapur	17/05/2007	90
7	Jennifer	Zhongyu	03/05/2007	78
7	Jennifer	Zhongyu	10/05/2007	77

2.5.6 Navigating Records in Queries

A query produces a set of results in a similar way to a table, but they should be regarded as being read-only and not changed. When a query is executed the results are normally shown in DataSheet View.

When viewing query results, the standard navigation toolbar is displayed at the bottom of the screen. Clicking the different sections of the toolbar, as shown below, will change the DataSheet View to move to another record and highlight it onscreen.

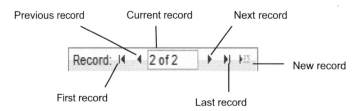

Practice Sequence		
1	Open the **Competitions Results** query in **Design View**.	☐
2	Modify the criterion to include scores between **75** and **80**.	☐
3	Retest the results.	☐
4	Modify the query again, and remove the criterion by deleting the text.	☐
5	Retest to verify that all records are once again returned.	☐

2.5.7 Editing a Query by Adding, Editing or Removing Criteria

The criteria for the query can be added to, changed to alter or further refine the results.

To amend the query that has just been created to include scores between 75 and 90, do as follows:

- Open the Query in **Design View.**
- Click in the criterion cell for the **Score** field.
- Change **>=75 And <=85** to **>=75 And <=90**
- Press **Enter** to register the change.
- Save the query.
- Rerun the query to test it.

To remove criteria, do the following:
- Open the query in Design View.
- Click anywhere in the **Criteria row** and in the **Query Setup** section of the ribbon select **Delete Rows**.

 note To delete one part of multiple criteria, place your cursor in the Criteria row beneath the field and delete it manually.

2.5.8 Editing a Query by Fields
It is possible to alter the fields in a query to further refine results.

Moving a Field
A field can be moved within a query to control where it is placed in the results.

To move the **Handicap** field so it appears after the **Score** field in the query that has been created, do the following:
- Open the query in **Design View**.
- Move the cursor over the narrow bar just above the **Score** field in the list of fields, until the cursor changes to a downward-pointing arrow.
- Click to select the column, as in the illustration on the right.

Cursor changes to an arrow

- With the column selected, left-click again in the same place and hold it down.
  The cursor changes to a move cursor.
- With the mouse button held down, drag the mouse to the right-hand side of the **Handicap** column, then release the button. The **Score** column will drop into place to the right of the **Handicap** column.
- Save and run the query and verify that the order of the fields has changed.

Cursor changes to a move cursor

Adding a Field
To add a field to a query, do the following:
- Open the query in **Design View**.
- In the column after **Score**, select **Competitions.Handicap** from the **Field** drop-down list.

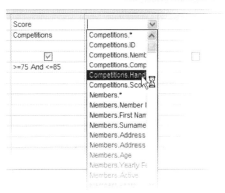

Removing a Field

To remove a field in a query, do the following:

* Click inside the field name textbox of the field to be deleted and delete the text.
* Press **Enter**.
  Alternatively, select the field's column and press the **Delete** key on the keyboard.

Hiding a Field

It may be necessary to include fields in a query, perhaps to add criteria to them, but stop them actually being included in the result.

To hide a field in a query, do the following:

* Open the query in **Design View**.
* Untick the **Show:** checkbox for the field that is to be hidden.

The **Show:** checkbox

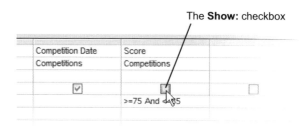

Unhiding a Field

To unhide a field in a query, do the following:

* Open the query in **Design View**.
* Tick the **Show:** checkbox for the field that is to be unhidden.

2.5.9 Wildcards

Wildcards can be employed in query criteria to perform partial comparisons, e.g. to perform a query on a specific section of the table.

In our example, we will return details about active members whose surname begins with **P**.

To add a wildcard, do the following:

* Open the **Active Members** query in **Design View**.
* Add **P*** as a new criterion to the **Surname** field. Access will change the entered text to **LIKE "P*"**.
* **Save** the query.
* **Run** the query.
  Only those active members whose surnames begin with P are returned.

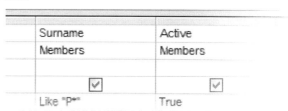

The asterisk means 'match any number of characters'. The criterion **LIKE "Sm*"** would return surnames such as "Smith", "Smedley", "Smyth" and "Smallwood". This wildcard character can appear either as the first or last character in the criterion, so **LIKE "*ley"** would match "Woodley", "Smedley" and "Godley".

* Another common wildcard character is the question mark (?).
  This is used to represent any single character. For example specifying **LIKE "B?rley"** as the Surname criterion would return "Barley" and "Borley".

2.6 Reports

Storing data in a database is a pointless exercise unless it can be extracted and presented in some human-readable way. Most often, this takes the form of **reports**, which can be printed to paper, PDF and other formats, or emailed, or exported to Excel and other formats.

2.6.1 Opening, Closing and Saving a Report

Opening a Report

To open a report, do the following:

- Start **Microsoft Access**.
- Open the desired database file as detailed above.
- The objects comprising the database are listed in the **Navigation Pane**.

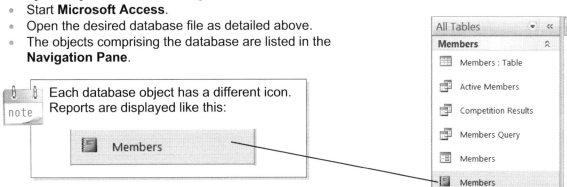

> note: Each database object has a different icon. Reports are displayed like this:

- Double-click the required report to open it in **Report View**.

Alternatively, right-click the report name and select **Design View** or **Layout View** to open in in that mode.

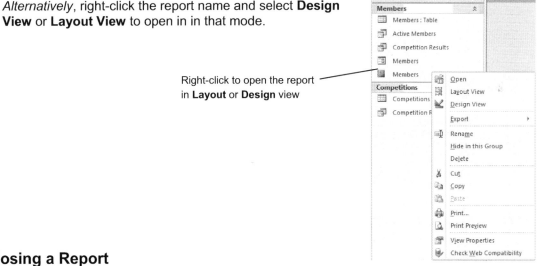

Right-click to open the report in **Layout** or **Design** view

Closing a Report

To close a report, do the following:

- Click the **Close X** button at the right of the report.

Close X button

Saving a Report

To save a report, do the following:

- Click the **Save** icon beneath the **File menu**.

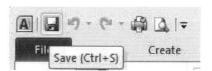

If this is the first time the report has been saved, a window will be displayed prompting for a name.

- Enter a name.
- Click **OK** to save.

2.6.2 Creating a Report

Reports are based on any **data source**. In Access terms, this means **tables** and **queries**. Creating a basic report is very similar to creating a form.

To create a report based on the Members table, do the following:

- In the **Navigation Pane**, click the **Members** table to select it.
- Click the **Create** tab on the ribbon.
- Click **Report** button in the **Reports** section.

A new report will be generated from the table, given the same name as the table, and displayed in **Layout View**.

The table has an active sort on the **Surname** field, hence the ordering.

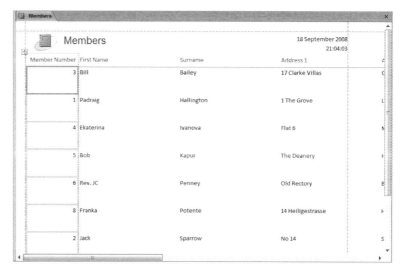

2.6.3 Changing the Arrangement of Data Fields

As with a form, the elements of the report can be positioned in Layout View by dragging them with the mouse.

The **First Name** and **Surname** fields on the report need to be switched. This can be done in Layout View, as follows:

- Change the view to **Layout View**.
- Click the heading text **First Name** and hold down the mouse button.
- The cursor changes to a cross.

Cursor changes to a cross

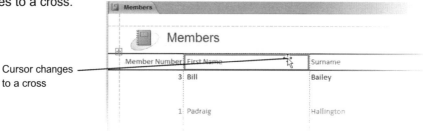

- With the mouse button held down, drag the cursor to the right-hand side of the **Surname** column heading.

- Release the mouse button. The order of the columns will change.

2.6.4 Adding, Modifying and Rearranging Text in Headers and Footers

Headers and footers can help identify a report by giving it an appropriate label.

In our example, the heading of the Members report needs to be amended to read **Members Report**.

Modifying Text in a Header

To modify the text in the header, do the following:
- Right-click the report in the **Navigation Pane**.
- Select **Design View** from the menu.

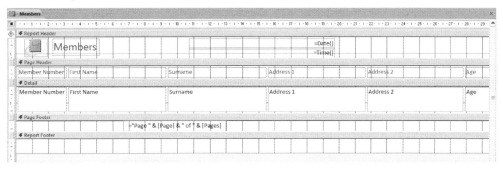

- The **Members** heading text is displayed using a **Label** control.
- Select this control by clicking its box.

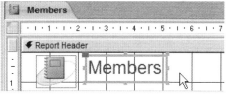

A **properties** list is visible on the right side of the Access window, listing the properties of the selected control.   If this is not visible, select the **Property Sheet** command from the **Report Design Tools/Design** tab.

- In the properties list, select the **Format** tab and then click to the right of the **Caption** property.
- Change the text to read **Members Report**.
- Press **Enter**. The report will change to reflect the new caption.

However, the label is too narrow to display all the text. To widen the label, do the following:
- Left-click the border on the right side of the label on the report design.
- Hold down the mouse button. The cursor changes to a resize cursor.

Resize cursor

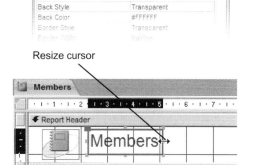

- Drag the mouse to the right to resize the label.

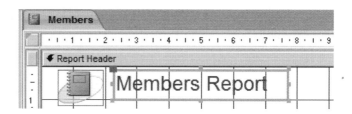

Adding Text to a Footer
The footer area of the report should display a copyright notice.

To add this text, do the following:
- Click the **Label** button **[Aa]** in the **Controls** section of the ribbon.

The cursor changes to a crosshair.
- Click in footer area of the report.
- Enter © **BEC 2008**.

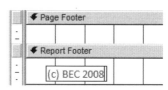

Rearranging Text in a Footer
The position of the text that has been added to the footer, or of any other item on the report layout, can be altered by dragging and dropping the item with the mouse.

To alter the position of the copyright text label that has just been added, do the following:
- Ensure the report is open in **Design View**.
- Click the label item to select it.
  A selection border will be shown enclosing it.

- Move the cursor over the top border line, until it changes to a move cursor.
- Click the mouse button, hold it down and drag the label to another position in the footer.
- Release the button to complete the move.
- Save the report and run it to verify the new position.

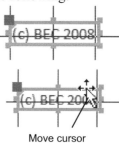

Move cursor

2.6.5 Grouping Records
In addition to simply displaying data, reports can employ **grouping**.
Records can be displayed together based on the contents of a
field or fields.
- Open the **Members** report in **Layout View**.
- Scroll across to view the other columns.
- Right-click the **Active** column and select **Group on Active** from the pop-up menu that appears.

The order of the records, and the layout, will change.

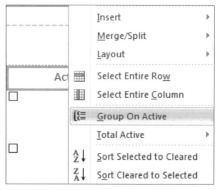

All records with **Active ticked** will be displayed together.
All records with **Active unticked** will be displayed together.

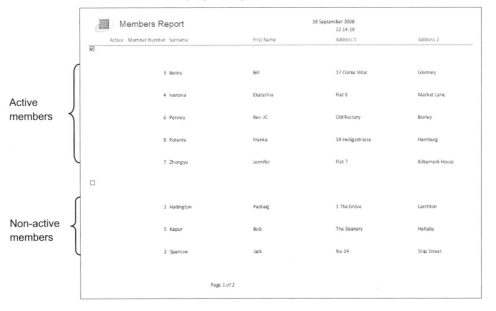

Totalling Options

When you present specific fields in a grouped report, you may avail of a number of options that summarise numeric information. These numeric fields will be located in the **Summary Options** section.

You can display numeric information by total (**sum**), mean (**avg**), maximum (**max**) or minimum (**min**).

- In **Layout View**, right-click the **Yearly Fees** column.
- Select the **Total Yearly Fees** menu option.
  The totalling options are listed on a sub-menu.
- Select **Sum**.

A total will be placed in the **Yearly Fees** column at each group break, and an overall total at the end of the report (circled below).

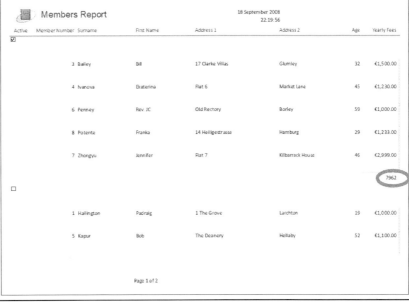

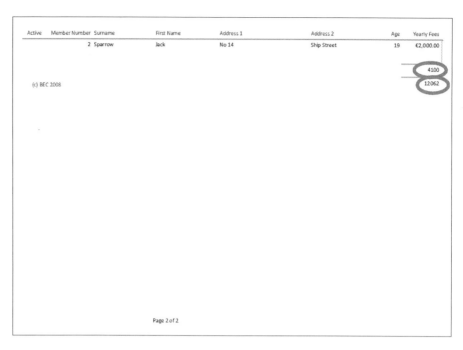

Further Examples of Totalling Options

- Consider the following simple table, called **Rep Sales**.
- It holds information about orders won by sales reps.

- A basic report can be created using this table, grouped by **Month Number**.

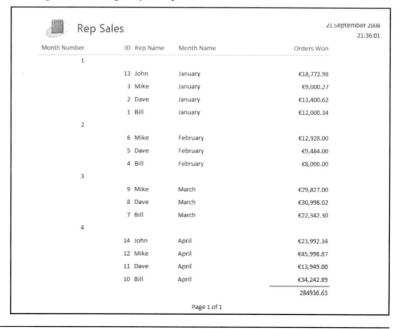

- Totalling the Orders Won column by **Sum** in the **Rep Sales** will produce a report, with sum totals for each group.

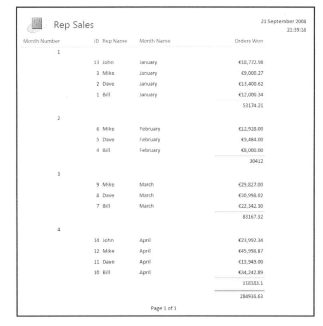

- Selecting **Average** will give the average order value for the month.

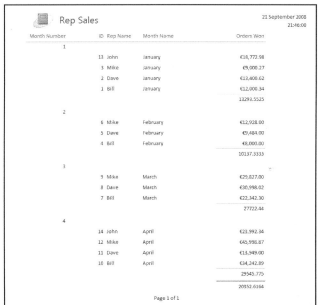

- Choosing **Count Records** will yield the number of records in each group.

- Selecting **Max** will show the highest value in the group, as shown on the right.
- Selecting **Min** will show the lowest value.

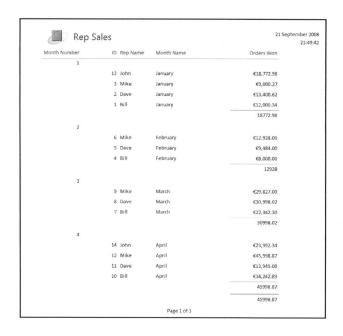

2.6.6 Viewing a Report

Apart from the Layout and Design Views, it is possible to view the records in Report View. Report View displays the report exactly as it will be output to a printer, screen or other output destination.

To view records in Report View, do the following:

- Double-click the report in the **Navigation Pane**. This will open it in **Report View**.

2.7   Defining a Relationship

Relationships are based on a field or fields that are common between two tables in a database and provide a method for linking the tables (see Section 1.6.11).

To create a relationship, do the following:

- Open the **Golf Club** database.
- Ensure that **no** tables, reports or other items are open.
- On the ribbon, select the **Database Tools** tab.
- In the **Relationships** group, click the **Relationships** option.

  If this is the first time that a relationship has been defined in the database, a **Show Table** window will be displayed.
- If the **Show Table** is not displayed automatically, click the **Show Table** option in the **Relationships** section of the ribbon.

- In the **Show Table** window, click the **Members** option in the list of tables to highlight it.
- Click **Add**.

- In the Show Table window, click the **Competition** option in the list of tables to highlight it.
- Click **Add**.
- Click **Close** to close the **Show Table** window.

The tables should now be
visible in the **Relationship
Designer**.

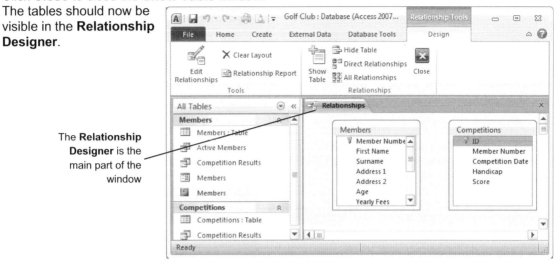

The **Relationship
Designer** is the
main part of the
window

As there can be many competition results for each individual member, a one-to-many relationship
is needed. The tables have a Member Number field in common, so this can be used to define the
relationship.

To create a one-to-many relationship, do the following.

- In the **Relationship Designer**, move the cursor over the **Member Number** field name in the
  Members table.
- Click and hold the mouse button.
- With the mouse button held down, drag the
  cursor to the **Member** number field in the
  Competitions table.
  The cursor changes to a pointer with a plus
  sign.

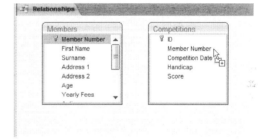

- Release the mouse button.
  The **Edit Relationships** window opens.
  The **Relationship Type** will be set automatically
  to **One-To-Many**.

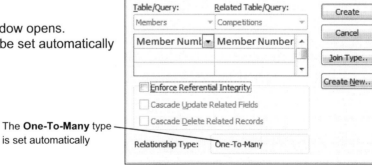

The **One-To-Many** type
is set automatically

- Click the **Enforce Referential Integrity** option.
- Click the **Create** button.
  The relationship will be created and the
  Relationship Designer window updated to
  reflect this. A line will be shown linking the fields.

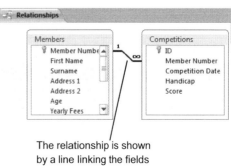

The relationship is shown
by a line linking the fields

note The line has a '1' on the Members side and the symbol for infinity on the Competitions side. This represents the one-to-many nature of the relationship.

- Save the relationship by clicking the **Save** icon above to the **File menu**.

One advantage of defining a relationship is that this automatically informs queries about how tables are linked.

To demonstrate this, do the following:
- Create a new query (see Section 2.5.4).
- In the **Show Table** window, add the **Members table** first, then the **Competitions table**.
- Close the **Show Tables** window.
  The tables are automatically joined
  using the relationship that was defined.
- Without defined relationships tables in queries, tables would
  have to be joined manually within the query every time they were used.
- Save or discard the query as required.

To demonstrate how enabling the **Referential Integrity** (see Section 1.6.12) option on the Relationship enforces data integrity, do the following:
- Open the Members table in Datasheet View.
- Highlight the record with the **Member Number** '1'.
- Press the **Delete** key.
  A message window opens indicating that the record will not be deleted or changed because the **Competitions** table includes related records. Deleting the record in the **Members** table would leave orphaned records in the **Competitions** table – records in the **Competitions** table with a **Member** number no longer existing in the members table.

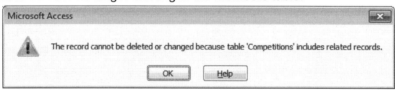

Datasheet View is also enhanced by a defined relationship. To see this, do the following:
- Open the **Members** table in **Datasheet View**.
- Each record now has an expansion box to the left of the **Member Number** field.
- Click this box to expand the grid to display the records related to that member that exist in the **Competitions** table.

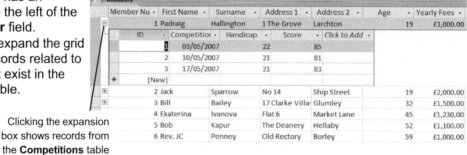

Clicking the expansion box shows records from the **Competitions** table

To delete a relationship, do the following.
- Open the **Relationship Designer**.
- Click the line joining the tables to select it.
- Press **Delete**.
  A confirmation window opens.
- Click **Yes**.
- Save the relationship.

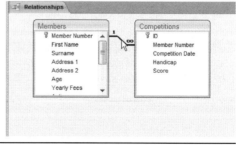

2.8   Printing

2.8.1   Previewing a Report, Form or Table

It is important to always view your table, form or report before you print it. This option is known as **preview**.

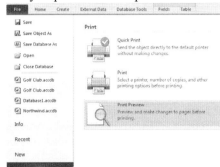

To use the preview option, do the following:
- Click the **File menu**.
- Select **Print** from the menu.
  Select **Print Preview**.

This will present the data in different ways depending on whether a report, form, table or query is involved.

A report will be exactly as it appears in **Report View**.

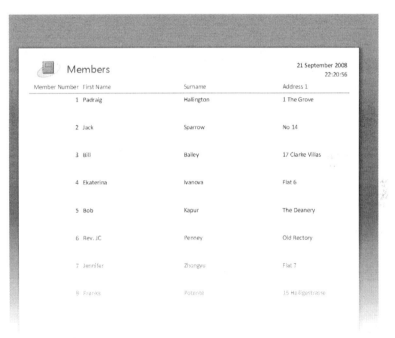

Previewing a table or query displays information in the way presented in the illustration below.

Previewing a form displays information in the way presented in the illustration on the right.

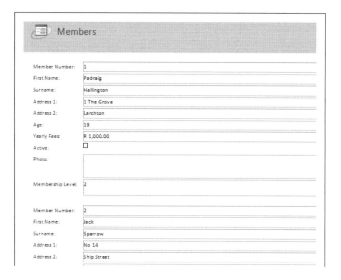

When in **Print Preview** mode, the ribbon changes to display a range of printing options.

To print from **Print Preview** mode, do the following:
- Click **Print** at the left of the ribbon.

2.8.2 Changing Orientation

There are two types of page orientation, **Portrait** and **Landscape**. Portrait is a vertical orientation. Landscape is a horizontal orientation.

This is landscape orientation

This is portrait orientation

To change the page orientation, do the following:
- In **Print Preview** mode, the ribbon has a **Page Layout** section.

  The orientation of the output can be changed between Portrait and Landscape using the appropriate command button.

2.8.3 Printing a Report, Form or Table

To print a report, form, table or query, do the following:
- Open the report, form, query or table from the **Navigation Pane**.
- Click the **File menu**.
- Select **Print** from the drop-down menu.
  A sub-menu with three options is displayed.
- Select the **Print** option to open the **Print** window.

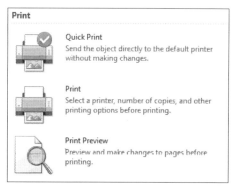

The **Print** window opens.
Use this window to select a printer, the number of copies required and pages to be printed.

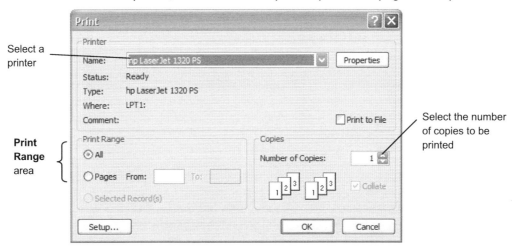

Select a printer

Print **Range** area

Select the number of copies to be printed

- Choosing the **All** option in the **Print Range** box means that all the contents of the table would be printed.

- Choosing the **Pages From** option means that you can choose which pages you want to print, i.e. if you type in 1 in the **From** box and type in 5 in the **To** box, pages 1, 2, 3, 4 and 5 would be printed.

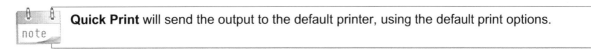

Quick Print will send the output to the default printer, using the default print options.

note

Any filters or ordering that has been imposed on tables, queries or forms will be maintained in the printed output.
- When all the printing options have been set, click **OK**.

2.8.4 Printing Selected Output from a Table
Sometimes, it is only necessary to print a selection of the data in a table.

To print a range of records, do the following:
- In **DataSheet View**, click one record to select it.
- Hold down the **Shift** key.
- Click a second record.
- Both the records, and any in between, will be selected.

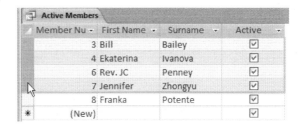

Selected Record(s) checkbox

- When the records have been selected, open the **Print** window by selecting **Print** from the menu in the **File** menu
In the Print window, click the **Selected Record(s)** option in the **Print Range** area.

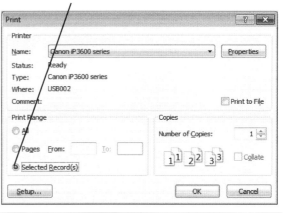

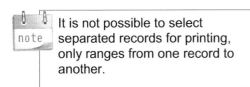

It is not possible to select separated records for printing, only ranges from one record to another.

note

1   Experiment with previewing and printing a report, form, query.

2.9   Exporting

In addition to printing, Access 2010 provides a range of options to **export** data to various formats. Exporting in different formats is useful if the information needs to be displayed in another application, such as Excel or Word.

Note that changes to the files produced by exporting are not reflected in the Access database itself.

To export, do the following:
* Open the table or query from the **Navigation Pane**.
* Click the **External Data** tab on the ribbon.
  An **Export** section will appear.

The most commonly used options have their own buttons.

Excel – will create a .XLSX file that can be used in Excel 2010.

	A	B	C	D	E
1	Member Number	First Name	Surname	Active	
2	3	Bill	Bailey	TRUE	
3	4	Ekaterina	Ivanova	TRUE	
4	6	Rev. JC	Penney	TRUE	
5	7	Jennifer	Zhongyu	TRUE	
6	8	Franka	Potente	TRUE	
7					

Word – creates a .RTF (Rich Text Format) file that can be used in Word 2010 or WordPad.

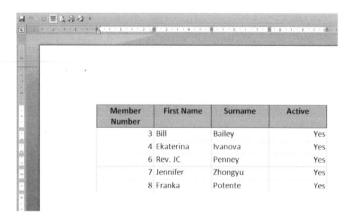

Member Number	First Name	Surname	Active
3	Bill	Bailey	Yes
4	Ekaterina	Ivanova	Yes
6	Rev. JC	Penney	Yes
7	Jennifer	Zhongyu	Yes
8	Franka	Potente	Yes

This illustration shows the results of exporting to text without formatting. This is called a **CSV** (Comma Separated Value) file, as the fields are separated by commas.

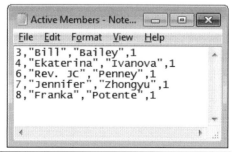

```
3,"Bill","Bailey",1
4,"Ekaterina","Ivanova",1
6,"Rev. JC","Penney",1
7,"Jennifer","Zhongyu",1
8,"Franka","Potente",1
```

Text – can create
a text file with
formatting, as in the
illustration on the right.

Clicking the **More** menu in the Export
section displays additional options.

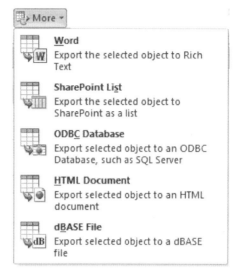

XML File – produces an .XML (Extensible Markup Language) file, a commonly understood
format for exchanging data between applications over the internet.

When an export is performed, an
Export Options wizard is displayed.

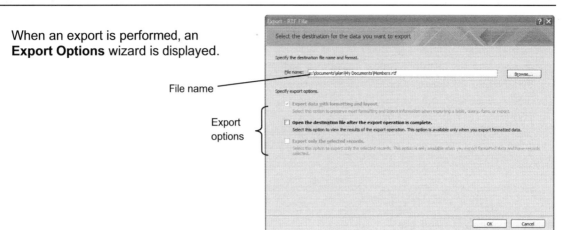

File name

Export
options

- The **File Name** section is where the name and location of the export file are specified.
- Below this are options.
  One or more of these may be unavailable depending on the type of export.
- Clicking **OK** may present further options, before actually producing the output file.

2.9.1 Exporting to a Location on a Drive

To export the Members table in Excel format to a specified location on a drive, do the following:

- Open the **Members** table in **DataSheet View**.
- Click the **External Data** tab on the ribbon.
- Click the **Excel** button in the **Export** section displayed on the ribbon.
- On the first Wizard page, click the **Browse** button beside the **File Name** textbox.

A **File Save** window opens.
- Navigate to the required folder and change the **file name** if necessary.

Navigate to
the required
folder

Enter a
file name

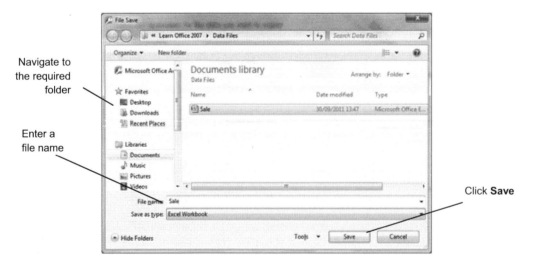

Click **Save**

- Click **Save** to save the file.

Practice Sequence

| 1 | Experiment with exporting a table and query to text with and without formatting (the **Export Data With Formatting And Layout** option on the wizard). | ☐ |
| 2 | Experiment with exporting a table and query to XML, then opening the .XML file in a web browser. | ☐ |

Presentations

module 6
Presentations

Module Goals for Module 6

Module 6 Presentations requires the candidate to demonstrate competence in using presentation software.

The candidate shall be able to:

- Work with presentations and save them in different file formats
- Choose built-in options such as the Help function within the application to enhance productivity
- Understand different presentation views and when to use them, choose different slide layouts and designs
- Enter, edit and format text in presentations. Recognize good practice in applying unique titles to slides
- Choose, create and format charts to communicate information meaningfully
- Insert and edit pictures, images and drawn objects
- Apply animation and transition effects to presentations and check and correct presentation content before finally printing and giving presentations.

Introduction

What is a Presentation?

A presentation is a set of slides that display on screen in sequence and present information to an audience. The subject matter can be aimed at a specific group, i.e. age and range of knowledge, or be aimed at the widest audience available. Presentations are created using an application such as **Microsoft PowerPoint** or similar software package. A slide show can be presented by a speaker or set to loop continuously. When presented by a speaker, the presentation can be projected onto a whiteboard so that it is visible to a large audience. A presentation needs to be presented with slides structured in a logical sequence.

A guide to PowerPoint

- What is PowerPoint?
- What is a presentation?
- Creating a slide show

Audience
and
Assimilation

6

Section 1 ▶   Using the Application

An **application** refers to the software package that is used to perform a task. The application that will be used for this training manual is Microsoft PowerPoint 2010. This is a comprehensive presentations package, capable of creating slide shows with multiple slides containing a variety of media, such as images, animations and effects.

1.1   Working with Presentations

A presentation consists of a set of slides in an ordered sequence that are all related to a specific subject.

In this section, you will learn about the following:

- Opening an existing presentation.
- Closing a presentation.
- Creating a new presentation.
- Switching between open presentations.
- Saving a presentation to a location on a drive and with a different name.
- Saving a presentation in another format, such as rich text format, template, show, image file format and version number.

1.1.1   Opening a Presentations Application

PowerPoint, the presentations application used in this module, will either be displayed as an icon on the desktop of your computer or found in the **Start** menu.

To open PowerPoint, do the following:

- Select the **Start** menu.
- Select **All Programs**.
- Select **Microsoft Office.**
- Select **Microsoft PowerPoint 2010**.

 ─── Select the Microsoft Office folder
and then Microsoft PowerPoint
20010

Alternatively, Microsoft PowerPoint may be displayed as a shortcut icon on the desktop of your computer.

- Right-click the icon and select **Open** from the shortcut menu (or double-click to open).

Microsoft Office PowerPoint 2010 opens.

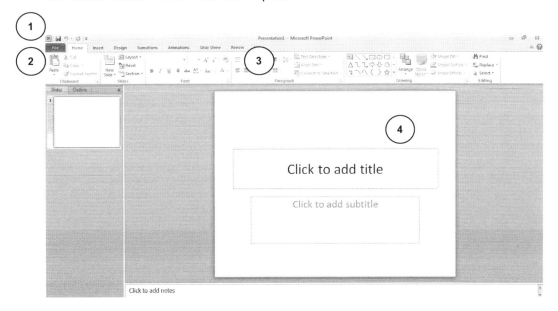

The screen layout will display the following:

① The Quick Access Toolbar.

② The File menu.

③ The ribbon.

④ A new, blank slide.

1.1.2 Closing a Presentations Application

To close PowerPoint, do the following:

- Select the **File menu**.
- Select **Exit**.

  The **PowerPoint** program will close.

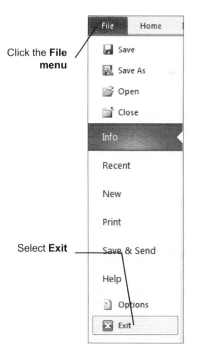

Alternatively, Select the **Close X** button in the top-right corner of the title bar.

Close X button

1.1.3 Opening a Presentation

To open an existing presentation, do the following:

- Open **PowerPoint**.
- Select the **File menu**.
- Select **Open**.

  The **Open** window opens.

File menu

- Select the location of the file by clicking the **Look in** arrow and choosing a drive and/or folder.
- Select the file.
- Click **Open**.

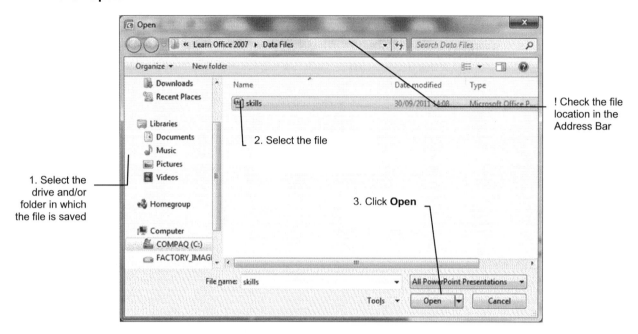

To display the Open window, press **CTRL + O**.

Opening Recent Presentations

Presentations, which have been opened recently, can be accessed more quickly than by using the Open option.

To view recently opened presentations, do the following:
- Select the **File menu**.
- Select the required file from the **Recent Presentations** list.

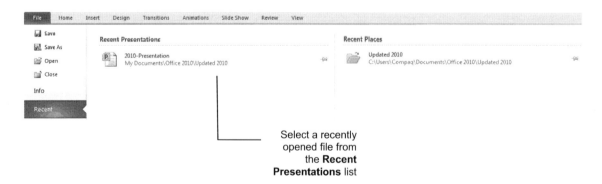

To change the number of documents listed in **Recent Presentations**, do the following:
- Select the **File menu**.
- Select **Options**.
- Select the **Advanced** command.

* Scroll down to the **Display** section of the window.
* Enter the number of recent documents that should display in the **File** menu.

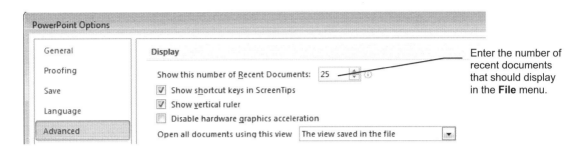

* Click OK.

1.1.4 Closing a Presentation

To close a presentation, do the following:

* Select the **File menu**.
* Click **Close**.

> If changes have been made to the file, a message will appear asking if you want to save the file before closing.
>
> * Click **Save** to save the file.
> * Click **Don't Save** to close the file without saving.
> * Click **Cancel** to cancel the message and return to the presentation.

1.1.5 Creating a New Presentation based on a Default Template

To create a new presentation, do the following:

* Select the **File menu**.
* Click **New**.
* Select **Blank Presentation**.
* Click **Create**.

- A new blank slide appears with a default slide layout (**Title Slide** layout).

1.1.6 Saving a Presentation to a Location on a Drive

To save a presentation for the first time, do the following:

- Select the **File menu**.
- Select **Save**.

  The **Save As** window opens.
- Select the correct drive and/or folder from the **Navigation Pane**.
- Enter a name in the **File name** box.
- Click **Save**.

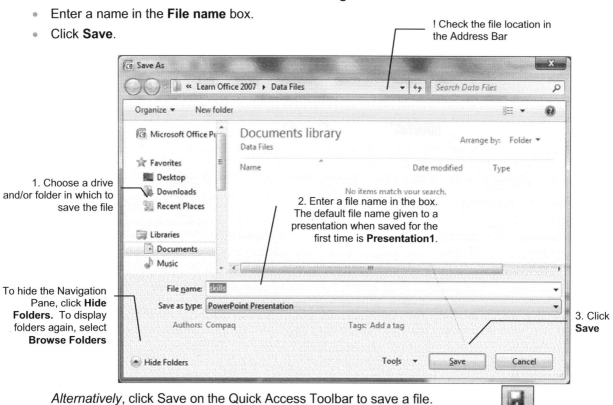

Alternatively, click Save on the Quick Access Toolbar to save a file.

> **note** When saving a presentation for the first time, clicking **Save** or **Save As** from the **File** menu will result in the **Save As** window opening. Subsequent changes to a presentation can be saved by selecting the **Save** option from the **File menu**. This will save the presentation with the same name and overwrite the original file.
>
> The keyboard shortcut to save is **CTRL + S**.

1.1.7 Saving a Presentation under Another Name

To save an existing presentation with a different name, do the following:

- Select the **File menu**.
- Select the **Save As** menu option.
  The **Save As** window opens.
- Select the correct drive and/or folder from the **Navigation Pane**.
- Ensure that **PowerPoint Presentation** is displayed in the **Save as type** box.
- Enter a name in the **File name** box and click **Save**.

1.1.8 Saving a Presentation as Another File Type

A presentation can be saved in a variety of different formats. See the different formats listed below.

PowerPoint format	Graphic format	Outline/Rich Text format
Presentation (.pptx)	Windows Metafile (.wmf)	Outline/rtf (.rtf)
Design Template (.potx)	GIF (.gif)	
PowerPoint Show (.ppsx)	JPEG (.jpg)	
	PNG (.png)	

Rich Text Format

When a presentation is saved in Rich Text Format, it retains all its formatting features and saves in a format that enables it to be opened and viewed in outline view. This format loses all the **graphical** content that exists in the presentation.

To save the presentation in Rich Text Format, do the following:

- Select the **File menu** and then select the **Save As** menu option.
  The **Save As** windows opens.
- Select the correct drive and /or folder from the Navigation Pane.
- Enter a file name into the **File name** box and then click the **Save as type** arrow.
- Select **Outline/RTF**.
- Click **Save**.

File name:	Windows Metafile
	Enhanced Windows Metafile
Save as type:	Outline/RTF
	OpenDocument Presentation

1. Select **Outline/RTF**

Template

A template contains standard content that will appear on all slides in a presentation. A template can be used repeatedly with other presentations. This saves time and effort when creating a new presentation. Templates are saved with a **potx** file extension and, unless another location is specified, will automatically save in the following location:

C:\Users\ *user name* \AppData\Roaming\Microsoft\Templates

To save a presentation as a template, do the following:

- Select the **File menu** and then select the **Save As** menu option.
  The **Save As** windows opens.
- Click the **Save as type** arrow.
- Select **PowerPoint Template**.
- Enter a file name into the **File name** box.
- Select the correct drive and/or folder from the Navigation Pane.
- Click **Save**.

6

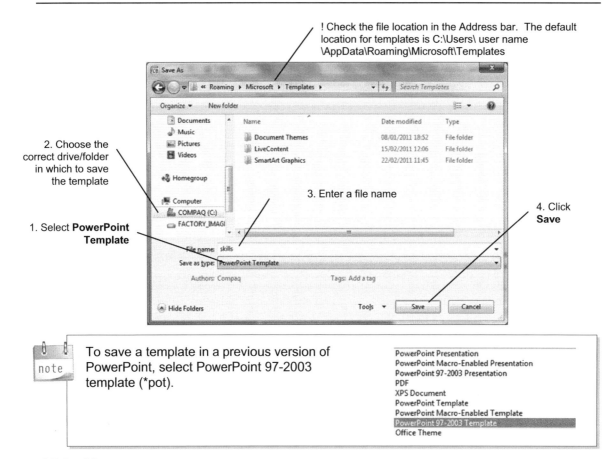

! Check the file location in the Address bar. The default location for templates is C:\Users\ user name \AppData\Roaming\Microsoft\Templates

2. Choose the correct drive/folder in which to save the template

3. Enter a file name

4. Click **Save**

1. Select **PowerPoint Template**

note

To save a template in a previous version of PowerPoint, select PowerPoint 97-2003 template (*pot).

PowerPoint Presentation
PowerPoint Macro-Enabled Presentation
PowerPoint 97-2003 Presentation
PDF
XPS Document
PowerPoint Template
PowerPoint Macro-Enabled Template
PowerPoint 97-2003 Template
Office Theme

Slide Show

A presentation saved in this format will be displayed as a full screen slide show when opened.

To save a presentation as a slide show, do the following:
- Click the **File menu**.
- Select the **Save As** option.
  The **Save As** windows opens.
- Select the correct drive and/or folder from the Navigation Pane.
- Enter a file name into the **File name** box.
- Click the **Save as type** arrow.
- Select **PowerPoint Show**.
- Select the **Save** button.

Select **PowerPoint Show**

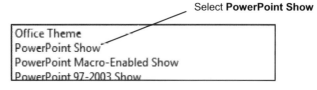

Office Theme
PowerPoint Show
PowerPoint Macro-Enabled Show
PowerPoint 97-2003 Show

Image File Format

A presentation can be saved in a variety of image file formats, such as jpeg, gif, png and wmf.

- A windows metafile (.wmf) image file is a drawn graphic made up of lines rather than picture elements. This means that the picture does not distort when it is resized.
- A bitmap image (such as jpg, gif or png), is a scanned or photographic image that is made up of small dots (or picture elements called pixels).
  To save a slide for use on the web, save in GIF, JPEG or PNG format.
  Jpeg is an image format used in the compression of photographic images. This format is suitable for on-screen display of low resolution photographs but unsuitable for high resolution commercial printing. **Gif** is an image format used for simple graphics with solid colour and is unsuitable for photographs. This format supports transparency and animation (non-photographic) and is best suited to on-screen display.

To save a presentation in image file format, do the following:
- Select the **File menu**.
- Click **Save As**.

  The **Save As** windows opens.
- Select the correct drive and/or folder from the Navigation Pane.
- Enter a file name into the **File name** box.
- Click the **Save as type** arrow.
- Select an image file format from the menu (i.e. jpg, .gif, .wmf or png).

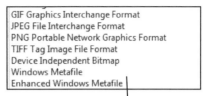

Select an image file format from the Save as type drop-down menu.

- Click **Save**.

  A confirmation window opens.
- To save only the current slide in image file format, select **Current Slide Only**.

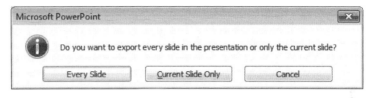

Version Number

Each version of PowerPoint has a different number. If the presentation needs to be opened and viewed in a previous version of PowerPoint it can be saved with a different version number.

To check the version number of the software on your computer, do the following:
- Select the **File** menu and select **Help**.
- Read the information in the **About Microsoft PowerPoint** section of the window.

- Check the version – it should be **Microsoft PowerPoint® 2010**.
- Click the **File** tab to close the menu.

To save the presentation with a different version number, do the following:
- Select the **File menu**.
- Select the **Save As** menu command.

  The **Save As** windows opens.
- Select the correct drive and/or folder.
- Enter a file name into the **File name** box.
- Click the **Save as type** arrow.
- Select **PowerPoint 97-2003 Presentation** to save a copy of the presentation that is fully compatible with PowerPoint 97-2003.

  Click **Save**.

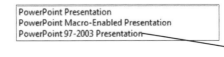

PowerPoint 97-2003 is an earlier version of the software

note PowerPoint 2010 does not support saving to PowerPoint 95 and earlier file formats. If you convert your presentation to a 95 or earlier file format, some Office 2010 formatting features may be lost during the conversion.

1.1.9 Switching between Open Presentations

Open presentations will be displayed as tabs on the taskbar.

To switch between open presentations, do the following:

- Select the **View** tab from the ribbon.
- In the **Windows** group, select the **Switch Windows** button.
  A tick will display beside the file name of the currently active presentation.
- Click another file name in the menu to make that the active presentation.

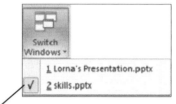

A tick beside the file name indicates that it is the active presentation, currently displayed on screen

Alternatively, open more than one presentation. The presentations will be displayed as tabs on the taskbar at the bottom of the screen. When the mouse is hovered over a tab, a thumbnail appears (not in Windows 7 Basic). Click a tab and then a thumbnail to open a presentation.

Tab and thumbnail on the Windows 7 taskbar

Thumbnails display differently in Windows 7 Basic

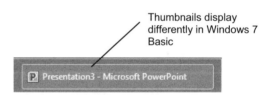

 note To switch between open presentations, using the keyboard, hold down the **ALT** key and press **TAB**.

1.2 Enhancing Productivity

Productivity can be increased by setting user preferences, such as adding a user name and/or creating a default folder from which to open and in which to save all presentations. Using the Help facility can also aid productivity by providing tips and advice on how to use the program effectively.

In this section, you will learn about the following:
- Setting user preferences.
- Using available Help functions.
- Using magnification/zoom tools.
- Restoring and minimising the ribbon.

1.2.1 Setting User Preferences

User preferences refer to the user name and the default location of opened and saved files. These can be changed as appropriate so that the user name is different or so that files can be opened or saved in another location.

To set user preferences, do the following:

User Name

- Select the **File** menu.
- Select **Options**.
- Select the **General** command.
- In the **Personalize your copy of Microsoft Office**, position the cursor in the **User name** box and delete the current uscr name.
- Enter the new user name.
- Click **OK**.

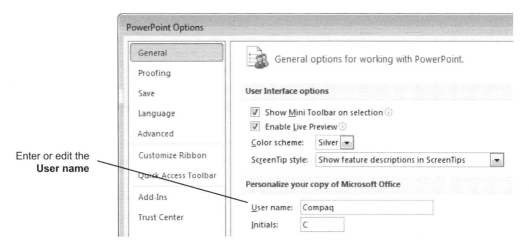

Enter or edit the
User name

Default File Location

- Select the **File** menu.
- Select **Options**.
- Select the **Save** tab.
- In the **Default File Location** box, enter the required file location of opened and saved files.
- Click **OK**.

Enter the file
location

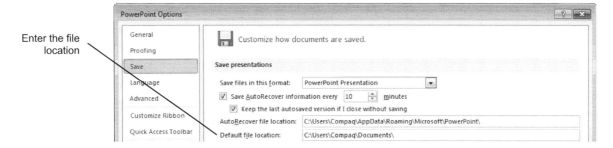

1.2.2 Using the Help Function

The Help function is available to give advice and help on aspects of the software that you are using. This is useful when you are trying to perform an action and don't know how to proceed further. Just ask the Help function a specific question and then select a relevant topic for the answer.

To use the Help function, do the following:

- Select the **Help** button.
  The **PowerPoint Help** window opens.
- Browse through the categories.
- Select a link to a relevant topic.
  A further set of links will appear that correspond with the selected topic.

- Select a relevant link to refine your search.
- Read the information on the chosen topic.
- Use the **Back** button to go back a step or the **Home** button to return to the first window of PowerPoint Help.

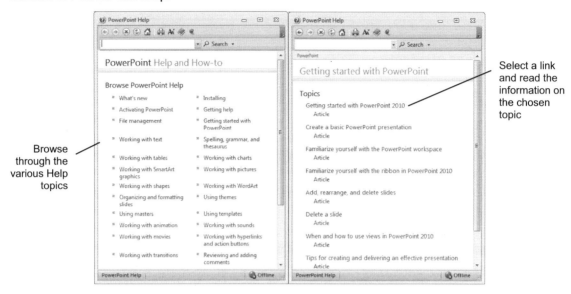

- Click **Print** to print a copy of the topic information.

You can also enter specific search criteria into the **Search** box to locate information on specific topics.

To enter search criteria, do the following:

- Enter a question in the **Search** box and click **Search**.
- A list of topic links relating to the search criteria will appear. Click a link to view the topic information.

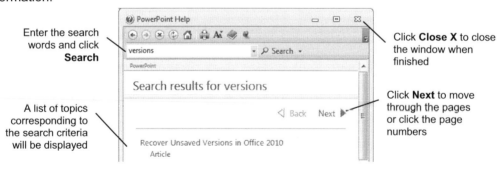

note   Press the **F1** key to display the **PowerPoint Help** window.

1.2.3 Using Magnification (Zoom)

The magnification tools are used to zoom in and out in a presentation.

To use the magification tools, do the following:

- Select the **View** tab from the ribbon.

- In the **Zoom** group, click **Zoom**.
  The **Zoom** window opens.
- Select **Fit** to ensure that the slide will fit the window.
- Select an option button to change the view percentage or use the scroll wheels to increase or decrease the percentage in the **Percent** box.
- Click **OK**.

Select a Zoom to: option button or use the scroll arrows to increase or decrease the percentage

Alternatively, using the Zoom bar at the bottom of the screen, select the **Zoom Out** button to reduce the view. Select the **Zoom In** button to enlarge the view.

Alternatively, drag the slider towards the Zoom Out or Zoom In buttons to decrease/increase the view.

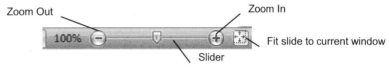

Zoom Out

Zoom In

Fit slide to current window

Slider

1.2.4 Minimising and Restoring the Ribbon

The ribbon can be minimised and then restored as required.

To minimise or restore the ribbon, do the following:

Minimising the Ribbon
- Right-click the ribbon bar.
- Select **Minimize the Ribbon**.
  The ribbon is hidden and only the tab headers are visible.

Restoring the Ribbon
- Right-click the bar containing the tabs.
- Click **Minimize the Ribbon** (note how a tick is displayed beside the menu command to indicate that it is active).

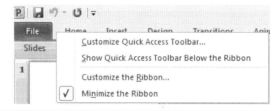

Practice Sequence

1	Open PowerPoint and create a new presentation.	☐
2	Save this presentation as **sale** in the default presentation format.	☐
3	Save another copy of the presentation in **RTF/Outline** format with the filename **saleRTF**.	☐
4	Reopen **sale** and practise switching between the two presentations.	☐
5	Zoom the **sale** presentation to **80%** and save.	☐
6	Use the **Help** function to find information on saving a presentation as a template.	☐
7	Close all presentations and exit PowerPoint.	☐

Section 2 ▶   Developing a Presentation

A presentation is developed in Normal View. When all slides have been added to the presentation they can be viewed in Slide Sorter view, which will display all slides as thumbnails, or viewed as outline displaying the titles on each slide. It is important that all slides have appropriate titles so that they are distinguishable in outline view. It also helps to have recognisable titles when navigating a presentation in Slide Show view.

2.1   Presentation Views

A presentation can be displayed in a variety of views: Normal, Slide Sorter, Slide Show and Outline. Normal view is displayed as a single slide and is used to create and edit a slide, Slide Sorter view displays miniature, thumbnails of all slides, making it easier to delete and move slides, and Slide Show view is used to view the presentation as a slide show. Outline view displays the titles only, making it easier to view and move slides.

In this section, you will learn about the following:

- Understanding the use of different presentation view modes.

- Recognising good practice in using different titles for each slide to distinguish it in outline view and when navigating in slide show view.

- Changing the presentation view modes.

2.1.1   View Modes

To change a presentation to Normal, Slide Sorter or Reading view modes, do the following:

- Select the **View** tab.

- Select a view mode, such as **Normal**, **Slide Sorter**, **Notes page** or **Reading View**.

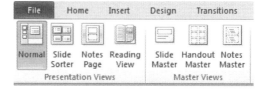

Normal View

Normal View enables the user to view an individual slide. The slide can be viewed with different magnification by zooming in or out using the Zoom buttons at the bottom of the screen. This view enables editing and formatting to be carried out on a single slide.

Slide Sorter View

Slide Sorter View enables the user to view all of the slides as thumbnails (miniature slides). This view is used to apply effects or timings to all slides. This view is also useful if you want to move slides to a different position.

Slide Show View

Slide Show View enables the user to view all of the slides as a slide show. In this view, you can navigate the slide show and pause or end the slide show.

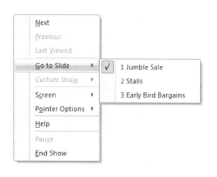

To navigate a slide show, do the following:

- Select the **Slide Show** tab and choose to start the slide show **From Beginning** or **From Current Slide**.

- Right-click the slide and a sub-menu will appear displaying options to move onto the next slide or enabling you to choose a specific slide.

- To move to the next slide, click **Next**.

- To select a specific slide, click **Go to Slide** and choose a slide from the list.

- To end the show, click **End Show**.

Outline View

To select Outline view, do the following:

- Selecting **Normal** from the **View** tab.

- Click the **Outline** tab.

  This view will only display the titles and text in each slide, with no graphical content. This view makes it easier to see the slide content at a glance and to edit the content on each slide. It is also easier to move slides to a different position using this view (more on moving slides later).

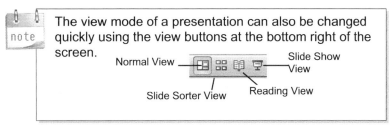

note   The view mode of a presentation can also be changed quickly using the view buttons at the bottom right of the screen.

2.1.2 Slide Titles

It is good practice to use different titles for each slide to distinguish them in Outline view and when navigating a slide show. For example, the following slides display bad practice and would be hard to distinguish when navigating a slide show.

When navigating these slides in a slide show, it would be difficult to distinguish between each slide as they would appear with the same title.

To ensure that each slide is easily distinguishable, use appropriate titles for each slide.

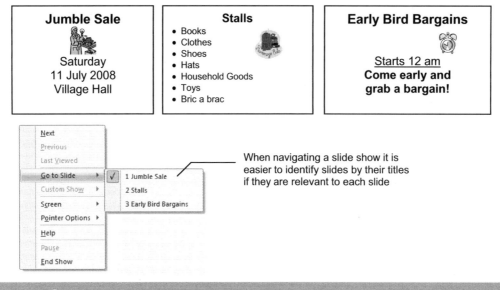

Practice Sequence

1	Open PowerPoint and then open the **skills** presentation.
2	View the presentation in **Slide Sorter View**.
3	View the presentation in **Outline View**.
4	View the presentation in **Slide Show View** and navigate the show using the **Go to slide** sub-menu: • Go to slide 3. • Go to slide 5. • Go to last viewed slide. • Go to next slide.
5	Pause the slide show.
6	Resume the show and go to slide 9.
7	End the show.
8	View the presentation in **Standard View**.
9	Close the **skills** presentation.

2.2   Slides

Slides can be formatted with different slide layouts, background colour or design. Slides can be copied and moved within and between presentations.

In this section, you will learn about the following:
• Choosing different slide layouts for a slide.
• Applying design templates to a presentation.
• Changing the background colour on specific slide(s).
• Adding a new slide with a specific slide layout.
• Copying and moving slides in and between presentations.
• Deleting slide(s).

2.2.1 Slide Layouts

The default slide layout in a new presentation is the **Title Slide** layout. This layout can be changed depending on the type of slide layout required. For example, you may want to create a slide to hold a title along with a graphic object, such as a picture or chart. For this you would select the **Title and Content** slide layout.

To change the layout of a slide, do the following:

- Select the **Home** tab from the ribbon.
- Select the **Layout** button.
- Select the required slide layout to match its content.
- The slide layout will be applied to the selected slide.

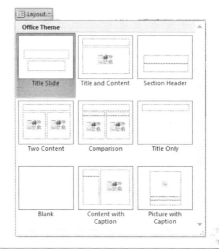

 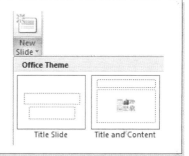

The default slide content for a slide in a new presentation is the **Title Slide**. Subsequent new slides will be inserted with the **Title and Content** slide layout, unless another layout is chosen from the **New Slide** menu.

2.2.2 Applying a Theme (Design Template)

A **theme** is a slide or set of slides that has been formatted with background colour, layout and theme fonts, and then saved as a theme. This theme can be applied to another presentation so that it displays the same formatting. In Office 2010, designs can be applied to a presentation by using a template that uses a customised theme. Themes can be customised to display different colours, fonts and effects and then saved as a custom theme or you can choose from various built-in themes that are available through the **Themes** command in the **Design** tab.

Standard content, such as the title, logo, text and background formatting are all applied to the template – this template can be used repeatedly with content, such as name and date being added to the slide as required

 Themes have replaced **design templates** used in previous versions of PowerPoint.

Applying a Built-In Theme

To apply a theme to a presentation, do the following:

- Open the presentation.
- Select the **Design** tab in the ribbon.
- The **Themes** group displays the built-in themes available for use with the current presentation. Move the mouse over a theme to see a preview of it applied to the current slide.

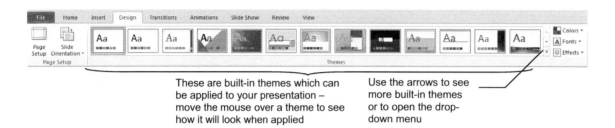

These are built-in themes which can be applied to your presentation – move the mouse over a theme to see how it will look when applied

Use the arrows to see more built-in themes or to open the drop-down menu

- The **Themes** menu displays the theme that is applied to the current presentation. The built-in themes are also displayed. More themes can be accessed by selecting **Enable Content Updates from Office.com**.

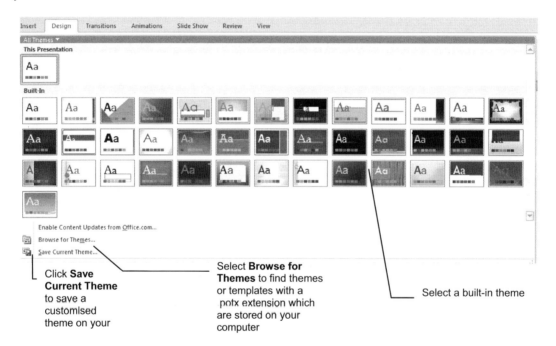

Click **Save Current Theme** to save a customised theme on your

Select **Browse for Themes** to find themes or templates with a .potx extension which are stored on your computer

Select a built-in theme

- The default theme is the **Office Theme**.
- Select a theme from the **Built-in** section of the menu.

Customising a Theme

The fonts, colours and lines/fill effects can all be changed to customise a theme.

To customise an existing built-in theme, do the following:

- Customise the theme by selecting formatting commands from the **Colors**, **Fonts** and **Effects** menus. The theme colours and fonts are indicated by the bar of colour and the lettering (Aa) on the **Theme** command.

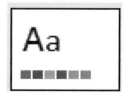

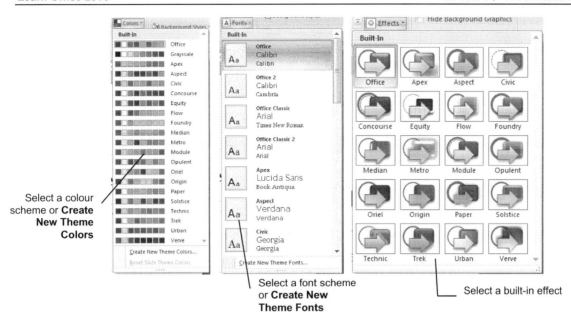

Select a colour scheme or **Create New Theme Colors**

Select a font scheme or **Create New Theme Fonts**

Select a built-in effect

- Click the **Colors** arrow.

  The theme colours currently applied to this theme
  are indicated by an outline around the menu command.

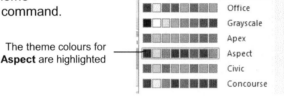

The theme colours for **Aspect** are highlighted

Theme colours consist of four text and background colours, six accent colours and two hyperlink colours.

To create a new theme colour, do the following:
- Select the **Colors** arrow.
- Click **Create New Theme Colors**.

  The **Create New Theme Colors** window opens.
- Choose the colours for the different elements of
  the theme and then enter a name for the new
  theme colour.
- Click **Save**.

  The theme currently applied to your
  slide displays the new theme colours.

Choose colours for the different elements of the theme

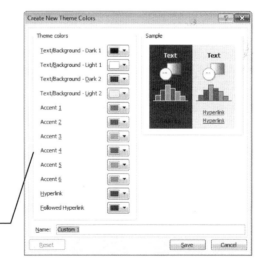

- Click the **Colors** arrow in the **Theme** group to see your
  custom colour.

The new theme colours
are displayed in the
Colors menu with the
saved file name

note   To return all theme elements to the original theme
       colours, select the **Reset** button and then **Save**.

To create New Theme Fonts, do the following:

- Select the **Fonts** arrow.
- Click **Create New Theme Fonts**.
- The theme fonts currently applied to this theme is highlighted in the menu.

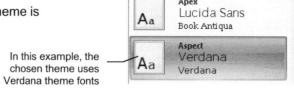

In this example, the chosen theme uses Verdana theme fonts

- To create new theme fonts, select the **Fonts** arrow and then click **Create New Theme Fonts**.
- Choose the fonts for headings and body text and then enter a name for the new theme font.
- Click the **Save** button.

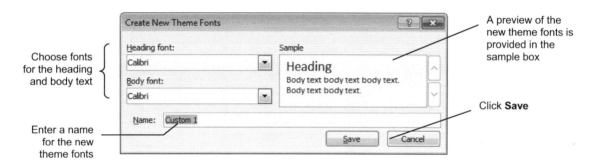

Choose fonts for the heading and body text

Enter a name for the new theme fonts

A preview of the new theme fonts is provided in the sample box

Click **Save**

- Click the **Fonts** arrow in the **Theme** group to see your custom fonts.

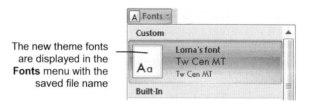

The new theme fonts are displayed in the **Fonts** menu with the saved file name

Theme effects consist of sets of lines and fill effects. To apply an effect, click the **Effects** button and then select an effect.

- The theme effects applied to the current theme is highlighted in the menu.

The chosen theme uses **Aspect Effects**

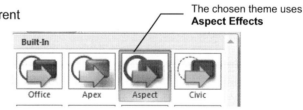

Saving a Theme

To save a customised theme, do the following:

More button

- In the **Themes** group on the ribbon, click the **More** button.
- Select **Save Current Theme**.
  The new theme will save in the **Document Themes** folder.

If you want to save the theme in a different location, do the following:

- Select a drive and/or folder in which to save the theme.
- Enter a name in the **File Name** box.
- The **Save as type** box will display the file extension associated with themes – Office Theme (*.thmx).
- Click **Save**.

Themes are automatically saved in the **Document Themes** folder – this location can be changed if required

Enter a file name for the new theme. It will save with a .thmx extension unless you change it

Click **Save**

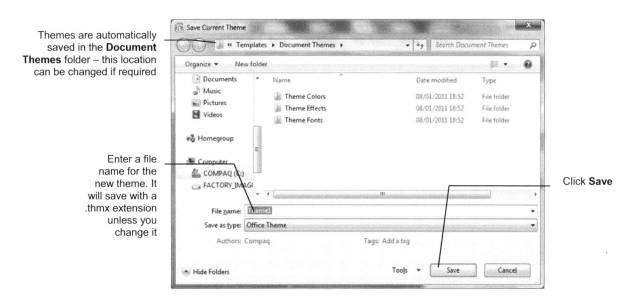

Applying a Saved Theme to a Presentation

To apply a theme that is stored on a drive on your computer, do the following:

- On the **Design** tab, in the **Themes** group, click the **More** button.
- Select **Browse for Themes**.
- Select a drive and/or folder from the Navigation Pane.
- Select the theme and then click **Apply** (or double-click the theme to apply it).

Choose the drive and/or folder

Select the theme

Click **Apply**

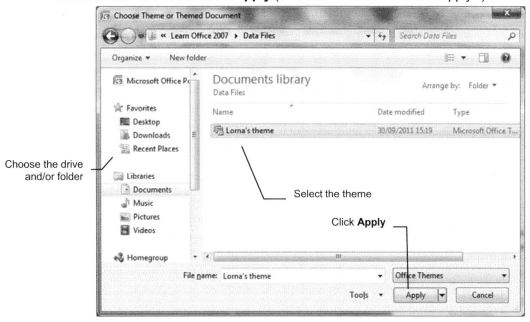

- Click the **More** button in the **Themes** group to see the customised theme.

 note   Click the **All Themes** arrow in the **Themes** menu to change how you view the menu items. You can choose to see all themes, including custom themes which you have applied, themes only in the current presentation or built-in themes.

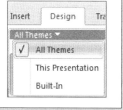

2.2.3 Background Colour

The background of a slide can consist of solid colour, gradient colour (using more than one colour), texture or picture. Background colour can be applied to one slide or all slides in a presentation.

To change the background colour, do the following:

- On the **Design** tab, in the **Background** group, click the **Background Styles** arrow.
- Select a colour from the menu or click **Format Background** to see the **Format Background** window.

  The **Format Background** window opens.
- Click the **Solid Fill** option button.
- Click the **Color** arrow.
- Choose a colour from the menu, or click **More Colors**.

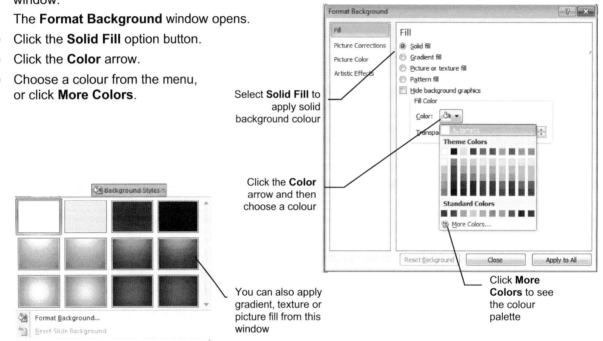

Select **Solid Fill** to apply solid background colour

Click the **Color** arrow and then choose a colour

You can also apply gradient, texture or picture fill from this window

Click **More Colors** to see the colour palette

- When **More Colors** is selected, the **Colors** window opens.
- From the **Standard** tab, select shades of different colours or click the **Custom** tab to mix colours together to create a custom colour.

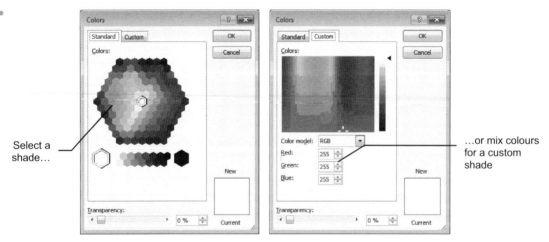

Select a shade...

...or mix colours for a custom shade

- Click **OK**.
- Click **Close** to apply the background colour to the current slide only or click **Apply to All** to apply the background to all slides in the presentation.

note

To return the background to the original background colour, click the **Reset Background** button before you click **Close**. Gradient, texture and picture fills can all be applied from the **Format Background** window.

Reset Background

2.2.4 Adding a New Slide

To add a new slide to a presentation, do the following:

- Select the **Home** tab and then, from the **Slides** group, click the **New Slide** arrow.
- Choose a slide layout to match the intended slide content.

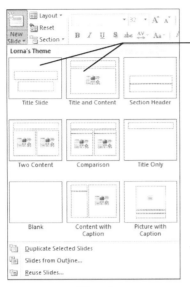

The two most commonly used slide layouts are **Title Slide** and **Title and Content**.

Title Slide provides placeholders (frames) for a heading and a subheading, **Title and Content** provides a title frame and also a frame to hold bulleted text, tables, spreadsheets and graphical data, such as images and charts

- Select the **Tile Slide** layout.

  The slide layout provides a placeholder (frame) for the heading and also a placeholder to hold a subtitle.

- To add a title, click into the placeholder and type the title text. Repeat this to add a subtitle to the subtitle placeholder

Click in the **Click to add title** placeholder and type the title text

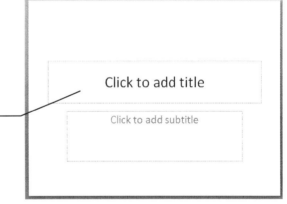

Click to add title

Click to add subtitle

- Select the **New Slide** arrow and choose the **Title and Content** slide layout.
- Add a title and then click into the second placeholder to add bulleted text or select one of the content icons.
- When the mouse is moved over an icon, a tag appears, describing its function.
- Double-click an icon to add content.

Table, Chart, SmartArt

Picture, Clip Art, Media Clip

Click to add a title, e.g. **Stalls**, and then either click to add bulleted text or double-click the relevant content icon in the centre of the slide to add a table, chart, graphic, etc.

Stalls

- Click to add text

Bullets

Bullets are used to define lists of information.

To add bulleted text to a slide, do the following:
- Click into the placeholder beside **Click to add text**.
- Enter the text – this will be displayed with the default bullet style.
- Press the **Enter** key to add another line of text – this will also display with a bullet.
- Repeat to add further text to the bulleted list.

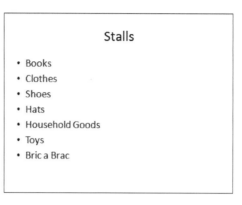

Tables

A table is used to display information in tabular format, i.e. in columns and rows. The intersection of a column and a row is called a cell.

To add a table to a slide, do the following:
- Click the **Insert** tab and then select the **Table** command. Select **Insert Table** from the drop-down menu.

  Alternatively, insert a slide with Title and Content layout and double-click the InsertTable icon.

  The **Insert Table** window opens.
- Select the number of columns/rows that are required.
- Click **OK**.

  The **Table Tools** contextual tab appears on the ribbon, holding the **Design** and **Layout** tabs which provide more tools for creating and formatting tables.
- From the **Design** tab, and in the **Table Styles** group, click the **More** button.
- Choose a table style.

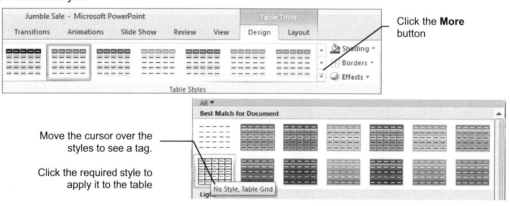

- Enter text into the first cell of the table.
- Press the **Tab** key on the keyboard to move to the next cell.

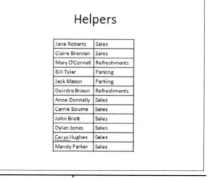

note | Pressing the **Tab** key at the end of the final row will insert a new row.
Press the **Shift** and **Tab** key to move to the previous cell in a table.

Charts

A chart is used to display information in graphical format, i.e. in bars/columns or segments or lines.

To add a chart to a slide, do the following:

- From the **Insert** tab, click the **Insert Chart** button on the ribbon.

  The **Insert Chart** window opens.

- Select the type of chart that you want (i.e. column, line, pie).

- Click **OK**.

  The window splits into two sections;
  one side displays the slide with chart and the second side displays
  a spreadsheet. The information that you enter into the spreadsheet will create the chart.

Insert Chart button

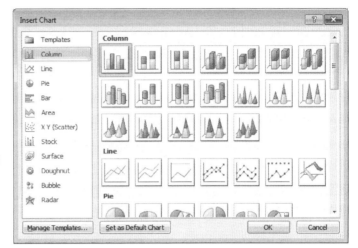

Note how the contextual **Chart Tools** tab appears on the ribbon, with **Design, Layout** and **Formatting** tabs containing more tools for creating and formatting charts.

- Add the data to the spreadsheet.
- Click the Close X button in the top right corner to close the spreadsheet.

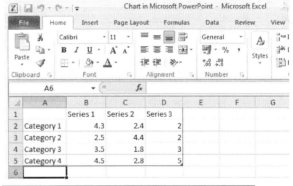

- The chart will display the data that was entered in the spreadsheet.

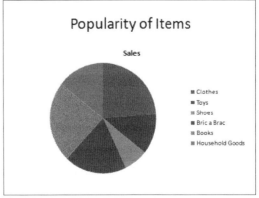

- Data labels and titles can be added to the chart (see sections 4.1.4 and 4.1.5).

2.2.5 Copying and Moving Slides

Slides can be copied or moved within a presentation or between open presentations.

To copy and move slides, do the following:

In the Same Presentation

- Select the **View** tab and then click **Slide Sorter** from the **Presentation Views** group.
  This view will display all of the slides in the presentation in thumbnail view.

To **copy** a slide, do the following:

- Select the slide and then, from the **Home** tab, select **Copy** from the **Clipboard** group.
- Select the slide that appears *before* the required position and then click **Paste** (slides will be pasted in position *after* the selected slide).
- The duplicated slide will appear in the new position.

To **move** a slide, do the following:

- Select the slide and then, from the **Home** tab, select **Cut** from the **Clipboard** group.
- Select the slide that appears **before** the required position and then click **Paste** (slides will be pasted in position **after** the selected slide).
- The moved slide will appear in the new position.
  Alternatively, use the **Drag and Drop** method of copying and moving slides by dragging the slide to the new position using the mouse. As you drag the slide observe the black vertical line that moves with it. This line should be placed in the required position before releasing the mouse button. To copy, hold down the **CTRL** key whilst dragging to the new position.

Between Open Presentations

- Open the required presentation files. Both files will be displayed as tabs on the taskbar at the bottom of the screen.
- Ensure that the presentation containing the slides to be copied, is the active presentation.
- Select the **View** tab and then click **Slide Sorter** from the **Presentation Views** group.
  This view will display all of the slides in the presentation in thumbnail view.

To **copy** a slide, do the following:

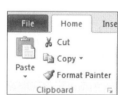

- Select the slide and then, from the **Home** tab, click **Copy** from the **Clipboard** group.
- Click the other presentation on the taskbar or select the **View** tab and **Switch Windows**. Choose the other presentation from the list.
- Ensure that you are viewing this presentation in Slide Sorter View.
- Click the mouse in the required position of the copied slide (a vertical line appears where you click) or click the slide that appears **before** the required position.
- From the **Home** tab, in the **Clipboard** group, click **Paste**.
- The slide will be duplicated in the selected position within the presentation.

To **move** a slide to another presentation, do the following:

- Select the slide and then, from the **Home** tab, click **Cut** from the **Clipboard** group.
- Click the other presentation on the taskbar or select the **View** tab and **Switch Windows**.
- Choose the other presentation from the list.
- Ensure that you are viewing this presentation in Slide Sorter View.

- Click the cursor in the required position of the copied slide (a vertical line appears where you click) or click the slide that appears **before** the required position.
- From the **Home** tab, in the **Clipboard** group, click **Paste**.

The slide will be moved to the selected position within the presentation.

> **note**
>
> If you want to copy or move more than one slide, select the first slide and then, holding down the **CTRL** key, click the other slides to copied/moved.
>
> The keyboard shortcuts are **CTRL + C** to copy, **CTRL + X** to cut and **CTRL + V** to paste.

2.2.6 Deleting Slides

Selected slides can be deleted within a presentation when they are no longer required.

To delete slides, do the following:
- Select **Slides** in Normal view (or view slides in Slide Sorter View)
- Right click the slide to be deleted and choose **Delete Slide**.

The selected slide will be deleted.

> **note**
>
> You can also press the **Delete** key on the keyboard to delete a selected slide.

Practice Sequence

1	Open PowerPoint and open a new presentation.
2	Ensure that the first slide has the **Title Slide** layout and enter the following title: **Jumble Sale**.
3	Enter the subtitle: **Saturday 11th July 2008** on one line and **Village Hall** on a separate line.
4	Create a new slide with the **Title and Content** slide layout and enter the title: **Stalls**.
5	Add the following bulleted text to the slide: ● Books ● Clothes ● Shoes ● Hats ● Household Goods ● Toys ● Bric a Brac
6	Create a new slide with **Title Slide** layout and the title: **Early Bird Bargains**.
7	Enter the subtitle: **Starts 12pm** on one line and **Come early and grab a bargain!** on a separate line.
8	Create a new slide with the **Title and Content** slide layout. Add the title: **Helpers**. Create a table with **9 rows/2 columns**. Add the data below into the table: Jane Roberts Sales Claire Brennan Sales Mary O'Connell Refreshments

Bill Tyler	Parking
Jack Mason	Parking
Deirdre Brown	Refreshments
Carrie Bourne	Sales
Dylan Jones	Sales
Cerys Hughes	Sales

9   Create a new slide with **Title Slide** layout and the title: **Popularity of Items**. ☐

Create a pie chart with the following data: ☐

10

Clothes	10
Toys	5
Shoes	3
Bric a Brac	8
Books	10
Household Goods	6

11   Apply the design template called **blue.potx** to the presentation. ☐

12   Change the background of slide 5 to a light blue solid colour. ☐

13   Copy slide 2 so that the duplicate slide appears before slide 5 (the chart). ☐

14   Move slide 4 so that it is the last slide in the presentation. ☐

15   Delete the duplicated slide (now slide 4). Save the presentation and keep open for the next step. ☐

16   Open a new presentation and copy slides 2 and 5 into it. ☐

17   Save this presentation as **manage** and close. ☐

18   Save the presentation as **Jumble Sale.pptx** and close it. ☐

2.3   Master Slides

To ensure consistency throughout your presentation it is advisable to create a master slide to contain standard content and formatting. A presentation can be produced by creating individual slides and applying formatting directly onto each slide. This can be time consuming if the presentation contains numerous slides and a more time effective method is to apply formatting and standard slide content once to a master slide.

In this section, you will learn about the following:

- Inserting a graphical object (picture, image, drawn object) onto a master slide.
- Removing a graphical object from the master slide.
- Entering text into the footer of specific slides and all slides in the presentation.
- Applying automatic slide numbering.
- Applying an automatically updated date and a non-updating date into the footer of specific slides and all slides in a presentation.

2.3.1 Creating a Master Slide

To create a master slide, do the following:

- Select the **View** tab and then, in the **Master Views** group, click the **Slide Master** button.

- The master slide opens.

2.3.2 Inserting a Graphical Object into a Master Slide

A graphical object refers to a picture, image or drawn object. If inserted onto a master slide, the graphical object will appear on all slides based on the slide master.

To insert a graphical object onto the master slide, do the following:

- Ensure that **Slide Master** view is selected.
- Select the **Insert** tab.
- From the **Images** group, click **Picture**.

The **Insert Picture** window opens.

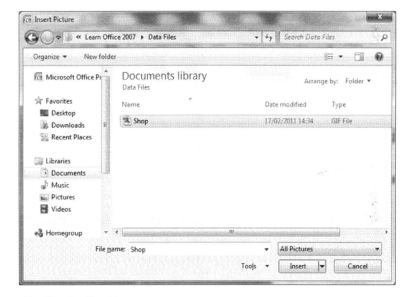

- Choose a drive and/or folder from the Navigation Pane.
- Select the picture file.
- Click **Insert**.
- Drag the picture to the required position on the slide.

Resizing a Graphical Object

The picture or drawn object may need to be resized so that it does not overlap text or other items on the slide. It is important that the original proportions of the object are maintained whilst resizing.

To resize a graphical object, do the following:

- Select the object – the object is surrounded by resizing handles.

- Position the mouse arrow over a corner handle (resizing from a corner handle will maintain the original proportions) and then drag in the required direction to either increase or decrease the size of the object.

Resize handles

6

2.3.3 Removing a Graphical Object from a Master Slide

Removing an object from the master slide will also remove it from any slides that are based on the slide master.

To remove a graphical object from the master slide, do the following:
- Open the Master Slide. Select the graphical object.
- Press the **Delete** key on the keyboard.

2.3.4 Inserting a Footer

A footer is an item of data that appears at the bottom of each slide that is based on the master slide. A footer may consist of a company name, the presenter's name or subject specific title.

To insert a footer on the master slide, do the following:
- Ensure that **Slide Master View** is selected.
- From the **Insert** tab, and the **Text** group, select **Header & Footer**.

  The **Header and Footer** window opens.

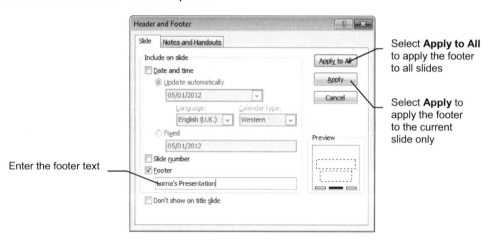

- Click the **Footer** checkbox to add a tick.
- Enter the text that you want to appear in the footer of each slide.
- Ensure that the **Don't show on title slide** tick box is unchecked if you want the footer to appear on all slides, regardless of slide layout.
- Select **Apply to All** to apply the footer to all slides in the presentation or **Apply** to apply the footer to only the current slide.

2.3.5 Inserting Automatic Fields

Automatic fields are items, such as dates and slide numbers, that update automatically. Some fields, such as fixed dates, do not update.

To insert an automatic field on the master slide, do the following:

Slide Numbering

- Ensure that **Slide Master View** is selected.
- From the **Insert** tab, and the **Text** group, select **Slide Number**.

- Select the **Slide Number** checkbox (to add a tick in the box).
- Ensure that the **Don't show on title slide** tick box is unchecked if you want the slide numbers to appear on all slides, regardless of slide layout.
- Select **Apply to All** to apply the slide number to all slides in the presentation or **Apply** to apply a slide number to only the current slide.

Automatically Updated Dates

- Ensure that **Slide Master View** is selected.
- From the **Insert** tab, and the **Text** group, select **Date & Time**.
- Select the **Date and Time** checkbox (to add a tick in the box).
- The **Update automatically** option button should be selected by default.
- Choose a date format from the drop-down list.
- Choose a language by selecting the **Language** arrow and choosing from the list.
- Ensure that the **Don't show on title slide** tick box is unchecked if you want the footer to appear on all slides, regardless of slide layout.

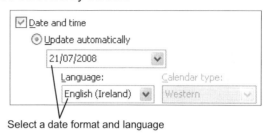

Select a date format and language

- Select **Apply to All** to apply an automatically updating date field to all slides in the presentation or **Apply** to apply a date to the current slide only.

Fixed Dates

- Ensure that **Slide Master View** is selected.
- From the **Insert** tab, and the **Text** group, select **Date & Time**.
- Select the **Date and Time** checkbox (to add a tick in the box).
- Choose a date format from the drop-down list.
- Choose a language by selecting the **Language** arrow and choosing from the list.
- Select the **Fixed** option button. This ensures that the date is fixed and will not update when the presentation is reopened on another date.

- Ensure that the **Don't show on title slide** tick box is unchecked if you want the footer to appear on all slides, regardless of slide layout.
- Select **Apply to All** to apply an automatically updating date field to all slides in the presentation or Apply to apply a date to the current slide only.

2.3.6 Closing the Slide Master

To close the Slide Master, do the following:

- From the **Slide Master** tab, click the **Close Master View** button.
- Ensure that the presentation is saved.

Close
Master View
Close

Practice Sequence

1	Open the **Jumble sale** presentation.	☐
2	Open the master slide and insert the image **shop.gif**. Position this image in the top right corner of the slide. To ensure that it will not obscure or overlap any other slide items, resize the image.	☐
3	Insert a footer that will appear on every slide in the presentation with your name.	☐
4	Insert an automatically updating date to appear on every slide.	☐
5	Insert slide numbers to appear on every slide in the presentation.	☐
6	Close the master slide and save the presentation with the same name.	☐
7	Close all open presentations.	☐

6

Section 3 ▶   Text

When entering text into a presentation, it is good practice to use short concise phrases, bullet points and numbered lists to display data. Bulleted and numbered lists can be indented and line spacing altered to enhance clarity. Text can be entered and edited within a *placeholder* (frame) in either standard or outline view. Editing text consists of deleting, adding and amending text. If you make a mistake whilst entering or editing text, the undo/redo functions enable the user to undo or redo a previous action. Text entered into a placeholder, as a bulleted/numbered list or a table, can be formatted to display with different fonts, sizes, colour and styles and in different alignments, such as left, right and centre. Tables can be further formatted and edited to insert and delete rows and columns and modify row/column height and width. Text can be copied or moved within and between presentations.

3.1   Handling Text

A presentation should contain short concise sentences or text broken down into bulleted or numbered lists. A presentation containing too much text may appear too busy and lose the attention of the audience. Large amounts of information should be summarised into brief sentences or bulleted lists for the benefit of the audience.

In this section, you will learn about the following:

- Recognising good practice in creating slide content: using short concise phrases, bullet points
  and numbered lists.

- Entering text into a placeholder in standard and outline view.

- Editing text in a presentation.

- Copying and moving text within and between presentations.

- Deleting text.

- Using the undo and redo commands.

3.1.1 Slide Content

Slide content may consist of text entered directly into a placeholder, in the form of titles, subtitles, phrases, bulleted or numbered lists, or entered into a table. The most important point to remember is that slide content should enable an audience to view and understand the information 'at a glance' without the need for reading large amounts of text. Text may be entered in Normal View in either Standard (Slide) or Outline View.

3.1.2 Entering Text in Standard View

Text may be entered in Standard View (Slide View). This view enables the user to see each slide individually.

To enter text in Standard View, do the following:

- Select the **View** tab and then, from the **Presentation Views** group, select **Normal**.

- Ensure that the **Slides** tab is selected.

- Enter text into the relevant placeholder (frame to hold title or subtitle or bulleted lists).

3.1.3 Entering Text in Outline View

Outline View gives an overview of all slides in the presentation and enables the user to see the titles, subtitles and text within each slide, without viewing the graphical content. This makes it easier to edit slide content.

To enter text in Outline View, do the following:

- Select the **Outline** tab.

  Existing slides will appear in the left hand pane, displaying text only.

- Click the mouse where you want to start typing and enter the required text.

3.1.4 Editing Text in a Presentation

Text can be edited within Standard or Outline View.

To edit text, do the following:

- Position the cursor within the placeholder and then make the necessary adjustments.

  In the example on the right, the text is edited to include the town in the second line of the subtitle text.

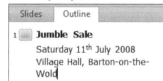

3.1.5 Selecting Text

Text must be selected before it can be formatted, copied, cut or deleted. Multiple items of text can be selected, whether adjacent or non-adjacent.

To select text, do the following:

Single Item of Text

- Position the cursor in front of the text and, holding down the left mouse button, drag to highlight the text. The text will display highlighted in grey/blue.

  Alternatively, position the cursor in the text to be selected and double-click the left mouse button.

Multiple Adjacent Items of Text

- Select the first item of text and then drag to highlight further items of text on the slide.

Multiple Non-Adjacent Items of Text

- Select the first item of text and then, holding down the **CTRL** key, select further items of text on the slide.

 Press **CTRL + A** to select all items within the selected placeholder.

Press **CTRL, SHIFT + END** to select all items from the current cursor position.

Hold down the **SHIFT** key and then press a directional arrow to select to the right, left, up or down.

You can also select a **placeholder** to format or copy/move the text within it. This method will select all of the text existing within the placeholder. To select a placeholder, click it.

Alternatively, select the **Home** tab and then the **Select** command from the **Editing** group. Select **Selection Pane** and then click the relevant placeholder from the task pane.

To select all items on a slide, click the **Select** command and then click **Select All**.

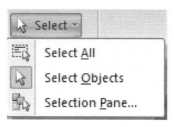

3.1.6 Copying and Moving Text

Text can be copied or moved within a presentation in Standard or Outline View. It can also be copied or moved between open presentations.

In the Same Presentation

- Select the **View** tab and then click **Normal** from the **Presentation Views** group.

  Text can be copied or moved using either Standard or Outline View.

To copy text, do the following:

- Select the text to be copied and then, from the **Home** tab, click **Copy** from the **Clipboard** group.

- Select the destination slide (the slide to which the text is being copied) and then position the cursor where the duplicated text is to display.
- Click **Paste**.

  The duplicated text will appear in the new position

To move text, do the following:

- Select the text to be copied and then, from the **Home** tab, click **Copy** followed by **Cut** from the **Clipboard** group.
- Select the destination slide (the slide to which the text is being copied) and then position the cursor where the duplicated text is to display.
- Click **Paste**.

  The moved text will appear in the new position.

  Alternatively, use the **Drag and Drop** method of copying and moving text by dragging the text to the new position using the mouse (in Standard View if copying or moving within the same slide or Outline View if copying/moving between slides in the same presentation). As you drag the text observe the vertical line that moves with it. This line should be placed in the required position before releasing the mouse button. To copy, hold down the **CTRL** key whilst dragging to the new position.

Between Open Presentations

- Open the required presentation files. Both files will be displayed as tabs on the taskbar at the bottom of the screen.
- Ensure that the presentation containing the text to be copied is the active presentation.

To copy text, do the following:

- Select the text and then, from the **Home** tab, click **Copy** from the **Clipboard** group.
- Click the other presentation on the taskbar or select the **View** tab and **Switch Windows**. Choose the other presentation from the list.
- Open the required slide in either Standard or Outline View.
- Click the mouse in the required position within the slide.
- From the **Home** tab, in the **Clipboard** group, click **Paste**.
- The text will be duplicated in the selected slide within the presentation.

To move text, do the following:

- Select the text and then, from the **Home** tab, click **Copy** followed by **Cut** from the **Clipboard** group.
- Click the other presentation on the taskbar or select the **View** tab and **Switch Windows**. Choose the other presentation from the list.
- Open the required slide in either Standard or Outline View.
- Click the mouse in the required position within the slide.
- From the **Home** tab, in the **Clipboard** group, click **Paste**.
- The text will be duplicated in the selected slide within the presentation.

note: If you want to copy or move more than one item of text, select the first item of text and then, holding down the **CTRL** key, click the other items of text to be copied or moved. Press **CTRL + C** to copy, **CTRL + X** to cut and **CTRL + V** to paste.

3.1.7 Deleting Text

Text can be deleted in either Standard or Outline View.

To delete text, do the following:
- Select the text to be deleted and then press the **Delete** key on the keyboard.

To delete one character at a time.
- Position the cursor in front of the character(s) to be deleted and press the **Delete** key (alternatively, position cursor behind the character(s) to be deleted and press the **Backspace** key on the keyboard).

To delete whole words without selecting text.
- Position the cursor in front of the word to be deleted and then, holding down the **CTRL** key, press **Delete** (or position cursor behind the word to be deleted and use **CTRL + Backspace**).

3.1.8 Undoing and Redoing

If a mistake is made when entering, editing or deleting text, it can be corrected by using the undo button. To redo the action, the redo button can be used.

To use undo and redo, do the following:
- To undo an action, click the **Undo** button from the **Quick Access Toolbar**.
- To redo an action, click the **Redo** button from the **Quick Access Toolbar**.

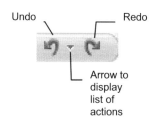

To see a list of actions that have been made recently, do the following:

- Click the arrow and select an action from the list.

Any actions that were completed before the selected action will also be undone.

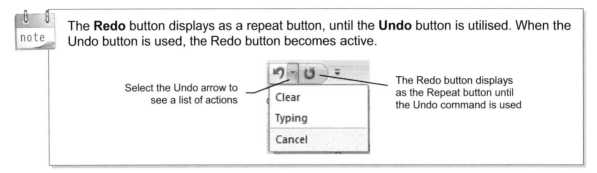

> **note** The **Redo** button displays as a repeat button, until the **Undo** button is utilised. When the Undo button is used, the Redo button becomes active.

Select the Undo arrow to see a list of actions

The Redo button displays as the Repeat button until the Undo command is used

Clear

Typing

Cancel

> **note** Press **CTRL + Z** to undo and **CTRL + Y** to redo.

Practice Sequence

1	Open the **Jumble sale** presentation and edit slide 1 by adding the name of the village **Barton-on-the-Wold** after the text **Village Hall**.	☐
2	Move the text **Come early and grab a bargain** from slide 3 to slide 1 so that it appears beneath the existing subtitle text.	☐
3	Open the presentation called **manage** and create a new slide with the **Title Slide** layout, with the title **Details**.	☐
4	Switch to the **Jumble sale** presentation. Copy the text **Saturday 11th July 2008** from slide 1 of the **sale** presentation and paste it into slide 1 of the **manage** presentation so that it appears beneath the title.	☐
5	Switch to the **Jumble sale** presentation. Copy the text **Starts 12am** from slide 3 so that it appears beneath the existing subtitle text on slide 1 of the **manage** presentation. Save the **manage** presentation and close.	☐
6	On slide 2 delete the text **Bric a Brac** from the bulleted list.	☐
7	Practise using the **Undo** command to return the text **Bric a Brac** to the bulleted list.	☐
8	Save and close the **Jumble sale** presentation.	☐

3.2   Text Formatting

Text formatting includes fonts, sizes, styles, colours, case and alignment. It is good practice to have consistent fonts and styles throughout a presentation; too many different formatting features, such as fonts, sizes and colours can detract from the presentation and appear unprofessional.

In this section, you will learn about the following:

- Changing text formatting: font sizes and font types.
- Applying text formatting: bold, italic, underline and shadow.
- Applying different colours to text.
- Applying case changes to text.
- Aligning text: left, centre and right in a text frame.

3.2.1 Font Types

Font types determine how the type face displays. Fonts can be *serif* or *sans serif*. A serif font is a font with 'tails' on the character.

Times New Roman

This is a serif font – the 'tails' are most apparent on the T and the N.

A sans serif font is a plain unadorned font without 'tails' on the character.

ARIAL

This is a sans serif font – this font is plain and without 'tails'.

There are many serif and sans serif fonts available for use.

To apply font types, do the following:

- Select the text to be changed.
- From the **Home** tab, click the **Font** arrow in the **Font** group.
- Choose a font from the list.

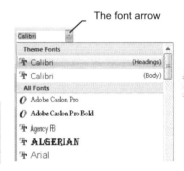

The font arrow

note

As the mouse is hovered over the font types, the selected text displays the font type. Click to make the selection.

3.2.2 Font Sizes

Font sizes determine how big or small the text appears and should vary for different slide elements. For example, titles should be displayed in a larger font size than subtitles which, in turn, should be a larger font size than bulleted list text or phrases. Font sizes should be consistent throughout the presentation to enhance clarity and provide a professional appearance, i.e. all titles should be the same size.

To change the font size, do the following:
- Select the text to be changed.
- From the **Home** tab, click the **Size** arrow in the **Font** group.
- Choose a size from the list.

The size arrow

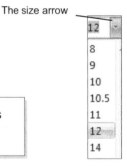

note

As the mouse is hovered over the sizes, the highlighted text displays the currently selected size. Click to make the selection.

3.2.3 Font Styles

Font styles can be used to enhance specific items of text within a slide. For example, you may wish to make a certain word stand out by making it **bold**, underlining it, or applying *italic* or shadow to it. Font styles should be used sparingly and be consistent throughout the presentation to enhance clarity and provide a professional appearance.

To change the font style, do the following:

- Select the text to be changed.
- From the **Home** tab, click the required style in the **Font** group.

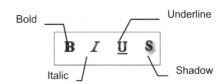

3.2.4 Font Colour

Font colour can be used to enhance specific items of text within a slide. Font colour should be used sparingly and be consistent throughout the presentation to enhance clarity and provide a professional appearance.

To change the font colour, do the following:

- Select the text to be changed.
- From the **Home** tab, click the **Font Color** arrow in the **Font** group.
  The menu will display the font colours used in the currently applied theme and also the standard colours.
- Select a colour from the menu or choose **More Colors** to see the colour palette.

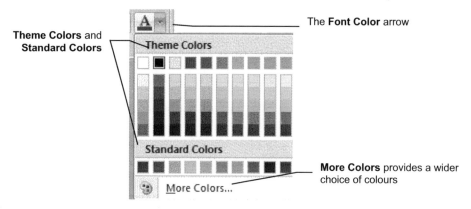

The **Colors** window opens when **More Colors** is selected.

- From the **Standard** tab, select a colour.
- Click **OK**.

  Alternatively, fonts, sizes, styles and colours can all be applied from the Font window. To open this window, select the Font window launcher in the **Home** tab.

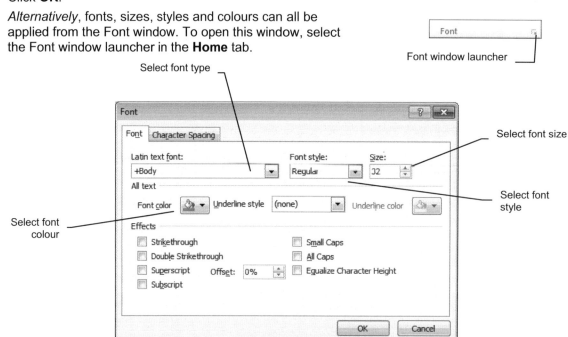

note   Press **CTRL + T** to open the **Font** window.

3.2.5 Changing Text Case

The term **case** refers to the capitalisation of characters. Text can be displayed in lower, upper or sentence case or you can choose to capitalise each word. Another feature is the Toggle case command which displays sentence case in reverse, with the initial letter of a sentence in lower case and the rest in upper case.

See the examples below.

- this is in lower case.
- This is in sentence case (initial character of each new sentence will appear in upper case).
- THIS IS IN UPPER CASE.
- Each Word Is Capitalized.
- tHIS IS TOGGLE CASE (initial character of each new sentence will appear in lower case).

To change the case of text, do the following:

- Select the text to be changed.
- From the **Home** tab, click the **Change Case** arrow in the **Font** group.
- Select a case from the list.

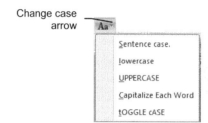

Change case arrow

note

To 'cycle' through lower, upper and sentence cases using the keyboard hold down the **Shift** key and press **F3**.

3.2.6 Aligning Text

Text can be aligned so that it is displayed on the left, right or centre of the slide.

See the examples below.

This text is left aligned.

This text is centred.

This text is right aligned.

This text is justified which provides a straight edge to both the left and right margins. Justification is only apparent on more than one line of text. The text is stretched so that it matches the line endings of other text in the paragraph.

To align text, do the following:

- Select the text to be aligned.
- From the **Paragraph** tab, click the required alignment button.

Left Justify

Centre Right

Alternatively, alignment can be applied from the **Paragraph** window. To open this window, select the Paragraph window launcher in the **Home** tab.

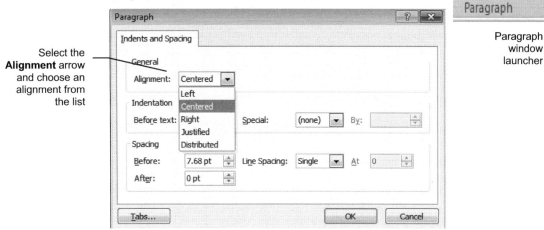

Select the
Alignment arrow
and choose an
alignment from
the list

Paragraph
window
launcher

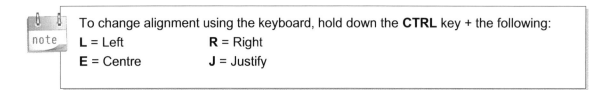

note   To change alignment using the keyboard, hold down the **CTRL** key + the following:
L = Left   **R** = Right
E = Centre   **J** = Justify

Practice Sequence

1	Open the **Jumble sale** presentation.
2	Format the bulleted list on slide 2 to be **Arial 28**.
3	Apply shadow to the bullet text on slide 2.
4	On slide 1, format the text **Come early and grab a bargain!** to display as bold and italics and with a dark blue font colour.
5	Change the text **Starts 12 am** on slide 3 so that it displays in upper case and format with an underline.
6	Change the alignment of the tabular data on slide 5 so that it displays in both columns with **Centre** alignment.
7	Save and close the **Jumble sale** presentation.

6

3.3 Bullet and Number Lists

Lists are bulleted or numbered ordered items of text. Bullets and numbers can be formatted to appear with a different symbol/number style and be indented by a specific measurement from the edge of the placeholder. Lists can also be enhanced by increasing or decreasing the line spacing between each line of text.

In this section, you will learn about the following:

• Indenting bulleted text.

• Removing bulleted text.

• Adjusting the line spacing before and after bulleted and numbered lists.

• Switching between different standard bullet and number styles in a list.

3.3.1 Applying and Removing Indents

The default indentation between a bullet and text, using the **Title and Content** layout with the standard Office theme, for a newly inserted bullet is 0.95cm. This can be altered to suit your presentation. Indentation can also be applied to the bullet or number itself so that it displays at a specific measurement from the edge of the placeholder.

To apply and remove indentation from a bulleted list, do the following:

- Select the bulleted/numbered list.
- Click the **Paragraph** window launcher icon.
  The **Paragraph** window opens.
- Using the **Before text** scroll arrows, select a measurement for the indentation **between** the bullet and text.
- Select the **Special** arrow and choose **Hanging** so that lines of text will indent beneath each other.
- Select the **By** scroll arrows to increase or decrease the measurement (the hanging indent should match the **Before text** indent).
- Click **OK**.

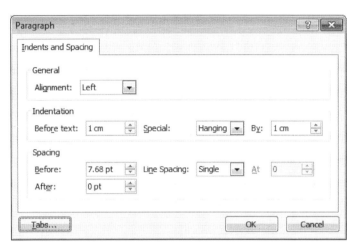

To remove indents, do the following:

- Open the **Paragraph** window.
- Decrease the indent measurements to **0cm**.

Alternatively, in the Paragraph group of the Home tab:

- Click the Increase List Level button to increase the indent.
- Click the Decrease List Level button to decrease the indent.
- Use the Ruler Bar to drag the indent markers to the required measurement.

First line indent

Hanging indent

3.3.2 Adjusting Line Spacing

Line spacing refers to the space before, after or between bulleted lines of text. The default line spacing between lines of text using the standard Office theme is **single**.

To adjust line spacing in a list, do the following:

- Select the bulleted/numbered list to be adjusted.
- Click the **Paragraph** window launcher icon.
  The **Paragraph** window opens.

- In the **Spacing** section of the window, use the **Before** scroll arrow to select a measurement for the spacing *before* bulleted text.
- Use the After scroll arrow to repeat this to increase the spacing *after* bulleted text.
- Select the **Line Spacing** arrow and choose an option from the list to change the line spacing *between* lines of bulleted text. If the **Multiple Lines** or **Exactly** options are selected, the **At** list box becomes active to choose a measurement from.
- Click **OK**.

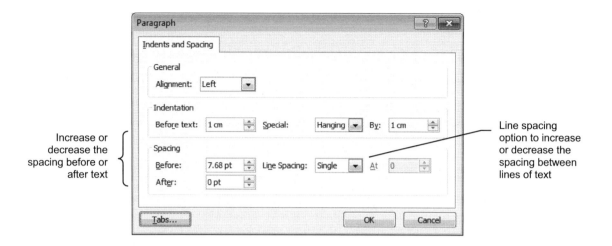

Increase or decrease the spacing before or after text

Line spacing option to increase or decrease the spacing between lines of text

3.3.3 Bullets and Numbering Styles

Bullet and numbering styles can be changed to display a different symbol or number style.

To change bullets and numbering styles, do the following:

Bullet Styles

* Select the bulleted list to be changed.
* Select the **Home** tab.
* Click the **Bullets** arrow in the **Paragraph** group.
* Select a bullet style from the menu or select **Bullets and Numbering** for more options.
* The **Bullets and Numbering** window provides more style options.
    ► Click the **Color** arrow and select a different colour for the bullet.
    ► Change the size of the bullet by a specified percentage of the text.
* Click **OK**.

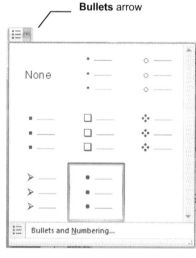

Bullets arrow

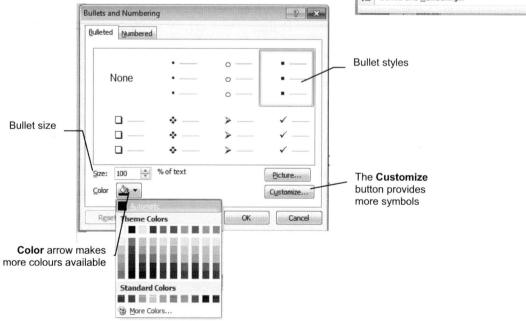

Bullet size

Bullet styles

The **Customize** button provides more symbols

Color arrow makes more colours available

Numbering Styles

- Select the numbered list.
- Select the **Home** tab.
- Click the **Numbering** arrow in the **Paragraph** group.
- Select a number style from the menu or select **Bullets and Numbering** for more options.
- The **Bullets and Numbering** window provides more style options. Ensure that the **Numbered** tab is selected.
  - ▷ Select a numbering style from the list.
  - ▷ Choose a different size for the numbers in relation to the text.
  - ▷ Click the **Color** button to change the colour of the numbers.
  - ▷ Select **Start at** to change the number sequence.
- Click **OK**.

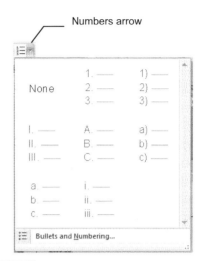

Numbers arrow

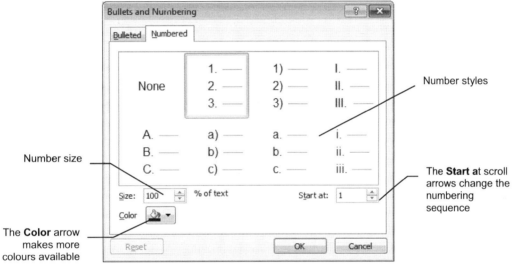

Number styles

Number size

The **Color** arrow makes more colours available

The **Start at** scroll arrows change the numbering sequence

> **note** The **Mini Toolbar** appears when text is selected. Formatting options such as font, sizes, styles, colour, alignment, indents and bullets can be accessed from this toolbar.

6

Practice Sequence

1	Open the **Jumble sale** presentation.	☐
2	Format the bulleted list on slide 2 so that the text is indented from the bullet with a hanging indent of 1cm.	☐
3	Format the bulleted list on slide 2 so that it displays with a square, pale blue bullet.	☐
4	Format the bulleted list on slide 2 that it displays with **4.5 pt** spacing *before* the bulleted text.	☐
5	Change the line spacing of the bulleted list on slide 2 to **1.5**.	☐
6	Save and close the **Jumble sale** presentation.	☐

3.4   Tables

A table displays text in tabular format, in rows and columns. The intersection between a row and a column is called a **cell**. Tables can be formatted to display with or without borders.

In this section, you will learn about the following:
- Entering and editing text in a table slide.
- Selecting rows, columns and an entire table.
- Inserting and deleting rows and columns.
- Modifying column width and row height.

3.4.1   Entering and Editing Text

To enter text in a table, do the following:
- Create a new slide with the **Title and Content** layout.
- Double-click the **Insert Table** icon.
- Choose the number of rows and columns required for the table.
- Click **OK**.
- Enter a title for the slide.
- Position the cursor within the first cell of the table and enter text.
- Press the **Tab** key to jump to the next cell in the same row and enter text.
- Repeat to enter text into the relevant cells (pressing the **tab** key at the end of the final row creates a new row).

To edit text in a table, do the following:
- Position the cursor in the cell and delete/amend text as appropriate (see Section 3.1.4).

3.4.2   Selecting Rows, Columns and an Entire Table

To select a table, or rows or columns in a table, do the following:

To select a row, do the following:
- Position the cursor so that it is pointing at the row.
  The cursor turns into a black arrow.
- Click to select the row.

To select a column, do the following:
- Position the cursor so that it is above the column.
  The cursor turns into a black arrow.
- Click to select the column.

To select an entire table, do the following:
- Position the cursor to the left of the first row to see the black arrow.
- Drag the mouse over the remaining rows.
  Alternatively, place the cursor in the table, row or column to be selected and, from the contextual **Table Tools** tab, select the **Layout** tab. Select the **Select** command and then choose **Row**, **Column** or **Table**.

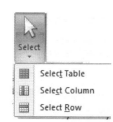

 note To select rows or columns using the keyboard, hold down the **Shift** key and use the directional arrow keys on the keyboard. To highlight the whole table, press **CTRL + A**.

3.4.3 Inserting and Deleting Rows and Columns in a Table

To insert rows in a table, do the following:

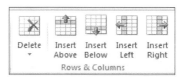

- Select the row *below* or *above* the intended position of the new row.

- From the **Table Tools** tab and the **Layout** tab, click the **Insert Above** or the **Insert Below** command from the **Rows & Columns** group.

To insert rows in a table, do the following:

- Select a column to the **left** or **right** of the intended position of the new column.

- From the **Table Tools** tab and the **Layout** tab, click the **Insert Left** or the **Insert Right** command from the **Rows & Columns** group.

To delete rows and columns in a table, do the following:

- Select the row or column to be deleted.

- From the **Table Tools** tab and the **Layout** tab, click the **Delete** command from the **Rows & Columns** group.

- Select **Delete Columns** or **Delete Rows**.

3.4.4 Modifying Row Height and Column Width

The rows and the columns in a table can be modified to increase or decrease the height of a row or width of a column. This is useful to ensure that all text is visible within the table.

To modify the height of rows in a table, do the following:

- Select the row or rows to be modified.

- From the **Table Tools** tab and the **Layout** tab, click the scroll arrows on the **Table Row Height** list box to increase or decrease the height of the row (in centimetres) from the **Cell Size** group.

To modify the width of columns in a table, do the following:

- Select the column or columns to be modified.

- From the **Table Tools** tab and the **Layout** tab, click the scroll arrows on the **Table Column Width** list box to increase or decrease the width of the column (in centimetres) from the **Cell Size** group.

Practice Sequence

1	Open the **Jumble sale** presentation.	☐
2	On slide 5 delete the row for **Dylan Jones**.	☐
3	Edit the name **Cerys** to read as **Cheryl**.	☐
4	Insert a new row above **Deirdre Brown** and enter details for **David Black, Sales**.	☐
5	Modify the row height of all rows in the table to **0.75cm**.	☐
6	Modify the column width of both columns in the table to **5cm**.	☐
7	Save and close the **Jumble sale** presentation.	☐

6

Section 4 ▶ Charts

Charts are visual graphical representations of numerical data, making it easier to see results 'at a glance'. Charts can be displayed in different formats, such as pie, bar/column and line and formatted with different colours and fonts, sizes and styles. Charts can also be created to display a hierarchical structure, such as organisational charts. This type of chart uses shapes and connecting lines to show the hierarchical relationship existing between different levels.

4.1 Using Charts

To use charts, you need to input data in a spreadsheet. This data is then displayed in chart format in the chart type that you specify. The chart can be modified if required to display a different chart type. Chart titles can also be added or removed as required. The chart data is described by the data labels that are applied. If no labels are applied, the chart is meaningless.

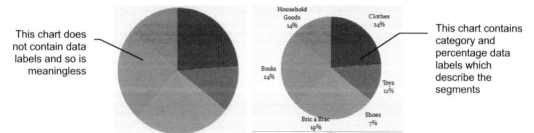

This chart does not contain data labels and so is meaningless

This chart contains category and percentage data labels which describe the segments

In this section, you will learn about the following:

- Inputting data to create built-in charts in a presentation: column, bar, line and pie.
- Selecting a chart.
- Changing the chart type.
- Adding, removing and editing a chart title.
- Adding data labels to a chart: values, numbers and percentages.
- Changing the background colour of a chart.
- Changing the column, bar, line and pie slice colours in a chart.

4.1.1 Creating Charts

To create a chart, do the following:

- Create a new slide with the **Title and Content** slide layout.
- Click the **Insert Chart** icon on the slide.
- Select a chart type, i.e. column, bar, line or pie, in the left hand pane.
- Select a chart sub-type in the right pane.
- Click **OK**.

Insert Chart icon

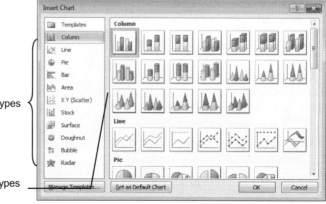

Chart types

Chart sub-types

- The screen will split so that both the slide and the spreadsheet are displayed.
- Enter data into the spreadsheet.

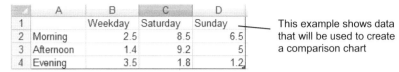

	A	B	C	D
1		Weekday	Saturday	Sunday
2	Morning	2.5	8.5	6.5
3	Afternoon	1.4	9.2	5
4	Evening	3.5	1.8	1.2

This example shows data that will be used to create a comparison chart

- Close the spreadsheet and return to the chart by clicking Close (X) in the top-right corner.

4.1.2 Selecting Charts

Before a chart can be edited or formatted, it must first be selected. When a chart element is selected, it can be deleted, resized, formatted and moved.

To select a chart do the following:
- Click the chart or chart element to select it.

  Alternatively, select **Chart Tools/Layout** and then, in the **Current Selection** group, click the **Chart Elements** arrow and select a chart element from the list.

  The selected chart element will display with handles surrounding it.

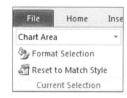

4.1.3 Changing the Chart Type

A chart can be modified to display a different chart type if required.

To change the chart type, do the following:
- Click the chart to select it.

  Alternatively, select **Chart Tools/Layout** and then, in the **Current Selection** group, click the **Chart Elements** arrow and select **Chart Area**.
- Select **Chart Tools/Design**.
- From the **Type** group, click the **Change Chart Type** button.
- Choose a chart type and sub-type.
- Click **OK**.

4.1.4 Chart Titles and Axis Titles

Chart titles help to describe the purpose of the chart. For example, a chart that displays the annual sales figures for a company in 2011 would be entitled: **Annual Sales Figures 2011**. Axis titles can also be used to identify each axis on the chart.

Add a Chart Title

To add a chart title, do the following:
- Click the chart to select it.

  Alternatively, in the **Chart Tools/Layout** tab, select the **Chart Elements** arrow and select **Chart Area** from the **Current Selection** group.
- Select the **Chart Tools/Layout** tab.
- Click the **Chart Title** command from the **Labels** group.
- From the menu you have the following options:
  - ▷ **None** (do not display a chart title).
  - ▷ **Centred Overlay Title**.
  - ▷ **Above Chart** (this is the usual position).
  - ▷ **More Title Options** (to format the chart title).

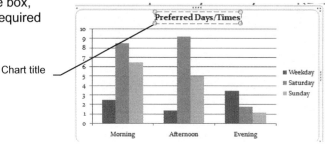

- Select **Above Chart** to add a chart title above the chart.
- Position the cursor within the chart title box, delete the existing text and enter the required chart title text.

Chart title

Edit a Chart Title

To edit a chart title, do the following:

- Position the cursor in the chart title box and amend, or delete, the existing text as necessary.

Format a Chart Title

To format a chart title, do the following:

- Click the title to select it.

  Alternatively, select **Chart Tools/Layout** and then, in the **Current Selection** group, click the **Chart Elements** arrow and select **Chart Title**.

- Select **Chart Tools/Layout** tab from the ribbon.
- Click the **Chart Title** command from the **Labels** group.
- Select **More Title Options** from the menu.

  The **Format Chart Title** window opens.
- Select the required formatting options.
- Select the **Home** tab.
- From the **Font** group, select a font, size, style and colour.
- Click **Close**.

From this window you can apply a solid, gradient picture or texture fill, a border with a specific colour and style or shadow effect

You can also apply a 3-D format to the chart title and change the alignment

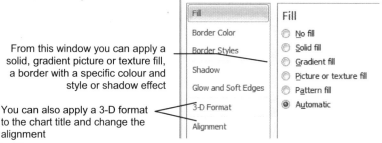

Remove a Chart Title

To remove a chart title, do the following:

- Click the chart title to select it.

  Alternatively, select **Chart Tools/Layout** and then, in the **Current Selection** group, click the **Chart Elements** arrow and select **Chart Title**.

- Select **Chart Tools/Layout** tab from the ribbon.
- Click the **Chart Title** command from the **Labels** group.
- Select **None**.

  Alternatively, select the chart title and press the **Delete** key.

Axis Titles

The methods above can also be used to add, format or delete axis titles by accessing the **Axis Titles** menu.

- Click the chart to select it.

Alternatively, select **Chart Tools/Layout** and then, in the **Current Selection** group, click the **Chart Elements** arrow and select **Chart Area**.

- Select **Chart Tools/Layout** tab from the ribbon.
- Click the **Axis Titles** command from the **Labels** group.
- Select an axis title option for the horizontal or vertical axis. A sub-menu opens to provide further options.
- Select an option from this sub-menu.
- Position the cursor within the **Axis Title** box.
- Delete the existing text.
- Enter the axis title text into the box.
- Repeat for other axes on the chart.

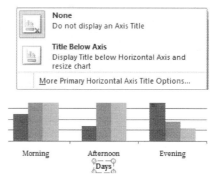

4.1.5 Adding Data Labels

Data labels help to identify the segment, line or column/bar in a chart.

To add data labels, do the following:

Values/Numbers and Percentages

- Click the chart to select it.
  Alternatively, select **Chart Tools/Layout** and then, in the **Current Selection** group, click the **Chart Elements** arrow and select **Chart Area**.
- Select **Chart Tools/Layout** tab from the ribbon
- Click the **Data Labels** button from the **Labels** group.
- Select an option from the drop-down list.
  - ▶ Select **None** if you don't want data labels or select one of the display options from the list.
  - ▶ Click **More Data Label Options** to see the **Format Data Labels** window.
- From this window, you can select the type of data label, such as **Value/number**, **Category Name**, **Series Name** or **Percentage**.
  You also have the option of changing the label position.
- Click **Close** when finished.

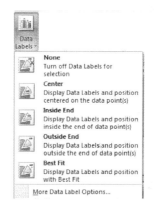

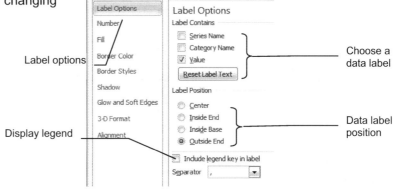

Examples of data labels, all with **Outside End** position.

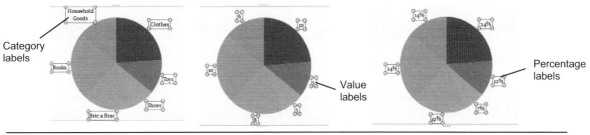

4.1.6 Background Colour

The background of a chart can be formatted to display a different colour.

To apply background colour, do the following:

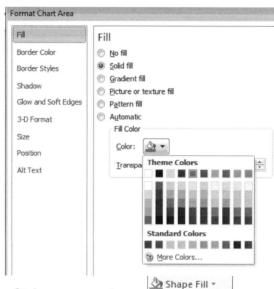

- Click the chart to select it.

  Alternatively, select **Chart Tools/Layout** tab and then, in the **Current Selection** group, click the **Chart Elements** arrow and select **Chart Area**.

- Select the **Format Selection** command from the **Current Selection** group.

- The **Format Chart Area** window opens.

- From the **Fill** command, select the **Solid fill** option button.

- Select the **Color** arrow and choose a colour from the palette or click **More Colors** to see a wider choice of colours. You also have the option of formatting the chart area with gradient, picture or texture fill.

- Click **Close**.

  Alternatively, select **Chart Tools/Format** tab and then click the **Shape Fill** arrow from the **Shape Styles** group and choose a colour.

4.1.7 Changing a Series Colour

The individual series on a chart can be formatted to display a different colour. For example, you may want to display each column in a column chart as a different colour to differentiate between the series. The individual series are the bar, lines, pie slices or columns that make up a chart.

To change the colour of a series, do the following:

- Click the series to select it.

  Alternatively, select **Chart Tools/Layout** tab and then, in the **Current Selection** group, click the **Chart Elements** arrow and select **Series 'series name'**.

- Select the **Format Selection** command from the **Current Selection** group on the ribbon

  The **Format Data Series** window opens.

- From the **Fill** command, select the **Solid fill** option button.

- Select the **Color** arrow and choose a colour from the palette or click **More Colors** to see a wider choice of colours.

- Click **Close**.

- Repeat this procedure to apply colour to each series in the chart.

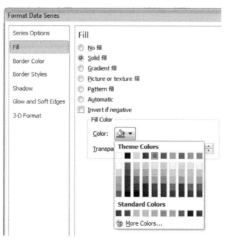

1   Open the **Jumble sale** presentation.

2   Create a new slide with the slide title **Preferred Days** and a **line** chart with the following data:

	Weekday	Saturday	Sunday
Morning	2.5	8.5	6.5
Afternoon	1.4	9.2	5
Evening	3.5	1.8	1.2

3   Add the following chart title: **Popularity of Days**.

4   Format the chart title to be Arial, 18, dark blue and italic.

5   Add a vertical rotated axis title: **Voting results**.

6   Add a horizontal axis title: **Days**.

7   Edit the chart title to read: **Preferred Days**.

8   Change the chart type to a column chart.

9   Remove the chart title form the chart.

10 Format each series in a different colour:
    Weekday=dark blue, **Saturday=green**, **Sunday=yellow**.

11 On slide 4, format the pie chart to display category and percentage data labels.

12 Change the background colour of the pie chart to white.

13 Save and close the **Jumble sale** presentation.

4.2   Organisation Charts

Organisation charts are used to display a hierarchical structure. This type of chart uses shapes and connecting lines to show the hierarchical relationship existing between different levels.

In this section, you will learn about the following:

- Creating an organisation chart with a labelled hierarchy by using a built-in organisation chart feature of PowerPoint 2010.
- Changing the hierarchical structure of an organisation chart.
- Adding and removing co-workers and subordinates in an organisation chart.

4.2.1   Creating an Organisation Chart

To create an organisation chart, do the following:

- Create a new chart with the **Title and Content** slide layout.
- Add a title for the slide.
- Select the **SmartArt** icon on the slide or, from the Illustrations group on the **Insert** tab, select the **SmartArt** button.

  The **Choose a SmartArt Graphic** window opens.

- Select a chart type, such as **Hierarchy**.
- Select a chart sub-type.
- Click **OK**.

Select a chart type

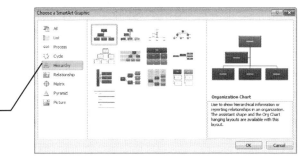

The organisation chart displays,
ready for inputting data.

Enter data into the
chart by clicking into a
box and typing

4.2.2 Changing the Structure of an Organisation Chart

An organisation chart can be modified to display a different hierarchal structure if required. For
example, a subordinate or co-worker may need to be moved within the structure if they are promoted.

To restructure the organisation chart, do the following:
- Select a level on the organisation chart.
- From the **SmartArt Tools/Design** tab and the **Create Graphic** group,
  select **Promote** to increase the level or **Demote** to decrease the level.
  Alternatively, drag a box to the required level and release

Changing Layout
- Select **SmartArt Tools/Design**.
- Click the **More** button in the **Layouts** group.

More button

- Choose a layout from the menu.

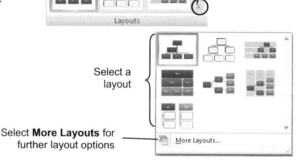

Select a
layout

Select **More Layouts** for
further layout options

- Select **Right to Left** to change the alignment of the chart.
- Select **Text Pane** to add text to the chart (or right-click within a box
  and select **Edit Text**).

Right to Left

4.2.3 Adding and Removing Levels

An organisation chart can be edited to display or remove specific levels in the hierarchy, such as
co-worker or subordinate.

To add or remove levels in an organisation chart, do the following:

Adding Co-workers or Subordinates
- Select a box on the level to which the co-worker will be added.
- Select **SmartArt Tools/Design**.
- Click the **Add Shape** button in the **Create Graphics** group.
- Choose an option from the menu:

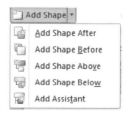

  ▷ **Add Shape After** (to add a co-worker after a selected box).
  ▷ **Add Shape Before** (to add a co-worker before a selected box).
  ▷ **Add Shape Above** (to add a higher level above the selected box).
  ▷ **Add Shape Below** (to add a subordinate below the selected box).
  ▷ **Add Assistant** (to add an assistant to the selected box).

A new box will be added to the chart.

- Right-click the box.
- Select **Edit text**.

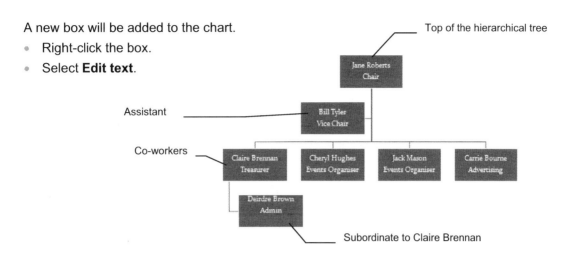

Removing Co-workers or Subordinates

To remove co-workers or subordinates in an organisation chart, do the following:

- Select the co-worker or subordinate to be deleted.
- Press the **Delete** key.

Practice Sequence

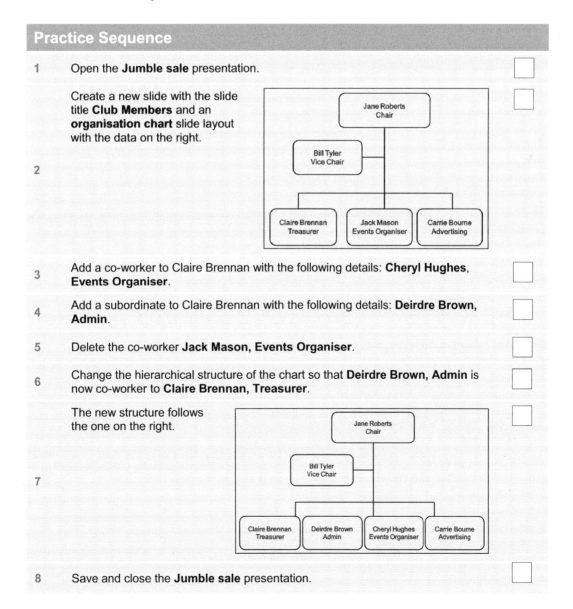

1	Open the **Jumble sale** presentation.
2	Create a new slide with the slide title **Club Members** and an **organisation chart** slide layout with the data on the right.
3	Add a co-worker to Claire Brennan with the following details: **Cheryl Hughes, Events Organiser**.
4	Add a subordinate to Claire Brennan with the following details: **Deirdre Brown, Admin**.
5	Delete the co-worker **Jack Mason, Events Organiser**.
6	Change the hierarchical structure of the chart so that **Deirdre Brown, Admin** is now co-worker to **Claire Brennan, Treasurer**.
7	The new structure follows the one on the right.
8	Save and close the **Jumble sale** presentation.

Section 5 ▶   Graphical Objects

A graphical object refers to an image, picture, drawn object, diagram or chart. Graphical objects can be manipulated by resizing, deleting, rotating and flipping, and by copying and moving between slides and between open presentations. Graphical objects can be aligned in a specified position relative to the slide.

5.1   Inserting and Manipulating Graphical Objects

In this section, you will learn about the following:

- Inserting a graphical object into a slide.
- Selecting a graphical object.
- Copying and moving graphical objects within a presentation and between open presentations.
- Resizing and deleting graphical objects in a presentation.
- Rotating and flipping a graphical object.
- Aligning a graphical object relative to a slide: left, centre, right, top and bottom.

note

In this module, the term 'picture' refers to a visual representation available from an inbuilt gallery, such the **ClipArt Gallery**. The term 'image' refers to a visual representation that is inserted from a **file**, such as a scanned photograph or drawing. For inserting drawn objects, see Section 5.2.

5.1.1   Inserting a Graphical Object into a Slide

Graphical objects – picture or image – can be inserted by creating a new slide with a slide layout that enables graphical content or by inserting a graphical object into a slide from a stored location on your computer.

To insert a graphical object into a slide, do the following:

Inserting a Clip Art Picture Using Slide Layout

- Create a new slide with the **Title and Content** slide layout and click the **Insert ClipArt** button.

  The **Clip Art** task pane opens.

- Find a picture in a specific category by positioning the cursor in the **Search for** box and entering a search word.

- Click **Go**.

  Pictures matching the search word will appear.

- Select a picture.

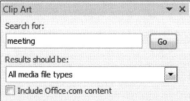

Inserting a Stored Image Using a Slide Layout

- Create a new slide with the **Title and Content** slide layout and click the **Insert Picture from File** icon.

The **Insert Picture** window opens.
- Locate the correct drive and/or folder from the **Look in** box.
- Select the image.
- Click **Insert**.

Clip
Art

Inserting a Clip Art Picture onto Any Slide
- Select the **Insert** tab.
- Click the **Clip Art** button in the **Images** group
  The **Clip Art** task pane opens.
- Find a picture in a specific category by positioning the
  cursor in the **Search for** box and entering a search word.
- Click **Go**.
- Pictures matching the search word will appear.
- Select a picture.

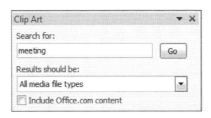

Inserting a Stored Image onto Any Slide
- Select the **Insert** tab.
- Click the **Picture** button in the **Images** group.
  The **Insert Picture** window opens.
- Locate the correct drive and/or folder from the **Look in** box.
- Select the image.
- Click **Insert**.

Picture

5.1.2 Selecting a Graphical Object
Before a graphical object can be edited, formatted or manipulated, it must first be selected.

To select a graphical object, do the following:
- Click the object.
  Handles appear around the object to indicate selection.
  Alternatively, from the **Home** tab, click **Select** and then **Selection Pane**. Select the picture placeholder from the list of slide elements.

5.1.3 Copying and Moving Graphical Objects
Graphical objects can be copied and moved in the same presentation or between different presentations.

In the Same Presentation
To copy graphical objects, do the following:
- Select the **View** tab.
- Click **Normal** from the **Presentation Views** group.
- Select the object.
- From the **Home** tab, click **Copy** from the **Clipboard** group.
- Select the destination slide (the slide to which the object is being copied) and click **Paste**.
  The duplicated object will appear in the new position.

To move graphical objects, do the following:

- Select the **View** tab.

- Click **Normal** from the **Presentation Views** group.

- Select the object.

- From the **Home** tab, click **Copy** and then **Cut** from the **Clipboard** group.

- Select the destination slide (the slide to which the object is being copied) and click **Paste**.

  The duplicated object will appear in the new position.

  Alternatively, use the **Drag and Drop** method of copying and moving objects within the same slide by dragging the object to the new position using the mouse. Drag the object to the required position before releasing the mouse button.

  To copy, hold down the **CTRL** key whilst dragging to the new position.

Between Open Presentations

To copy graphical objects, do the following:

- Open the required presentation files.

  Both files will be displayed as tabs on the taskbar at the bottom of the screen.

- Ensure that the presentation containing the objects to be copied is the active presentation.

- Select the object.

- From the **Home** tab, click **Copy** from the **Clipboard** group.

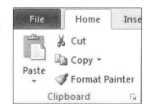

- Click to the other presentation on the taskbar or select the **View** tab and **Switch Windows**.

- Choose the other presentation from the list.

- Open the required slide in standard view.

- Position the cursor in the required position within the slide.

- From the **Home** tab, in the **Clipboard** group, click **Paste**.

  The object will be copied in the selected slide within the presentation.

To move graphical objects, do the following:

- Open the required presentation files.

  Both files will be displayed as tabs on the taskbar at the bottom of the screen.

- Ensure that the presentation containing the objects to be copied is the active presentation.

- Select the object.

- From the **Home** tab, click **Cut** from the **Clipboard** group.

- Click to the other presentation on the Taskbar or select the **View** tab and **Switch Windows**.

- Choose the other presentation from the list.

- Open the required slide in standard view.

- Position the cursor in the required position within the slide.

- From the **Home** tab, in the **Clipboard** group, click **Paste**.

  The object will be copied in the selected slide within the presentation.

 Images, drawn objects and charts can all be copied and moved in the same way. If you want to copy or move more than one object, select the first object and then, holding down the **CTRL** key, click the other objects to be copied/moved.

Press **CTRL + C** to copy, **CTRL + X** to cut, **CTRL + V** to paste

5.1.4 Resizing Graphical Objects

Graphical objects can be resized to increase or decrease the size. It is important to ensure that the original proportions of a graphical object are maintained.

To resize a graphical object, do the following:

Using the Mouse

- Select the object.

  It will be surrounded by handles.
- Position the cursor over a corner handle.
- The cursor turns into a double headed black arrow.
- Left-click the mouse.
- Drag the cursor inwards or outwards to decrease/increase the size.
- Release the mouse when the object is the required size.

 note Always resize from a corner handle to maintain the original proportions of the image.

Using Picture Tools

- Select the object.

  It will be surrounded by handles.

  The **Picture Tools/Format** tab becomes available.
- Click this tab to see the picture formatting tools.
- Use the scroll arrows on the **Height** and **Width** list boxes to increase or decrease the size of the object.

  Alternatively, click the **Size** window launcher icon.
- Enter a measurement into the **Height** and/or **Width** boxes.
- To maintain the original proportions, only change the height or the width and ensure that the **Lock Aspect Ratio** button is selected.
- Click **Close**.

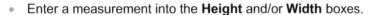

Change height or width of image

Select **Lock Aspect Ratio** to ensure that the width is resized in proportion to the height

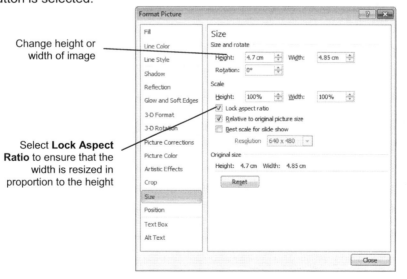

5.1.5 Deleting Graphical Objects

To delete graphical objects, do the following:

- Select the object, it will be surrounded by handles.
- Press the **Delete** key on the keyboard.

5.1.6 Rotating and Flipping a Graphical Object

To rotate and flip graphical objects, do the following:

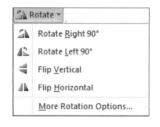

- Select the object, it will be surrounded by handles.
  The **Picture Tools/Format** tab becomes available.
- Click this tab to see the picture formatting tools.
- Click the **Rotate** arrow to see a list of rotation and flip commands.
- Select an option from the list or click **More Rotation Options** to rotate by specified degrees.
- Click **Close** when finished.

Use the scroll arrows on the **Rotate** list box to select a specific measurement

Alternatively, objects can also be rotated by using the **Rotate** handle on a selected object. Position the mouse arrow over the rotate handle and drag in the required direction.

Rotate handle

5.1.7 Aligning a Graphical Object

A graphical object can be aligned horizontally on the left, centre or right of the slide, or aligned at the top or bottom of a slide.

To align an object, do the following:

Relative to a Slide
- Select the object to see the handles surrounding it.
  The **Picture Tools/Format** tab becomes available.
- Click this tab to see the picture formatting tools.
- From the **Arrange** group, select the **Align** command to see the menu.
- Select the **Align to Slide** menu option (a tick beside a menu option indicates that it is active).
- The object will align relative to the slide.

Alignment (Left, Right, Centre, Top and Bottom)
- Select the object to see the handles surrounding it.
  The **Picture Tools/Format** tab becomes available.
- Click this tab to see the picture formatting tools.
- From the **Arrange** group, select the **Align** command to see the menu.
- Choose an alignment option from the menu.

6

Practice Sequence		
1	Open the **Jumble sale** presentation.	☐
2	Create a new slide with a **Title and Content** slide layout and the title **ClubMeeting**. Enter the bulleted text: **Next meeting 30th December 2008**.	☐

3	Insert a relevant picture from ClipArt.	☐
4	Insert the picture called **sell.gif** into slide 1 so that it displays beneath the title.	☐
5	Resize the picture so that the height is **3cm** and the width will alter proportionally.	☐
6	Insert the picture called **clock.gif** on slide 3 so that it appears on the right side of the subtitle text.	☐
7	Resize the picture so that the height is **5cm** and the width will alter proportionally.	☐
8	Rotate the clock so that it is displayed at **35°** clockwise.	☐
9	Flip the picture horizontally on slide 1.	☐
10	Copy the picture on slide 1 of the **Jumble sale** presentation into slide 3 of the **manage** presentation.	☐
11	Save and close the **manage** presentation.	☐
12	Save and close the **Jumble sale** presentation.	☐

5.2   Drawn Objects

Drawn objects can be added to a slide in a variety of shapes and sizes. Drawn objects can be formatted with colour, shadow effect, borders and line style. Multiple drawn objects can be ordered so that specific shapes appear in front of or behind other objects or they can be grouped together to create one single object.

In this section, you will learn about the following:

- Adding different types of drawn object to a slide: line, arrow, block arrow, rectangle, square, oval, circle and text box.
- Entering text into a text box, block arrow, rectangle, square, oval, circle.
- Changing the background colour, line colour, line weight, line style of a drawn object.
- Changing arrow start style and arrow finish style.
- Applying a shadow to a drawn object.
- Group and ungroup drawn objects in a slide.
- Bringing a drawn object one level forward, one level backward, to the front and to the back of other drawn objects.

5.2.1 Drawn Objects
To add a drawn object to a slide, do the following:

Line
- Select the **Insert** tab from the ribbon.
- From the **Illustrations** group, click the **Shapes** command.
- Select the **Line** tool from the **Lines** section of the drop-down menu.

Click the **Line** tool

The cursor turns into a black crosshair symbol (+).

- Position the crosshair symbol where you want the
  line to start and then drag the mouse to create the line.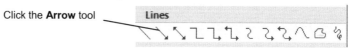

Arrow

- Select the **Insert** tab from the ribbon.
- From the **Illustrations** group, click the **Shapes** command.
- Select the **Arrow** tool from the **Lines** section of the drop-down menu.

Click the **Arrow** tool

The cursor turns into a black crosshair symbol (+).

- Position the crosshair symbol where you want the
  arrow to start and then drag the mouse to create the arrow.

 Hold down the **Shift** key to create a line or arrow that is straight.

Block Arrow

- Select the **Insert** tab from the ribbon.
- From the **Illustrations** group, click the **Shapes** command.
- Select one of the **Block Arrow** tools from the **Block Arrow** section
  of the drop-down menu.

Click a **Block
Arrow** tool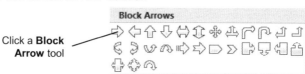

The cursor turns into a black crosshair symbol (+).

- Position the crosshair symbol where you want the arrow to start
  and drag the mouse to create the block arrow.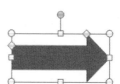

Rectangle

- Select the **Insert** tab from the ribbon.
- From the **Illustrations** group, click the **Shapes** command.
- Select one of the **Rectangle** tools from the **Rectangles** section
  of the drop-down menu.

Click a
Rectangle tool

The cursor turns into a black crosshair symbol (+)

- Position the crosshair symbol where you want the rectangle
  to start and then drag the mouse to create the rectangle.

 Drawing a square: Follow the instructions to draw a rectangle, but hold down the **Shift**
key whilst dragging to create a perfect square.

Oval

- Select the **Insert** tab from the ribbon.
- From the **Illustrations** group, click the **Shapes** command.
- Select the **Oval** tool from the **Basic Shapes** section of the drop-down menu.

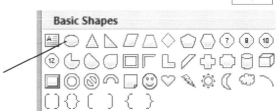

Click the **Oval** tool

The cursor turns into a black crosshair symbol (+).

- Position the crosshair symbol where you want the oval to start and then drag the mouse to create the oval.

 Create a circle: Follow the instructions to create an oval, but hold down the **Shift** key whilst dragging the shape to create a perfect circle.

Text Box

- Select the **Insert** tab.
- From the **Illustrations** group, click the **Shapes** command.
- Select the **Text Box** tool from the **Basic Shapes** section of the drop-down menu.

Click the **Text Box** tool

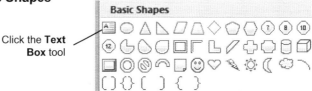

The cursor turns into a black crosshair symbol (+)

- Position the crosshair symbol where you want the text box to start and drag the mouse to create the text box.

Text box

5.2.2 Entering Text into a Drawn Object

Text can be entered directly into a drawn object as required.

To enter text into a drawn object, do the following:

- Click the drawn object to select it.

  The cursor appears within the drawn object ready for text insertion.
- Enter the required text into the drawn object.
- Click outside the drawn object to continue.

What's on offer

 To edit or format the text in a drawn object, right-click on the object and select Edit Text from the pop-up menu that appears. The cursor appears within the text.

5.2.3　Formatting a Drawn Object

To format an object with background colour, line colour, line weight and line style, do the following:

Background Colour

- Select the object.
- From the **Drawing Tools/Format** tab on the ribbon, select the **Shape Fill** command from the **Shape Styles** group.
- Select a colour or choose **More Fill Colors** for a wider choice of colours or select **No Fill** to remove colour.

  From this menu, you also have the choice of formatting the shape with a picture, gradient or texture.

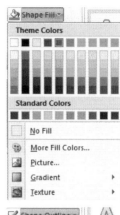

Line Colour

- Select the object.
- From the **Drawing Tools/Format** tab on the ribbon, select the **Shape Outline** command from the **Shape Styles** group.
- Select a colour or choose **More Outline Colors** for a wider choice of colours or select **No Outline** to remove the line.

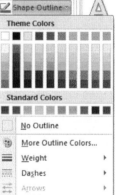

Line Weight

- Select the object.
- From the **Drawing Tools/Format** tab on the ribbon, select the **Shape Outline** command from the **Shape Styles** group.
- Select **Weight** and choose a weight from the list.

  The weights are displayed in points (pt).
- Select **More Lines** to see more line options.

Line Style

- Select the object.
- From the **Drawing Tools/Format** tab on the tab, select the **Shape Outline** command and then the **Dashes** command from the **Shape Styles** group.
- Select a style or click **More Lines** to see more line options.

  The **Format Shape** window opens.
- Select the **Line Style** command.
- Format the line using the **Line Style** options (width, type, etc.).
- Click **Close**.

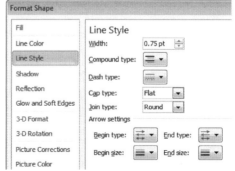

5.2.4 Arrow Styles

An arrow can have an arrow shape at the start and/or at the end of the line.

To apply styles to the arrow, do the following:

- Select the arrow.
- From the **Drawing Tools/Format** tab from the ribbon, select the **Shape Outline** command from the **Shape Styles** group and choose **Arrows**.

- Select an arrow style from the sub-menu or click **More Arrows** for further formatting options.

  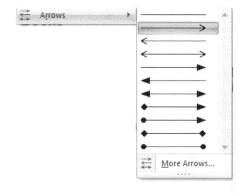

  The **Arrow Settings** in the **Format Shape** window enable **Begin** and **End** types to be applied to arrows (a double headed arrow would have both).

- Select a **Begin Type** or **End Type** and then choose a size for the **Begin/End** types.
- Click **Close**.

5.2.5 Applying a Shadow to a Drawn Object

To apply shadow to a drawn object, do the following:

- Select the object.
- From the **Drawing Tools/Format** tab, select the **Shape Effects** command from the **Shape Styles** group.
- Select **Shadow**.
- Select a shadow style from the sub-menu.

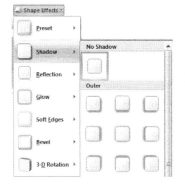

5.2.6 Grouping a Drawn Object

Multiple drawn objects can be grouped together into one single object, making it easier to manipulate. The grouped object can be ungrouped when required for editing and modification.

To group or ungroup a drawn object, do the following:

Group

- Select the first object.
- Holding down the **CTRL** key, click the other objects to be grouped.
- From the **Drawing Tools/Format** tab from the ribbon, select the **Group** command from the **Arrange** group.
- Select **Group** from the drop-down menu.

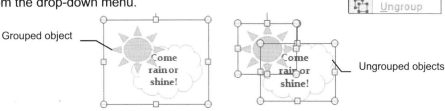

Ungroup

- Select the object.
- From the **Drawing Tools/Format** tab from the ribbon, select the **Group** command from the **Arrange** group.
- Select **Ungroup**.
  The objects will display as individual objects.

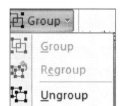

Regroup

Objects can be regrouped without selecting each individual object.

To regroup the objects, do the following:
- Select an object (there is no need to select each of the objects to be regrouped).
- From the **Drawing Tools/Format** tab from the ribbon, select the **Group** command from the **Arrange** group.
- Select **Regroup**.
  The objects will display as one single object.

  Alternatively, selected objects can be grouped, ungrouped and regrouped by right-clicking the selected objects and selecting **Group** and then an option from the pop-up menu that appears.

5.2.7 Ordering a Drawn Object

Drawn objects can be ordered so that objects appear in front of or behind specified objects. This is useful when creating a picture consisting of multiple objects.

To order objects, do the following:

Bring Forward One Level

- Select an object.
- From the **Drawing Tools/Format** tab on the ribbon, select the **Bring Forward** command from the **Arrange** group to bring the selected object forward by one level.

Send Back One Level

- Select an object.
- From the **Drawing Tools/Format** tab on the ribbon, select the **Send Backward** command from the **Arrange** group to send the selected object backward by one level.

Bring to the Front of Other Objects

- Select an object.
- From the **Drawing Tools/Format** tab on the ribbon, select the **Bring Forward** arrow from the **Arrange** group.

- Select **Bring to Front** from the menu to bring the selected object forward to the front of all objects.

Send to the Back of Other Objects

- Select an object.
- From the **Drawing Tools/Format** tab on the ribbon, select the **Send Backward** arrow from the **Arrange** group.
- Select **Send to Back** from the menu to send the selected object behind all other objects.

Alternatively, selected objects can be ordered by right-clicking the selected objects and selecting **Bring to Front** or **Send to Back** from the pop-up menu, followed by an option from the sub-menu.

Practice Sequence

1	Open the **Jumble sale** presentation.	☐
2	Using drawing tools on slide 2, add a block arrow positioned at the right side of the bulleted text. The tip of the arrow should be pointing at the bulleted text.	☐
3	Format the block arrow with a red solid fill colour, a dashed line style with **3pt** weight and grey line colour.	☐
4	Apply a **Perspective** shadow effect to the arrow.	☐
5	Add the following text to the arrow shape: **What's on offer**. Format the text to display with a white font colour and Comic Sans MS, 18, bold.	☐
6	Using the drawing tools create a cloud shape (from Basic shapes) and format with white solid fill colour and a pale grey outline. Position the cloud shape so that it slightly overlaps the end of the block arrow.	☐
7	Add the following text to the cloud shape: **Come rain or shine!**	☐
8	Format the text to display in **Comic Sans MS**, **18**, **blue**, **bold** and **italic**.	☐
9	Using the drawing tools create a sun shape and format with a yellow fill colour and a pale grey outline. Position the sun image on the left side of the cloud.	☐
10	Order the cloud shape so that it displays behind the other shapes.	☐
11	Group the 3 shapes as one object.	☐
12	On slide 1, draw a solid line to separate the title and image from the subtitle text. Format the line to be dark blue with a weight of 4½ pts.	☐
13	Format the line to display as a double headed arrow.	☐
14	On slide 7 insert a text box with the following text: **2008-2009**.	☐
15	Save and close the **Jumble sale** presentation.	☐

6

Section 6 ► Preparing Outputs

Output refers to the way that the presentation is viewed, either on screen or as printed hard copy. Both types of output require preparation by applying effects and choosing an appropriate output format for slide presentation, such as overhead, handouts or on-screen show. Slides can be hidden as part of a slide show if required and presenter notes can be added to specific slides in the presentation. It is good practice to check spelling and proofread a presentation to ensure it is error free and presented to a professional standard. The layout of a presentation can be altered so that it displays in a different orientation and paper size and then printed in a variety of formats, such as specific slides, handouts, notes pages or Outline View.

6.1 Preparation

In this section, you will learn about the following:

- Adding and removing transition effects between slides.

- Adding and removing preset animation effects to different slide elements.

- Adding presenter notes to slides.

- Selecting an appropriate output format for slide presentations, e.g. overhead, handout or onscreen show.

6.1.1 Transition Effects

A transition is the effect that displays between each slide in a slide show. There are a variety of slide transition effects to choose from.

To add or remove a transition effect, do the following:

Adding a Transition

- Select the **Transitions** tab from the ribbon.

- From the **Transition to This Slide** group, select the **More** button.

Click the scroll button or the **More** button to see more transition effects

The **None** (No Transition) command is selected by default

- Click a transition to select it.

- The transition will be applied to the currently selected slide.

- To apply the selected transition to all slides in the presentation, click the **Apply to All** command.

- To specify the length of the transition use the scroll arrows on the **Duration** list box.
  Automatic transition timings can be set by selecting a time in the **After** box (or choose to control the slide show by **On Mouse Click**).

- An effect can be applied to each transition by selecting the **Effect Options** command.

- In the example on the right, the Wipe Transition Effect can appear from different directions on the slide. The Effect Options differ depending on the currently selected transition effect.

- A transition effect is indicated by the following symbol beneath a slide (in Slide Sorter view).

- Click this symbol to see a preview of the transition effect.

> A slide show presented by a speaker should be controlled by mouse click. A self-running slide show that is looped to play continuously (such as displaying services in a reception foyer), can be set to play with automatic timings.

Removing a Transition

To remove a transition, do the following:

- Select the **Transitions** tab from the ribbon.
- From the **Transition to This Slide** group, select the **None** command.
- Select **Apply to All** to remove the transition from all slides in the presentation.

6.1.2 Animation Effects

An animation effect is applied to individual slide elements. The animation effects are displayed when the slide is viewed in Slide Show View.

To add and remove animation effects to slide elements, do the following:

Adding a Preset Animation Effect

- In **Normal View**, select the **Animations** tab from the ribbon.
- Select the slide element(s) to which the animation effect is to be applied.
- From the **Animation** group, select an animation (the default animation effect is **None**).

- Repeat this procedure to apply animation effects to different slide elements.
  Alternatively, animation effects can be applied to slide elements by selecting **Add Animation** and choosing an animation effect.

- Select the **Effects Options** command to see different effects that can be applied to the chosen animation.

- In the example on the right, the direction can be changed for the Fly In animation effect.

- The Effect Options differ depending on the currently applied animation effect.

- Timing, duration and start trigger can all be applied from the commands in the Timing group.

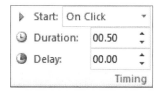

Re-order Animation Effects

- In **Normal View**, select the **Animations** tab from the ribbon.
- Select the **Animation Pane** command from the **Advanced Animation** group.

- Animation effects which are applied to elements on the current slide will be displayed.

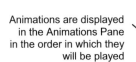

Animations are displayed in the Animations Pane in the order in which they will be played

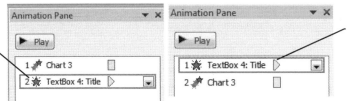

Animations can be re-ordered as shown – see how the textbox animation is now above the chart animation

- Select the animation to be re-ordered and select a command from the Reorder Animation group (choose Move Earlier to move up one level and Move Later to move down one level).

Removing a Preset Animation Effect

- In **Normal View**, select the **Animations** tab from the ribbon.
- Select the slide element(s) from which the animation effect is to be removed.
- From the **Animations** group, select **None**.

6.1.3 Presenter Notes

Presenter notes are added below a slide and do not display when the slide show is running. Presenter notes can be viewed in standard view and Note Pages view, and can be printed with the slides if required.

To add presenter notes to a presentation, do the following:
- In **Normal View**, select the notes pane beneath the slide.
- Enter the notes text.

Click in the **Notes Area** to add presenter notes

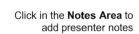

- To see the full notes pane, select the **View** tab and then **Notes Page**.

  The notes page will appear, displaying the slide above and the notes pane below.

- Enter text as required and format in the same way as normal text.
- Click **Normal View** to close **Note Pages View**.

Note Pages View displays the notes pane beneath the slide

Click in the note pane to add text

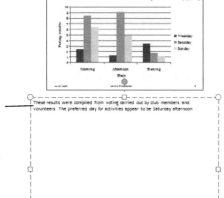

6.1.4 Presentation Output

The default presentation output format is **On-Screen Show**. If the presentation is to use overhead transparencies, select the **Overhead** output format. **Handouts** from the presentation can be created and given out to audience members so that they can follow the presentation or be provided for future reference. Handouts can be printed with 1, 2, 3, 4, 6 and 9 slides to a page. The 3 slide handout provides space for the audience to add notes.

To select appropriate output formats for a slide presentation, do the following:
- Select the **Design** tab.
- From the **Page Setup** group, click the **Page Setup** command.
  The **Page Setup** window opens.

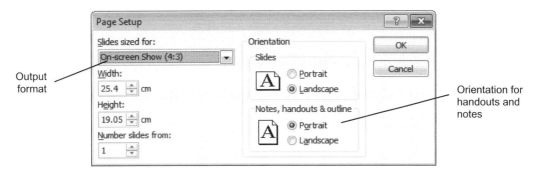

- Select the **Slides sized for:** arrow and choose an option, such as **On-screen Show** or **Overhead** from the list.
- Use **A4 Paper (210 x 297)** to format the slides for A4 paper or select **Custom** if you want to set the measurements yourself.
- Click **OK**.

6.1.5 Hiding and Showing Slides

Specific slides in a presentation can be hidden if required. This is useful when presenting a slide show to different audiences as you can hide certain slides that should only be viewed by a specific audience (for example, sensitive material such as personnel records or accounts).

To hide or show a slide, do the following:

Hiding Slides
- In **Slide Sorter View**, select the slide or slides to be hidden.
- Select the **Slide Show** tab from the ribbon.
- From the **Slide Setup** group, click the **Hide Slide** command.
  The hidden slide(s) will display in **Slide Sorter View** with a line through the slide number to indicate it is hidden.

Showing Slides
- In **Slide Sorter View**, select the slide or slides to show.
- Select the **Slide Show** tab on the ribbon.
- From the **Slide Setup** group, click the **Hide Slide** command (this is a *toggle* button, which means that each time it is clicked it turns on/off).

Practice Sequence

1	Open the **Jumble sale** presentation.	☐
2	Add a **Dissolve** transition effect to all slides in the presentation.	☐
3	On slide 2, apply a **Wipe** (**All at Once**) animation effect to the bulleted text.	☐
4	On slide 2, apply a **Fly In** animation effect to the grouped drawn object.	☐
5	On slide 4, apply a **Wipe** (**By Category**) animation effect to the pie chart.	☐
6	On slide 6, apply a **Fade** (**By Series**) animation effect to the column chart.	☐
7	On slide 7, apply a **Fly In** animation effect to the title **Club Members**.	☐
8	Add the following notes to slide 6: **These results were compiled from voting carried out by club members and volunteers. The preferred day for activities appears to be Saturday afternoon.**	☐
9	Add the following notes to slide 8: **This meeting is to plan the Spring Fair in March 2009.**	☐
10	Check that the current output format for your slide show presentation is **On-screen Show**.	☐
11	Hide slides 7 and 8.	☐
12	Show slide 7.	☐
13	Save and close the **Jumble sale** presentation.	☐

6.2   Checking and Delivering

It is good practice to spell check and proofread your presentation prior to showing or printing, to ensure that it is error free and presented to a professional standard. Slide setup should be modified before printing to ensure that an appropriate orientation and paper size is applied to the presentation. A presentation can be printed as specific individual slides, as handouts (miniature thumbnails), notes or in outline format (this format will only display text but not graphics that appear in the presentation). Once checked, the presentation can be delivered in slide show format. A slide show can be started from any slide and navigated using a shortcut menu.

In this section, you will learn about the following:

- Spell checking a presentation and make changes, e.g. correcting spelling errors and deleting repeated words.
- Changing the slide setup and the slide orientation to portrait or landscape.
- Changing the paper size.
- Printing the entire presentation, specific slides, handouts, notes pages and outline view of slide and choosing the number of copies of a presentation.

6.2.1 Spell Checking a Presentation

It is important before showing or printing a presentation to check the spelling on each slide and correct errors or repeated words.

To check spelling, do the following:

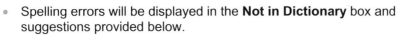

- Select the **Review** tab from the ribbon.
- From the **Proofing** group, click the **Spelling** button.
- Spelling errors will be displayed in the **Not in Dictionary** box and suggestions provided below.
- Select the correct suggestion and click **Change** to correct the spelling.
- Some words that are not in the Spelling dictionary are incorrectly flagged as errors. When this happens, click **Ignore**.

The spelling error is flagged

Suggestions are provided for the correct spelling of the word

Click **Change** to change to the suggested spelling or **Ignore** to retain the current spelling

You are given the opportunity to delete or ignore repeated words.

- Click **Delete** to delete a repeated word or **Ignore** to keep the repeated word and continue the spelling check.

Repeated words are displayed in the **Repeated Word** box

Click **Ignore** to retain the repeated word or **Delete** to delete the repeated word

- When the spell check is complete, a confirmation window opens.
- Click **OK**.

6.2.2 Slide Setup

Slide setup should be performed to change the orientation and paper size before the presentation is printed. Slide orientation refers to portrait or landscape. Portrait is taller than it is wide and landscape is wider than it is tall.

This orientation is landscape

This orientation is portrait

- Select the **Design** tab on the ribbon.
- From the **Page Setup** group, click the **Page Setup** command.
    The **Page Setup** window opens.

Select the paper size

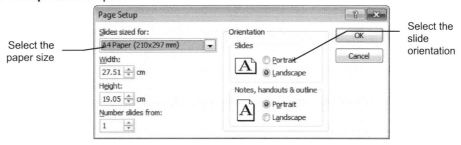

Select the slide orientation

- Select a slide orientation option button.

Alternatively, select the **Design** tab and then, from the **Page Setup** group, click the **Slide Orientation** command. Choose **Portrait** or **Landscape**.

- Select a paper size from the **Slides sized for** box.

- Slides can be sized for the various paper sizes.

- Click **OK**.

```
Letter Paper (8.5x11 in)
Ledger Paper (11x17 in)
A3 Paper (297x420 mm)
A4 Paper (210x297 mm)
B4 (ISO) Paper (250x353 mm)
B5 (ISO) Paper (176x250 mm)
```

6.2.3 Printing a Presentation

To print a presentation, do the following:

Entire Presentation

- Select the **File menu** and then select **Print**.

- Ensure that the **Print All Slides** option is selected from the **Slides** menu in the **Settings** section and that **Full Page Slides** is selected from the **Print Layout** menu.

- Select the **Print** command.

Select **Print All Slides** to print all slides in the presentation

Select **Full Page Slides** to print 1 slide per page

Specific Slides

- Select the **File menu** and then select **Print**.

- Select the **Custom Range** option from the **Slides** menu in the **Settings** section of the window and enter the slide numbers that you want to print (separate the slides with a comma, i.e. 1, 2, 5).

- Ensure that **Full Page Slides** is selected.

- Click **Print**.

Click the **Custom Range** option and enter the slide numbers, separated by commas

Click **Current Slide** to print the currently selected slide

Current Slide

- Select the **File menu** and then select **Print**.

- Select **Print Current Slide** from the **Slides menu** in the **Settings** section of the window.

- Click **Print**.

Handouts

- Select the **File menu** and then select **Print**.
- Select the **Print Layout** menu from the **Settings** section.
- From **Handouts** select the required amount and orientation of slides per page.
- A preview of the handouts will be displayed in the right-hand section of the window.
- Click **Print**.

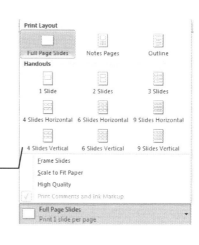

Select the number of slides per page

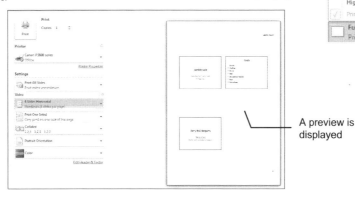

A preview is displayed

Notes Pages

- Select the **File menu** and then select **Print**.
- Select **Notes Pages** from the **Print Layout** menu in the **Settings** section.
- Click **Print**.

Outline View

- Select the **File menu** and then select **Print**.
- Select **Outline** from the **Print Layout** menu.
- Click **Print**.

Number of Copies

- Select the **File menu** and then select **Print**.
- Use the scroll arrows on the **Copies** list box to increase/decrease the required amount of printed copies.
- Click **Print**.

Print

Copies: 1

Print

note   If you want hidden files to print, select the **Print Hidden Slides** option in the **Print Layout** menu.

6.2.4 Starting a Slide Show

A slide show can be started from any slide in the presentation.

To start a slide show, do the following:

From the Start

- Select the **Slide Show** tab on the ribbon.
- From the **Start Slide Show** group, select **From Beginning**.
  The slide show will start from the first slide in the presentation.

From Beginning

From the Current Slide

- Select the slide from which you want the slide show to start.
- Select the **Slide Show** tab on the ribbon.
- From the **Start Slide Show** group, select **From Current slide**.
- The slide show will start from the currently selected slide.

6.2.5 Navigating a Slide Show

You can navigate between different slides in a slide show by selecting a specific slide title or by selecting the next or previous slide.

To navigate a slide show, do the following:

- Run the slide show.
- Right-click the slide to see a shortcut menu.
- Select **Next** to go to the next slide in the slide show or **Previous** to go to the previous slide. To go to a specific slide, click **Go to Slide** and select a slide title.
- Press **Esc** or click away to close the menu without selecting an option.

Practice Sequence		
1	Open the **Jumble sale** presentation.	
2	Spell check the presentation to ensure that there are no spelling errors or repeated words.	
3	Practise changing the orientation of the slides to **Portrait** and **Landscape**. Ensure that the slide orientation is Landscape before continuing the task.	
4	Change the paper size to A4 Paper (210 x 297 mm).	
5	Print one copy of slides 1, 2, and 5.	
6	Print all slides in the presentation in handout format, with 6 slides per page.	
7	Print slides 6 and 8 in notes pages format.	
8	Print 2 copies of all slides within the presentation in Outline View.	
9	Start the slide show from the first slide and navigate to slide 5 **Helpers**.	
10	Go to previous slide.	
11	Select slide 4 and start the slide show from this slide.	
12	Go to slide 8 and end the show.	
13	Save and close the **Jumble sale** presentation and exit PowerPoint.	

Web Browsing and Communication

module 7
Web Browsing and Communication

Module Goals for Module 7

Web Browsing and Communication is divided into two sections. The first section, Web Browsing, requires the candidate to know about the internet and to use a web browsing application.

The candidate shall be able to:

- Understand what the internet is and common terms associated with it. Be aware of some security considerations when using the internet.
- Accomplish everyday web browsing tasks including changing browser settings.
- Complete and submit web-based forms and search for information.
- Save web pages and download files from the web. Copy web content into a document.

The second section, Communication, requires the candidate to understand some of the concepts of electronic mail (e-mail), to know about other communication options, and to appreciate some security considerations involved in using e-mail.

The candidate shall be able to:

- Understand what e-mail is and know some advantages and disadvantages of its use. Be aware of other communication options.
- Be aware of network etiquette and security considerations when using e-mail.
- Create, spell check and send e-mail. Reply to and forward email, handle file attachments and print an e-mail.
- Be aware of ways to enhance productivity when working with e-mail software. Organise and manage e-mail.

7

Section 1 ▶   Web Browsing

1.1   Internet Concepts and Terms

1.1.1   The Internet

The internet facilitates various services, ranging from the transfer of files from one place to another, to e-mail, the World Wide Web, chat rooms and notice boards, as well as a whole range of online services from shopping to entertainment. In addition, thousands of government, educational and commercial institutions as well as millions of individuals have information that is stored on computer systems and can be accessed over traditional telephone lines, fibre optic cables, satellite communications and almost any other means of telecommunications that is available.

The internet is a global network of computer networks. The computers connected to it communicate with one another and it also provides the infrastructure that converts the information and provides the routes through which the information flows. In the early 1960s, J.C.R. Licklider of the Massachusetts Institute of Technology wrote about a concept he termed Galactic Networks. He envisaged a network of computers on a worldwide scale, across which information would be transferred an idea that eventually became the internet as we know it today.

It is generally accepted that the initial development of the internet was prompted by the Cold War between the US and Russia. To ensure that information could continue to flow should elements of the communications structure be destroyed in a nuclear strike, the US decided to decentralise its information storage and to create a system where information could be accessed through a number of different routes. At the same time, US universities were demanding access to these powerful computers for research purposes. In the late 1960s, super-computers were installed by the military in a number of locations around the US and a network was designed to enable the universities to use its resources.

The main users of this fledgling internet were scientists, engineers and technical experts. During the 1960s and 1970s, US libraries automated their indexes and, over the next decade, made their catalogues available online. Being online was the reserve of technical, scientific and research experts for quite some time as the system was complex to use. As well as the military, the educational community, government bodies and research institutions dominated the internet's use. Mail services emerged in the early 1980s and were predominantly used by educational institutions that engaged at an international level in information exchange.

The growth of accessible databases on the internet grew substantially in the late 1980s and early 1990s and the difficulty of tracking through the huge volume of information prompted the development of catalogues. Throughout the 1990s, the development of systems that could retrieve information links from web-based indexes began to emerge. Parallel to this, technological developments in computing saw greater processing speeds and more user-friendly computer interfaces, telecommunications and cable companies increased capacities and high-speed fibre optic cable networks were being rolled out. The commercial use of the internet did not really begin until the early 1990s and, by the late 1990s, particularly with the commercial provision of internet services, business traffic on the internet was widespread. More recent developments in the internet are attempting to address the challenges presented by even greater capacity demands in the delivery of multimedia, enticing more home users online and an ever increasing growth in online service provision from government, educational and commercial agencies.

7

1.1.2 The World Wide Web

The World Wide Web (www) is a collection of interlinked documents on the internet. It was conceived by Tim Berners-Lee who wanted to create a virtual space in which information could be shared or exchanged. It required a generic approach to the processing of information from different networks so that different computers could present and locate documents on the **www**. To facilitate this, a code, or computer language, referred to as hypertext mark-up language (HTML) was developed.

The invention of HTML greatly enhanced and eased the access across the web. Typically, clicking a piece of text or an image in a HTML document, called a link, moves to another page, which can be on the same website or a different one entirely. This convenience revolutionised web use, enabling users to browse a myriad of related topics.

1.1.3 Uniform Resource Locators (URLs)

A **URL**, or **Uniform Resource Locator**, is a text address that uniquely identifies a web page on the internet. URLs are not usually case sensitive. They are made up of a number of different parts separated by dots (full stops) and slash marks.

A typical URL is shown on the right.

- **http** stands for hypertext transfer protocol.
- **www** indicates that this is a world wide web address.
- The **domain name** is a principal part of the address. (A domain is a location or area where the pages are stored.)
- The **top-level domain** often refers to a country or is one of a number of international domains, such as .com (commercial), .net (network), .org (organisation, usually non-commercial), .gov (governmental).

1.1.4 Hyperlink

As the cursor is moved around a web page, it will occasionally change to a hand with a pointing finger. This indicates that this particular piece of text or graphic is a hyperlink.

A hyperlink is a piece of text, an object or a graphic that acts like a button. Clicking a hyperlink performs an action such as moving to a different part of the same page, displaying a new page or moving to another site altogether.

Anything that changes the cursor to the hand cursor as you move over it is normally a hyperlink. Graphics that include a hyperlink will also change to the hand cursor.

1.1.5 Internet Service Providers (ISPs)

An internet service provider is a business that supplies internet services to individuals, businesses and organisations. Typically, they host websites, provide connectivity services and offer worldwide delivery of e-mails and access to information on the web. There is usually a fee charged for the access facility and setup.

An ISP typically provides the customer with software, a username, a password and a number to enable access through their particular service. With large companies, ISPs often provide direct connection between the company's networks through leased lines. The term internet access provider (IAP) is frequently used for ISP.

1.1.6 Web Browsers

A web browser is an application that enables users to view individual web pages or the collections of linked web pages that comprise websites. These can be accessed on the internet, on a local network or on an individual computer. The browser also facilitates navigating through websites, the use of hyperlinks, and so on. In Microsoft Windows, the most commonly used browser is Internet Explorer, although popular alternatives, such as FireFox and Opera, are also available.

Screenshots and examples in this module are taken from Internet Explorer Version 8.

1.1.7 File Transfer Protocol (FTP)

File transfer protocol (FTP) is a recognised format that enables users to transfer files between different computers on the internet. FTP works in much the same way as HTTP works for transferring web pages from a server to the user's browser.

* Transferring a file from a remote computer to your own computer is called downloading the file.
* Sending a file to a remote computer is called uploading the file.

1.1.8 An Overview of Search Engines

A **search engine** is a website that helps users to find other websites using a searchable database. Different search engines use different approaches and some concentrate on particular types of search, so it may be possible to find information using one that will not be found using another.

Almost all modern search engines use programs called **spiders** or **automated crawlers** to visit as many other websites as possible, and catalogue their contents to produce a searchable index. When a search engine is used as a result of a user entering a **search term** or terms on the relevant website, powerful **search algorithms** query this index and return results or **hits**.

There are also **meta-search engines** that automatically perform searches against many normal search engines and collate the results together in attempt to provide the largest set of results possible.

Some examples of different search engines are given below.

Automated
Google http://www.google.com.
Microsoft Live Search http://search.live.com.
Yahoo! Search http://www.yahoo.com.
Lycos http://www.lycos.com.

Meta-Search
DogPile http://www.dogpile.com.
IxQuick http://www.ixquick.com.
MetaCrawler http://www.metacrawler.com.

Searching for information involves entering a search term on search engine page. A list of websites that the search engine has determined meet those criteria is then displayed. The individual sites can then be accessed as required. Searching the web is described in detail in Section 1.7 of this module.

1.1.9 Cookies and Caches

A cookie is a small identifier file. Cookies are placed on the hard disk by the website being visited. When the same website is browsed again later, the cookie notifies the website and often a customised version of the page is returned in response. For example, if a user submits their name and requests information from a web-based book vendor, they will often be presented with a personalised version of the website the next time they return to the site.

Each time a site is visited, the browser saves the contents of the visited pages into a temporary storage area on the hard disk, usually a folder dedicated to temporary internet files called a cache. This speeds up the future downloading of these pages. It is possible to adjust the amount of space used to store these pages, as they can take up large amounts of disk space.

1.1.10 Really Simple Syndication (RSS) Feeds

The large amount of ever-changing content on the web means that it is increasingly difficult for web users to keep up with the various websites and other resources that they may be interested in. Really Simple Syndication (RSS) addresses this problem. Many if not all popular websites now provide one or more feeds or channels that can be subscribed to.

To read this information, an aggregator or feed reader is used. This can be a stand-alone application or integrated into a web browser. The aggregator will handle all RSS subscriptions and automatically check them from time to time, presenting any new items in summary form. This usually happens in the form of small pop-up windows on the screen, which removes the need to check these websites. The summary items can be clicked on to open them and the full item can be read as it appears on the originating website.

Subscribing to an RSS feed can be as simple as visiting a website that is displaying the RSS feed icon although the exact method will vary depending on the application being used as a feed reader.

The illustration on the right shows the **SharpReader** application.

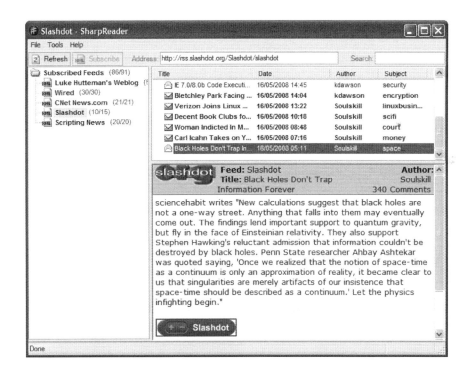

A desktop pop-up appears at the bottom right of the desktop when a new item appears on a feed.

The feed can be opened and items read by clicking the pop-up. In normal operation, the RSS reader window is not visible, and all that will be seen is the occasional pop-up as items come in, enabling users to stay up-to-date but not requiring them to switch applications and check websites constantly.

1.1.11 Podcasts

The term podcast is an acronym for Portable On-Demand Broadcast. Podcasting is an extension of the RSS concept (see Section 1.1.10), where content in any type of file, often music or video, can be subscribed to and automatically downloaded.

In a typical scenario, the following happens:

- Media content, such as episodes of a television show, are made accessible from the internet. Their location is published in a special file called a **feed** which is linked to by a URL.
- Users subscribe to the feed on their computer using a specialised feed reader called a **podcast client** or, sometimes, **podcatcher**.
- The podcast client software takes care of automatically downloading new episodes, files etc. as they become available.
- Users transfer these media files to their portable device for accessing later. Usually, the podcast client software performs this download automatically.

The illustration on the right shows the Juice application with some subscribed feeds.

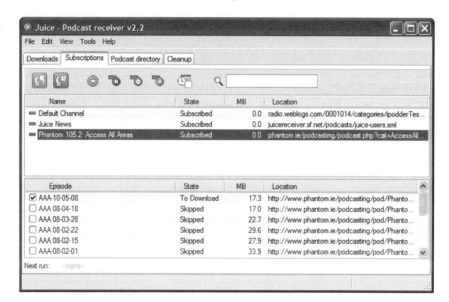

1.2   Security Considerations

1.2.1 Usernames and Passwords

Almost any network, from a home network, to an office or educational establishment network, to the internet itself will require a **username** and **password** to gain access. The use of password security makes it possible to restrict access to authorised entities, and also makes it possible to track user activity. In corporate or educational environments, usernames and passwords are generally issued by IT departments and users are allowed to change their passwords but not their usernames.

It makes sense to choose a strong password, containing a lengthy mixture of upper and lower case letters, numbers and non-alphabetic characters, such as underscores. Many networks will now actively enforce the choosing of strong passwords and require that users change them on a regular basis.

1.2.2 Secure Websites

Buying something online with a credit card or banking online involves using a secure website. These sites employ encryption (see Section 1.2.4) to protect the information being transferred. Web browsers will indicate that a secure section of a website is being viewed.

Internet Explorer shows a padlock icon to the right of the URL.

 The URL begins with **https://** rather than the normal http://. This indicates that the **secure** version of the HTTP protocol is being used.   https://

Not all parts of a website will be secure. For example, on shopping sites the sections where products are selected are normally unsecured and secure pages only appear at the checkout section, where personal information must be entered.

 The Firefox browser will display a padlock icon in the bottom right of the window, and show the page URL in yellow in the address bar along with another lock icon.

1.2.3 Digital Certificates

When goods are being bought on the internet or when confidential information is being exchanged, there is a need to establish that agencies are authentic and the transfer of data is secure. Digital certificates verify that users are who they claim to be. Digital certificates offer the additional assurance that information sent across the internet between parties is encrypted and that only the authentic person, company or authority has the appropriate mechanism to decode or access the information.

Typically, users will register with an organisation that issues digital certificates. This registration usually requires the checking of confidential information, e.g. credit card numbers and companies, to confirm identity. Companies conducting business across the internet will also register in a similar manner. The certifying authority then facilitates the secure communication between users and the recipient when, for example, a hotel booking is being paid for online.

1.2.4 Encryption

Encrypting files ensure that they cannot be accessed or utilised except by the person for whom the communication is intended. If there is any attempt to intercept a file as it is being transferred across the internet, the encryption offers a high level of security. Encryption is extensively used to protect information such as credit card numbers and sensitive information such as personal data or company secrets.

1.2.5 Malware

The term malware is used to describe a range of unsolicited and usually malicious software programs. They transfer between computers across networks and the internet using various methods – for example from malicious websites and e-mail attachments – by infecting program files or by exploiting security weaknesses in operating systems. Some actively destroy data, some steal passwords and private information, and some remain dormant until they are activated to use the host computer as part of a huge attack on a corporate or government network.

7

They are generally grouped into the headings of **viruses**, **worms**, **spyware** and **trojans**.

- **Virus**: This is a type of software that spreads from an infected program to other programs. Generally, viruses can be found in executable programs (.exe files). When the infected executable program is run, the virus spreads to other programs and performs a damaging function. Whatever function the virus performs is known as a **payload**. A payload can be anything that the virus is programmed to do, such as delete data from the hard drive or flash a message on users' screens.

- **Worm**: This is a type of software that spreads across computer networks. Similar to viruses, worms have a payload. One of the most common worm payloads is to use up network bandwidth and slow down the transfer of data across a network.

- **Spyware**: This refers to a range of programs that monitor and collect users' personal information and behaviour. This information is then used for marketing purposes or to redirect users to a specific website. Spyware can also have undesirable effects, such as slowing down an internet connection or a computer's performance in general. Most spyware programs infect a computer by getting users to install them unknowingly, much like Trojan horses.

- **Trojans**: This is a type of program that is designed to resemble another type of software. By deceiving users, a Trojan horse actually gets them to install malicious code on their computers in the belief that they are actually installing a different program. Once installed, the Trojan horse doesn't spread like a virus or worm, but creates what is known as a 'backdoor' that enables access to the infected hard drive without detection.

1.2.6   Antivirus Software

To combat the effectiveness of malware, **antivirus software** can be used. This type of software uses a database of known malware and resides in memory inspecting files as they are accessed on a computer. Problem files can be automatically deleted or placed in **quarantine**. An antivirus application will periodically update its threat database via the internet from a central location – this is vital as new threats appear on a daily basis.

1.2.7   Firewalls

A computer connected to the internet is connected to millions of other computers worldwide. This carries a huge risk of unauthorised access by malicious individuals or criminal organisations. **Firewalls** act as a barrier between individual computers or computer networks and the wider internet, and essentially make them invisible. Firewalls can exist in hardware, for example inside a **broadband router**, or in software. They can be configured to provide **alerts** if someone attempts to intrude.

1.2.8   Risks with Online Activity

Taking part in chat rooms and online discussions can be an engaging and rewarding experience where new friends can be made with people all over the world. Unfortunately, there is an element of risk involved in these types of online activities from cyber-bullies or online predators who seek to gain personal information to harass or cause other types of abuse.

Online harassment might seem rather unlikely because of the anonymous nature of the internet, but it is that anonymity that enables cyber-bullies and online predators to operate successfully. These criminals often masquerade as seemingly harmless people asking normal questions based on genuine interest. In other instances, cyber-bullies and online predators target a specific victim by gathering personal information from online profiles or websites that might contain contact details. Never provide your phone number, postal address or e-mail address on any public profile.

Fortunately, following some simple rules and employing common sense will minimise these risks.

- Use antivirus software and keep it up to date.
- Never reveal your entire name, full date of birth, contact details or other personal information to anyone whose identity you are not absolutely certain of.
- Use strong passwords and change them frequently.

- Ensure the operating system is kept up to date, especially with updates designed to fix security loopholes.
- Never open an unexpected e-mail attachment, even if it appears to be from a known sender.
- Learn to recognise phishing attempts (see Section 2.2.2).
- Where possible and appropriate, avoid entering real personal details, such as name, age, sex or location, into forms on websites. It is necessary, for example, to use correct personal information for banks or where credit card details are needed, but an invented online identity, called an **alias** or **handle** should be used for web forums, etc.

1.2.9 Parental Controls

As computers and high-speed internet connections become increasingly prevalent in homes, so do the dangers posed to younger users. As with the threat from malware, common sense coupled with correct use of the technology can reduce or eliminate these risks.

- **Supervision** of online activity can be effective, perhaps including having the internet computer located in the kitchen or other busy room in the house.
- **Education** is vital for both parents and children. Make sure younger users trust no one outside their own circle of friends, and never release their age, sex or home address in chat rooms, etc. Parents should learn to spot inappropriate behaviour.
- E-mail clients can use a **blacklist** to block e-mails from unwanted senders, or alternatively block all e-mails except those from senders on a **whitelist**.
- As with television, time limits should be established for computer usage and other activities should be encouraged.
- Investigate **parental control software**. This can take the form of stand-alone applications that constantly monitor online activity, or **plug-in** additions to web browsers, such as the free Parental Control Toolbar (http://parentalcontrolbar.org/). These programs sometimes check websites against online blacklists, or search for certain keywords on the site and block based on those.
- **Games** are not just for children, and many contain adult situations and themes. Games software is rated in a similar manner to films by various organisations such as PEGI (http://www.pegi.info). Use the ratings, and search for reviews online to establish a game's suitability.

1.3 First Steps with a Web Browser

Websites on the internet, in offices, on college networks or even individual computers are accessed using an application called a **web browser**, or just **browser**.

1.3.1 Opening and Closing a Web Browser

The first step in accessing the internet is to open the browser.

To open the Internet Explorer browser, do the following:

- Click the **Start** button.
- Select the **All Programs** group, then the **Internet Explorer** option.
  Alternatively, click the Internet Explorer icon on the desktop if it is present.

- If a **broadband** internet connection is being used, the browser window will appear almost immediately.
- If a **dial-up** internet connection is being used, there may be a prompt to use the connection.
  - ▷ The **Connect name bar** usually displays the name of your ISP.
  - ▷ Your **username** and **password** – received from the ISP upon setup – may be entered automatically. Note that the 'connect' window may vary in its appearance according to connection type and the version of software being used.

▷ Click **Connect**.

The computer modem dials the ISP number and makes the connection. When the connection is successful, the connection window closes and Internet Explorer opens a preset home page (or start page).

Enter a **username** and **password**

Click **Connect**

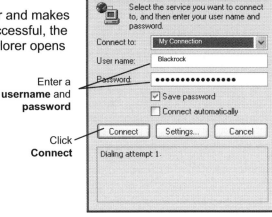

The first web page that appears is called the **home page**, initially it is chosen by your computer, but you can change it to a page that is more relevant for you (see Section 1.4.1).

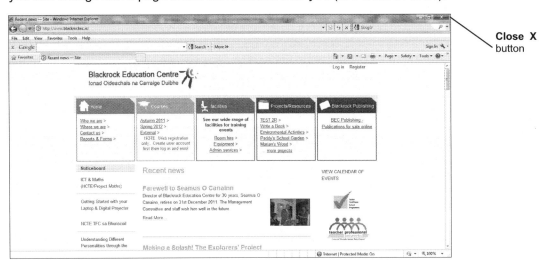

Close X button

At the end of the browsing session, the browser should be closed.

To close the browser, do the following:

- Click the **Close X** button in the top right of the window.
  Alternatively, select **Exit** from the **File** menu (if the Menu Bar is not visible, right click the Command Bar and select **Menu Bar**).

| note | If a dial-up connection is being used, one of these actions may or may not close the connection as well. |

1.3.2 Displaying a Web Page in a New Window or Tab

New web pages can be viewed in a number of ways. Two of the most useful are by opening a new window or opening a new tab. Using one of these methods means that it is possible to view more than one website without having to close one before opening another.

Tabbed browsing enables multiple pages to be open in one Internet Explorer window, but on separate tabs. This is an invaluable feature that reduces desktop clutter.

Address bar changes to reflect the URL of the active tab.

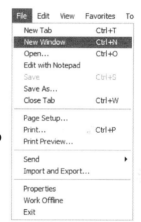

In the above image, there are three separate websites open on different tabs. Each tab can be clicked to make it active, and the address bar will change to reflect its URL.

To open a new window in Internet Explorer, do the following:
- Click the **File** menu and select **New Window**.
  Alternatively, use the keyboard shortcut **CTRL + N** or select **New Window** from the **Page** menu on the **Command Bar**.
  A separate Internet Explorer window opens.

To open a new tab, do the following:
- In the **File** menu, select **New Tab**.
  Alternatively, use the keyboard shortcut **CTRL + T** or click the **New Tab** button:

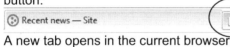

A new tab opens in the current browser.

To open a hyperlink (see Section 1.1.4) in a new window, do the following:
- Right-click the link and select **Open in New Window**.
  A new Internet Explorer window with the linked URL opens.

  A similar procedure is used to open pages in new tabs, except **Open in New Tab** would be chosen.

1.3.3 Stopping a Page from Downloading
Some pages may take a long time to download due to their size, the speed of the internet connection, problems on the website, problems on the internet generally or any combination of the above.

To stop a page from downloading, do the following:
- Click the **Stop** icon at the end of the Address Bar.

1.3.4 Refreshing a Web Page

All browsers use caching to some extent, especially if they are being used with a dial-up network connection. This means that pages and images from pages are stored locally on the computer to save downloading them again every time the page is visited. Sometimes, it is necessary to refresh a web page to make sure it is the most up-to-date version, or if the page initially failed to load.

To refresh a page, do the following:
- Click the **Refresh** icon at the end of the Address Bar.
  Alternatively, press **F5**.

1.3.5 Using Help Functions

If you wish to find assistance with different aspects of the browsing application, choose **Help**. This is available to you as you work with the Help function in one of two ways.

- Choose the **Help** menu on the **Menu** bar.
  Alternatively, use the **F1** key on your keyboard.

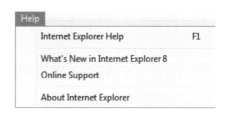

The Help facility can also be opened by clicking the **Help** button on the **Command Bar**:

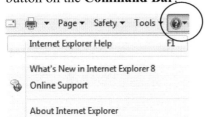

Using the Help function is described in detail in Section 7 of the Before You Begin module.

1.4 Adjusting Settings

1.4.1 Setting the Home Page

The first page displayed when the browser is launched is called the home page. In Internet Explorer, this is initially set to an information page stored locally. It is possible to change the home page to something that is more relevant and useful to the individual user, such as a search engine.

To change the home page, do the following:
- Start **Internet Explorer**.
- Go to the web page that is to be set as the new home page.
- From the **Tools** menu select **Internet Options**. The **Internet Options** window opens.
- In the **Home Page** section, click the **Use Current** button.
- Click **OK**.

Click **Use current**

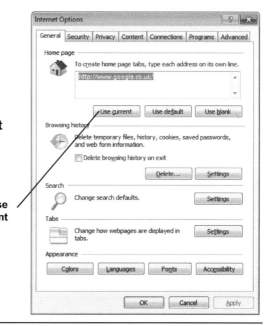

Multiple home pages can also be specified, with each opening in a different tab when Internet Explorer is launched.

To set multiple pages, do the following:
- Start **Internet Explorer**.
- Go to the web page that is to be set as the new home page.
- From the **Tools** menu select **Internet Options**. The **Internet Options** window opens.
- In the **Home Page** box, enter the URLs of the pages on separate lines.
- Click **OK**.

Enter URLs

Alternatively, navigate to the page which is to be set as the home page; select the **Home** button on the **Command Bar** and select **Add or Change Home Page**. Select one of the option buttons in the window that appears, and then click **Yes**.

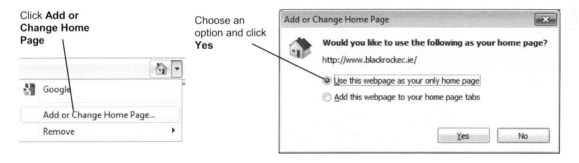

Click **Add or Change Home Page**

Choose an option and click **Yes**

1.4.2 Allowing or Blocking Cookies

Cookies are small files that may be saved on the computer by websites. If personal details are entered in an online form, for example, some may be stored in a cookie so that the next time the website is visited, the information can be filled in again automatically, thus saving time. They can also be used to provide personalised versions of websites.

Cookies can also be used to track what sites have been visited, and this information can be used to target advertising at users. This makes them a potential security concern.

Internet Explorer can be configured to use cookies in various ways.
- Start **Internet Explorer**.
- Click the **Tools** button and select **Internet Options** from the menu.
  The **Internet Options** window opens.
- Click the **Privacy** tab.
- In the **Settings** section, the slider can be moved up and down to select more or less strict rules for allowing cookies to be stored on the computer.

note   Higher settings may cause some websites to function incorrectly.

Slider

The cookie settings as described above can be overridden on a site-by-site basis. For example, it might be necessary to always accept cookies from a banking site.

To set this option, do the following:
- Start **Internet Explorer**.
- Click the **Tools** button and select **Internet Options** from the menu.
  The **Internet Options** window opens.
- Select the **Privacy** tab.
- Click the **Sites** button.
  The **Per Site Privacy Actions** window opens.
- Enter a website URL in the **Address of website** field.
- Click **Block** or **Allow** for all cookies from that site to be blocked or allowed regardless of the global cookie settings.
- Click **OK**.

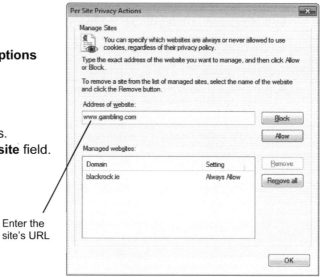

Enter the site's URL

1.4.3 Clearing the Browser Cache and Temporary Internet Files

During normal web browsing, copies of the files that make up the websites visited are sometimes stored in an area of the computer called the cache. These files include any graphics and the HTML or similar files that define the layout of the websites. The reason this is done is to increase performance – if these files are present already on the computer, they do not have to be downloaded every time the website is visited. Similarly, the history of visited sites, the usernames and passwords used, and other items of information are stored in the temporary internet files folder. In Windows 7, this is a hidden folder.

All this stored information takes up disk space, and also creates security and privacy concerns. For this reason, the contents of the cache and the temporary internet files can be deleted.

To delete temporary internet files, do the following:
- Start **Internet Explorer**.
- Click the **Safety** button from the **Command bar**.
- Select **Delete Browsing History** from the menu that opens.
  The **Delete Browsing History** window opens.
- Select the items to be deleted.
- Click the **Delete** button.

Click **Delete**

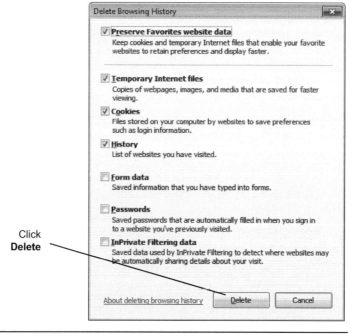

1.4.4 Deleting All or Part of the Browsing History

As websites are visited, each address is stored in the browsing history file.

This history can be viewed in Internet Explorer and can be useful in finding sites that have been visited but whose URL has been forgotten.

However, keeping a browsing history means a privacy, and possibly a security, risk is created, so Internet Explorer can be set to clear addresses after a certain number of days.

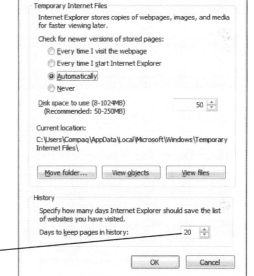

To set the limit to clear the browsing history, do the following:

- Start **Internet Explorer**.
- From the **Tools** menu, select **Internet Options**.
- In the Browsing history section, click the Settings button. The **Temporary Internet Files and History Settings** window opens.
- In the **History** section, enter the number of days for which the browsing history should be kept.

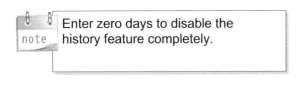

> **note** Enter zero days to disable the history feature completely.

Enter number of days

To manually clear the history completely, do the following:

- Click the **Safety** button on the **Command bar**.
- Select **Delete Browsing History** from the menu that appears. The **Delete Browsing History** window opens.
- Select the **History** tick box.
- Click **Delete**.

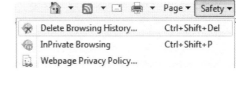

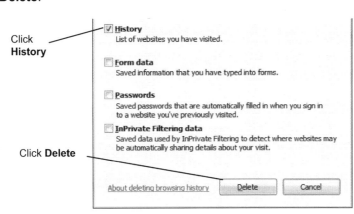

Click **History**

Click **Delete**

1.4.5 Allowing or Blocking Pop-Ups

Pop-ups are browser windows that automatically appear within the main Internet Explorer window when certain websites are visited. They are often used for intrusive advertising or even the delivery of malware. Internet Explorer version 7 and above has built-in pop-up management capabilities to allow them to be blocked.

Some sites, such as banking sites, however, use pop-ups legitimately to provide a richer user experience, and Internet Explorer can also allow pop-ups where disabling them would make a website unusable.

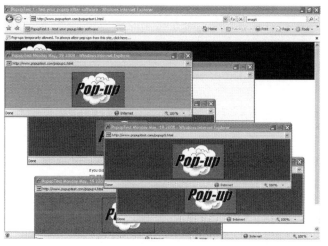

When a website is visited, Internet Explorer will intercept any attempts by the site to show pop-up windows and display a **pop-up bar** to highlight this.

The bar appears under the Command bar, as below:

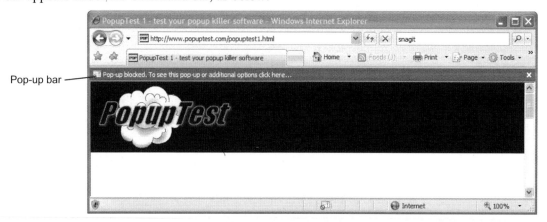

The site used in the above illustration (http://www.popuptest.com) is useful for testing pop-up blocking. In the above example, if the pop-up bar is clicked, a menu opens allowing pop-ups to be enabled for the current site on a temporary or permanent basis.

You can adjust the filter level of the pop-up blocker to regulate what type of pop-ups you want to block. To adjust the filter level, do the following:
- Start **Internet Explorer**.
- In the **Tools** menu, select **Pop-up Blocker**.
  A sub-menu appears.
- Select **Turn On Pop-up Blocker** from the sub-menu to block pop-ups.
  OR
- Select **Turn Off Pop-up Blocker** from the sub-menu to allow pop-ups.
  The desired setting is applied.

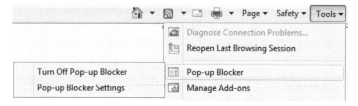

You can adjust the filter level of the pop-up blocker to regulate what type of pop-ups you want to block.

To adjust the filter level, do the following:

- In the **Tools** menu, select **Pop-up Blocker**. A sub-menu appears.
- Select **Pop-up Blocker Settings** from the sub-menu.
  The **Pop-up Blocker Settings** window opens.
- In the **Notifications and blocking level** section, select the desired setting from the **blocking level** box.

> **note** Be sure to select **Show Information Bar when a pop-up is blocked**. Some pop-ups are legitimate features of a web page. If a legitimate pop-up is blocked, you can use the Information Bar to view that pop-up.

1.4.6 Displaying and Hiding Toolbars

By default, Internet Explorer displays various bars such as the **Navigation/Address bar**, **Search bar** and the **Command bar**.

- The **Navigation/Address bar** is where website URLs are entered, and the arrow buttons for navigation are located.
- The **Search bar** to the right enables a search to be performed using the default Search Provider.
- The **Command bar** contains the tabs for any websites that are open, and the Home, Feeds, Print, Page and Tools buttons.

Additional bars such as the **Favorites bar, Menu bar** and **Status bar** can be displayed or hidden by right-clicking on a blank area of the Command bar and ticking or unticking the relevant option on the menu that opens.

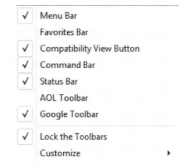

1.5   Web Navigation

1.5.1 Go to a Uniform Resource Locator (URL)

Every website has a unique address – its Uniform Resource Locator, or URL.

To access a website using its URL, do the following:
- Enter the **URL** in the browser **address bar** (located at the top of the browser window).
- Press **Enter**.
  Alternatively, click the green arrow to **navigate** to that website.

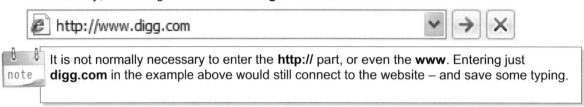

> note It is not normally necessary to enter the **http://** part, or even the **www**. Entering just **digg.com** in the example above would still connect to the website – and save some typing.

The address bar always displays the URL of the page being viewed. It will change to reflect a change to a new website during browsing.

1.5.2 Accessing Previously Visited URLs

Internet Explorer keeps a history of the locations visited as the browser is used (see Section 1.4.4). This list can be accessed by using the Forward and Backward buttons (see Section 1.5.4) or by clicking the downward arrow to the right of the area where the URL is entered.

Individual URLs in the drop-down list can be clicked to revisit them. Only URLs that were manually typed into the Address Bar are available here – any visited by clicking on hyperlinks are not.

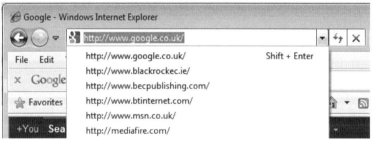

The browsing history can also be permanently displayed in a **History** panel to the left of the Internet Explorer window.

To display the browsing history, do the following:
- Start **Internet Explorer**.
- Click the **Favorites** button to the left of the **Command bar**.
  The **Favorites Center** opens to the left of the Internet Explorer window.
- Click the **History** tab to change to history view.
  Select a time limit (e.g. Today) to see previously viewed websites.
  The URLs of previously visited websites can be accessed.
- Clicking the **Pin** button will cause the **Favorites Center** to be permanently locked in place.

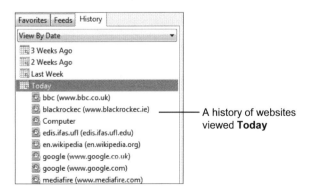

A history of websites viewed **Today**

Pin button

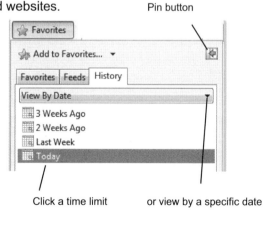

Click a time limit   or view by a specific date

1.5.3 Activating a Hyperlink

The use of **hyperlinks** is one of the things that make the internet revolutionary. These enable users to move instantly to new pages of information by clicking on special areas in the pages they are currently viewing. This, coupled with the ability to open links in **tabs** (see Section 1.3.2), means an experienced user can browse a huge amount of information very quickly.

Hyperlinks tend to come in two forms.

In a text link the text is underlined in a different colour to the surrounding text, and the cursor changes to a pointing finger icon when moved over it.

Images can also be used as links, and the cursor will change in the same way when moved over them.

Single-clicking a hyperlink will navigate to the **linked location** and display the contents, whether that location is somewhere else on the same page, on a different page on the current website or on a different website altogether. The **linked location** can be displayed either in the current browser window or in a new browser window or a new tab (see Section 1.3.2).

1.5.4 Navigating Backwards and Forwards

In addition to hyperlinks, it is possible to navigate through web pages using the Forward and Backward buttons on the **Navigation bar**.

* The arrow pointing left is the **Backward** button – it goes back to the page that was being viewed before the current one. If the current page was the first to be viewed, this button will be greyed out.
* The arrow pointing right is the **Forward** button. If the Backward button has been used to find previous pages, clicking this button will take the user forward again, through the chain of pages that have been viewed.

In addition, the Backward and Forward buttons both have smaller arrows to the right side. Clicking these arrows will display a menu showing the list of visited locations, enabling one to be clicked on.

1.5.5 Navigating to the Home Page

The home page can be returned to at any time by clicking the home page icon on the Command bar.

1.5.6 Web-Based Forms

Web-based forms are just like real-world forms and are most often used by websites where information must be submitted by the user.

Examples include:
- Booking flights – items such as name, address and contact phone numbers are required.
- Ordering groceries – name, address and a list of items must be supplied.

Web forms often include a variety of **controls** designed for users to enter or select information. All of the common elements that will be encountered are included in the sample form below.

- The **Text Box** enables any text to be entered, for example a name. If a password is being entered, the textbox will display the * character instead of the actual letters, for added security.

  First Name: John

  Surname: Smyth

- The **Drop-Down Menu** allows the selection of one item from a list. Only the currently selected item is displayed. The list is 'dropped down' by clicking the arrow, and another item can then be chosen.

- The **List Box** displays a list of items with multiple items being visible at the same time. If there are more items than will fit, a scroll bar will be displayed to the right of the control. Some list boxes allow the selection of multiple items by holding the CTRL key when clicking.

- The **Check Box** is used for simple 'yes or no' choices. Clicking the box will alternate between ticked and unticked states.

  ☑ Receive Updates by Email.

- The **Radio** (or **Option**) **Button** presents a range of mutually exclusive choices. At least one must be selected and only one can be selected. Selecting an item will unselect any previously selected item.

  ◉ Married ○ Single

1.5.7 Submitting a Web-Based Form

When a web-based form has been completed, it can be submitted either by clicking the **Submit** button on the web page or by pressing the **Enter** key on the keyboard.

In some cases, it may be necessary to complete a CAPTCHA before submitting a form. This is a test to verify that the form is being submitted by a human rather than an automated program and is usually a series of slightly distorted letters and numbers that users have to enter into a text field to verify that the submission is authentic.

Character string shown: 36LX4X

If the form is either incorrect or incomplete, there is usually a prompt to correct or complete the form before resubmitting it. To reset a web-based form and clear all the fields, either the **Reset** or **Cancel** button can be clicked on the web page.

Practice Sequence

1	Start **Internet Explorer**.	☐
2	In the Address bar, type in the address: **www.becpublishing.com**.	☐
3	Click the blue **Online Practice** button on the right-hand-side of the home page. A login box opens, which has to be completed before the website can be accessed.	☐
4	In lower case, type the word **blackrock** in the **username** field.	☐
5	In lower case, type **practice** in the **password** box.	☐
6	Click **OK**. The support website window opens.	☐
7	Go to the **Complete a Form** link in the frame to the left-hand side of the page.	☐
8	When the cursor crosses the link, it changes to a hand.	☐
9	Click the left mouse button at this point. The form window will open.	☐
10	Type fictitious information as required into the different boxes.	☐
11	Click **Next** to proceed to the next set of information items.	☐
12	Carry on until a confirmation window opens to indicate the form has been completed.	☐

1.6   Using Bookmarks

1.6.1   Adding Bookmarks (Favorites)

It is convenient to store frequently used URLs so that they do not have to be remembered. This is achieved by creating a **favourite**.

To create a favourite, do the following:
- Browse the website that will be added to the favorites list.
- Click the **Favorites** button and then select **Add to Favorites**.

The **Add a Favorite** window opens.

The **Name** will have been filled in automatically with the name of the website, but this can be changed if needed.
- Click **Add**.

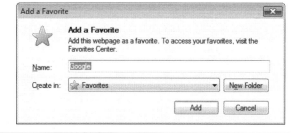

1.6.2 Displaying a Bookmark (Favorite) Web Page

Bookmarks can be viewed in the **Favorites Center** in Internet Explorer.

To open it, do the following:

- Click the **Favorites** button.

The **Favorites Center** opens.

- Click the **Favorites** tab to display the **Favorites** list.

1.6.3 Deleting Bookmarks (Favorites)

To delete favorites, do the following:

- From the **Favorites Center**, click the **Add To Favorites** arrow.
- Select **Organize Favorites** from the menu that opens.

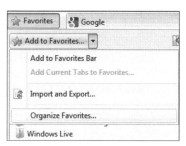

The **Organize Favorites** window opens.

- Highlight the Favorite to be deleted by clicking it once.
- Click **Delete**.
- Click **Close**.

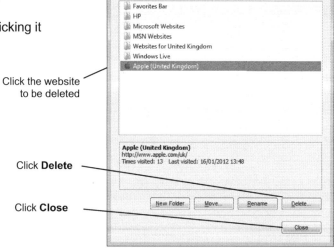

Click the website to be deleted

Click **Delete**

Click **Close**

1.6.4 Organising Bookmarks (Favorites)

Creating Favorite Folders

If favorites are always added to the main list, the list will soon become very long and unwieldy. It is therefore good practice to group favorites for similar types of websites into folders.

To create a Favorites folder, do the following:

- From the **Favorites Center**, click the **Add To Favorites** arrow.
- Select **Organize Favorites** from the menu that opens.
  The **Organize Favorites** window opens.
- Click the **New Folder** on the menu bar.
- A new folder is added to the list.
- Type a name for the new folder.
- Press **Enter**.

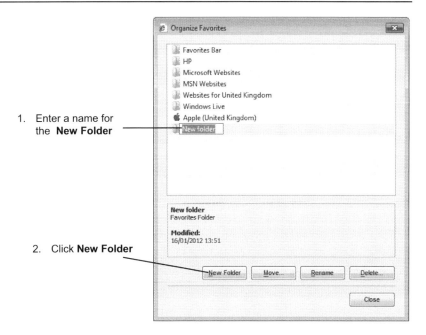

1. Enter a name for
    the **New Folder**

2. Click **New Folder**

Adding URLs to a Favorites Folder

To add websites to a Favorites folder rather than to the main list, do the following:

- Browse to the website to be added to the favorites folder.
- From the **Favorites** Center, click the **Add to Favorites** button.

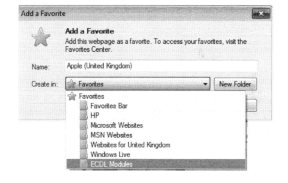

  The **Add a Favorite** window opens.
- Select the correct **Favorites** folder from the
  Create In list.
- Click **Add**.

Deleting a Bookmark Folder

To delete a bookmark folder, do the following:

- From the **Add to Favorites** menu, select
  Organize Favorites.
  The **Organize Favorites** window opens.
- Click the desired folder to select it.
  The folder is highlighted.
  All web pages contained in the folder
  are displayed beneath it.
- Click **Delete**.
- A **Confirm Delete** window opens.
- Click **Yes**.
- The selected folder is deleted.
- Click **Close** to close the **Organize
  Favorites** window.

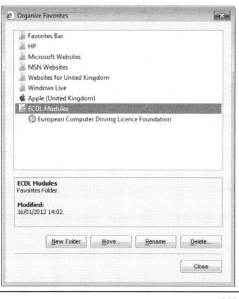

1.7   Search Engines

1.7.1 Selecting a Specific Search Engine

A **search engine** is a program that helps you to find information on the web. It stores listings of websites from all over the world and makes them easily available. There are many different search engines associated with the internet, such as AltaVista, Yahoo!, Google and Webcrawler.

To open the Google search engine, do the following:

- Click the **Address bar** with your mouse.
- Type **www.google.ie**.
- Click the **Go** button to right of the Address bar.
  The web page for **Google** will be displayed.

1.7.2 Searching by Keyword and Phrase

To perform a general search enter a search word or phrase, also known as a **search term**, in the search box. The number of results returned depends on the words and phrases used and how specific they are.

Using Google Instant

Google Instant lets the user see predicted searches and results as they type. To search for a phrase using **Google Instant**, do the following:

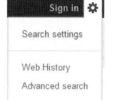

- Open **www.google.co.uk, www.google.com** or **www.google.ie**.
- Select the Options button (gear icon ✿ at the top right of the page) and select **Search Settings**
- The Search Settings page opens.

Click on

- Select the **On** button.
  The **On** button will display

  Select the **Save** button at the bottom of the page to save the new setting.
- Click **OK**.
- Open **www.google.co.uk, www.google.com** or **www.google.ie**.
- In the search box, enter **blackrock education**.

Enter search term

Predictive results are displayed as the search criteria is entered and the Search button displays as a magnifying glass:

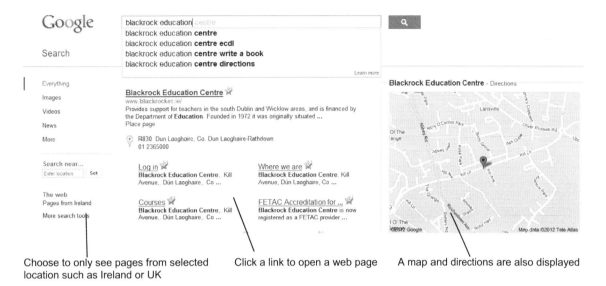

Choose to only see pages from selected location such as Ireland or UK

Click a link to open a web page

A map and directions are also displayed

- Select the magnifying glass or click one of the menu options.

The results page will show the number of **hits** – the web pages that the Google search algorithms decide match the words **blackrock** and **education**, with the most relevant listed first.

Number of **hits** in total and time taken to find results

Turning off Google Instant
To turn off Google Instant predictive results and search for a phrase using **Google**, do the following:

- Open **www.google.co.uk, www.google.com** or **www.google.ie**.
- Select the gear icon ✿ at the top right of the page and select **Search Settings**
- The Search Settings page opens.
- Select the **Off** button [ON].   Off
- The **Off** button will display [OFF].
- Click the **Save** button at the bottom of the page and then click OK.
- Open **www.google.co.uk, www.google.com** or www.google.ie.
- In the search box, enter **blackrock education**.
- Select **Google Search**.

Enter search term

The results page will show the number of **hits** – the web pages that the Google search algorithms decide match the words **blackrock** and **education**, with the most relevant listed first.

There are various options to select a result.
- Click one of the 10 or 20 most relevant pages that are listed.
- Click a page number in the navigation control at the bottom of the list.

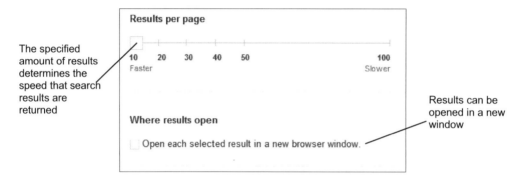

- Click the **Next** or **Previous** links to move back or forwards through the page numbers.
- To choose the number of results that are displayed each time a search is performed, select the Options button (gear icon) and then **Search Settings**.
- In the results per page section of the Settings window, select the amount of results to be returned when a search is performed. Click Save and then click OK.

A specific location can be specified.
- To choose a specific location from which pages are displayed each time a search is performed, select the Options button (gear icon) and then **Search Settings**.
- Select the **Location** link and enter a location in the **Where are you?** box. Click Save and then click OK.

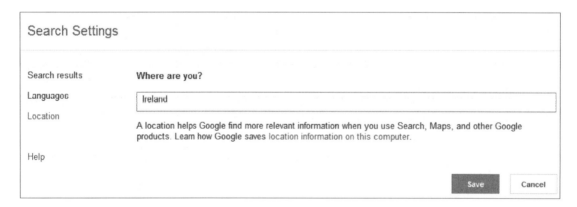

1.7.3 Using Advanced Search Features
Advanced search features work by enabling users to set filters that refine searches and achieve more accurate results. Some common advanced search features include refining searches to match an exact phrase or to exclude certain words in the search. The more precise the keyword or phrase that is used, the more relevant the results found will be. It is also possible to refine searches to match a specific date or file format.

To search for an exact phrase, do the following:
- Open **www.google.co.uk**, **www.google.co.uk** or **www.google.ie**.
- Click **pages from (location)**.

- Type **blackrock +education** in the search box.

Typing a **+** sign before a word means that the word must be included in the results.
Typing a **–** sign means the word must be excluded (e.g. the search term **spaniel –cocker** will find all spaniels *except* for cocker spaniels).
- Click the **Search** button.
  Different pages will be returned.
  Alternatively, go to www.google.com, www.google.co.uk or www.google.ie.
- Click the **Advanced Search** link at the bottom of the page.

The **Advanced Search** page opens.
- In the **Find Results** section, enter the phrase you are searching for in the **with exact phrase** text box.

- Click **Advanced Search**.
  The search results are displayed on the page.

To exclude certain words, do the following:
- Go to **Google**.
- Click **Advanced Search**.
  The **Advanced Search** page opens.
  In the **Find Results** section, enter the phrase you do not want to include in the search in the **without the words** text box.
- Click **Advanced Search**.
  The search results are displayed on the page.

To match a specific date, do the following:
- Go to **Google**.
- Click **Advanced Search**.
- The **Advanced Search** page opens.
- In the **Date** section, click the arrow to display the drop-down list.
- Select the desired date range from the list.
- Click **Advanced Search**.
  The search results are displayed on the page.

To match a specific file format, do the following:

- Go to **Google**.
- Click **Advanced Search**.
- The **Advanced Search** page opens.
- In the **File Format** section, click the arrow to display the drop-down list.
- Select the desired file type from the list.
- Click **Advanced Search**. The search results are displayed on the page.

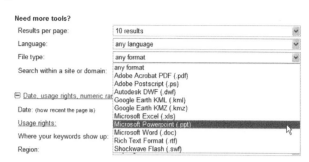

Some tips for using Google are:

- Narrow searches by using + and -.
- To search for an exact phrase, enclose it in double quotation marks. For example, **"blackrock education centre"** will find that exact sequence of words. Searching for **Blackrock education centre** will find pages with the word **Blackrock**, pages with the word **education** and pages with the word **centre**.
- Use wildcards. Searching on **program*** will find **programming**, **programs**, **programme**, etc.
- Search on synonyms by using a tilde (~) before the word.
- Google has various conversions that can be performed in addition to searches. Try typing **convert 100 euro to dollars** in the search box for example.
- Google can search images, books and many other specialised areas using the links at the top of the page.

1.7.4 Web-Based Encyclopaedias and Dictionaries

Search engines provide generic searching capabilities. There are also online encyclopaedias and dictionaries that can be used in the same way as their printed counterparts.

Encyclopaedias

Wikipedia has become a very popular free online encyclopaedia.

To access Wikipedia, do the following:

- Open **Internet Explorer**.
- Browse to **www.wikipedia.org**.
- Enter a search term (in a similar manner to Google – see Section 1.7.1).
- Click the search button and a list of results will be returned.

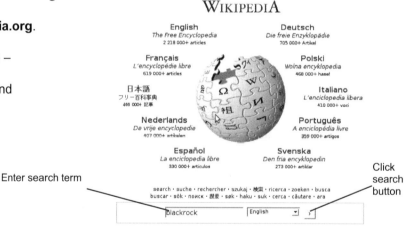

While it provides similar searching functionality to a search engine, the searches in online encyclopaedias are performed against a database of articles rather than web pages.

Dictionaries

To use an online dictionary, do the following:

* Go to **www.askoxford.com**.
  A search box is provided to enter a word.
* Enter the word to search, e.g. **heliotrope**.

* A search will be performed and the definition returned.

Search results

heliotrope

/ˈheelɪtrop/

• **noun** a plant of the borage family, grown for its fragrant purple or blue flowers.

— ORIGIN Greek *heliotropion* 'plant turning its flowers towards the sun', from *helios* 'sun' + *trepein* 'to turn'.

1.8   Saving Files

1.8.1   Saving a Web Page to a Location on a Drive

Web pages can be saved for offline viewing if required. One reason to do this might be if they need to be accessed during periods when an internet connection is not available.

A web page displayed in the browser is built from a variety of files behind the scenes. Any graphics present are not embedded in the page but exist as separate files on the **web server** that the website resides on. When saving, either the page text only can be saved, or the page and all the supporting files that go with it can be saved.

To save a web page in its entirety, do the following:

* Open the website and page that are to be saved.
* On the **Command bar**, click the **Page** button.
  The **Page** menu opens.
* Select **Save As** from the menu.
  The **Save Webpage** window opens.
* Browse to the drive and folder to which the page will be saved.
* Ensure the **Save as Type** drop-down menu has **Web Archive, Single File (*.mht)** selected.
* Click **Save**.

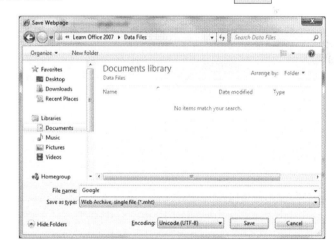

 To save the page text alone, follow the same steps as above but choose **Webpage, HTML Only (*.htm, *.html)** from the **Save as Type** list.

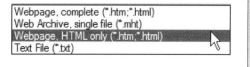

1.8.2   Saving Individual Files from a Web Page

Many websites have files that can be saved, or **downloaded**, to a local computer. They can be in many different formats and, as a result, the relevant software used to open them must be installed on the computer. For example, PDF files require Adobe Acrobat Reader and MP3 files will require a media player application that supports that format.

7

To practise downloading a text file, image file, sound file and video file, go the website **www.becpublishing.com**, click on the blue **Online Practice** button and enter the username **blackrock** and password **practice** as required.

Choose the **Download Media Files** link on the web page you access to choose from a variety of information that you can download as practice.

To download an item, do the following:
- Right-click on the link.
- Select **Save Target As** from the menu.

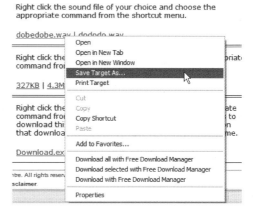

The **Save Web Page** window opens.
- Choose your location from the Navigation Pane.
- Choose a name for the file in the **File name** box.
  If you want to save with the graphics, you can use the **Web Page complete (*.htm, *.html)** file type option.
  If you want to save the web page without the graphics, you can choose to save it as a **Text File (*.txt)**.
- Click **Save**.

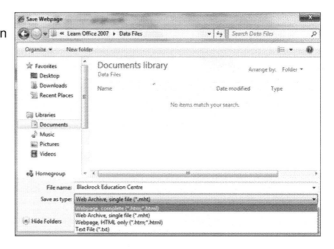

Experiment with the different options and files available on the site.
- Go to the web page **www.becpublishing.com**.
- Click the blue **Online Practice** button on the right-hand-side of the home page.
  A login box opens, which has to be completed before the website can be accessed.
- Enter the username **blackrock** and the password **practice**.
- Click the **Download Media Files** link.
- In the **Type Of Media** column, scroll down to **Video File**.
- Right-click a link and select **Save Target As**.

During the download, a monitoring window normally opens to show the progress of the downloading. Upon completion, you may close the **Download complete** window and proceed according to the choice you made.

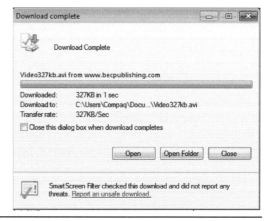

1.8.3 Copying Text, Images and URLs to a Document

All material that is accessible on the internet is covered by international copyright, therefore permission must be sought from the copyright owners before any data can be used. A simple e-mail to the owners will usually get a positive response. In order to avoid problems at a later stage, copies of the responses should be kept in a safe location.

Go to **www.becpublishing.com** to practise (remember click the blue Online Practice button and enter the username **blackrock** and the password **practice** in the login box).

Follow the steps below to copy text from a web page to a document.
* Click the **Learn About Text** link.
* Highlight the text by dragging the mouse over it.
  There is usually an **Advanced Search** button. Note the links that help with advanced searches.
* Right-click the selected text and select **Copy**.
* Open a word processing document in an application such as Microsoft Word.
* In the **Clipboard** group (Home tab) in the word processing document, select **Paste**, or press **CTRL + V**.

To copy an image, do the following:
* Click the **Download Media Files** link.
* Right-click the image.
  A shortcut menu opens.
* Choose the **Copy** command.
* Open a word processing document.
* In the **Clipboard** group (Home tab) of the word processing document select **Paste**, or press **CTRL + V**.
  If the Word Processing file is saved, the image will be included in the saved file.

To copy a URL, do the following:
* Click the **Download Media Files** link.
* Right-click on any link and select **Copy Shortcut**.
* Open a word processing document.
* In the **Clipboard** group (Home tab) select **Paste**, or press **CTRL + V**.

1.9 Preparing and Printing Web Pages

1.9.1 Preparation
Before printing a web page, it is good practice to preview the output and make any necessary adjustments.

In Internet Explorer, print options are accessed by clicking the **Print** button on the **Command bar** (or click the **Print** arrow and then **Print**).

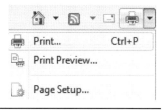

1.9.2 Print Preview

To open the Print Preview window, do the following:
- Click the **Print** arrow on the **Command bar**.
- Select **Print Preview** from the menu that opens. The **Print Preview** window opens.

The preview window has a toolbar that provides printing, page set-up and navigation options.

Print   Page Setup

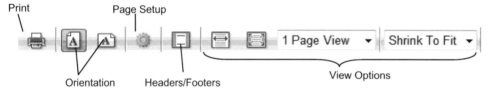

Orientation   Headers/Footers   View Options

1.9.3 Print Options

To change the print options that are available under the General tab, paper size and so on, do the following:

Changing Orientation

There are two types of page orientation, **Portrait** and **Landscape**. Portrait is a vertical orientation. Landscape is a horizontal orientation.

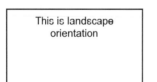

This is landscape orientation

This is portrait orientation

To change the page orientation, do the following:
- Open the desired web page in the Print Preview.
- Click the **Portrait** or **landscape** button on the **Print Preview** toolbar.
  Alternatively, click the **Page Setup** button on the **Print Preview** toolbar. The **Page Setup** window opens.
- Click **Portrait** or **Landscape**.
- Preview the changes in the top right of the **Page Setup** window.
- Click **OK**.

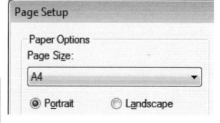

> note   The Page Setup window can also be accessed via the Print menu on the Command Bar.

Adjusting Margin Settings

Margins refer to the amount of space that appears at the top, bottom, left and right of a page.

To adjust margin settings, do the following:
- Open the desired web page in Print Preview.
- Select the **Page Setup** button
- Alternatively, from the **Print** menu on the Command Bar, select Page Setup.
  The **Page Setup** window opens.
- In the **Margins** (millimeters) section, type in the desired margins.
- Preview the changes in the top right of the **Page Setup** window.
- Click **OK**.

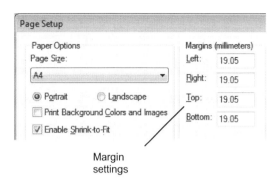

Margin settings

Paper Size

To change the paper size, do the following:
- Open the desired web page in Print Preview.
- Select the **Page Setup** button
- Alternatively, from the **Print** menu on the Command Bar, select Page Setup.
  The **Page Setup** window opens.
- In the **Paper Options** section, click the **Page Size** box to display the drop-down list.
- Select the desired **Paper size** from the list.
- Click **OK**.

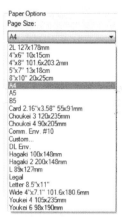

1.9.4 Additional Options

After the page orientation, margins and paper size are specified the page can be printed. This can be done from the Print Preview window by clicking the Print button on the toolbar. This displays the Print window, the main points of which are described below.

General Tab: Select Printer

This area of the window displays printers that are installed in Windows. The printer to be used can be selected by clicking it.

General Tab: Page Range
- **All** – This option prints the entire document.
- **Current Page** – Prints the current page only.
- **Pages** – Allows a range of pages to be printed, for example **1,3,5,6-12** would print pages 1,3,5 and 6, then all pages between 6 and 12.

Select a printer

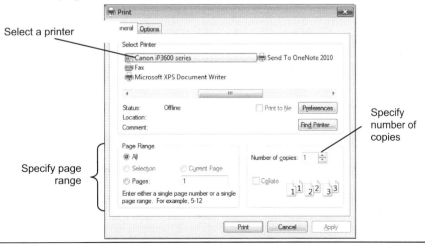

Specify page range

Specify number of copies

7

General Tab: Number of Copies

Specify the number of copies to be printed here. If more than one copy of a printout that requires more than a single printed page is specified, the **Collate** options section will become available to allow a collation sequence to be chosen.

Options Tab

Some web pages use **frames**, which are multiple sections each having its own scroll bar and which can be scrolled independently. In effect, they are separate small web pages all displayed on the same screen.

If frames have been used, the **Print Frames** option will be available in the Print window under the Options tab.
* Each frame can be printed on a separate sheet.
* The selected frame can be printed.
* The page can be printed as it appears on screen.

Visit **www.becpublishing.com** for an example of the use of frames. Click the blue Online Practice button and enter the username **blackrock** and password **practice** in the login box.

Section 2 ▶   Electronic Communication

2.1   E-Mail Concepts and Terms

2.1.1 History

In 1971, Ray Tomlinson, working in a technology company called Bolt, Beranek and Newman, sent the first example of what we would recognise as an e-mail – in other words a message between computers using an address where the recipient's name and their computer were separated by the characteristic @ symbol.

The number of e-mails now sent every day is hard to estimate but at the time of writing in 2010, there could be as many as 62 billion.

2.1.2 Advantages of E-Mail

Electronic mail, or **e-mail** as it is commonly known, is the most widely used facility available on the internet. Mail programs such as **Microsoft Outlook, Outlook Express, Netscape Mail, Eudora** and **Pegasus Mail**, enable messages to be received locally or internationally for the price of a local telephone call. E-mail is fast, cheap and convenient. You can send an e-mail to an individual or to a group of people at the same time. You can create mailing lists that send mail automatically to particular groups of people. In addition, you can attach files such as spreadsheets, pictures and sounds to your e-mail messages.

E-mail messages can be prepared in advance before you go online or connect via your ISP. This saves on telephone costs when using a dial-up connection. When you are preparing mail without being connected, you are working **offline**. When you are connected, you are **online**.

A different way to use e-mail is by using **webmail**. This provides huge flexibility, because all e-mail is stored on a remote computer belonging to the webmail provider. All that is needed to use it is a web browser, meaning that these e-mails can be read and sent from any location that has a browser and any sort of internet connection – a hotel departures lounge, for example, or a portable device such as an iPhone. There are many webmail providers offering free accounts – examples include **www.googlemail.com** and **www.fastmail.fm**. You should note, though, that mail service providers normally have limitations on the size and number of e-mails you can store.

Traditionally, software applications called **e-mail clients** have been used to receive, store, read, send and organise emails. Some examples are **Windows Live Mail, Microsoft Outlook** and **Thunderbird**.

To use e-mail the following are required:

- **An internet connection**: This can be broadband or dial-up. With dial-up, there are considerations to do with the low speed of data transfer involved. It may be easier to compose e-mails when not connected to the internet (offline) and then send them as a batch when connected (or online). Also with dial-up connections, there will be a limit to the size of files that can be attached when sending a message, or that can be received.

- **An e-mail account with an e-mail provider**: Generally the Internet Service Provider (ISP) will allow some e-mail addresses to be set up, and take care of routing messages to and from the customer's computer. In a business or educational establishment, e-mail addresses are usually provided by the IT department.

- **An e-mail client**: E-mail client software must be configured with the details provided by the ISP, including a username and password.

7

2.1.3 Network Etiquette

The development of the internet has created a true global village, bringing together people with varying views, ideas and customs. In order that everyone can communicate without undue misunderstanding, a loosely defined set of rules has emerged to form a convention for online communication, including e-mail and instant messaging. This is known as **netiquette**, a shortening of **network etiquette**.

Some basic guidelines for using e-mail are:

- Use accurate and brief descriptions in subject lines.
- Keep messages brief.
- Reply promptly.
- Don't 'reply to all' unless necessary.
- Spell check outgoing e-mails.
- Remember that tone can be hard to convey, especially to recipients in other cultures. Something said ironically or jokingly may not be read that way. In personal e-mails, use **emoticons** or **smileys** to infer meaning. For example the characters **:)** look like a smiling face when viewed from the side, and can be used to indicate humour.
- Don't forward chain letter e-mails.
- UPPERCASE IS SHOUTING!

2.1.4 The Structure of an E-Mail Address

An e-mail address is required before email can be sent or received. The address is usually written in lower case letters and contains no spaces. A distinctive feature is the @ symbol that separates the username from the domain part of the address.

In this example, Ethna Boland has an e-mail address in Ireland with Blackrock Education Centre. She has chosen **ethnab** as her username. Her address would be read aloud as 'ethna b at blackrockec dot ie', but written as shown below.

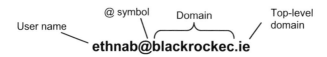

Each e-mail address must be unique. The part after the @ symbol is usually the same for a particular ISP or company, so the person's actual name – before the @ symbol – cannot be duplicated. People often use a variation of their actual name to distinguish them from others with similar names. For example, if Ethna Boland wanted to have the name eboland, she may discover that this particular name has already been taken. She would then have to choose another name.

2.1.5 SMS Messages

The term **SMS (Short Message Service)** refers to the technology used to send short (maximum 170 character) text messages across mobile phone networks. Sending SMS messages from mobile phones is commonly referred to as **texting**. Usually, the messages are sent to another mobile phone, although it is possible to send messages to other devices or to send SMS messages from a computer.

note   Some mobile devices, such as the Blackberry and the iPhone, can send and receive e-mails in the true sense – this is not the same as SMS.

2.1.6 VoIP

VoIP (Voice over Internet Protocol) refers to the use of the internet, and digital equipment connected to it, to transmit voice traffic rather than using a traditional telephone. The advantage is usually cost. A business may have its own private network connecting offices worldwide – if telephone traffic can be transmitted over the same network as data then that business will not have to incur the costs involved if a person in one country calling someone in another country using the normal telephone system. The business will use normal desktop telephones that connect directly into its data network.

The free **Skype** application is popular among home users. Using a headset with a microphone it enables:

- Free voice and video calls to other Skype users worldwide.
- Calls from Skype to normal telephones at much cheaper rates than those offered by telephone companies.

2.1.7 Virtual Communities

Virtual Communities are communities in which people interact with each other in various ways over the Internet, including keeping in touch with their friends, finding new friends, asking advice, playing games, and taking part in discussions and debates.

Some of the most popular examples of virtual communities are **social networking websites** like MySpace and Facebook. On these websites, registered users can add photos and enter personal information to create a unique webpage that represents them to the other members of the community. Users are able to search for people that they know and list them as a friend so that they can easily stay in contact. Users can interact in a variety of ways, including sending e-mails and instant messages, uploading digital photos, music, and videos and playing computer games.

Other types of virtual communities include **internet forums**, where users can ask questions and receive answers or discuss a particular subject. **Chat rooms** are a virtual community where users can send and receive messages, and participate in discussions and private conversations in real time. Internet forums and chat rooms are often controlled by moderators who ensure that no users violate the rules of the community or send abusive or inappropriate messages.

Online computer games often create virtual communities where the members play games against each other. These types of virtual communities can vary in size from a small number of players to a global game involving thousands of players scattered across hundreds of countries. Online computer games are often character-based, role-playing games, but also include games such as chess and tennis as well as even casino games where users can register their credit card details and gamble online.

7

2.1.8 Instant Messaging

Instant messaging (IM) enables computer users to communicate in real time in the form of a 'chat', and is one of the oldest forms of communication using a computer. Messages entered are sent instantly to the other user, who can then reply. It is also possible to transfer files. On a broadband internet connection, there is no cost involved in using IM and it provides an experience closer to a normal conversation than e-mail.

Windows Live Messenger is one such application that is used widely. It provides the user with several facilities including web mail, file sharing online, telephone calls over the web and online chat. The application has a set of convenient icons to display either your own availability or that of others who are on your contact list, e.g. whether you are away from your computer, online and available, and so on.

There are two main ways to use instant messaging.

- **User to User**: This type of instant messaging takes the form of a closed conversation between two users of the same IM network, for example the MSN Messenger network.
- **Chat rooms**: These are virtual rooms that enable many users to connect and chat together at the same time. Normally, chat rooms are based around a topic.

The illustration on the right depicts a chat room used for technical support.

2.2 E-mail Security Considerations

2.2.1 Fraudulent and Unsolicited E-Mail

E-mail is a popular form of communication and is a powerful tool for targeting advertising messages directly at users. Unwanted e-mail, known as spam or junk mail, has become an increasingly common and controversial way for companies to reach people.

Most e-mail client software applications have a built-in facility for filtering out junk mail. The software will guess whether or not a message is junk based on the contents of the subject line and other indicators. It will then be moved to a junk mail folder if necessary. Periodically, users check the junk mail folder and can either confirm messages as being junk mail or legitimate. In this way, the e-mail client can learn over time to identify unwanted mail. In business and educational networks, this e-mail filtering generally takes place at the point of entry and the individual users may see little or no junk mail at all.

Unsolicited e-mail is a major problem – it has been estimated at times that up to 75 per cent of all e-mails during a given period are spam. Never reply to unsolicited e-mail messages, even those that claim to offer a method of unsubscribing. All this will do is indicate to the sender that they have hit a 'live' e-mail address. Distribute personal and business e-mail addresses extremely carefully. When using online forms supply a fake e-mail address where possible to reduce the risk of the address being harvested for use by spammers.

2.2.2 Phishing

Phishing is in essence impersonation. A user may receive emails supposedly from their bank or major online entities such as PayPal or eBay. The e-mail will detail some reason or other that requires the user to re-enter their username and password, and a link to the bank website will be provided. However, the link will actually go to a different website that has been cloned to look like the real thing. In this way, any usernames and passwords entered are stored away and used for criminal purposes later. Some examples of phishing attempts purporting to be e-mails from eBay are displayed at: http://pages.ebay.com/education/spooftutorial/.

Most modern e-mail clients and web browsers can spot attempted phishing attempts and alert the user, however, these are not foolproof and so it falls on the user to employ caution. Some online banks, for example, will ask for a piece of personal information that a third party could not know, and include this in their e-mails.

No legitimate online entity such as a bank will ever ask for personal details in an e-mail.

The following images illustrate a phishing scam that resembles the Paypal login webpage. Paypal is an internet-based financial service that enables registered users to make secure transactions online. The phishing scam worked by sending e-mails worded to lure recipients into believing the email was from Paypal. The e-mail also stated that the recipient should go to the Paypal site to update their personal details. The e-mail contains a link that appeared legitimate.

`https://www.paypal.com/us/cgi-bin/webscr?_cmd=_login-run`

However, the actual link differed from the displayed link and, once clicked, took recipients to a website designed to resemble the legitimate PayPal login page.

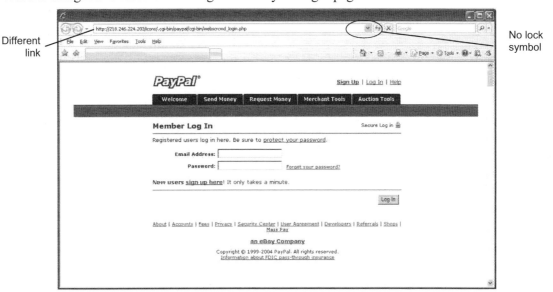

There are two indications that a link or website is a phishing scam. The first thing to look for is the **link**. The displayed link should be the same as the actual link. In the example, the displayed link is as follows: **https://www.paypal.com/us/cgi-bin/webscr?_cmd=_login-run**.

However, the actual link of the website is as follows:

http://218.246.203/icons/.cgi-bin/paypal/cgi-bin/webscrcmd_login.php.

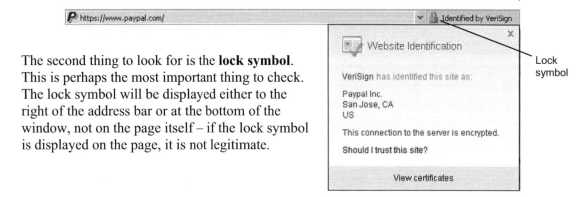

The second thing to look for is the **lock symbol**. This is perhaps the most important thing to check. The lock symbol will be displayed either to the right of the address bar or at the bottom of the window, not on the page itself – if the lock symbol is displayed on the page, it is not legitimate.

Clicking the lock symbol will display the website's certificate which is designed to authenticate the website's legitimacy. The certificate will display the issuing authority, usually VeriSign, as well as the website the certificate is issued to.

2.2.3 Malware Threats from E-Mail

Malware is an umbrella term that describes a variety of security threats in the form of unwanted programs, including viruses and Trojans. One of the ways that these programs spread is via e-mail. These e-mails will generally come from an unrecognised source, but sometimes they will appear to come from known contacts by using **address spoofing**.

The malicious software will sometimes come in the form of an **executable attachment**, in other words a program that can be saved or run directly from the e-mail. It may appear to be a game, or a joke thus leading the recipient to believe it is harmless but it will in fact introduce malware into the system when executed. Other malware has spread via e-mail by taking advantages of security flaws or bugs in the operating system, for example by including a graphic file that when opened can create a hidden method of entry for an attacker.

Fortunately, the threat of malware spreading via e-mail under Ubuntu is minimal compared to other operating systems because of its secure design. Users should still be careful, however, never to open unexpected executable attachments, even if they are from a known sender.

2.2.4 Digital Signatures

A digital signature is an electronic message or tag that may be used to validate the identity of the source of a message. It also certifies that the original matter of the message or document is intact.

When working with e-mail over the internet, security and privacy are particularly important. Digital signatures associated with reputable sources of information provide a level of guarantee in this regard.

2.3 First Steps with E-Mail

2.3.1 Opening and Closing an E-Mail Application

There are various e-mail clients available that will work with Microsoft Windows. This text will be centred around Microsoft Outlook 2010.

Opening Microsoft Outlook 2010

To open Outlook 2010, do the following:

- Double-click the desktop icon.

  Alternatively, open the Start Menu, click **All Programs** and select **Microsoft Outlook 2010** from the Microsoft Office folder.

When Outlook 2010 opens, it will look similar to the following illustration.

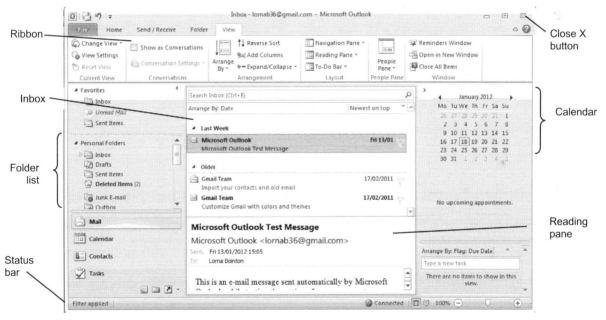

Closing Microsoft Outlook 2010

To close Outlook 2010, do the following:
- Click the **Close X** button in the top-right of the Outlook 2010 window.

2.3.2 Opening E-Mails

E-mails are stored in different folders, which are on the left of the Outlook 2010 window. Incoming messages go to the **Inbox**.

To open an e-mail, do the following,
- Click **Inbox** in the folder list to select it.
  Messages in the Inbox are listed on the right of the window, showing things such as the Sender, Subject and Date.
- Double-click a message to open it.
  The e-mail will open in a new window.

> Clicking the e-mail once will display the message in the **Reading Pane** (which is can be displayed at the bottom or the right of the Outlook window).

2.3.3 Closing E-Mails

When you are finished with an opened message, it should be closed.

Close X button

To close an e-mail, do the following:
- Click the **Close X** button on the e-mail's title bar.

2.3.4 Using Help Functions

A range of Help options are also available from the Help button on the Ribbon in the Outlook window (or of any e-mail message). Clicking the question mark button opens a fully searchable Help file for Microsoft Outlook 2010 and its functions.

Help button

Alternatively, press F1 to open **Outlook Help**.

note   This help is online, so an internet connection is needed.

2.4 Adjusting Settings

2.4.1 Managing Inbox Headings

The column headings at the top of messages in the Inbox can be changed to suit users' particular requirements.

To change these headings, do the following:
- Ensure the **Inbox** is selected in the folder list to the left in the **Outlook 2010** window.
- Right-click any column header in the list of messages.
- Select **Field Chooser** from the pop-up list.

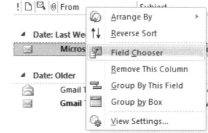

The **Field Chooser** window opens.

- Drag and drop the required column name to its position in the **Outlook** window. Red arrows will indicate where the column will appear in the window.

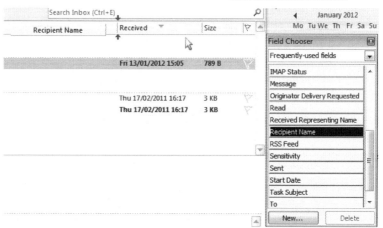

note   To remove a heading either drag the column header out of the Outlook window or right-click on the header and select Remove this column from the pop-up list.

The results of adding the **Recipient Name** column as the seventh column are shown below.

2.4.2 Displaying and Hiding the Ribbon

The Ribbon at the top of the Outlook 2010 window can be displayed or hidden depending on a user's need.

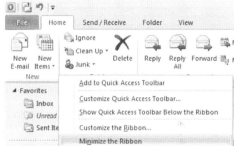

To display or hide the ribbon do the following:
- Right click the ribbon and select **Minimize the Ribbon**.
- The ribbon is minimized (hidden).
- To display the ribbon, right click the Ribbon Bar.
- Select **minimize the Ribbon**. Note that a tick means that the menu item is active.

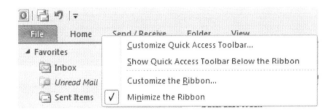

In common with most Windows applications, commands can also be added to and removed from the ribbon.

To add or remove commands, do the following:
- Right click the ribbon..
- Select **Customize the Ribbon**.
- Select a command from the **Choose Commands** list on the left of the **Outlook Options** window to display on the ribbon.
- Click **Add** to add the selected command to the ribbon.
- Select a command from the **Customize the ribbon** list on the right of the **Outlook Options** window to remove it from the ribbon
- Click **Remove** to remove the command from the ribbon.
- Click OK.

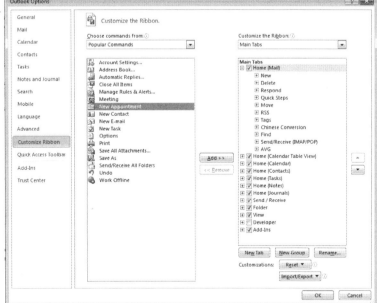

note Commands can be added to the Quick Access Toolbar by selecting the arrow at the end of the toolbar and selecting **Customize Quick Access Toolbar** Click More Commands to see the Customize window

2.5   E-Mail Options

2.5.1   Flagging E-Mails

Received e-mails can be flagged for attention later. Placing a flag next to an e-mail makes it easier to identify these types of message in a long list.

To flag a message, do the following:
- Click in the flag column towards the right of the message.
  A red flag will appear in the flag column for that message.

Red flag

To un-flag a message, do the following:
- Click the red flag to remove it.

2.5.2   Read and Unread

When messages are received into the inbox in Outlook, they are displayed as **unread**. This is shown by the display text in the message list being **bold** and a **closed envelope** icon being used. After an e-mail has been read, the display text automatically changes to **regular** and the envelope icon changes to an **open envelope**.

! □ ⊠ ⚲ From ▲	Subject	Received	Size
◢ From: Gmail Team (2 items, 1 unread)			
Gmail Team	Import your contacts and old email	Wed 18/01/2012 16:17	3 KB
Gmail Team	**Customize Gmail with colors and themes**	**Wed 18/01/2012 16:17**	3 KB

To mark messages as read or unread manually, do the following:
- Right-click the message.
- Select **Mark as Unread** or **Mark as Read** from the menu that appears.

note

> To mark all messages in the Inbox as read, right-click the particular folder in the folder list and select **Mark All As Read**.

2.5.3   Prioritising E-Mails

Prioritising an e-mail means that it will appear in the recipient's e-mail application with an indicator that it is of a higher (or lower) priority or importance than other e-mails. It does not mean that the message is sent more quickly.

There are three priority levels:
- **Normal Importance** (no symbol).
- **High Importance** (often a red exclamation mark).
- **Low Importance** (often a blue arrow).

To send an e-mail with a high priority, do the following:
- Create a new e-mail in Outlook (see Section 2.6.1).
- Before sending, click the **High Importance** button in the **Tags** group (Message tab).

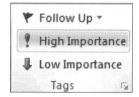

An indication of the higher priority will appear at the top of the address section of the e-mail.

High priority indicator

- When the message appears in the recipient's Inbox, there is an indicator (the exclamation mark in the illustration) that it is high priority.

Different e-mail clients have different ways of indicating the importance of the message.

To send an e-mail with a low priority, do the following:
- Create a new e-mail in Outlook.
- Before sending, click the **Low Importance** button.

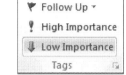

2.5.4 Saving an E-Mail as a Draft

Sometimes, it is necessary to compose an e-mail, but not send it immediately. In this situation, a new message can be saved as a **draft**. It will then be stored in the **Drafts** folder until needed again.

To save a message as a draft, do the following:
- Using Outlook, compose a new e-mail message (see Section 2.6.1).
- Click **Save** on the Quick Access Toolbar.

The message will be stored in the **Drafts** folder.
The message can then be reopened as it is needed and can be amended further and saved as a draft again, or sent.

The amount of messages saved in the Drafts folder is indicated by the number displayed in brackets beside the folder. The example on the right shows that 1 message is saved within the Drafts folder.

2.6 Creating and Sending E-Mails

2.6.1 Composing a New E-Mail

It is important to note that the procedure for setting up an e-mail account is not part of the ICDL syllabus. It is assumed that an e-mail account has been set up with an authorised ISP and that Microsoft Outlook 2010 is being used as the default mail application.

To create (or **compose**) a new e-mail, do the following:
- Open **Outlook 2010**.
- Click **New E-mail** from the **Home** tab.

A **New Message** window opens.
- In the **To** field, enter a recipient's e-mail address, e.g. **bec@blackrockec.ie**.
- In the **Subject** field, enter a subject that describes the content of the e-mail.
- Enter the message text, or **body text**, in the main part of the window.

Additional recipients can be entered in the **To**, **Cc** and **Bcc** fields (to insert the Bcc field; select the Bcc command from the Options tab and Show Fields group). Addresses should be separated by semi-colons.

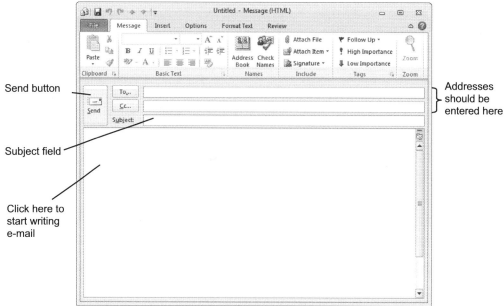

Send button

Addresses should be entered here

Subject field

Click here to start writing e-mail

To send the message, do the following:

* Click **Send** on the New Message window toolbar.

1	Open **Outlook** and click **New E-mail** on the **Home** tab.
2	In the message window that opens, write **mailtest@blackrockec.ie** in the **To** field.
3	In the **Subject** field, write **Test**. Write some text in the message window.
4	Press **Send**. You will receive a reply to this email in your inbox.

2.6.2 Recipients

When composing an e-mail there can be three categories of recipient.

* **To**:   The **To: list** contains the main recipients that are affected by the message. In the example below, '5-a-side football' is a mailing list, containing multiple recipients, while mpatton@fnm.com' is an individual recipient.

* **Cc**:   The **Carbon Copy list (Cc:)** is for recipients who may be indirectly affected by the message or that need to be kept 'in the loop'.

* **Bcc**: Recipients in the **Blind Carbon Copy list (Bcc:)** receive the e-mail, but the recipients in the To and Cc lists will not be aware of this. One use of Bcc is for mailings to large numbers of recipients where the identities of the others must be hidden.

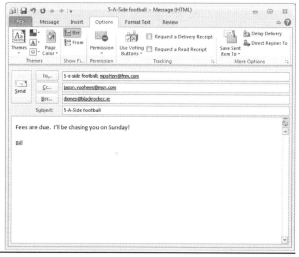

2.6.3 Copying Text from Another Source into an E-Mail

Text can be copied from other documents into an e-mail using the usual cut and paste method.

To copy text from a Microsoft Word document, do the following:
- Open **Outlook 2010** and create a new e-mail message.
- With the new e-mail message still open, start **Microsoft Word** and open the document that contains the text to be copied.
- In **Microsoft Word**, select the text and copy it to the clipboard using **CTRL + C**, or by selecting **Copy** in the **Clipboard** section of the **Home** tab on the ribbon.
- Locate the window for the new e-mail message, and click in the main body text section.
- Press **CTRL + V** to paste the text.
  Alternatively, select **Paste** in the **Clipboard** group on the **Message** tab.
  The text is copied into the e-mail message.

2.6.4 Replying to E-Mails

An e-mail that is received can be replied to directly, without the need to create a new e-mail and address it to the original sender.

There are two types of reply.
- A normal reply is to just the sender.
  If the message was sent to many recipients, they will not receive the reply.
- A **Reply All** reply will send your reply to all recipients of the original message.

To reply to an email, do the following:
- Select the **Inbox** on the folder list to the left of the Outlook window.
- In the message list, click the message to be replied to once.
- From the **Home** tab and **Respond** group, click either **Reply** or **Reply All**.

A new message window opens.

The e-mail addresses of the original sender will be in the **To** field.
If **Reply All** was clicked, and the original e-mail was sent to multiple recipients, the e-mail addresses for these recipients will also appear in the **To** field.

The subject box will have the text **Re:** and the original subject line.

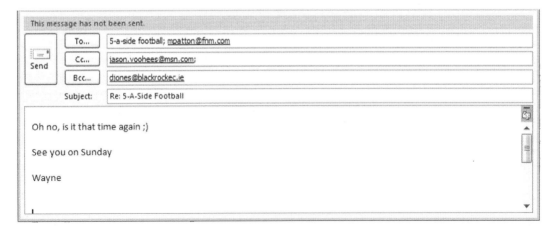

- Enter the text of the reply in the body section. Whether or not it should be entered above or below the quoted text is the subject of much debate, but for most users entering it above the quoted text is the standard, especially for long messages.
- Click **Send**.

2.6.5 Controlling Original Message Quoting when Replying

When replying to e-mail messages, text of the original message will be automatically quoted in the reply (see Section 2.6.4).

To stop this happening, do the following:
- In the Outlook window click **File** and select **Options** from the menu. The **Outlook Options** window opens.
- In the **Mail** tab, In the **Replies and forwards** section, select **Do not include original message** from the **When replying to a message** drop-down list.
- Click **OK**.

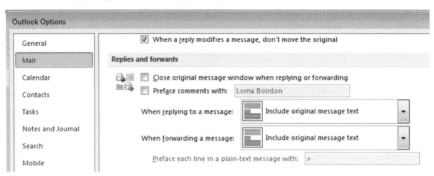

note | Use the Outlook Options window to control quoting the original message when forwarding an e-mail.

2.6.6 Forwarding E-Mails

Forwarding an e-mail involves a person receiving an e-mail and passing that message on to a further recipient who was not included on the original message. It is a very similar action to replying to an e-mail.

To forward an e-mail, do the following:
- Open **Outlook 2010**.
- Select the **Inbox** on the folder list to the left of the Outlook window.
- In the **Message** list, double-click the message to be forwarded to open it.
- From the **Home** tab and **Respond** group, click the **Forward** button.

The body text of the original message is quoted in the message to be forwarded.
- Enter a recipient, or recipients, e-mail address in the **To:** box.
- Click **Send**.

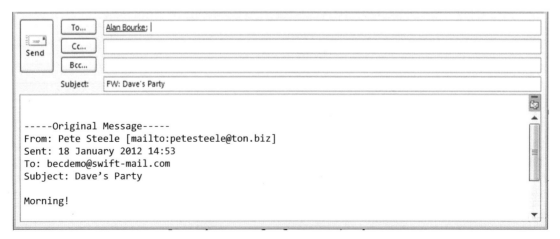

2.6.7 Spell Checking E-Mails

As with any document, it is good practice to spell check e-mails before they are sent. By default, spelling is checked automatically as a message is typed but not before the e-mail is sent.

To set spelling options, do the following:
- In the Outlook window click the **File** menu and select **Options** from the menu.
  The **Outlook Options** window opens.
- In the **Mail** tab and **Compose Messages** section, select or de-select the options for checking the spelling of e-mails.
- Click OK.

To set the **Check spelling as you type** option, do the following:
- In the Outlook window click the **File** menu and select **Options** from the menu.
  The **Outlook Options** window opens.
- In the **Mail** tab and **Compose Messages** section, click the Spelling and AutoCorrection button.
  The **Editor Options** window opens.
- Ensure the **Check spelling as you type** has been selected in the **When correcting spelling in Outlook** section of the window.

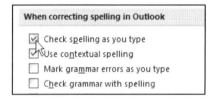

Incorrectly spelled words in the message body text or subject lines will be underlined in red.
- Right-clicking the underlined word will display a pop-up menu with suggestions as to the correct spelling.
- Selecting an item from this menu will replace the incorrect word.

Right-click the misspelled word for a range of alternative spellings

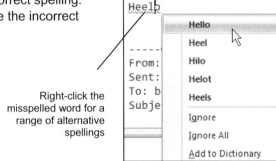

Clicking the **Spelling and AutoCorrection** button, opens the **Editor Options** window.

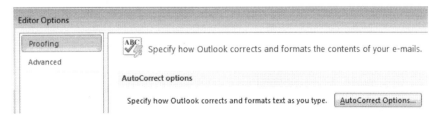

Clicking the **AutoCorrect Options** button in the **Editor Options** window opens the **AutoCorrect** window in which different options can be selected.

- To select them, tick the box next to the option.
- The language of the dictionary used in the spell check can also be set in this window.
- Click **OK** to apply the settings.

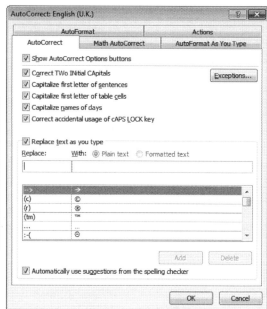

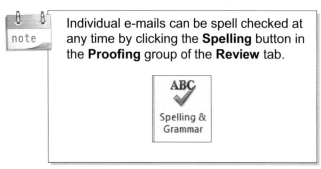

> Individual e-mails can be spell checked at any time by clicking the **Spelling** button in the **Proofing** group of the **Review** tab.

2.7   Attachments

2.7.1   Sending an E-Mail with an Attachment

Files can be attached to e-mails and will be available to all recipients (see Section 2.7.3). As part of this exercise, identify a previously created document file to use as an attachment.

Inserting an Attachment

To attach the file to an e-mail, do the following:

- Create a new e-mail message in **Outlook 2010**.
- Enter a recipient e-mail address in the **To:** field, and a subject in the **Subject** field.
- Enter some body text.
- Click the **Attach File** button in the **Include** group of the **Message** tab. The **Insert File** window opens.
- Locate the file to attach.
- Click **Insert**.

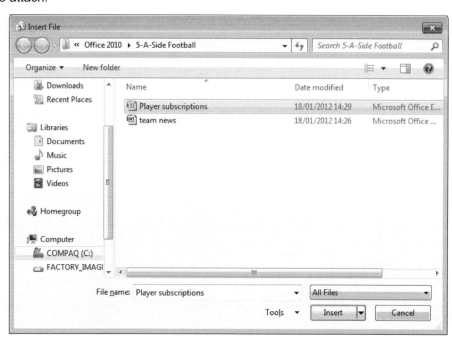

- The attachment or attachments will be displayed below the subject field.

Removing an Attachment

To remove an attachment, do the following:

- Right-click the attachment in the attachment list.
- Select **Remove** from the menu.

2.7.2 Saving Attachments

When an e-mail with an attachment or attachments is received, the message displayed in the inbox folder will have a paperclip icon indicating that there are attachments.

Paperclip icon

To save the attachment so that it can be opened, do the following:

- Open the e-mail message.
- In the message window, the attachments and their size will be displayed in the header area.

There is one attachment called **Player subscriptions.xlsx** in the illustration on the right.

Attachment

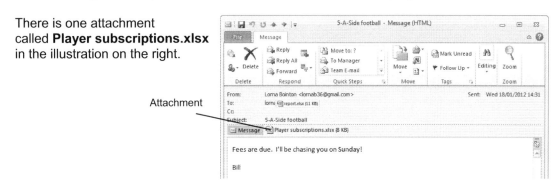

- Right-click the attachment.
- Select **Save As** from the menu that opens.
  The **Save Attachment** window opens.
- Choose a location to save the file and give the file a meaningful name.
- Click **Save**.
- When an attachment has been saved, it can be opened in the same way as any file.

When an attachment is received, it can also be opened straight from the e-mail message.
- Right-click the attachment and choose **Open** from the pop-up list.
  The **Opening Mail Attachment** window opens giving options to open the file or save it.
- Click **Open**.
  The file opens in the appropriate application (e.g. Excel or Word).

2.7.3 Considerations when Attaching Files
One of the most powerful features of e-mail is the ability to attach files to messages. However, there are some things that need to be considered to avoid problems with attachments.

- **File size**: Be aware of the size of attachments and the likely types of internet connection used by recipients. It is all too easy for a user in a business, educational or home situation with a high-speed internet connection to attach a multi-megabyte file to an e-mail and send it to multiple recipients without considering the use of bandwidth involved, or that recipients not using a high-speed internet connection may not be able to receive it. If the attachments seem too large, they can be compressed using special software. Image, sound and video files can be created in formats that have compression built in, such as PNG or MP4. The result is much smaller files resulting in much faster transmission via e-mail, but with the same content.

- **File type**: E-mail is a common cause of malware propagation (see Section 1.2.5). As a result, some e-mail clients or e-mail servers may actively strip certain types of attachment out of e-mails due to the security risks they pose. So it may not be possible to send executable attachments to some recipients, for example.

2.8 Mail Management

2.8.1 Efficient E-Mail Management
In Section 2.6.4, the Outlook Options window was opened to control the option of including a received message in an outgoing reply. The Outlook Options window, also contains other options that can be chosen which help the efficient use of **Microsoft Outlook 2010**.

To choose these settings, do the following:
- In the Outlook window, click the **File** menu.
- Click **Options**.
  The **Outlook Options** window opens.
- Select the **Mail** tab.

Select or deselect the options you prefer by clicking in the check boxes.

To activate a choice, click an empty item check box. This will place a check mark in the box, indicating that the option has been activated. Clicking a box that is already checked removes the check mark and deactivates the option.

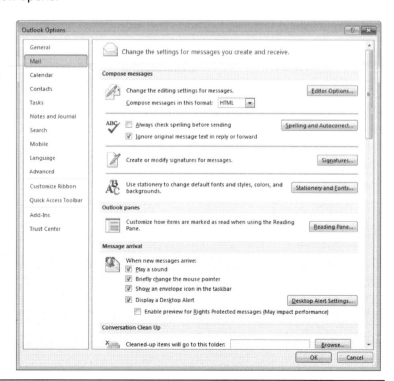

Some of the options available are as follows.

- **Save copies**: This keeps a copy of all messages that you send.
- **Automatically save**: This automatically saves unsent messages.
- **Close original message**: This ensures an e-mail message window is closed as soon as the **Reply** or **Forward** buttons are selected.

2.8.2　Creating E-Mail Folders

As the **Inbox** and **Sent Items** folders can become cluttered very quickly, messages can be stored in a tidier and more accessible manner using dedicated folders to collect e-mails covering particular subjects. Folders used to collect similarly themed e-mails or e-mails from particular senders should be named appropriately.

To create a new folder in the Inbox, do the following:
- Right-click the Inbox folder in the **Folder** list on the left of the **Outlook** window.
- Select **New Folder**.

A **Create New Folder** window opens.
- Enter a name for the folder.
- Click **OK**.

A new sub-folder is created within the **Inbox** folder.

2.8.3   Deleting E-Mail Folders

To remove the folder and all the items in it, do the following:

- Right-click the folder in the folder list that is to be deleted.
- Select **Delete Folder** from the pop-up menu, A confirmation window opens.
- Click **Yes**.

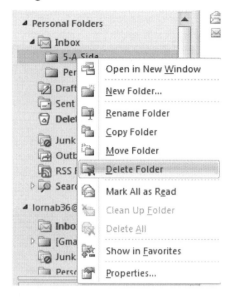

2.8.4   Moving E-Mails to E-Mail Folders

To move a message from the inbox into another folder (e.g. from the **Inbox** to the **5-A-Side** folder created in Section 2.8.2.), do the following:

- Click the message to be moved.
- With the mouse button held down, drag the message to the target folder in the folder list. The cursor has a small rectangle attached and the folder will be highlighted.

- Release the mouse button. The message will disappear from the **Inbox** message list.
- Click the **5-A-Side** folder to view the message.

You can also move a message to folders in other ways from the Outlook window.

1.   Using the Move command
Select the message to be moved. In the **Home** ribbon, click the **Move** arrow and then select **Other Folder** to move the message or **Copy to folder** to copy the message from the drop-down list. Choose the folder to which the message should be moved/copied from the **Move Items** window that opens.

2.   Using right-click
Right-click the message to be moved and select **Move** and then select **Other Folder** to move the message or **Copy to folder** to copy the message from the drop-down list. Choose the folder to which the message should be moved/copied from the **Move Items** window that opens.

If a message has been opened it can be moved to a folder by clicking the **Move** button in the **Move** group of the **Message** tab. The folder to which the message is to be moved can then be selected from the pop-up menu that opens.

To copy the message instead of moving it, do the following:
- Click the message to be copied so that it is highlighted.
- Hold down the **CTRL** key.
- With the **CTRL** key held down, left-click the message and drag it to the target folder in the folder list.
  The folder will be highlighted.
- Release the mouse button.
  The message will be in both the Inbox and the folder, e.g. in the **5-A-Side** folder.
- Click the **5-A-Side** folder to view the message.

2.8.5 Deleting E-Mails

E-mail builds up quickly and can take up a lot of disk space, especially if large attachments are involved. It is good practice to periodically clear out old messages from e-mail folders.

To delete an e-mail, do the following:
- Click the e-mail to be deleted to highlight it.
- Click the **Delete** button on the toolbar.

The e-mail will be sent to the **Deleted Items** folder in the folder list at the left of the Outlook window.

2.8.6 Restoring Deleted E-Mails

When an e-mail is placed in the **Deleted Items** folder, it is not actually deleted and can still be read and returned back to another folder in the inbox.

To restore a deleted e-mail, do the following:
- Click the **Deleted Items** folder to view the message.
- Drag the message from of the **Deleted Items** folder and drop into the **Inbox** (or other folder).

2.8.7 Emptying the Deleted Items Folder

E-mail is stored in the Inbox and other folders until you decide to delete it. The first step in deleting an e-mail does not remove it altogether, but keeps it in the **Deleted Items** folder.

To delete mail permanently, do the following:
- Right-click the **Deleted Items** folder.
- Select **Empty folder** in the pop-up menu that opens.
  A confirmation window opens.
- Click **Yes**.
  Alternatively, open the **Deleted Items** folder and delete the e-mails individually (see Section 2.8.5).

When the **Deleted Items** folder has been emptied, the e-mails are deleted permanently.

2.9 Distribution Lists

Outlook 2010 offers a **Contacts** function, which is a database of e-mail addresses and other information for individual people or groups.

2.9.1 Adding an Address to Contacts

To add a new contact, do the following:
- Click the **Contacts** button at the bottom left of the **Outlook** window.

The **Contacts** window opens.
- On the **Home** ribbon, click **New Contact**.
  The **New Contact** window opens.
  The default view is **General**.
- When all the details have been added, click **Save & Close** to save.
- Click **New Contact** to add a further contact and repeat the steps above.
- Click the **Mail** tab in the lower left pane of the Contacts window to return to the Inbox.

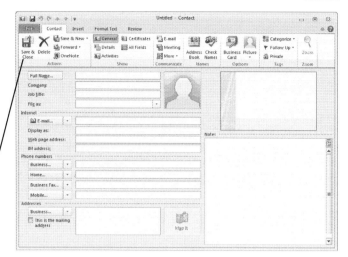

Click **Save & Close**

Contacts are displayed in the **Contacts** window. The example below displays contacts in Business Card view. The view can be changed in the Current View group:

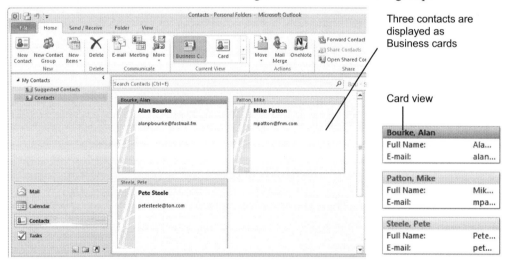

Three contacts are displayed as Business cards

Card view

2.9.2 Deleting a Contact

To delete a contact, do the following:
- Open the main **Contacts** window.
- Select the contact to be deleted.
- Click the **Delete** button on the **Home** ribbon.

2.9.3 Updating Contacts with an Addresses from Incoming E-Mails

A contact can be created directly from a received e-mail. This ensures the correct e-mail address is added.

To add a contact from an incoming e-mail, do the following:
- Open the e-mail message from the contact whose details are to be added to **Contacts**.
- Right-click the sender's e-mail address.
- Select **Add to Outlook Contacts** from the menu that opens.

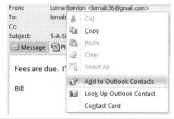

The **Contact** window opens.
- The name and e-mail address of the contact are added automatically.
- Add other details about the contact as required (see **Section 2.9.1**)

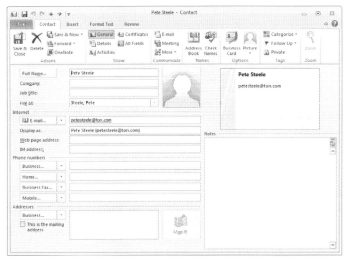

2.9.4 Creating Contact Groups

Contact (or Distribution) groups can be used to group contacts together so that a single e-mail can be sent to them as a group, without having to enter each e-mail address individually.

To create a contact group, do the following:
- Open the **Contacts** window.
- Click **New Contacts Group** on the **Home** ribbon.

New Contact Group

The **Contact Group** window opens.

- Enter an appropriate name in the **Name** box.
- Click **Add Members** from the **Members** group and select **From Outlook Contacts**

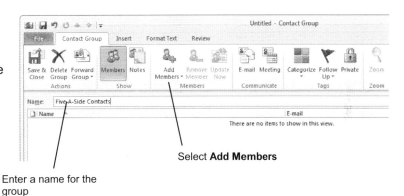

Enter a name for the group

Select **Add Members**

- From the addresses listed in **Contacts**, select those that are to be included in the group.
- After selecting the name and address, click Members.
- Repeat the above steps to add more members.
- When all the members have been added, click **OK**.
- Click **Save & Close** to create the group.

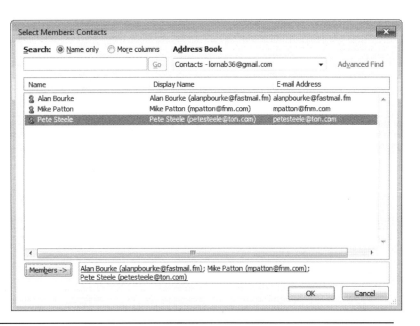

7

To send a new e-mail to the group, do the following:

- Compose a new message as normal.
- In the **To:** field, enter the name of the list, e.g. Five-A-Side, as the recipient (a tag will appear containing the full contact name as the contact name is entered – click this tag to enter the contact name in the To: field).

Alternatively, select the **To:** field and choose the contact group name from the list of contacts and click OK:

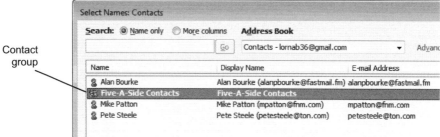

The contact group name will be displayed in the **To:** field. Enter a subject and message text and click **Send**. The message will be sent to each of the contacts listed in the Contacts List.

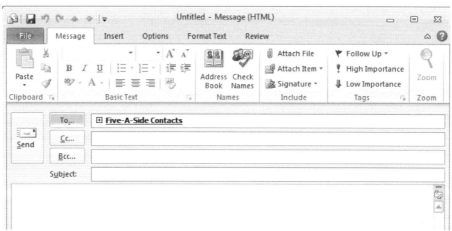

2.9.5 Updating Distribution Lists

To change a contact group (also referred to as a Distribution List), for example to add or remove a contact within it, do the following:

- Open the **Contacts** window.
- Double-click the required group to display the **Group** window.
- Add or remove **Contacts** or change the **Group name** as required.
- Click **Save & Close** to save any changes.

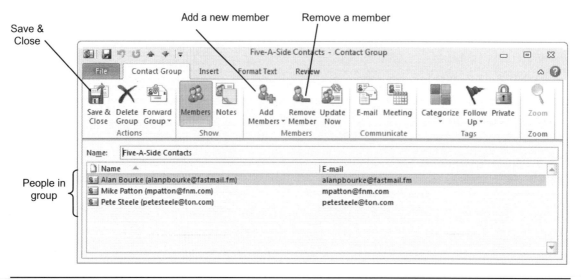

2.10   Searching and Sorting E-Mails

2.10.1   Searching for E-Mails

Microsoft Outlook has the ability to search emails using a range of criteria.

Instant Search

There is an 'Instant search' field above the message section of the Outlook window.

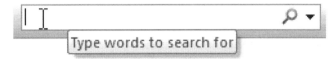

This will search the subject lines of the messages in the currently selected folder for the text entered, returning a list of matching messages which can be opened or replied to as normal. To clear the search and return to the normal message list, click the **X** button to the right of the search field.

Advanced Search

More thorough searching is available whereby other parts of the Outlook folders can be searched.

To refine search criteria, do the following:
* When criteria is entered into the **Instant Search** box the **Search Tools** ribbon becomes available.
* Choose to search within only the currently selected folder (e.g. Inbox) or search all subfolders or Outlook Items.
* Refine the search criteria by searching by sender's address; the subject; message attachments; importance; flag status or a specific time frame in which a message was received.
* Choose to search using Recent Searches or select options from the **Search Tools** drop-down menu.
* Close the search tools ribbon by selecting **Close Search**.

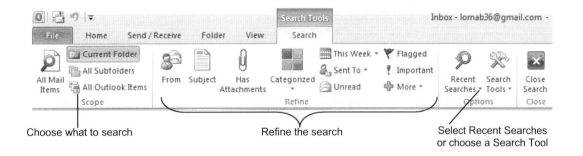

Selecting **Advanced Find** from the **Search Tools** menu will open the **Advanced Find** window:

Choose an
Outlook item in
which to
search

Click **Browse...** to
change the folder
to be searched

Enter word to be
searched for

Click to begin
search

Click **From...** or
Sent to... to
open Contacts
and select
contact name

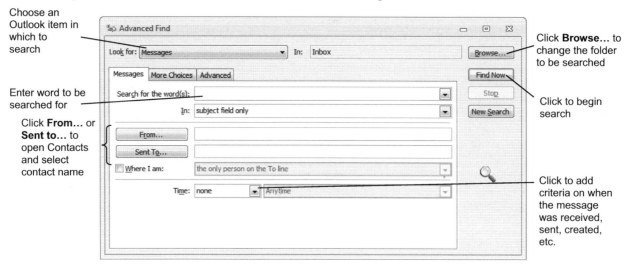

Click to add
criteria on when
the message
was received,
sent, created,
etc.

▷ **Look for**: This field indicates the part of Outlook to be searched (contacts, messages, etc.).

▷ **In** (to the right of **Look for**): Using this field, the
   folder to be searched can be identified. Clicking
   Browse... opens the **Select Folder** window.
   Select the folder by placing a tick next to its name.

▷ **In** (underneath **Search for the word(s)**):
   Using this field, the part of the message
   to be searched can be specified.

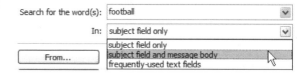

▷ **From.../Sent...**: These options open the **Contacts** window so that the names of senders
   and recipients can be entered to narrow the search and make it more focused.

▷ **Time**: This option allows users to enter details
   about the time the message being searched for
   was sent, created, received, etc. Click the arrow to
   the right of the Time: box to show the options.
   Click to select an option.

▷ When the **Time**: option has been selected the
   second box is activated. Click the arrow to the
   right of this box to specify a timescale.

If there are results from the search, the bottom of the window will expand to list them. Messages in this list can be opened, replied to, etc. in the normal way.

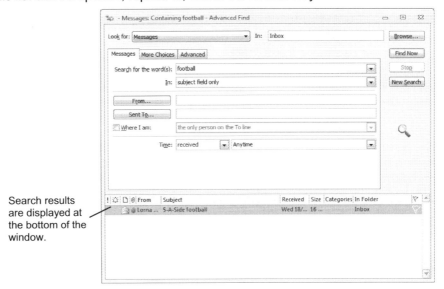

Search results are displayed at the bottom of the window.

2.10.2 Sorting E-Mails

The contents of the Inbox or other folders can be sorted by clicking the column headers in the message list.

To sort messages by sender, do the following:
- Ensure the required folder is open in the **Outlook** window.
- In the message list, click the column header to be used to sort the messages, e.g. **From**. The messages are sorted by the chosen column.

When messages have been sorted by a specified header, the messages are grouped together, e.g. all messages from the same sender will be grouped together if the **From** field is sorted.

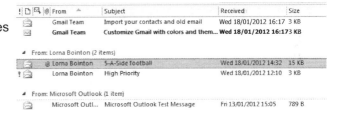

note

The column being used to sort the messages is indicated by an arrow in the column header.

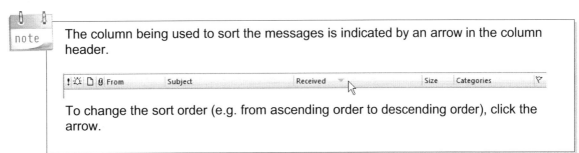

To change the sort order (e.g. from ascending order to descending order), click the arrow.

Messages can be sorted on any column displayed in the message list in the same way.
- To sort by subject, click the title of the **Subject** column.
- To sort by the received date, click the title of the **Date** column.
- To sort by message size, click the title of the **Size** column.

note

It is also possible to change the current sort by right-clicking the required column header and selecting **Reverse Sort** from the pop-up list.

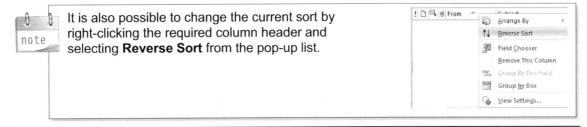

2.11   Printing E-Mails

2.11.1   Printing E-Mails

To print an e-mail, do the following:

- Select the **Inbox** in the folder list to the left of the **Outlook** window.
- Select the message to be printed in the message pane on the right of the window.
- Click the **File** menu and choose **Print**. Choose print settings and then click the **Print** button. The message will print to the default printer.

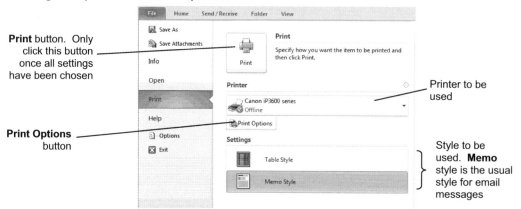

The message is previewed in the **Preview** pane of the Print window:

Clicking the **Print Options** button opens the **Print** window:

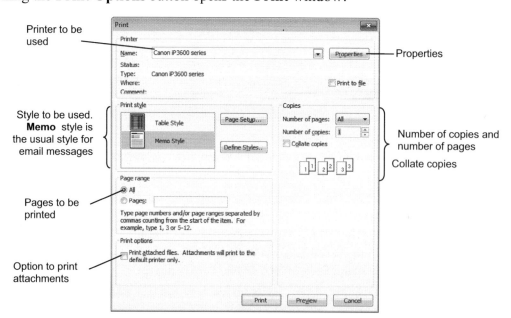

- Clicking the **Properties** button displays advanced settings.
- When your preferences have been entered, click **OK**.
- Click **Print** to print to the default printer. To close the Print window, click the **File** menu.

Glossary
and Index

Glossary and Index

ASCII (American Standard Code for Infor-mation Interchange) Text saved in ASCII format can be used by most word processors without the need for translators, but any layout or styles are lost.

backup To keep a copy of a file or files for safekeeping in the case of loss or damage to the original.

barcode A pattern of black and white lines that can be scanned and read by computer, as seen at supermarket checkouts.

bit (BInary DigiT) One of the two digits (0 or 1) used in the binary counting system used by computers. Bits are commonly used in sets of 8, called bytes.

bitmap The arrangement of a collection of dots to form a picture on a computer screen. When bit-mapped images are enlarged, the individual dots can be seen and appear jagged.

browse to locate a web page, or to work through a program or presentation.

browser A program enabling users to view pages on the world wide web.

byte A set of (usually) 8 bits. A byte can represent a single character of the alphabet or a 'normal' number.

cache memory A special type of memory between the CPU and the main memory chips that stores frequently used data to save time, thus increasing the speed of the computer.

CAD See Computer Aided Design

CAM See Computer Aided Manufacture

CD-ROM (Compact Disk Read-Only Memory) A storage medium with the same size and appearance as normal music CDs, used for storing large amounts of information. The data is optically encoded and read by a laser beam.

cell A single 'box' on a spreadsheet. Each cell has its own unique address derived from the letter of the column (A, B, C…) and the number of the row (1, 2, 3…) i.e. B3, etc.

centring Aligning text or objects to be centred on the page between the margins.

central processing unit (CPU) The principal part of a computer. It performs all the activities required by the instructions input from the keyboard or mouse, for example, and displays the result on the screen. Also used to describe the actual microprocessor chip that does the work, or the box in which it is contained.

click Pressing (and releasing) the mouse button to give a command to the computer.

ClipArt Collections of professionally drawn illustrations from which the user can select for use in his/her own work.

compression A technique for reducing the space occupied by files to maximise storage or for transmission over a network, for example. Compressed files have to be decompressed before they can be used.

computer aided design (CAD) A specialised drawing program that enables users to simplify the production of complex drawings and designs.

computer-based training (CBT) The use of the computer to provide (usually) interactive instruction to students, but often used for more specialised purposes.

computer graphics Illustrations drawn on or by a computer.

configure To set up hardware or software so that it operates as required.

Control Panel On a computer, a piece of software that can be used to set various options, such as the number of colours displayed on the screen, the printer to be used, etc.

copy and paste A technique where data is copied from one location and pasted into another, e.g. text in a document. The original data remains in place when a copy is made, unlike Cut and Paste.

corruption Damage to computer files that may render them unusable, caused by malfunction, mechanical failure, magnetic fields, etc.

CRM See customer relationship management

cursor An icon on the screen that shows where the next action will begin, such as where typed text will appear. Often called a pointer.

customer relationship management (CRM) Support systems that monitor and direct a company's interaction with its client base, from contract management to call manage-ment. May include on-line ordering, soft-ware updates, etc

cut and paste A technique for transferring data from one location to another. When cut, the original data is removed and pasted into its new position, unlike copy and paste.

data A term used for an item or items of information.

Data Protection Act A government act controlling the use and control of data stored on computer systems.

database A large collection of information. A computer database brings the computer's speed and versatility to finding, sorting and presenting information in a variety of ways.

default A setting that is used in the absence of Any instructions to the contrary. Default settings can be thought of as 'factory' settings which remain in force unless changed by the user.

desktop A term used to describe the computer screen on which icons represent items as if they were arranged on a 'real' desktop.

desktop publishing (DTP) The use of personal computers, page layout programs, laser printers, scanners, etc. to produce high-quality documents, as distinct from sending the original material to a commercial typesetter.

dictionary A list of words in a computer's memory which it uses to check spelling, e.g. in a word

G

processing document. Words not in the original list can be added to create a custom dictionary.

digital Commonly used to describe data in digital format, i.e. a string of ones and zeros, that can be used by a computer to reconstruct the original image, whether it be text, sound, video, etc.

directory A collection of files and/or folders stored under a common name. Also know as a folder. A directory or folder can contain sub-directories or folders as well as files.

download To transfer data from a remote computer – i.e. the internet – to your own computer.

dragging Pointing to an object, holding down the mouse button and moving the mouse to perform an action on the screen, then releasing the mouse button.

encryption A method of encoding data for security purposes so that it can only be accessed by authorised users.

error message A message displayed on the screen when something goes wrong or a problem occurs. There may also be buttons to click which offer various options for resolving the problem.

export The ability to send or save a file from one application in a format that can be used in another.

field A part of a database record that contains a single item of information, such as a person's surname or a telephone number.

file Can be either a set of data, such as a document, or a program such as a word processor.

font The set of characters and numbers of a particular design and style that determines the overall appearance of text, more correctly described as a typeface, e.g. Arial and Times New Roman.

format The structure of a file depending on the application that produced it. Microsoft Word files, for example, are stored in a different format from files produced by other word processors, making them mutually incompatible unless special translators are used.

formatting The process of changing text, images, charts, tables, etc. by altering the font, font size, colour or style.

formula An instruction used in a spreadsheet to perform a calculation, such as adding a series of numbers.

function A preset formula used in a spreadsheet which saves the user from having to devise and insert the formula, e.g. =sum(A3:A15) calculates the sum of the numbers from cells A3 to A15.

graphical user interface (GUI) A system of pictures or icons on a screen that enable users to control the computer by clicking them with the mouse, in contrast to typing in commands from a keyboard.

graphics Drawings, illustrations, diagrams etc.

hacking A term used to describe (usually) unlawful attempts to gain access to protected computer systems.

hard copy Computer file printed out on paper as distinct from the soft copy on the computer's hard disk.

hard disk The principal storage device in a computer. Data is stored magnetically on a spinning metal disk.

hardware The physical computer equipment and peripherals, such as keyboards, scanners, monitors, as distinct from the computer programs or software.

Help system A series of files included with many application packages which the user can call on for assistance on screen.

highlight To select an object or text so that an action can be performed with it.

icon A small picture or symbol used to represent a feature or activity on the screen. Clicking on an icon with the mouse is a way of giving a command to the computer.

import To include a file from an outside source in an application. For example, to take a piece of Clip Art into a document or records from one database into another.

information communication technology (ICT) The use of technology, such as computers, telecommunications and other electronics technology, to process information

inkjet printer A type of printer that sprays tiny drops of ink onto the paper to build up an image. Inkjet printers give high quality but are generally slower and more expensive to run than laser printers.

input device A device such as a keyboard, scanner etc. for entering data in the computer.

install To transfer software from the medium on which it has been bought –CD ROM, etc – to the computer's hard disk.

interactive The ability of users to interact with a program to alter and select its progress in contrast to, for example, a film or TV program over which users have no control.

interface The system used to aid the transfer of data from one environment to another. The human interface between the user and the CPU includes the keyboard, mouse and monitor. A modem is the interface between a computer and the telephone system, for example.

justification Aligning text so that it lines up neatly at the left or right margins, or both, or in the centre of the page.

LAN (Local Area Network) A computer network confined to a local area, such as a single building or group of buildings close together.

laser printer A printer that uses electrostatic charges to transfer toner powder to paper in the manner of a photocopier, giving a very high quality.

logging off The process of disengaging from a system to which you have logged on.

G

logging on The process of gaining access to a protected system, usually involving entering a username and/or password.

mail merge Combining data such as names and addresses from a database file with a document such as a letter in a word processor so that individualised documents can be printed.

manual line break Forcing a new line in a word processing document without creating a new paragraph.

memory Electronic chips that can store information on the computer while it is being used. Devices that store information when the computer is switched off, such as hard disks, are sometimes referred to as secondary memory.

menu A list of actions or choices from which the user makes a choice. Commonly displayed on a Menu Bar.

merge To combine two or more files to form a single file.

modem A device that enables computer signals to be transmitted to remote computers using the telephone system. It does this by superimposing the computer signals on an audible tone: it *modulates* the tone, which is then *demodulated* by the remote computer.

monitor The screen on which the computer displays information. It 'monitors' what the CPU is doing and displays the results for users.

mouse A hand-controlled input device for giving instructions to the computer. A ball in the base of the mouse rolls along the surface of the mouse mat and this moves the cursor on the screen. Buttons can be clicked to perform further actions and a wheel between the forward buttons can be used for scrolling through documents and windows. They are normally connected to the computer with a USB cable, but some cordless and use radio or infrared technology to communicate with the computer.

network A number of connected computers through which data can be exchanged. A network can consist of a small number of computers in the same building or a world-wide system such as the internet.

operating system A collection of programs that controls the entire computer and the way the user operates it. Major Operating Systems are DOS, UNIX, Windows and Mac OS. All these are mutually incompatible, in that applications designed for one will not run on the others, but files can be exchanged between different operating systems.

output device A device such as a monitor or printer on which the output of the CPU is displayed or made available.

palette A selection, usually of colours, avail-able to the user.

password A security feature requiring a series of characters to be entered to gain access.

peer-to-peer network A simple computer network in which the computers exchange files directly with one another.

peripheral A piece of equipment such as a printer, scanner or external hard drive that can be attached to a computer.

pixel A single 'dot' on a computer monitor. Each pixel's colour and brightness is controlled by the computer to produce the complex images you see on the monitor.

point To move the mouse so that the cursor rests on an object on the screen, e.g. an icon.

port A socket on the computer into which external cables or devices can be plugged.

primary key In a database, a special field such as an ID number, used to identify a record.

program A set of instructions, written in a programming language, used by the computer to perform an action.

prompt A flashing cursor on a screen that indicates to users that the computer is expecting some input, e.g. entering text.

RAM (Random Access Memory) A memory chip in which the computer stores and retrieves data. RAM needs a constant power supply so any data in it is lost when the computer is switched off.

record The basic unit in a database system, containing various fields, equivalent to a paper catalogue card.

relational database A database that uses several related files, e.g. a company might keep a list of customers in one file and a list of products in another and addresses in third. The database can extract and combine data from the different files as the user requires.

ribbon A strip of tabs across of application windows containing all the actions needed to create files in that application.

ROM (Read Only Memory) A memory chip containing permanent data which is retained when the computer is switched off. The computer cannot alter the contents of ROM; it can only 'read' it.

RTF (Rich Text Format) A format for exchanging text between different word processors without losing the layout or style content.

run To run a program is to start it operating.

scanner Converts an illustration on paper into a digital file that can then be edited and manipulated on the computer.

scroll bar A bar along the side or bottom of a window enabling the contents of the window to be viewed by moving the scroll bar up or down or from side to side when the window is too small to display all of it at once.

scrolling Moving the contents of a window to view parts that are hidden because of the small size of the window.

G

server A computer that acts as a storage or processing unit for other computers on a network.

software A computer program of any kind. word processors, database packages, graphics manipulation packages, games, and so on are all examples of software.

software piracy The illegal copying and use of software, whether for personal or commercial use or for sale.

sort To arrange items in a distinct order, the most common are alphabetical or numerical.

spell check A program that checks the spelling in a document against a built-in dictionary and facilitates the correction of errors.

spreadsheet An application program used to display and manipulate financial or statistical information. The program performs calculations and can produce charts.

system software The set of programs that a computer uses to operate, as distinct from programs such as word processors used by users.

touch screen A special screen that responds to users' fingers touching the surface, replacing the mouse or keyboard, e.g. in kiosk-type public information systems.

touchpad An input device that replaces the mouse on laptop computers.

trackball An input device for controlling the computer; essentially an 'upside down' mouse with the ball on top instead of underneath.

uninstall To remove unwanted software from the computer's hard disk.

upload To transfer data from a user's computer to a remote computer over a network, e.g. the internet.

virus A software program written with malicious intent. A virus interferes with the normal operation of the computer and may display a harmless message on the screen or cause serious corruption of files, depending on the virus.

WAN (Wide Area Network) A computer network in which the computers are geographically remote from each other e.g. the ATM system used by banks, or even world-wide as in the internet.

window A clearly defined area on the screen in which information is displayed. Several windows can open at a time and they can be individually moved and resized.

wizard A feature in some applications that helps users through a series of tasks by displaying a series of choices on the screen to choose from.

word processor A computer program used to prepare, edit, format and produce documents in a sophisticated way.

world wide web (www) A collection of interlinked documents on the internet. It was conceived by Tim Berners-Lee who wanted to create a virtual space in which information could be shared or exchanged.

WYSIWYG Pronounced 'wizzy-wig'. Describes a screen display that accurately matches the eventual paper version produced on the printer. Literally, 'What-You-See-Is-What-You-Get'.